Critical Survey of Long Fiction

Psychological Novelists

Editor

Carl Rollyson

Baruch College, City University of New York

Salem Press

Ipswich, Massachusetts • Hackensack, New Jersey

Cover photo:
Monaco (© Swim Ink 2, LLC/Corbis)

978-1-4298-3682-1

CONTENTS

CONTRIBUTORS

Thomas Banks
Ohio Northern University

Cynthia A. Bily
Adrian, Michigan

Randi Birn
Original Contributor

J. Madison Davis
Original Contributor

Thomas Di Napoli
Original Contributor

Margot K. Frank
Original Contributor

Sheila Golburgh Johnson
Santa Barbara, California

Harland W. Jones III
University of South Carolina

Anna B. Katona
Original Contributor

Rebecca Kuzins
Pasadena, California

John D. Lyons
Original Contributor

Charles E. May
California State University, Long Beach

Laurence W. Mazzeno
Alvernia College

Sally Mitchell
Original Contributor

Robert A. Morace
Daemen College

George O'Brien
Original Contributor

Janet Pérez
Original Contributor

Dorothy Dodge Robbins
Louisiana Tech University

Joseph Rosenblum
Original Contributor

John K. Saunders
Original Contributor

Jan Sjåvik
Original Contributor

Katherine Snipes
Original Contributor

William B. Stone
Original Contributor

Stan Sulkes
Original Contributor

Ronald G. Walker
Original Contributor

Jaquelyn W. Walsh
McNeese State University

James Whitlark
Texas Tech University

Roger E. Wiehe
Original Contributor

Psychological Long Fiction

From the ancient belief in humors to the twentieth and twenty-first centuries' psychoanalytic and pharmacological methodologies, diverse theories about the mind have affected the literary production of novelists. Categorization according to these theories is difficult, because authors tend to mix them and use more than they admit. Hermann Hesse's works, for example, began to overflow with the analytical psychology of Carl Jung after the latter treated him, yet Hesse tended to belittle that influence and spoke of being closer to Sigmund Freud. Consequently, psychological long fiction is most easily categorized not according to medical theories but according to four literary techniques: playful etiology, unrepentant confession, stream of consciousness, and Kafkaesque fantasy.

Playful etiology

Charles Baudelaire's novella *La Fanfarlo* (1847; the flaunter) attributes the idiosyncrasies of the protagonist, Samuel Cramer, to his mixed parentage (German and Chilean), his French education, and his heaven-bestowed partial genius. Baudelaire is thus practicing etiology—diagnosing the causes of a condition—but not with the seriousness a physician would adopt. Instead, he explains a condition through a whimsical mixture of rationales based on nature, nurture, and God. Such jocular syncretism (or, indeed, any extensive etiology) is common in fiction only from the eighteenth century onward. In Ovid's *Metamorphoses* (c. 8 C.E.; English translation, 1567), Myrrha's incestuous passion for her father creates the kind of situation that later fascinated psychologists, but the narrator simply comments on that passion as criminal and disgusting without investigating why Myrrha had such an unusual craving. Presumably, fate or the gods are somehow responsible.

With the rise of the sciences in the eighteenth century, however, tacit reference to supernatural influence was not enough to explain personality differences. Before the Romanticism of the early nineteenth century, the characters to be diagnosed seldom deviated far from normality and thus were little in need of lavish elucidation. Thereafter, however, neurotics and psychotics began multiplying through a growing interest in extreme expressions of individuality.

To demonstrate this individuality, authors must at some point diagnose characters' deviance from the norm; paradoxically, since what can be thus cataloged is not uniquely individual, the authors must also show a distaste for diagnosis itself. In *Washington Square* (1880), Henry James's narrator details the characters' psychological quirks quite directly, yet the story turns against such insights. The shrewd Doctor Sloper, known for diagnosing in too much detail, ruins his daughter's life by exposing her fiancé's temperament. In later works, James continues to provide etiological information, but it is filtered through points of view that render it ambiguous, as in his novella *The Turn of the Screw* (1898), which never establishes whether its ghosts are real or symptoms of a governess's hysteria.

Even more complexly, the narrator of Thomas Mann's *Doktor Faustus: Das Leben des deutschen Tonsetzers Adrian Leverkühn, erzählt von einem Freunde* (1947; *Doctor Faustus: The Life of the German Composer Adrian Leverkühn as Told by a Friend*, 1948) tries to demonstrate that the genius and mental illness of the composer Adrian Leverkühn are symptoms of both Germany's brilliance and its degeneration. Moreover, the narrator's mannered prose undercuts faith in his judgments. As Mann's essays also demonstrate, he considered the complexity of life to transcend simple categories. On a somewhat less sophisticated level, his method (obsessive use of etiology, yet skepticism about its conclusions) also appears in many thrillers, including Thomas Harris's *Red Dragon* (1981) and *The Silence of the Lambs* (1988). In these works, both a psychoanalyst-turned-cannibal and the investigating detectives employ psychological profiling. To this guesswork (which is not always accurate), Harris counterpoints pervasive religious imagery, meant to give the evil an apocalyptic quality, but without reducing it to any single theory, either psychological or theological.

In *Against Interpretation, and Other Essays* (1966), Susan Sontag combats the psychological and particularly the biographical study of literature. Accordingly, she peoples her novels with misfits on whom she comments in a manner that is more a parody of psychology than a reliance on it. Comparably, Thomas Pynchon took imagery from Jung's psychological introduction to the Tibetan Book of the Dead and travestied it in his comic novel *The Crying of Lot 49* (1966). As do others of Pynchon's fictions, it treats all analysis as itself a form of paranoia. Causing controversy, the New Novelist Alain Robbe-Grillet placed obvious allusions to Oedipus (a basic pattern in the Freudian system) throughout *Les Gommes* (1953; *The Erasers*, 1964); he denied publicly that they were there. In her essays, Nathalie Sarraute, another New Novelist, has explained that her characterization describes tropisms (behaviors with which people try to control one another), but she believes that no depths lie beneath these. Citations of psychological diagnoses merely to deny or ridicule them occur on a popular level in such novels as Ken Kesey's *One Flew over the Cuckoo's Nest* (1962), in which the character Nurse Ratched embodies a health care system eager to label patients as a way of demeaning and bullying them.

UNREPENTANT CONFESSION

In classic psychoanalysis, discovering etiology is largely the doctor's role. The patient engages in a secular form of confession, as a result of which (unlike the religious version) no one is required to repent. Literature has followed a similar path. In Fyodor Dostoevski's *Zapiski iz podpolya* (1864; *Letters from the Underworld*, 1913; better known as *Notes from the Underground*), the narrator's almost gloating self-exposure, without purgation or salvation, broke with Christian contrition and set a model for twentieth century confessional fiction. According to literary theorist Mikhail Bakhtin, Dostoevski's later novels, at their best, consist of a dialogue of voices presented without a commenting narrator. This would make Dostoevski's works confessional throughout, but, as Bakhtin admits, Dostoevski sometimes resorts to diagnosis and etiology, as in the epilogue to *Prestupleniye i nakazaniye* (1866; *Crime and Punishment*, 1886), with an obtrusive psychology based on Christianity.

At the beginning of the twentieth century, André Gide's *L'Immoraliste* (1902; *The Immoralist*, 1930) took the confessional mode further toward the secular. Until near the book's conclusion, its protagonist, Michel, is unaware of his homosexuality, so he cannot divulge it, except by reporting behavior he understands less than do the readers. Furthermore, since homosexuality in the novel is not an action but a tendency, it is not, in Christian terms, a sin; despite the guilt it instills, it does not seem susceptible to purgation. By persuasively associating the human condition with embarrassing impulses, *The Immoralist* sets a despairing tone for French fiction.

This tone continued at least as late as Albert Camus's *La Chute* (1956; *The Fall*, 1957). Its protagonist, Jean-Baptiste Clamence, is unwilling to risk his life to save a drowning man. Disillusioned by his own cowardice, Clamence abandons conventional behavior and slips into cruelty, intent on convincing everyone that his imperfection springs from an ineradicable strain within humanity itself: a fall for which there is no savior. Like Michel's homosexuality, Clamence's sadism is one of the conditions that the first half of the twentieth century brought to psychological attention. That age, shocked by the repressed, appears again in Kazuo Ishiguro's nostalgic novels. They show how reluctant people were to discover their own destructiveness, as shown in the disguised sadomasochistic relationship between Sachiko and Mariko in *A Pale View of Hills* (1982), or in the self-delusions of character Christopher Banks in *When We Were Orphans* (2000). Although Freud argued that aggressive and sensual drives might be sublimated into cultural achievements, novelists, along with the public, tended to be dismayed at psychology's disclosure of an unconscious prone to irrationality.

With the exception of such nostalgic works as Ishiguro's, confessional fictions in the twentieth century's second half were not as easily dismayed by implacable instincts. In Anthony Burgess's *A Clockwork Orange* (1962; reprinted with final chapter, 1986), the narrator, Alex, is a rapist and murderer who is treated with aversion therapy so that he becomes nauseated at the thought of sex or violence. In other words, he has been coerced into being as repressed as a stereotypical Victorian. Readers are expected to condemn his psychological castration. In a victory of free will, however, he overthrows the conditioning and returns to committing mayhem.

Comparably, in Orson Scott Card and Kathryn H. Kidd's *Lovelock* (1994), the narrator is an artificially enhanced capuchin monkey, who, like Alex, must overcome his conditioning to be capable of sex and violence. Here, even more clearly than in *A Clockwork Orange*, evil is an animal side of the mind to be freed. Liberation of the bestial permeates many first-person works that were popular in the 1960's, such as Jack Kerouac's *The Dharma Bums* (1958) and John Barth's *Giles Goat-Boy: Or, The Rev. New Syllabus* (1966). Although more conscious of evil than Kerouac, Barth makes psychological liberation sound relatively innocent compared with Burgess, whose acute awareness of human destructiveness is more typical of British fiction, such as J. G. Ballard's *Crash* (1973), which is about taking sadomasochistic joy in automobile accidents.

Perhaps because the nature of drama predisposes it to public rituals, in such plays as Peter Shaffer's *Equus* (pr., pb. 1973) and in countless films, psychoanalysis itself forms a setting for confession. In first-person fiction, however, the closest analogy to it is the relationship between narrator and reader. When psychoanalyst-like figures are present in fiction, they are often disguised to emphasize either the negative or positive associations of psychiatry. Thus, fresh from a productive therapy with Jung, Hesse made the rebellious, precocious title character of *Demian* (1919; English translation, 1923) into its narrator's unofficial analyst. Similarly, in J. D. Salinger's Glass family saga (such as in *Seymour: An Introduction*, 1963), although family members sometimes find themselves on a psychiatrist's couch, the older brothers, one of whom commits suicide, combine the functions of guru and therapist. Whether the analyst is a cannibal or a friend who helps people live with their sins, the process has less to do with penitence and forgiveness than with providing the readers entertainingly shocking revelations about what Joseph Conrad, in his 1902 novel of the same name, termed humanity's "heart of darkness."

STREAM OF CONSCIOUSNESS

According to Keith M. May, stream of consciousness—an attempt to represent barely conscious thinking—belongs to a relatively brief period when the two world wars led people to once again recognize human irrationality. Significantly, May omits mention of Édouard Dujardin's stream-of-consciousness novel *Les Lauriers sont coupés* (1887, serial; 1888, book; *We'll to the Woods No More*, 1938; also known as *The Bays Are Sere*, 1991), which was published generations before World War I. More perceptively, Dorrit Cohn contends that ungrammatical fragments in stream of consciousness approximate a deep stratum of the mind, since the psycholinguist Lev Vygotsky has demonstrated such incoherence to be its nature.

According to Shiv Kumar, psychologist-philosopher William James originated the phrase "stream of consciousness" in 1890, but it was introduced to literary criticism in a 1918 article by May Sinclair about the novels of Dorothy Richardson. In *Pilgrimage* (1938, 1967), Richardson confines herself to her protagonist's consciousness, without providing the customary information readers expect early in a book. Fifty pages into the novel, the reader learns the character is a teenager. As Katherine Mansfield did for the short story, Richardson brought to the English novel the technique of stream of consciousness, whose major practitioners were Virginia Woolf, James Joyce, and William Faulkner.

The first of Woolf's novels to employ the technique is *Jacob's Room* (1922), about the life of an Englishman who dies in World War I. It repeatedly marks characters' inattention to traditional religion even when church bells chime in the background. (Her generation associated stream of consciousness with a world that was replacing theology with psychology.) By focusing on a single day, her next novel, *Mrs. Dalloway* (1925), achieves greater intensity in the depiction of relatively plotless mental flux. A unifying element, though, is repeated reference to Septimus Smith, who consults a psychiatrist and kills himself to avoid another physician. On an extreme level, his suicide parallels the importance that internal events have for the other characters.

Although stream of consciousness means something slightly different in each novelist's works, Joyce shows the greatest range of techniques. In his *A Portrait of the Artist as a Young Man* (serial 1914-1915, book 1916), most sections are in third person, but they are so attuned to their protagonist's developing mind that they range from baby talk (in the earlier ones) to the erudition of an educated young man (in the concluding ones). Joyce's *Ulysses* (1922), however, unifies each section by parodying some genre or style, such as journalistic prose or expressionist drama. The last section, rendering the mind of Molly Bloom as she falls asleep, is a flow of words without punctuation that particularly suits the term "stream of consciousness." Her monologue should not be confused with works whose authors simply provide their own musings.

In the first draft of *On the Road* (1957), Kerouac, at maximum speed, wrote the whole work as a single, unedited sentence to achieve spontaneous self-revelation. In contrast, Joyce is distancing himself from Molly's irrationality and somnolence. If stream of consciousness means representation of one mind at a time, then Joyce's monumental last work, *Finnegans Wake* (1939), has moved beyond it to a very nonlucid dream that takes incoherence almost to unintelligibility. Its readers enter something like Jung's collective unconscious: the whole human race's heritage of symbols.

After treating Joyce's daughter, Jung misunderstood even *Ulysses*, which he considered the spontaneous outpourings of hereditary madness, exacerbated by alcohol. Although no proof of its authors' insanity, the incoherence of stream of consciousness can well portray characters' mental aberrations. The first section of Faulkner's *The Sound and the Fury* (1929) records the barely comprehended sensory impressions occurring to Benjy, an idiot. Readers then encounter the mental contents of other witnesses to the same story, including a young man who killed himself because of incestuous feelings for his sister. Similarly, in Faulkner's next novel, *As I Lay Dying* (1930), Darl, a clairvoyant headed toward madness, is the character whose mind is most often sampled. Although interest in stream of consciousness was fostered by the rise of psychology, the technique itself implies that a mind is being observed not clinically but telepathically; thus, Darl's clairvoyance has much in common with those who write or read stream of consciousness.

Stream of consciousness began attracting a new generation of writers at the end of the twentieth century. Two examples are Patrick McCabe, whose narrator in *The Butcher Boy* (1992) is a young boy who deals with a troubled family by retreating to a fantasy world, and Irvine Welsh, whose *Trainspotting* (1993) is narrated by several drug users from the same town. Novels that employ wordplay, nonlinear structure, and footnotes in addition to stream of consciousness include Mark Z. Danielewski's *House of Leaves* (2000), Jonathan Safran Foer's *Everything Is Illuminated* (2002), and Junot Díaz's *The Brief Wondrous Life of Oscar Wao* (2007). The most celebrated example, however, is Toni Morrison's *Beloved* (1987), winner of the Pulitzer Prize and numerous other awards. Its protagonist is Sethe, an escaped slave traumatized by the brutality she endured and by the despair that led her to murder her daughter, Beloved. Sethe's narration is fragmented, like the woman herself, and Morrison's use of stream of consciousness helps readers understand Sethe's psychological state.

KAFKAESQUE FANTASY

Stream of consciousness views characters' minds as if the author were separate from them. In Kafkaesque literature, however, characters and their authors converge. Indeed, Kafkaesque writers tend to place images of themselves within their works. Franz Kafka names the protagonist of *Das Schloss* (1926; *The Castle*, 1930) with the initial K., while the main character of *Der Prozess* (1925; *The Trial*, 1937) is Joseph K. (Kafka was named Franz for the emperor Franz-Joseph). Kurt Vonnegut puts himself in his own novel, *Slaughterhouse-Five: Or, The Children's Crusade, a Duty-Dance with Death* (1969), as a minor character who describes the book's composition and thereby tells the readers that the action is imaginary. Billy Pilgrim slips back and forth through time because of an association of ideas in Vonnegut's mind.

Milan Kundera makes his part in composition even more explicit by interrupting action with essays explaining how he created one character or another. In his novel *L'Insoutenable Légèreté de l'être* (1984; *The Unbearable Lightness of Being*, 1984; in Czech as *Nesnesitelná lehkost bytí*, 1985), he shapes the protagonist through meditations on living in truth as this idea is expressed by Kafka and Václav Havel. Although Kafka himself was subtler, examination of his works demonstrates that he structured events in quite as artificial a way as Kundera, with almost no attempt at verisimilitude. Rather, Kafkaesque fiction is like a lucid dream or nightmare in which the action, however exciting, is never quite real.

In non-Kafkaesque fiction, the work is a buffer between author and reader, so that they lose sight of each other. The Kafkaesque creates at least the illusion of transparency, where author and reader may glimpse one another as if they were characters. In Italo Calvino's *Se una notte d'inverno un viaggiatore* (1979; *If on a Winter's Night a Traveler*, 1981), readers take an active part in the plot; indeed, a male reader of Calvino's book is described as having a romance with a female reader. *If on a Winter's Night a Traveler* is one of the most elaborate attempts to make "you" a character, but other notable novels that do this include Michel Butor's *La Modification* (1957; *Second Thoughts*, 1958; better known as *A Change of Heart*) and Carlos Fuentes's novella *Aura* (1962; English translation, 1965).

In Kim Newman's second-person novel *Life's Lottery: A Choose-Your-Own Adventure Book* (1999), the reader is invited to become Keith, the protagonist, and to make decisions on Keith's behalf; choosing one path over another directs the reader to another section of the novel. Kafka's fragmentary *Beim Bau der Chinesischen Mauer: Ungedruckte Erzählungen und Prosa aus dem Nachlass* (1931; *The Great Wall of China, and Other Pieces*, 1933) has both a first-person narrator, related complexly to Kafka himself, and a "you" as protagonist.

Like characters in nightmares, Kafkaesque protagonists may sometimes lack individual depth. Nonetheless, in its detailed probing of the authorial mind's dreaming its fictions, the Kafkaesque mode is at least as introverted and self-reflexive as are the other forms of psychological narrative.

James Whitlark

BIBLIOGRAPHY

Cohn, Dorrit. *Transparent Minds: Narrative Modes for Presenting Consciousness in Fiction*. Rev. ed. Princeton, N.J.: Princeton University Press, 1988. Cohn divides the fictional rendering of consciousness into three modes: "psycho-narration," which is both diagnosis and summary of mental contents; quoted (interior) monologue; and narrated monologue, a third-person narration that adopts the style of the character described.

Crosthwaite, Paul. *Trauma, Postmodernism, and the Aftermath of World War II*. New York: Palgrave Macmillan, 2009. Argues that the postmodern novel is not, as many critics claim, ahistorical, but deeply attuned to the cultural and social significance of trauma. Postmodernism has "reformulated" history in terms of a trauma "that is traceable, time and again," to the psychological horrors of World War II.

Edel, Leon. *The Modern Psychological Novel*. Reprint. Gloucester, Mass.: Peter Smith, 1973. This revision of Edel's *The Psychological Novel, 1900-1950* (1955) concerns modes of subjectivity in early twentieth century fiction, particularly stream of consciousness.

Hume, Kathryn. *American Dream, American Nightmare: Fiction Since 1960*. Urbana: University of Illinois Press, 2000. Analyzes the psychological responses of both writers and their fictional characters to the false promises of the American Dream in nearly one hundred novels.

May, Keith M. *Out of the Maelstrom: Psychology and the Novel in the Twentieth Century*. New York: St. Martin's Press, 1977. Ranging from the beginning of the twentieth century to the fiction of Jean-Paul Sartre in the 1960's, this study suggests analogies between psychology in novels and in the writings of psychologists contemporary with them.

Rosenberg, John. *Dorothy Richardson, the Genius They Forgot: A Critical Biography*. New York: Alfred A. Knopf, 1973. Aptly parallels events in Richardson's *Pilgrimage* to the writer's life. Concludes with an analysis of Richardson's pioneering impact upon the development of the modernist novel in general and stream of consciousness in particular.

Schur, Owen. *The Regulation of Consciousness in the English Novel: Desire and Power.* Lewiston, N.Y.: Edwin Mellen Press, 2002. Examines desire, consciousness, and hierarchies of power in the social practices of protagonists in the English novel. Covered novelists include Jane Austen, Charles Dickens, and Virginia Woolf.

Weinstein, Arnold L. *Recovering Your Story: Proust, Joyce, Woolf, Faulkner, Morrison.* New York: Random House, 2006. Analysis of eight novels, including *Mrs. Dalloway* by Virginia Woolf, *The Sound and the Fury* by William Faulkner, and *Beloved* by Toni Morrison, to show how fiction can help readers understand their own perceptions and dreams.

Whitlark, James. *Behind the Great Wall: A Post-Jungian Approach to Kafkaesque Literature.* Rutherford, N.J.: Fairleigh Dickinson University Press, 1991. Whitlark analyzes the psychological implications of Franz Kafka's fictions and of works by thirty-six authors influenced by him.

AYI KWEI ARMAH

Born: Takoradi, Gold Coast (now Ghana); 1939

PRINCIPAL LONG FICTION

The Beautyful Ones Are Not Yet Born, 1968
Fragments, 1969
Why Are We So Blest?, 1972
Two Thousand Seasons, 1973
The Healers, 1978
Osiris Rising, 1995
KMT in the House of Life: An Epistemic Novel, 2002

OTHER LITERARY FORMS

Although Ayi Kwei Armah (awr-MAW) is primarily a novelist, he has written and published in other forms as well. Among his short stories, "Yaw Manu's Charm" appeared in *The Atlantic Monthly* (1968) and "The Offal Kind" in *Harper's* (1969). His poem "Aftermath" is included in *Messages: Poems from Ghana* (1970). Armah also has worked as a translator for *Jeune Afrique* and the Algerian-based *Révolution Africaine*. His polemical essay "African Socialism: Utopian or Scientific?" appeared in *Présence Africaine* (1967).

ACHIEVEMENTS

Ayi Kwei Armah has become Ghana's best-known writer on the international scene, but he would probably prefer to measure his achievement by the reception of his African audience. He has been vulnerable to suspicion and resentment both in Africa and abroad. Not only has he been in exile from his own nation, choosing to live in other African countries, in Paris, and in the United States, but he has also attacked virulently the corruption and materialism of his country's elite and has absolutely condemned the white race (whether European or Arab) for its perverted mentality and for its past and present role in the destruction of African culture.

There is an abrasive quality about Armah's early novels—their oppressive naturalism, their sadomasochistic sexuality, their melodramatic casting of blame—that demands more than mere tolerance on the part of his audience. These novels require the reader to go beyond the vehicle to the attitude and the argument that it reveals. A reasonably careful reading will get beyond this abrasiveness and may even dispel the suspicion and resentment, because Armah's real achievement lies in his making the novel not a simple outlet for his venom but a functional instrument in the African cause. Armah is one of the few truly experimental African novelists. He takes a Western literary form and shapes it into a voice for the African in the modern world.

In his first novel, Armah turns naturalism and romantic irony into a symbolic, existential statement. In the next two novels, he experiments with narration through multiple points of view. In all three cases, his purpose is to explore the isolation of the individual African in his transformed society. It is evident that Armah is searching for a voice. In his later novels the voice is that of the traditional historian and storyteller of the tribe. The Western concept of point of view merges with the oral tradition, and fictional realism merges with history, legend, and myth. In *Osiris Rising*, his sixth novel, Armah returns to the realism of his earliest work but imbues this with a new symbolic undercurrent based on the Osiris and Isis myth cycle, one of Africa's earliest foundational stories. Armah does not engage in experimentation for its own sake: Technique and form are in the service of the larger human concern, the preservation of a culture and the fulfillment of his role within it.

BIOGRAPHY

Ayi Kwei Armah was born in 1939 in the seaport town of Sekondi-Takoradi in western Ghana. Unlike the unnamed protagonist of his first novel, Armah was able to attend mission schools and Achimota College, near the capital city of Accra. He then received scholarships to continue his education in the United States. Like the "man" in his first novel, *The Beautyful Ones Are Not Yet Born*, however, his early life was dramatically influenced by the effects of colonial rule. During World War II, the British sent Ghanaians to fight in Burma (Myanmar) and on other battlefields; the postwar period in Ghana was marked by economic crises, social unrest and strikes, the rise of political parties, and the achieving of independence.

Armah did not experience directly the events after independence. In 1959, he received a scholarship to attend Groton School in Massachusetts. He went on to Harvard, where he graduated summa cum laude in sociology. In 1963, he visited Algeria and worked as translator for *Révolution Africaine*. He saw firsthand what was happening in African countries after independence: a continuation of the old policies, of African subservience, and of poverty. The novel *Why Are We So Blest?* appears to be a distillation of Armah's experiences during these years.

During his brief return to Ghana in 1966, Armah attempted to apply his American education and his talents as a writer in various ways. He was a research fellow at the university, a journalist, a teacher of English, and a television scriptwriter. His second novel, *Fragments*, appears to be a spiritual biography of this frustrated attempt to adapt himself again to his society. In 1967, Armah was again in the United States, attending Columbia University on a writing fellowship, and then in Paris as editor-translator for the newsmagazine *Jeune Afrique*. In 1968, he taught at the University of Massachusetts and published *The Beautyful Ones Are Not Yet Born*, which traces the Ghanaian experience from World War II to the overthrow of Kwame Nkrumah in 1966 but concentrates on the corruption in Ghanaian society around the time of the coup.

Armah continued to teach at universities in diverse locales, both in Africa and abroad.

He held academic appointments at the Teachers' College in Dar es Salaam, Tanzania; the University of Lesotho; the University of Wisconsin at Madison; and in Nigeria. Armah settled in Popenguine, Senegal. In the mid-1990's, he and some friends formed a cooperative printing and publishing company dedicated to the promotion of the local African book industry.

Analysis

Ayi Kwei Armah's novels have provoked conflicting reactions. On one hand, one can argue that Armah is essentially Western, not African. He is certainly not African in the manner of the Nigerian novelist Chinua Achebe. While Achebe's works are to some degree "social documents," Armah moves rapidly from social realism to a symbolic level, even within his first novel. His succeeding novels move away from external detail toward the inner life and the idealism of legend and myth. Achebe is a realist, Armah a romantic. Achebe maintains an objective stance in his analysis of the colonial and postcolonial eras in Nigeria, while Armah's voice is strident and polemical. Whereas Achebe is likely to make the society itself as important a "character" as the individual protagonist, Armah, in his early works at least, focuses on the individual consciousness.

Armah's novels thus bear the obvious marks of contemporary European and American fiction. His protagonists are alienated antiheroes who deserve sympathy and who are essentially correct in their moral attitudes, but who are ineffectual misfits. The society itself is clearly wrong but defeats the individual moral person through sheer force of numbers, viewing such protagonists as mad or criminal. In fact, this society is the typical twentieth century wasteland, whether it is in Ghana, northern Africa, or the United States. Armah's Ghanaians resemble black Americans trying to be white in order to participate fully in the technological age. Finally, the protagonist within this society resembles, and often in fact is, the isolated artist—a typical Western figure, not at all African.

One can easily argue that if these are not incidental features, they are at least sketched into a larger picture that identifies Armah with an essentially African sensibility. Judging from his first five novels and not emphasizing simply the early works, one could conclude that Armah is an African writing for Africans. For him, the identity of the African artist is inseparable from the society that he serves. He would not want to be judged according to the Western criterion of art for its own sake, or by Western standards of what makes a satisfactory novel. He tries to make his novels functional within an African context. His primary stress is on the individual African sensibility isolated from his society. His novels are a search not so much for private redemption as for communal salvation, and in this respect he reflects an essentially African rather than Western mentality.

Armah is a philosophical novelist: Realism is in the service of, or sacrificed to, an idea. He is a social critic searching for a philosophical and historical framework. His protagonists are social failures but heroes in the cause of the greater Africa. His ultimate purpose is pan-African in scope, and his experimentation with technique and form, even though the source may be Western, is a search for the appropriate voice to further the end of common understanding.

Although each novel individually could not be called a bildungsroman, together they appear, in retrospect, to trace the individual protagonist from confusion and frustration to a sense of wholeness and communal belonging. The "man" in *The Beautyful Ones Are Not Yet Born* cannot be sure of his own identity or his moral values because he receives no reinforcement from his society, while Densu in the fifth novel, *The Healers*, rejects his immediate society and joins a small outcast community that understands the larger African tradition.

Armah has some interesting things to say sociologically as well. Like most contemporary African novelists, he deals with the traumatic experience of colonialism, the rapid change from traditional to modern society, the effects of the slave trade and of Western influence in general, the difficulties of adapting to the technological age, the political corruption immediately after independence, and the cultural vacuum. His novels move from the narrow confines of one Ghanaian city in *The Beautyful Ones Are Not Yet Born* to the larger international scene of America, Europe, and North Africa, to show at first hand those forces that helped create the filth and artificiality surrounding his protagonist. In *Two Thousand Seasons* and *The Healers*, Armah leaves the 1960's to give a picture of African society in the distant and recent past. In general, he argues that foreign exploitation has perverted the traditional communal values, which are, if anything, superior to the ones that have replaced them. What seems to concern Armah particularly, however, are the psychological implications of this displacement.

The protagonists of the second two novels are mentally disturbed and require professional therapy or convalescence. Juana of *Fragments* is a psychologist, and the outcast priests of *Two Thousand Seasons* and *The Healers* are practitioners of traditional therapies. The essential problem that Armah identifies is the impotence and extreme depression of the sensitive individual rejected by the westernized African society. In addition, Armah explores the nightmares and dreams of his frustrated protagonists, and in his novels he seeks an answer to frustration through the revival of racial consciousness in myth and legend. The ultimate purpose of his novels is therapeutic.

THE BEAUTYFUL ONES ARE NOT YET BORN

If the central issue in Armah's novels is the relationship between the individual and his (or her) community, then *The Beautyful Ones Are Not Yet Born* is a depressing omen. The main character, the center of consciousness, has no name—not so much because he represents all men or even because he represents the man of integrity, though these are possible readings, but because he is anonymous. Society does not recognize his existence. He is an outcast because he attempts to hold on to moral values while the rest of society has succumbed to bribery, corruption, and materialism. This isolation is total. Even his own family urges him to advance himself for their benefit within the corrupt system. The isolation, however, extends beyond family and community. Even in this first novel, Armah introduces the historical context. The "man" is trapped within the present. He has no sense of belonging to a Ghanaian or to an African tradition. He cannot identify the source of his integrity or of his moral judgment. Hence, he resides in a historical void, which makes him question the very values that give him sustenance. Honesty seems unnatural, cruel, obstinate, even criminal and insane.

The story evolves at a specific time in the contemporary history of Ghana. Though Armah does not give dates, it is clear that the early episodes (chapters 1-12) take place late in Kwame Nkrumah's reign, in the mid-1960's. The final three chapters deal with the hours just after Nkrumah's fall in February, 1966. The "man" is a controller for the railroad, a husband, and the father of two children. Armah describes in naturalistic detail a day in the man's life, his journey to and from work, the oppressiveness of the physical surroundings, the boring and insignificant responsibilities of his job, and the return home to an unsympathetic and accusing wife. The only dramatic event in these first chapters is the man's rejection of a bribe.

To seek relief and reassurance, he pays a visit to his former teacher, who shares his moral awareness and can explain to some extent the origin of the present malaise, but who has withdrawn from society. The teacher has no family and hence no compelling responsibility. He refuses to participate in the corruption but also declines to fight it. All he can do for the man is understand his situation. He is, nevertheless, the first of a series of figures in the five novels who represent the wisdom of a way of life that Ghana no longer knows. Within this realistic and cynical first novel it is not surprising that the teacher lacks the confidence and the vision necessary to save the man or his society. In spite of this, Armah leaves no doubt as to the importance of the teacher and his philosophical appraisal of contemporary Ghana. He places the visit at the very center of the novel. From this point, the man must accept total isolation. He cannot lean on his elder and former guide: He must find his own solution.

The problem that faces the man in the final third of the novel involves him in the corruption of an old classmate who is a minister under Nkrumah. His wife and mother-in-law agree to participate in the illegal purchase of a fishing boat, which is primarily for the benefit of Minister Koomsan. When the man refuses complicity, he becomes even more of an outcast within the family. His wife constantly measures him against the successful Koomsan, who has surrounded himself with the things of modern civilization. The last three chapters, however, reverse the situation. Nkrumah falls. Koomsan, a pitifully frightened victim of the coup, comes to the man for aid. The two escape from the house just as the authorities arrive, and the man leads him to the fishing boat and to exile. The man himself swims back to shore and to his family. Though he has involved himself in the corruption he despises, the act of saving Koomsan must be seen as a heroic and humane gesture. The man's wife, at least, now recognizes his courage and his worth. The novel thus moves from almost total submergence in the repulsive details of daily life to a romantic but ironic act of heroism, whose ultimate significance is nevertheless left ambiguous.

Armah is already suggesting the larger movement from realism to myth in the figurative and even symbolic dimension of the narrative. What first strikes the reader's attention, in fact overwhelms him or her, is the vivid and disgusting insistence on the filth, the excrement, and the vomit that one touches and breathes in the city. Yet this physical reality is at the same time the political and moral corruption that the society discharges as it continues to pursue and consume the "things" of Western technology. Koomsan's escape through the latrine is symbolically a wallowing in his own excrement. A second symbol special to this novel is the chichi dodo bird, which despises excrement but subsists on the worms that the excrement nourishes: the man, as much as he may try to remain free of taint, is implicated in the social guilt.

Finally, Armah uses a third image, the stream, that recurs in all the other novels. He seems to identify water in a traditional way as a purifying agent. During one of his walks, the man notices, in an otherwise muddy stream, a perfectly clear current that seems to have no source. He associates it with a gleam of light—his own moral awareness—a clarity of vision that he cannot trace to any source. He sets this clarity against the brightness of new things imported from the West, but it is not strong enough or permanent enough to give him hope. In spite of his heroism, his baptismal dip in the ocean, and his "rebirth," he still must recognize at the end that "the beautyful ones are not yet born."

FRAGMENTS

In *Fragments*, Armah continues the exploration of the individual and his obligation to both family and community. The scene again takes place in the later 1960's, but the situations are considerably changed. Baako Onipa (the hero now has a name, which means "Only Person") is a "been-to," a member of the educated elite who has spent five years studying in the United States. In this respect, he resembles Armah himself, an American-educated intellectual who must have had similar difficulties readjusting to Ghanaian society.

Like Armah, Baako is a writer searching for a role within his newly independent nation. No longer is the protagonist buried in lower-class poverty. His education gives him access to prominent men in the community and to the things of modern technology. He thus has the means to satisfy the expectations of his family, especially his mother. He resembles the man, however, in his inability to sacrifice his personal integrity to take advantage of his opportunities. In a sense, his situation is even more critical than that of the man. He is a highly sensitive artist. Whereas the man has perceived the "madness" of his obstinacy, Baako has already experienced insanity in America and is on the edge of it again throughout this novel, the title of which, *Fragments*, is thus particularly appropriate.

The story does not follow a clear chronological path, because Armah has chosen to present it through three centers of consciousness. The emphasis is thus not on the exterior world but, much more obviously than in *The Beautyful Ones Are Not Yet Born*, on the psychological responses to the world of the two main characters, Baako and Juana, a Puerto

Rican psychologist who becomes Baako's confidant, and of Baako's grandmother, Naana, who represents the traditional wisdom of the people. The novel opens with Naana recalling Baako's ritual departure five years before and her anticipation of his cyclical return. Baako does return, unannounced, however, to avoid the inevitable ritual ceremony. He dreads to face his family because he brings no gifts and because he knows that he will be unable to fulfill his mother's expectations. His mother expects what the man's wife expected in *The Beautyful Ones Are Not Yet Born*, money and the comforts of the modern age. Baako, in his rebellion against this imitation of Western values, goes to his former teacher, Ocran, for advice. Ocran has himself chosen to pursue his profession as an artist in solitude, because he sees no possibility for useful work within contemporary Ghanaian society.

Against Ocran's advice, the less experienced Baako has decided to make the attempt by turning his talents as novelist to a more public role as a television scriptwriter. He hopes to transform popular Ghanaian myths into scripts for television, and in general to raise the consciousness of the people by introducing them to the true traditions of Ghana. The authorities, preferring to use the television screen as an instrument of propaganda, reject this proposal as dangerous. Baako goes back to the privacy of the writing table and, thus isolated, gradually loses his mind. His family places him in an asylum, from which he is about to be rescued by Juana as the novel closes.

The threat of insanity, in fact, has plagued Baako from the very beginning. He goes to Juana for help early in the novel. She becomes his lover and, along with Ocran, his spiritual guide. The novel thus ends as does *The Beautyful Ones Are Not Yet Born*, ambiguously—but with a note of hope, and with the nucleus of a new community, two Ghanaians and the outsider, Juana, who represents not the evils of white society but the sensitivities of a minority. Furthermore, Ocran seems to offer a temporary compromise between the two extremes that have driven Baako to insanity, a compromise that Armah develops in the later novels. Whereas society and family demand that Baako yield to their values, and Baako, while recognizing his inherent need for identity within the community, must maintain his integrity, Ocran proposes a kind of synthesis: Baako cannot expect to achieve his goal immediately. He must submit to a temporary isolation from the present society and work for the larger community of the future. Naana reinforces this view as her commentary closes the novel with a picture of contemporary Ghana in fragments. This novel thus has raised the argument to a more philosophical level than that of *The Beautyful Ones Are Not Yet Born* by using four different characters who reflect on the problem of the perceptive individual within a materialistic society.

In other ways, too, Armah moves away from the naturalism of his first novel. Even the naturalistic scenes, such as the killing of the "mad" dog, are obviously symbolic of something beyond themselves. Just as Juana observes a crowd of soldiers who close in on a dog that they only suspect to be mad, so she watches the community and the family judge and incarcerate Baako for his "insane" ideas. The novel also incorporates ritualistic and religious elements. Naana contrasts the unifying role of traditional ritual with the fragmentation of the present. The mother appeals to an itinerant, spiritualist preacher to aid her in praying for Baako's return. Baako and Juana discuss the similarities between Catholicism and animism, as opposed to the isolating force of Protestantism. Baako is concerned in particular with myth: He contrasts his overseas experience with the traditional hero's departure and triumphal return to save the community. He and Juana repeat the myth of Mame Water, who rises from the sea periodically to meet her lover and give him special powers, but at the same time leaves him with an excruciating sense of isolation. The water itself, like the stream from *The Beautyful Ones Are Not Yet Born*, flows into *Fragments*. Baako pictures himself swimming upstream against a cataract; water still seems to be a purifying force and the stream itself the natural flow of history.

WHY ARE WE SO BLEST?

In retrospect, *Why Are We So Blest?* appears to be a transition between Armah's first two novels and the mythical ones to follow. It continues the trend away from realistic description toward a study of multiple consciousness, a philosophical reflection, a larger international context, and an emphasis on personal relationships. The time of the novel, however, remains the same, the mid- to late 1960's, as does the central premise: the individual isolated from his community and hence from his own identity.

Again, Armah seems to be drawing from his own experience, this time as a student in an American university, and from the guilt feelings that inevitably arise in one who is given special treatment while his country suffers from the very hands that feed him. In a sense, the Ghanaian character, Modin, is Baako receiving the education that is so useless to him upon his return, though Armah has a far different fate for this avatar. The other major African character, Solo, shares with Modin a situation that Armah has not created in the first two novels. They both remain abroad, completely detached from their societies, Modin as a student and would-be revolutionary, Solo as a disillusioned revolutionary in exile. Solo, the dispassionate observer, finds in Modin a reincarnation (with variations) of his own past fascination with revolution and with a Western woman. This third major character is Aimée Reitsch, a white American of German ancestry, whose perverted fascination with Africa and with Modin precipitates his destruction.

The narrative in *Why Are We So Blest?* resembles that of *Fragments* in that it, too, has three centers of consciousness. The two principal actors in the drama, Modin and Aimée, have kept journals about their experiences, which Aimée leaves with Solo after Modin's death. Solo thus functions as editor, providing personal information and commentary and arranging the journal entries to reconstruct the story of their lives and his encounter with them in northern Africa. He opens the novel with an account of his own life before he met them and fills out this autobiography at intervals throughout the book. He is a reviewer of books eking out an existence in the fictional town of Laccryville (Algiers) and making occasional visits to the headquarters of a revolutionary organization that he once wished to join.

The story of Modin and Aimée, as Solo reconstructs it, goes back to Modin's days as a scholarship student in African studies at Harvard. Immediately after arriving, he receives a warning from Naita, the black secretary of his sponsor, that he must not trust those who have brought him to the United States. They actually consider him their property. Modin eventually realizes that she is right about the white race in general being the black person's destroyer, but makes the mistake of considering Aimée an exception. He leaves for Africa with her to join the revolutionary organization in Laccryville. Its leaders are suspicious of Aimée and hence reject them both. Solo meets them and would like to do something to save Modin, but realizes that he is doomed. Modin and Aimée take off on a futile hitchhiking journey across the Sahara, only to be picked up by white male racists who sexually abuse them and leave Modin to die. Aimée returns to her middle-class life in America and Solo is left frustrated in his isolation. It would seem, however, that Solo as author has finally found his voice, and is fulfilling a useful function after all in this "book" that he is offering to the public. That is, Solo has discovered the role that Armah himself has chosen.

In this respect, *Why Are We So Blest?* looks forward to the positive and hopeful tone of the next three novels. What the "man" and Baako lacked, Solo has discovered. In other ways, too, this novel looks forward. The stream as a motif reappears, but it is no longer muddy as in *The Beautyful Ones Are Not Yet Born*, and the swimmer is no longer fighting against the current. Instead, Solo is observing its continuous flow and waiting for a place to enter and become a part of it. Madness, obsession, and psychological tension continue to be significant motifs, but while *Fragments* ends with Baako in an asylum, this novel opens with Solo's overcoming a bout of mental depression by committing himself to a month's convalescence in a hospital. His return to health accompanies a transformation in his view of society, the nature of revolution, and the role of militants.

By this third novel, also, Armah has transformed the African female figure into a kind of soul mate. Naita possesses sexual purity, a natural grace, and a wisdom that could have been Modin's salvation. She attains an almost mythical dimension. The most significant symbol in the novel, in fact, is sexuality. Through it, Armah exposes the selfish aggressiveness of the white female and the cruel fascism of the white male. The novel announces with violent acerbity a thesis that appears for the first time in Armah's fiction, the essential animosity between black and white. It bears the sure stamp of the Black Muslim movement that must have deeply affected him in America. The white race becomes identified as the destroyer, the enemy. The African has lost his or her identity because the white race has taken away the tradition and the community that gave him or her meaning.

TWO THOUSAND SEASONS

In *Two Thousand Seasons*, Armah prophesies a more fruitful course. He makes a leap of faith in his narrative style and, more important, in his promise of an answer to the frustrated heroes of the first three novels. This novel has no hero, unless it be the community itself. No isolated personality is trapped within his own consciousness. The narrator, as character, is the ubiquitous member of every generation who knows the true history of the tribe. He is the griot, the tribal historian, the wise man, the poet. He is a member of the select few whose task it is to maintain the spiritual coherence of the group. The story he tells is the group's chronicle. Thus Armah, as author, effaces himself by adopting the traditional and anonymous role of historian—a significantly symbolic act since Armah must recognize that he too finds his identity only if he merges with the community.

The chronicle begins one thousand years (two thousand seasons) ago, when the Akan tribe, probably intended to represent the black race, living in peace, harmony, and "reciprocity" on the edge of the desert, succumbs to the "predators" of the north, the Arab-Muslim civilization of North Africa. The narrator describes the destruction of the social order and the enslavement of the people. It is here that the community first loses its cohesiveness. A small nucleus of people, particularly women of the tribe, initiate and lead a revolt, and then a migration away from the desert toward the south. The eventual destination is present-day Ghana, but the people arrive only to find another threat from the sea. The Europeans have begun their exploitation of the continent.

The last half of the novel concentrates on the disintegration of the tribe as the forces from without create division within. The narrator focuses on one particular period, when one generation of youths undergoing initiation escapes into the forest and organizes a resistance movement. A seer named Isanusi leads them and trains them in the "Way," the traditional values of the tribe. Their king, Koranche, subsequently persuades them to return, deceives them, and sells them into slavery. They are able to escape from the slave ship and make their way back to the forest retreat, bringing with them new recruits. These guerrilla warriors, the "beautyful ones," operate against the oppressive authorities who have betrayed the tribal traditions.

Armah has thus solved the essential problem facing the protagonists of the early novels. He has achieved the synthesis adumbrated by Ocran in *Fragments*. Though it may be impossible to join and serve the particular society in Ghana today, it is possible to participate spiritually in the larger society and in the genuine traditions of the people. This solution certainly explains the mythical and romantic mode of this novel in contrast to the naturalism or realism at the base of the first three. No longer caught within the contemporary world of the 1960's, the initiates of *Two Thousand Seasons* belong to an ancient tradition. A mythical pattern controls the novel. The tribe begins in Eden, falls from grace, and moves toward the cyclical return. It is this confidence in the future and in the total pattern of life that separates this novel from its predecessors.

The racism of *Why Are We So Blest?* becomes a struggle for cultural identity on a panoramic scale. The whites, whether Muslim or Christian, are the enemy. Their culture is oppressive and destructive to blacks. They represent class divisions and hierarchical structures. The African "way" is reciprocity, equality, and a sharing of responsibility and power. Armah is obviously dealing in romantic terms. He is also trying to find his own modus vivendi: a justification of his "exile" and a role within the larger pattern of his nation's fate.

The Healers

Armah called *The Healers* a historical novel. It is, to be sure, based on particular events in the 1870's during the Second Asante War, and Armah's purpose—as in the previous novels, especially *Two Thousand Seasons*—is to offer an interpretation of Ghanaian (African) society and to reevaluate African history. His method, however, is not so much historical as romantic and mythical. The story is a mixture of fact and fiction, and the characters and events conform to an idea of the essential African mentality and the future of the African continent. It thus continues the optimistic chronicle of the previous novel.

The storyteller is again the "anonymous" griot. The tale begins as an epic, in medias res. It proceeds immediately to narrate the initiation of nine Asante boys into manhood. Densu is obviously a young man of heroic proportions. He refuses to engage in the wrestling contest because the competition required violates the spirit of cooperation that he values. He nevertheless demonstrates his superior strength and grace in this and other games, while finally refusing to win to avoid being named the next chief in the tribe. He resists this temptation held out by Ababio, the evil adviser who remains Densu's nemesis throughout the novel. Densu's ambition is to join the spiritual ones, the "priests" or "healers" who live as outcasts in the forest and who preserve the values of the community that are being perverted by ambitious men such as Ababio. Before he can realize this goal, however, he must not only convince Damfo, the chief healer and his spiritual guide, that he can truly sacrifice the things of common life but also overcome Ababio's scheme to condemn him falsely for murder and to engage in the war against the British as General Nkwanta's aid. The novel ends melodramatically, with the betrayal and defeat of the Asante army, the last-minute acquittal of Densu at the murder trial, and the various African tribes dancing on the beach, ironically brought together by the invading British.

Armah thus suggests a future pan-African unity. For the present, however—if the events of the 1870's offer a paradigm for the contemporary situation—the solution to the sociological and psychological problems facing Ghanaians is much the same as that proposed in *Two Thousand Seasons*. The perceptive individual who works for a solution must not expect an immediate communal identity. Again, Armah clarifies the choices available through romantic simplification. In *Two Thousand Seasons*, the proponents of the Way face a challenge from the white predators and destroyers and from the zombies among their own people. In *The Healers*, the choice is between competition and manipulation on one hand and cooperation and inspiration on the other. Densu chooses to leave his tribe because he knows that the leaders and the people are not ready for the essential virtues of the true community. Instead, he is initiated by Damfo into the community of healers. Damfo, in his dealings with other people, never resorts to manipulation or even persuasion, but rather relies on spiritual understanding and respect. This is presented as the only way to establish a genuine community.

In this fifth novel, Armah seems to be consciously drawing in all the threads from his early works. The beautyful ones, it would seem, are born, but they reside outside the society itself, preparing for the future. Unlike the "man," they fully accept the pain of nonconformity. The healer, Damfo, fulfills the tasks that frustrate the teacher, Ocran, Juana, Naana, and Solo. In his conversations with Densu, he employs a method of instruction that is both Socratic and therapeutic. The philosophical and psychological conflicts that plague the early heroes thus find their resolutions in the spiritual communication and intimate friendship between priest and initiate. Nightmares become dreams of self-discovery. Body, mind, and spirit achieve harmony in Densu. He sees the chaos of the present within the perspectives of history. He is also at home in the natural world.

The stream that flows as a minor motif through the other novels is a significant part of the setting in *The Healers*. Densu wins the swimming contest not by competing but by becoming at one with the natural element. He later escapes arrest by holding on to roots at the bottom of the stream and breathing through a hollowed-out cane. Even later, he and Damfo master the stream in a long journey against the current. Finally, in this river of life Densu contemplates his own image and purpose. Clearly, Armah creates a hero in *The Healers* who has found his place in the stream of history, a hero who gives meaning to Armah's own chosen role in his community.

OSIRIS RISING

Osiris Rising, Armah's sixth novel—and his first in seventeen years—represents a further evolution of his perspective along this axis. The old themes are once again in evidence: pan-African unity, historical consciousness, intellectual nonconformity, and disgust with the corrupt African leadership. The Osiris and Isis myth alluded to in the title provides an important symbolic background for this otherwise realistic text. As a genuinely African myth of origin, the Osiris legend mirrors a major theme of the novel, which explicitly deals with the need for Africa to put its own culture at the center of its historical consciousness. The magnificence of ancient Egypt then serves as the perfect and natural locus for this shift. The novel tells the story of Ast, a young African American Egyptologist who feels displaced in America and thus "goes home" to Africa in search of her roots and a sense of belonging. She is also following Asar, her college lover who has returned to his homeland in Africa to fight against the injustices of the postindependence puppet regimes. Significantly, the country to which she travels (and where the rest of the novel takes place) is never named directly. Armah's pan-Africanism makes him more interested in the symbolic aspects of the story than in its relevance to any single national entity. In Africa, Ast comes across another acquaintance from her university days, Asar's longtime rival and countryman Seth, who has risen in the corrupt administration to become chief of security for the entire nation. The action of the novel revolves largely around Ast's and Asar's grassroots political organizing on the campus where they both teach, set against the insipid political machinations of Seth, who sees Asar in particular as a threat to his way of life. Ultimately, Seth appears to "win" at the close of the novel as Asar's body is literally blown into fragments by the guns of Seth's death squad.

When considered alongside the informing Osiris myth, however, Seth's victory is exposed as transitory and futile against the greater advances for which Asar's teaching has set the stage. The myth tells of Osiris and his sister and wife Isis, who ruled Egypt as king and queen. Their brother Seth murdered Osiris and scattered fragments of the body across Egypt, which historically accounted for the spread of the Osiris cult. Isis then raised their son, Horus, to manhood, at which time he avenged his father's murder by deposing Seth and assuming power as king of the living. Osiris, reassembled by Isis, became lord of the underworld. With this in mind, an allegorical reading of the novel becomes clear: Asar, who has clearly stated throughout the novel that his death would be an insignificant obstacle for the widespread communal movement for African unity, is the martyr Osiris, and the rising alluded to in the title suggests that indeed the movement will yet prevail. Likewise, that Ast is pregnant with Asar's child would seem to prophesy the child's ultimate defeat of Seth and victory for the representatives of African justice.

OTHER MAJOR WORKS

SHORT FICTION: "Yaw Manu's Charm," in *The Atlantic*, 1968; "The Offal Kind," in *Harper's*, 1969.

POETRY: "Aftermath," in *Messages: Poems from Ghana*, 1970.

NONFICTION: "African Socialism: Utopian or Scientific?," in *Présence Africaine*, 1967; *The Eloquence of the Scribes: A Memoir on the Sources and Resources of African Literature*, 2006.

Thomas Banks
Updated by Harland W. Jones III

BIBLIOGRAPHY

Fraser, Robert. *The Novels of Ayi Kwei Armah: A Study in Polemical Fiction*. London: Heinemann, 1980. An excellent starting place for general readers. The first chapter provides the context of liberation and resistance informing Armah's work and is followed by five chapters on individual novels. Includes a bibliography and an index.

Lazarus, Neil. *Resistance in Postcolonial African Fiction*. New Haven, Conn.: Yale University Press, 1990. Full-length study that focuses on the politics and ideology of Armah's first three novels. A cogently argued critique of early postcolonial nationalism.

Ogede, Ode. *Ayi Kwei Armah: Radical Iconoclast*. London: Heinemann, 1999. Full-length study of Armah's entire oeuvre, from one of the most prolific Armah scholars. Focuses on the juxtapositions of "imaginary" worlds with the "actual." A volume in the Studies in African Literature series.

Okolo, M. S. C. *African Literature as Political Philosophy*. New York: Palgrave Macmillan, 2007. While focusing on works by Chinua Achebe and Ngugi wa Thiong'o, Okolo places these writings within the broader context of postcolonial African literature, including a discussion of Armah's work. Okolo argues that Armah, Achebe, and Thiong'o have been profoundly affected by the continent's political situation and have helped create a new African political philosophy.

Palmer, Eustace. "Negritude Rediscovered: A Reading of the Recent Novels of Armah, Ngugi, and Soyinka." *International Fiction Review* 8 (1981): 1-11. This discussion of the concept of negritude pays particular attention to three works: Soyinka's *Season of Anomy*, Ngugi's *Petals of Blood*, and Armah's *Two Thousand Seasons*. Includes notes.

Research in African Literatures 18 (Summer, 1987). A special issue on Ayi Kwei Armah that includes three articles, a bibliography of studies in African literature, and seventeen book reviews.

Wodajo, Tsegaye. *Hope in the Midst of Despair: A Novelist's Cures for Africa*. Trenton, N.J.: Africa World Press, 2004. Examines five novels—*The Beautyful Ones Are Not Yet Born*, *Fragments*, *Two Thousand Seasons*, *The Healers*, and *Osiris Rising*—to focus on the characters' protests against Africa's sociopolitical and economic institutions. Wodajo argues that the first two novels meticulously describe the deterioration of these institutions, providing a rationale for the protagonists of the last three novels, who openly resist the continent's corrupt ruling elite and the complicity of their foreign collaborators.

Wright, Derek. *Ayi Kwei Armah's Africa: The Sources of His Fiction*. London: Hans Zell, 1989. Traces the African background of Armah's fiction, particularly the early novels, and provides a broad cultural and anthropological context. Useful for the student and reader already familiar with Armah's work and seeking more specialized analysis. Includes chapter notes, a bibliography, and an index.

_______, ed. *Critical Perspectives on Ayi Kwei Armah*. Boulder, Colo.: Three Continents Press, 1992. Collection of twenty-two essays on Armah's early career. Includes four general essays and seven on *The Beautyful Ones Are Not Yet Born*, with the rest evenly distributed among four other early novels. Extensive and valuable bibliography and notes on contributors.

Yankson, Kofi E. *The Rot of the Land and the Birth of the Beautyful Ones: The World of Ayi Kwei Armah's Novels*. Accra: Ghana Universities Press, 2000. A text of a lecture delivered in 1994, in which Yankson critiques *The Beautyful Ones Are Not Yet Born*, *Fragments*, *Why Are We So Blest?*, *Two Thousand Seasons*, and *The Healers*. Maintains that these novels depict two types of souls—diseased and healthy. Focuses on the nature and causes of the diseased souls who, according to Armah, constitute the rot of the African continent.

HERMANN BROCH

Born: Vienna, Austria; November 1, 1886
Died: New Haven, Connecticut; May 30, 1951
Also known as: Hermann Joseph Broch; Vergil Bertrand

PRINCIPAL LONG FICTION

Die Schlafwandler, 1931-1932 (*The Sleepwalkers,* 1932)
Die unbekannte Grösse, 1933 (*The Unknown Quantity,* 1935)
Der Tod des Vergil, 1945 (*The Death of Virgil,* 1945)
Die Schuldlosen, 1950 (*The Guiltless,* 1974)
Der Versucher, 1953 (revised as *Demeter,* 1967, *Bergroman,* 1969, and *Die Verzauberung,* 1976; English translation, *The Spell,* 1986)

OTHER LITERARY FORMS

Although his fame and reputation as a writer rest on his two major novels, *The Sleepwalkers* and *The Death of Virgil,* Hermann Broch (brawk) was in fact a multifaceted author of truly eclectic interests—interests ranging from literature per se in almost every genre to literary criticism, from philosophical and sociopolitical essays to incisive psychological studies of mass hysteria. Broch's earliest publications were poems and essayistic studies submitted to some of the local journals in Vienna. A sonnet, "Mathematisches Mysterium" (mathematical mysterium), and two essays—one a review of Thomas Mann's novella *Der Tod in Venedig* (1912; *Death in Venice,* 1925)—appeared as early as 1913 in the liberal journal *Der Brenner,* which was noted for publishing such influential writers of the period as Karl Kraus, Mann, Georg Trakl, Franz Werfel, and Stefan Zweig.

In fact, it was the essay, as a vehicle for the expression of both literary and philosophical thought, that would become Broch's preferred medium over the years, although one that was long overshadowed in the minds of the reading public by his two major novels. At the end of World War I, in 1919, Broch published the essay "Konstitutionelle Diktatur als demokratisches Rätesystem" (constitutional dictatorship as a democratic soviet-system), which outlines his belief that a sort of Nietzschean will to power was required if constitutional governments were to bring about a true democracy based on humanist, egalitarian ideals. Other important essays of the early 1930's by Broch include his "Logik einer zerfallenen Welt" (logic of a fallen world) and "Das Böse im Wertsystem der Kunst" (evil in the value system of art); both indicate their author's lifelong search for human values in a world gone awry.

One of Broch's more incisive essays to appear in English was titled "The Style of the Mythical Age," published in 1947; in the early 1950's there followed such essays as "Einige Bemerkungen zum Problem des Kitsches" (observations on the problem of kitsch), "Hofmannsthal und seine Zeit" (Hofmannsthal and his age), and "Study on Mass-

Hysteria," posthumously published in 1959. Broch's essays occupy two volumes of the ten-volume edition of his collected works, *Gesammelte Werke*, published by Rhein Verlag of Zurich over a nine-year period beginning in 1952: The first volume of essays, published in 1955, bears the title *Dichten und Erkennen: Essays I* (poetry and perception); the second volume, also published in 1955, is titled *Erkennen und Handeln: Essays II* (perception and deed).

Broch also tried his hand at drama, writing three plays between 1933 and 1934. His first play, *Die Entsühnung* (pb. 1933; *The Atonement*, 1972), premiered at the prestigious Schauspielhaus in Zurich, Switzerland, on May 15, 1934, under the title . . . *Denn sie wissen nicht, was sie tun* (for they know not what they do). It deals with workers' problems and stems from Broch's experience as a skillful and respected mediator in labor disputes within the textile industry. As one indication of the continuing interests even in Broch's minor works, this early play was successfully adapted for radio by Ernst Schonwiese in 1961.

Broch's second work for the theater, *Es bleibt alles beim Alten* (1934; the same old thing), was a musical farce written with his son, Hermann Friedrich Broch de Rothermann (1910-1994). Broch's third work in this genre bore the rather baroque title *Aus der Luft gegriffen: Oder, Die Geschèfte des Baron Laborde* (1934; pulled out of thin air: or, the affairs of Baron Laborde); once again, Broch's son was named coauthor, though the actual extent of his participation is in dispute. It was apparently the father's wish that his son embrace a theatrical career, so he listed him as a collaborator in the writing of these plays. It is interesting to note that, in a later version of this play, Broch replaced both his name and his son's name with the pseudonym Vergil Bertrand—a name made up of those of two of the chief protagonists in *The Death of Virgil* and *The Sleepwalkers*, respectively.

Finally, Broch was also a skillful writer of short stories; a collection, *Short Stories*, edited by Eric Herd, appeared in 1966. Some of Broch's most famous stories are "Der Meeresspiegel" (1933; "The Ocean's Mirror"); "Die Heimkehr des Vergil" (1933; "The Homecoming of Virgil"), which foreshadows the larger novel of 1945; and "Der Steinerne Gast" (1941; "The Stony Guest"), the germinal story of the novel *The Guiltless*.

ACHIEVEMENTS

Hermann Broch must surely be counted among such other major German novelists of the twentieth century as Franz Kafka, Mann, Robert Musil, Heinrich Böll, and Günter Grass, alongside such other creative artists as Wassily Kandinsky, Gustav Klimt, Oskar Kokoschka, Gustav Mahler, Egon Schiele, and Arnold Schönberg—in terms of both the committed humanist stance he assumes in his writing and the purely technical mastery of his craft. In this latter regard, Broch has been compared justifiably to James Joyce and William Faulkner in his use of interior monologue and stream of consciousness to capture the reality of life—and death—that he perceived all around him. For Broch, such techniques reflect the age in which he matured. William James's *Principles of Psychology*, which includes a chapter titled "The Stream of Thought," had been published in 1890. It was James who had advanced the concept of stream of consciousness, as later adapted for fiction. Sigmund Freud's *Die Traumdeutung* (*Interpretation of Dreams*), which called attention to the irrational inner life of humans, appeared in 1900, and his *Zur Psychopathologie des Alltagslebens* (*Psychopathology of Everyday Life*) was published in 1904. Albert Einstein's theory of relativity, which called into question the very certainty with which humans could know the "real" world, was published in 1905. All these works fostered, indeed necessitated, a preoccupation with subjective truth on the part of intellectuals of the day.

Given his early training as an engineer and his more than passing interest in science, Broch was acutely conscious of such revolutionary theories concerning reality and was able to translate the scientific and psychological principles being developed at that time into viable literary devices. His most successful literary endeavor, *The Death of Virgil*, is a compelling tour de force, lyric in its elegiac sense of loss, dreamlike in its irreal transcendence of time and space, yet actual in its uncompromising depiction of the artist's fate.

Broch's lifework was the quest for meaning in a world in which all certainties were open to question. Though he did not begin his full-fledged literary career until he was in his forties, he was spiritually a part of that generation of apocalyptic writers and artists who bore witness to the crisis facing Western European culture in the first decades of the twentieth century. While other artists of the day may have contributed their share to the erosion of cultural values (the Dadaists, for example) or sought order and meaning in an irrational realm beyond the visible world of shared human experience (the Surrealists), Broch, to his credit, stood firmly in this maelstrom of eroding values, seeking to recover a sense of absolute totality in the simultaneity of universal human actions. To perceive reality, to plot an ethical course of behavior based on one's perceptions, and to act with conviction for the betterment of humanity was Broch's sustaining motivation in all of his writing, regardless of genre.

Finally, insofar as Broch reached maturity as an author well after such spiritual contemporaries as Kafka (1883-1924), Rainer Maria Rilke (1875-1926), and Hugo von Hofmannsthal (1874-1929), Broch must be regarded as a vital link to such important Austrian writers as Thomas Bernhard and Peter Handke—writers who are similarly concerned with the debilitating effect of modern civilization on the individual psyche, writers committed as Broch was to sociopolitical, cultural critique, using literary methods that owe their effectiveness in part to extraliterary disciplines such as psychology, sociolinguistics, and cultural anthropology.

BIOGRAPHY

Hermann Joseph Broch was born in Vienna, Austria, on November 1, 1886, the first son of Joseph Broch, a wealthy Jewish textile manufacturer, and Johanna, née Schnabel, who came from an old and affluent Viennese Jewish family. Three years later, Broch's brother, Friedrich, was born.

In a symbolic sense, Hermann Broch was very much a child of his times. He grew up in fin de siècle Europe, experiencing all the hopes and fears, the sense of irrevocable loss coupled with the dreams of unlimited fulfillment, then manifest. It was a time of transition, of outward progress, yet it was a time when people began to call into question the very basis of life, which for centuries had rested upon a foundation of unshakable absolutes. To an entire generation that prided itself on its modernity, the nineteenth century must have seemed strangely anachronistic; the fin de siècle was a period of uncertainty and anxiety—the "gay apocalypse," as Broch himself termed it—one that seemed relativistic and devoid of absolutes. As such, it would leave its stamp on all of Broch's writing, ultimately finding its most eloquent expression in *The Death of Virgil*. Further, it is this crisis in values that accounts in large measure for the boundary situations of all of Broch's fictional characters.

It was in this fragile world that Broch entered adulthood. In 1903, he graduated from the public school system and advanced to the Vienna Institute for Weaving Technology. Further study followed at the Textile Institute in Mülhausen (Alsace-Lorraine)—a period in Broch's life that would provide the background for the third part of *The Sleepwalkers*. Upon graduating in September of 1907 with a degree in textile engineering, Broch journeyed to the United States for two months to familiarize himself with cotton farming and milling procedures in the South, particularly in New Orleans, Louisiana. Upon his return to Austria, Broch entered his father's firm and became active in its management. As an administrator in the local textile union, Broch also gained a reputation for his equitable decisions in labor disputes. The plight of the worker in a society, changed overnight by rapid industrialization, was familiar to Broch from not only personal experience but also his reading of German naturalists such as Gerhart Hauptmann, Arno Holz, Johannes Schlaf, and Hermann Sudermann.

In 1908, Broch served for a time as a volunteer with the military stationed in Zagreb. In December of 1909, he married Franziska von Rothermann, despite the objections of both families. He continued to work in his father's firm, educating himself by reading widely in many fields. From 1915 to 1921, he pursued more formal studies in logic, mathematics, and physics at the University of Vienna, all the while working on a personal theory of values and his own philosophy of history. He began to immerse himself in ideas of Immanuel Kant, Søren Kierkegaard, Friedrich Nietzsche, Arthur Schopenhauer, Karl Kraus, and Otto Weininger. Oswald Spengler's *Der Untergang des Abendlandes* (1918-1922; *The Decline of the West*, 1926-1928), in particular, prompted Broch to develop his ideas on the necessity of the heroic quest on the part of the isolated and alienated individual if humankind should rise from the abyss of shattered values. Paradoxically, for Broch, the search for personal values served only to exacerbate the collapse of communal values. Years later, as a refugee from Adolf Hitler's Third Reich, Broch would seek a resolution of this paradox in the individual's pursuit of universal humanist goals.

During World War I, Broch served as an administrator for the Austrian Red Cross until he was discharged for medical reasons in 1916. He assumed control of his father's business and continued to write essays on philosophical and sociopolitical issues. As an indication of the direction his thought took at this time, one finds Broch turning for publication to such journals as *Die Rettung* and *Der Friede*. It was also at this time that Broch began to gain entry into the leading literary and intellectual circles active in Vienna at this time: the circles around Freud, the acerbic critic Karl Kraus, the writer Robert Musil, and the philosopher Ludwig Wittgenstein.

The crisis in values that began to manifest itself in nearly every phase of human endeavor during the hectic 1920's proved especially critical for Broch. His twelve-year marriage to von Rothermann ended in divorce in 1922, after a year's separation. The fear of impending inflation as well as a desire to devote more and more time to purely intellectual pursuits prompted Broch to give up the directorship of the family firm in 1927. From 1927 to 1931, he enrolled in courses at the University of Vienna, studying mathematics, philosophy, philology, and psychology. He began writing in earnest, seeing in literature the chance to resolve those of life's questions incapable of being answered adequately by rational science alone. His first major success, *The Sleepwalkers*, was completed during these years.

In later years, particularly after the publication of *The Death of Virgil*, Broch would once again return to his roots in science, devoting his attention almost exclusively to the social sciences. He came to view science as a sort of metapolitics, better able to redeem humankind than art, having grown skeptical once again of the efficacy of art to explain life, to posit values adequately for the masses. Ironically enough, it is in his most ambitious work, *The Death of Virgil*, that Broch eloquently expresses in art his apprehension and uncertainties about art. So great, in fact, was his conviction in this regard that he went so far as to associate the art for art's sake aesthetic of a poet such as Stefan George, for instance, with that sort of pseudo-art that has come to be known as kitsch. The personal crisis in his life worsened and, in 1928, he sold the family textile mills, despite the opposition of relatives, and returned to the University of Vienna to pursue a doctorate in philosophy and mathematics.

The situation for Jews grew worse daily—the first laws against the Jews were passed in 1933—and study at the university became increasingly difficult (even though Broch had converted to Catholicism in the early twentieth century). In 1935, he moved to Mösern near Seefeld in the Tyrolean Alps to work on his so-called mountain novel, *Bergroman*. It is a work that attempts to express the demoniac personality of the protagonist, who captivates an entire village, subjecting it entirely to his will. It was meant to present in miniature an idea of the mass hysteria of the fascist era. In its setting, the novel owes much to Mann's *Der Zauberberg* (1924; *The Magic Mountain*, 1927), though it is fragmentary and far inferior to Mann's monumental effort. Broch had met Mann in 1932 and had been influenced by him as early as the first decade of the century. He wrote a review of Mann's *Death in Venice* in 1913 and would undoubtedly have been familiar with Mann's first major success as a writer, *Buddenbrooks* (1900), which details the decline and fall of one family amid that of an entire age and way of life. Personal matters deteriorated for Broch during the late 1930's. He was arrested and held in detention by the Gestapo; through the intervention of such well-known figures as Joyce and Mann, Broch's release was secured and permission was granted for him to emigrate.

Traveling by way of England and Scotland, Broch finally arrived in New York on October 9, 1938, to begin a new life. While in England, he received assistance from the PEN Club of London, which enabled him to continue work on *The Death of Virgil*. Once in the United States, Broch was aided by the American Guild for German Cultural Freedom in New York and by the Oberlaender Trust of Philadelphia. Other grants that he received over the years came from the American Academy of Arts and Letters, the John Simon Guggenheim Memorial Foundation (1939) for work on *The Death of Virgil*, the Rockefeller Foundation (1942), and the Bollingen Foundation (1946-1947), the latter two being granted so that Broch could continue his research in mass psychology. Offers also came in from major universities. Broch worked at the Princeton Office of Public Opinion Research and accepted a professorship in German literature at Yale University. In addition, he received an invitation to teach at East Germany's prestigious Jena University, but he declined this offer to continue his work at Yale.

With the publication in 1945 of *The Death of Virgil*, Broch's place in the history of German—and world—literature was secure. His reputation during his last years in the United States grew steadily, though it never rivaled that of such other noted émigrés as Bertolt Brecht and Mann. In 1950, Broch was nominated by the Austrian delegation of the PEN Club, an international writers' association, as well as by literary circles in the United States, for the Nobel Prize in Literature. Thus, Broch was on the threshold of a much-deserved worldwide recognition when he succumbed to a heart attack on May 30, 1951, in New Haven, Connecticut; burial followed in nearby Killingworth.

ANALYSIS

THE SLEEPWALKERS

Hermann Broch's first novel, *The Sleepwalkers*, is a psychological-historical novel that explores the gradual disintegration of values beginning in the latter half of the nineteenth century and culminating in the Armageddon that was World War I. The work is a trilogy whose main sections bear the names and the worldviews of each section's protagonist: "Pasenow, or the Romantic," "Esch, or the Anarchist," and "Huguenau, or the Realist."

Specifically, the work depicts the degeneration of German society from 1888 to 1918—a thirty-year period of crucial and inevitable change, as Hannah Arendt describes it in her 1949 article "The Achievement of Hermann Broch":

> 1888, when the Romantic finds himself in the not yet visible decay of the old world; 1903, when the Anarchist gets entangled in the prewar confusion of values; 1918, when the Realist becomes the undisputed master of a nihilistic society.

Part 1 of *The Sleepwalkers* presents the reader with the fragile world of the Junker Joachim von Pasenow, a Romantic in the sense that he inhabits an otherworldly realm of sterile conventions and anachronistic Prussian values, a realm of facades and titular masks whose symbol is the uniform. The protagonist is a man of honor, a believer in order and tradition. He loses his brother, Helmuth, in a senseless duel over family honor and so assumes responsibility for the family estate. In his task of maintaining the property and privileges of the landed aristocracy to which his family belongs, he is helped by his close friend, Eduard von Bertrand, who has risen to become a leading industrialist in Berlin. The first part comes to a close with Pasenow's marriage to Elisabeth, who, as the daughter of a wealthy neighbor, is well within Pasenow's social circle. The founding of this new family, particularly after the birth of a child, seems to promise the continued growth and prosperity of Pasenow's class and way of life. As Broch's readers will come to discover, this is not to be.

In part 2, a petit bourgeois bookkeeper by the name of Esch makes his appearance. A malcontent, he is called an anarchist because, unlike Pasenow, he has lost faith in the old values and is seeking a new faith at any cost. Yet, like the hero of part 1, Esch is presented as a victim of circumstances, of a process of general social and cultural decline destined to run its full course. Having become a small-time variety-show entrepreneur, Esch, who is a social climber, will use any means at his disposal to get ahead—bribery and blackmail included. He is an impetuous man, settling accounts with real or imagined adversaries in confrontations contrived and acted out in his mind. Such interior dialogues only exacerbate Esch's inability to act. Though drawn to political agitators, his attraction, like his dreams, is so unrefined as to inhibit effectively any consequent action. Rather, Esch destroys things and people who are seen to stand in his way. Foremost among them is Pasenow's friend, Bertrand, whom Esch tries to blackmail for his homosexuality. Bertrand, a man positively portrayed as someone in charge of his fate, a man against whose actions those of the other characters are to be gauged, commits suicide rather than submit to the intrigues of a person such as Esch. His death must be viewed as the death of all that is decent and worthwhile in the novel. At the close of part 2, Esch takes the widow Hentjen in marriage in a near parody of Pasenow's marriage at the close of part 1.

In part 3, the reader is confronted with the total triumph of amorality. Although Huguenau, the realist, is the nominal hero of this last section, he shares center stage with Pasenow, who has gone on to become a major in the war and is now governor of the town in which Esch is serving as editor of a Socialist newspaper. Through a twist of fate—Pasenow publishes an idealistic article in Esch's paper—the two men become allied across class boundaries and against Huguenau, who, after deserting from the same army in which Pasenow had served so honorably, has become a successful businessman. He is a realist in the sense that his approach to every situation in life is cold, methodical—in short, businesslike. Such a worldview allows Huguenau to manipulate life dispassionately to his own advantage. Huguenau ends up slandering Pasenow and murdering Esch—both of whom, like sleepwalkers, are oblivious to events around them—yet still manages to become a leading member of the society that has emerged after the war.

The destinies of Pasenow and Esch are those of Romantic tradition and mere anarchy: the Romantic past is over; anarchy, as a precondition for the emergence of a new social order, has spent its energy. The fascist state is being born. On a technical level, the form of the novel perfectly reflects its content. Traditional nineteenth century epic narration—reminiscent, for example, of the mature Theodor Fontane—dominates the first portion of the novel. Gradually, however, this ordered, objective style becomes transformed into a more subjective narrative style. The tightly woven and objectively related plot incidents of part 1 give way to the imaginative musings of Esch in part 2, where stream of consciousness and interior dialogue mirror the growing emphasis on subjective reality and its concomitant skepticism, prevalent around the beginning of the twentieth century.

In part 3, the narration has become even more fragmented; it has disintegrated into a series of epic, dramatic, or lyric episodes bound loosely by the destinies of Pasenow, Esch, and Huguenau. Through the juxtaposition of seemingly objective dialogue and stream of consciousness, Broch skillfully plays off one view of reality against another. The resulting discrepancy between outer and inner reality reveals, according to Arendt, "the fundamental fragility of the time, the insecurity and convulsiveness of those who were its representatives." Through his use of various narrative perspectives to relate main and subordinate plot lines, Broch creates multiple levels of action and reality as his characters emerge, recede, and interact with one another. This technique effectively reflects the general collapse of an integrated worldview and results in a true multiple perspective, each character, each social sphere declaring its own relative values to be absolute.

THE DEATH OF VIRGIL

The Death of Virgil, which was recognized with both Guggenheim and Rockefeller awards, was originally written in the form of an eighteen-page story in 1936. The story was modified and lengthened as a direct result of Broch's detention and the very real threat of death at the hands of the Nazis in 1938. As Theodore Ziolkowski points out, "Whereas [Broch] had previously considered Vergil primarily as a prototype of the artist in a valueless society, he now devoted his attention to the *death* of Vergil." Broch himself said of the genesis of the work that "*Virgil* was not written as a 'book,' but (under Hitler's threat) as my private discussion with death." Broch continued to work on *The Death of Virgil* after his release from prison—revising and expanding the work's central idea—and by 1940, he had compiled the major part of the novel. He continued to refine the work until 1945, when it was published simultaneously in English and German. As the title indicates, the story deals with the death of the poet Vergil; his meditations on self and society, art and human activity, and life and death constitute the bulk of the novel.

The story takes place in the year 19 B.C.E., in the ancient port city of Brundisium in Italy; in an obvious parallel to Joyce's *Ulysses* (1922), the work covers only the final eighteen hours of Virgil's existence. This unity of time and place indicates the hero's (and the author's) anguished quest for unity, despite all of life's apparent dissonance, despite the chaos that death seems to herald. It is this nearness to death that sets life into sharp focus for author and hero alike.

The plot is straightforward and easily summarized. The work opens with the dying poet's return from Greece to Italy with the imperial navy. What follows and what takes up the greater part of five hundred pages until Virgil's death is anything but straightforward. Broch has created an intensely lyric work that, in its approximation of poetic, even musical form and structure, has expanded the very notion of the modern novel.

Broch himself described his work as being

> a poem, though not in the sense of a single lyrical outburst and also not in the sense of a poem cycle on a central theme, yet a poem and moreover, one that extends in a single breath over more than five hundred pages.

The entire work, in fact, is one long interior monologue, in which the thoughts and visions, the feverish dreams and repressed fears of Virgil are all called forth from the depths of his subconscious; in order to capture their reality and truth, the poet must articulate them by means of language.

The point of view throughout is that of Virgil himself, a poet, paradoxically enough, in despair of poetry. In the face of his imminent death, Virgil comes to question the relevance, the validity, indeed the morality of his entire lifework. Is a life given over to purely contemplative activity enough to justify it, given the need for committed action in a valueless world marked by enmity, war, poverty, and death? It is on his way from the ship to the emperor's palace that Virgil encounters all the ill-fated members of humanity. Where, he wonders, is the dignity and meaningfulness of life? Where is the beauty that he desperately sought to reproduce in poetry? Has he not, in his work, neglected fully half of life's total reality: namely, its horror, its evil, its ugliness? These are existential questions that the poet Rilke posed in his *Die Aufzeichnungen des Malte Laurids Brigge* (1910; *The Notebooks of Malte Laurids Brigge*, 1930) and in his *Duineser Elegien* (1923; *Duino Elegies*, 1931) and that Kafka raised in many of his diary entries and letters.

In fact, Kafka's request to his longtime friend and literary executor, Max Brod, to destroy his works after his death finds its parallel in Broch's novel when Virgil reveals to friends his wish to destroy the *Aeneid*. His reasons are that as a work of art, of beauty, it fails to represent the totality of truth and reality adequately; because it is "only" beautiful, he feels it to be of little benefit to humankind. Kafka's doubts were those of Broch as well, as evidenced in part by Broch's lifelong vacillation among a wide variety of forms: short story, drama, poetry, novel, philosophical essay, sociological case study, and so on. In *The Death of Virgil*, however, Broch confronted the problem of artistic validity head-on, and in so doing, he created a soul-searching work of literature, which, had he written nothing else, would have sufficed to add his name to the history of world literature. As Broch himself put it, expressing a kinship with Kafka, "We live and write, and that's all."

Broch completed his monumental novel precisely at a time in history when humanity seemed to have reached its lowest point. With death and destruction all around him, Broch, with all the conviction he could muster as a humanist, posited life and human creativity as counterweights. Virgil gives in to the pleas of his friend, Emperor Octavianus Augustus, and entrusts his *Aeneid* to him for safekeeping. He does so because he comes to realize that it is the task of the poet to offer humans, if ever so vaguely, a small glimpse of the eternal, which is theirs—and perhaps theirs alone—to perceive. As the harbinger of eternal, metaphysical order, Virgil sees the poet as the spiritual counterpart to Emperor Augustus, who embodies the temporal order.

Structurally, the novel is divided into four parts: "Water, the Arrival"; "Fire, the Descent"; "Earth, the Expectation"; and "Air, the Homecoming." Each section thus corresponds to a phase in the hero's perception of creation. In part 1, Virgil becomes aware of life's polarities while aboard the ship taking him back to Italy. He becomes conscious of the contrast between the limitless heavens above and the dark, murky, unfathomable waters below; he sees the noble passengers above deck and the pitiful slaves below; there is the sea itself signifying life and man's seemingly endless journey toward a shore that represents for the poet his inevitable death, his homecoming. On his journey through the dark and narrow streets of Brundisium, he sees the slums of the poor, which contrast sharply with the emperor's palace. For Virgil, it is his arrival at the threshold of self-awareness that serves as a catalyst for all the self-doubts faced and ultimately resolved in the rest of the novel.

Book 2 depicts in rhapsodic monologues and long lyric sequences Virgil's descent into the hellfire of self-recrimination. Book 3, which is the most narrative section of the work, presents in Virgil's discussions with his friends the poet's earthly expectations for himself as a poet, for his art, and his subsequent despair over his actual achievements. Part 4 brings a resolution to all of Virgil's doubts. Through his debate with Augustus, he comes to realize that a greater sacrifice is needed for him *not* to burn the *Aeneid*. Destruction of the work would bring fleeting self-satisfaction. Allowing it to exist elevates this work of aesthetic beauty to the status of all of those creative works that bear witness to one man's less-than-perfect quest for unity and truth.

In a final, grand vision leading from death's door back through life to birth and beyond into the order-generating act of creation itself, Virgil comes to realize the totality of life, precisely in the affirmation of all of life's apparently irreconcilable opposites, including life and death themselves. It is a vision of life that nearly defies verbal articulation. For this reason, Broch described the novel's structure in musical terms, comparing it to a traditional symphony in four movements. He even ascribed musical designations to three of the four sections: 1—"andante"; 2—"adagio"; and 4—"maestoso." Language as music is what Broch had in mind—music not only because of language's sonorous qualities but also, and more important, because of the lyric language's universal, timeless power to enchant.

It is the language that Hofmannsthal sought to describe in his famous *Brief des Lord Chandos an Francis Bacon* (1905; first published as "Ein Brief" in *Der Tag*, 1902; *The Letter of Lord Chandos*, 1952) and to which Rilke gave voice in his *Duino Elegies* and *Sonette an Orpheus* (1923; *Sonnets to Orpheus*, 1936). It is lyric language, self-reflective in its anxious attempt to crystallize the most fleeting of life's moments, the moment between that which has not yet dawned and that which is irrevocably lost—Broch's famous "no longer and not yet." In *The Death of Virgil*, Broch has captured many such moments in the life and gentle death of a man who, like himself, sought to understand life and death, to perceive their meaning, to discover their intrinsic order and unity, and then to create the language commensurate to the task of conveying his vision to others.

Thomas Di Napoli

Other major works

short fiction: *Methodologische Novelle*, 1933; *Methodisch konstruiert*, 1949; *Short Stories*, 1966 (E. W. Herd, editor).

plays: *Die Entsühnung*, pb. 1933 (also known as . . . *Denn sie wissen nicht, was sie tun*; English translation, *The Atonement*, 1972).

nonfiction: "James Joyce und die Gegenwart," 1936 ("James Joyce and the Present Age," 1949); *Dichten und Erkennen: Essays I*, 1955; *Erkennen und Handeln: Essays II*, 1955; *Brief*, 1957; *Massenpsychologie*, 1959; *Hofmannsthal und seine Zeit*, 1964 (*Hugo von Hofmannsthal and His Time: The European Imagination, 1860-1920*, 1984); *Zur Universitätsreform*, 1969; *Gedanken zur Politik*, 1970; *Hermann Broch-Daniel Brody: Briefwechsel, 1930-1951*, 1970 (Bertold Hack and Marietta Kleiss, editors); *Menschenrecht und Demokratie*, 1971; *Briefe über Deutschland, 1945-1949*, 1986; *Geist and Zeitgeist: The Spirit in an Unspiritual Age*, 2002 (John Hargraves, editor).

miscellaneous: *Gesammelte Werke in zehn Bänden*, 1952-1961 (10 volumes); *Die Heimkehr*, 1962; *Kommentierte Werkausgabe in dreizehn Bänden*, 1974-1981.

Bibliography

Bartram, Graham, and Philip Payne. "Apocalypse and Utopia in the Austrian Novel of the 1930's: Hermann Broch and Robert Musil." In *The Cambridge Companion to the Modern German Novel*, edited by Graham Bartram. New York: Cambridge University Press, 2004. *The Sleepwalkers* and *The Death of Virgil* are analyzed and placed within the wider context of 1930's Austrian literature in this essay about novelists Broch and Robert Musil.

Broch de Rothermann, H. F. *Dear Mrs. Strigl: A Memoir of Hermann Broch.* Translated by John Hargraves. New Haven, Conn.: Beinecke Rare Book & Manuscript Library, Yale University, 2001. Broch's son recalls his father's personal life. Describes Broch's relationship with his father, his exile in the United States, and other aspects of Broch's often difficult life. In both English and German.

Halsall, Robert. *The Problem of Autonomy in the Works of Hermann Broch.* New York: Peter Lang, 2000. Halsall argues that concerns about autonomy are central to understanding Broch's literature and philosophy and demonstrates how these concerns are evident in his novels, including *The Sleepwalkers* and *The Guiltless.* Includes bibliographical references and an index.

Hargraves, John A. *Music in the Works of Broch, Mann, and Kafka.* Rochester, N.Y.: Camden House, 2001. Although this book examines music as an aspect of the work of three German writers, Hargraves's study concentrates on Broch, arguing that of the three writers, Broch was the most interested in expressing the primacy of music in his writing. Essays discuss Broch's discursive writings on music and the musical elements in several of his novels.

Horrocks, David. "The Novel as Parable of National Socialism: On the Political Significance and Status of Hermann Broch's *Bergroman.*" *Modern Language Review* 86, no. 2 (April, 1991). A critical study of *The Spell*, focusing on themes of Nazism. Horrocks examines why Broch portrayed the rise of Nazism in an oblique way and the novel's significance as a political statement.

Lützeler, Paul Michael. *Hermann Broch: A Biography.* Translated by Janice Furness. London: Quartet, 1987. Lützeler, who has edited the seventeen-volume collected works of Broch and written extensively on his life, provides a comprehensive general biography. Includes an index.

_______, ed. *Hermann Broch, Visionary in Exile: The 2001 Yale Symposium.* Rochester, N.Y.: Camden House, 2003. Contains papers delivered at an international symposium that present a wide range of interpretations of Broch's work. Several papers analyze various elements of *The Sleepwalkers*, *The Death of Virgil*, *The Guiltless*, and Broch's early novels.

Simpson, Malcolm R. *The Novels of Hermann Broch.* Las Vegas, Nev.: Peter Lang, 1977. A useful general introduction to Broch, providing an interpretation of each of his novels in relation to the author's life. Evaluates Broch's literary status and contribution to the modern novel.

Strelka, Joseph P. "Hermann Broch." In *Major Figures of Modern Austrian Literature*, edited by Donald G. Dariau. Riverside, Calif.: Ariadne Press, 1988. An overview of Broch's life and work is included in this collection of essays about Austrian authors who began their literary careers before World War II, were driven into exile after Austria was annexed to Germany, and became prominent figures after the war.

JEAN COCTEAU

Born: Maisons-Laffitte, France; July 5, 1889
Died: Milly-la-Forêt, France; October 11, 1963
Also known as: Jean Maurice Eugène Clément Cocteau

Principal long fiction

Le Potomak, 1919
Le Grand Écart, 1923 (*The Grand Écart*, 1925)
Thomas l'imposteur, 1923 (*Thomas the Impostor*, 1925)
Le Livre blanc, 1928 (*The White Paper*, 1957)
Les Enfants terribles, 1929 (*Enfants Terribles*, 1930; better known as *Children of the Game*, 1955)
Le Fantôme de Marseille, 1933
La Fin du Potomak, 1939

Other literary forms

Never limited by distinctions among genres, Jean Cocteau (kawk-TOH) was an important figure in many arts. After an early and not particularly interesting "dandyistic" phase in his poetry, including *La Lampe d'Aladin* (1909; Aladdin's lamp), *Le Prince frivole* (1910; the frivolous prince), and *La Danse de Sophocle* (1912; the dance of Sophocles), he was influenced by Futurism, Dadaism, and Surrealism, and he developed a classical rigor and purity mingled with linguistic and imaginative originality. *Le Cap de Bonne-Espérance* (1919; the Cape of Good Hope), for example, glorifies pilots and flying, emphasizing sensation. *L'Ode à Picasso* (1919; ode to Picasso) seeks the wellspring of creativity in the great artist. *Vocabulaire* (1922; vocabulary) exhibits further linguistic creativity, and *Discours du grand sommeil* (1922; discourse on the great sleep) explores the experience of World War I. Later works use the suggestions of mythology, classical simplicity, and the subconscious, particularly *Plain-Chant* (1923), *L'Ange Heurtebise* (1925), *Mythologie* (1934), *Allégories* (1941), *La Crucifixion* (1946), *Clair-obscur* (1954; chiaroscuro), *Gondole des morts* (1959), and *Cérémonial espagnol du phénix* (1961).

Cocteau was a witty playwright on similar themes in *Orphée* (pr. 1926; *Orpheus*, 1933), *La Voix humaine* (pr., pb. 1930; *The Human Voice*, 1951), *La Machine infernale* (pr., pb. 1934; *The Infernal Machine*, 1936), *Les Chevaliers de la table ronde* (pr., pb. 1937; *The Knights of the Round Table*, 1955), *Les Parents terribles* (pr., pb. 1938; *Intimate Relations*, 1952), *Les Monstres sacrés* (pr., pb. 1940; *The Holy Terrors*, 1953), *La Machine à écrire* (pr., pb. 1941; *The Typewriter*, 1948), the verse drama *Renaud et Armide* (pr., pb. 1943), *L'Aigle à deux têtes* (pr., pb. 1946; *The Eagle Has Two Heads*, 1946), and *Bacchus* (pr. 1951; English translation, 1955). He was director or writer, or both, of a number of films that have become classics because of their striking visual imagery and their evocation of the archetypal and mythological. *Le Sang d'un poète* (1930; *The Blood of a Poet*, 1949), *La Belle et la bête* (1946; *Beauty and the Beast*, 1947), *Les Parents terribles* (1948; *Intimate Relations*, 1952), *Les Enfants terribles* (1950), *Orphée* (1950; *Orpheus*, 1950), and *Le Testament d'Orphée* (1959; *The Testament of Orpheus*, 1968) are considered his best. He also wrote ballet scenarios, including those for Erik Satie's *Parade* (pr. 1917), Darius Milhaud's *Le Boeuf sur le toit* (pr. 1920), and Les Six's *Les Mariés de la Tour Eiffel* (pr. 1921; *The Wedding on the Eiffel Tower*, 1937), and two musical dramas, *Antigone* (pr. 1922; English translation, 1961), with music by Arthur Honegger, and *Oedipus-Rex* (pr. 1927; English translation, 1961), with music by Igor Stravinsky.

Cocteau's nonfiction is witty and incisive and usually based on his life and role as a poet in the control of forces he does not understand. The books in this category include *Le Rappel à l'ordre* (1926; *A Call to Order*, 1926), *Lettre à Jacques Maritain* (1926; *Art and Faith*, 1948), *Opium: Journal d'une désintoxication* (1930; *Opium: Diary of a Cure*, 1932), *Essai de la critique indirecte* (1932; *The Lais Mystery: An Essay of Indirect Criticism*, 1936), *Portraits-souvenir, 1900-1914* (1935; *Paris Album*, 1956), *"La Belle et la bête": Journal d'un film* (1946; *"Beauty and the Beast": Journal of a Film*, 1950), *La Difficulté d'être* (1947; *The Difficulty of Being*, 1966), and *Poésie critique* (1960).

ACHIEVEMENTS

Twentieth century art in many areas is indebted to Jean Cocteau. His accomplishments span the artistic and literary activities of his times, the diversity unified by his vision of all art as facets of the purest form: poetry. Whether working in film, fiction, theater, drawing, or verse, he considered himself to be revealing the poet in him. Critics now generally agree that his finest achievements are in the novel and the cinema. One of the most crystalline stylists among French writers of the twentieth century, Cocteau employed brilliant imagery and extraordinary visual qualities that make his novels powerfully evocative despite their terse style. Some regard him as a dilettante interested only in stylishness and facile demonstrations of his gifts; his classical style, however, allows him to transcend the limitations of ordinary novelists and their message-oriented prose to explore the resonances of mythology and archetype in a modern context. His versatility, irony, and playfulness encouraged his contemporaries to dismiss him, and he received few honors other than his 1955 election to the Académie Française. His novels are quirky, experimental, often chaotic, but filled with intriguing imagery and wit. *Children of the Game* is almost universally agreed to be his masterpiece.

BIOGRAPHY

Jean Cocteau's background was solidly Parisian bourgeois. Georges and Eugénie Lecomte Cocteau, his parents, were a cultivated couple who introduced Jean, his brother Paul, and his sister Marthe to the fine arts. Near their suburban home, Cocteau would re-

Jean Cocteau
(National Archives)

call, the children played on the grounds of a "magical" castle designed by François Mansart. When living in the city with his grandparents, Cocteau would wander through rooms that contained classical busts, vases, a painting by Eugène Delacroix, and drawings by Jean-Auguste-Dominique Ingres. The celebrated violinist Pablo de Sarasate often visited Cocteau's grandfather, who was a cellist, and they would play music together. What impressed the young Cocteau most, however, were his trips to the circus, the ice palace, and the theater, particularly the Comédie-Française. His memories of these trips, he would later come to realize, were even brighter than the real experiences. In his own productions years later, he would ask technicians to duplicate the lighting or brilliance of childhood theatrical events and be told it had been technically impossible to create such effects when he was a boy. Memory had heightened the splendor of the past, including the recollections of the castle and of his grandparents' house; his own life began to assume mythological dimensions.

At the Petit Lycée Condorcet, Cocteau was a poor student, especially after his father killed himself in 1899 because of financial pressures. He did, however, meet the haunting Pierre Dargelos, who would become the dark "god" of *Children of the Game*. At the Grand Condorcet, Cocteau was frequently truant, exploiting his illnesses to stay home. Like many creative people, he was irritated by institutions, and he much preferred having his German governess sew doll clothes for a model theater to sitting behind a school desk. Réné Rocher, one of his best friends, often played with Cocteau's miniature theaters and, in adulthood, became a director himself.

Cocteau traveled with his mother to Venice, then began study for his *baccalauréat*. He was more interested, however, in his first love affair—with Madeleine Carlier, ten years his senior—and his deepening involvement in theater. He became a protégé of Édouard de Max, who acted opposite Sarah Bernhardt. All of these diversions contributed to Cocteau's failing the *bachot*.

De Max, however, thrust Cocteau into the public eye by organizing a reading of Cocteau's poetry by de Max, Rocher, and other prominent actors and actresses, at the Théâtre Fémina, on April 4, 1908. Several important literary critics and many of the elite of Paris attended. Cocteau's debut was a great success, and reviewers compared him to Pierre de Ronsard and Alfred de Musset. Subsequently, Cocteau met many literary notables, including Edmond Rostand, Marcel Proust, Charles-Pierre Péguy, Catulle Mendès, and Jules Lemaître. Comtesse Anna de Noailles particularly enchanted him, and he tried to write refined and sensual poetry like hers. He helped found the literary magazine *Schéhérazade*, dedicated to poetry and music, and moved into the Hôtel Biron, whose residents at the time included Auguste Rodin and his secretary, Rainer Maria Rilke.

Meeting the great impresario Sergei Diaghilev of the Ballets Russes caused Cocteau to abandon his previous enthusiasms for a while. He begged Diaghilev to let him write ballets. Diaghilev eventually said, "Étonne-moi!" ("Astonish me!"), perhaps to quiet him, but Cocteau took it as an order and a goal for the rest of his life's work. Though Diaghilev produced Cocteau's first ballet, *Le Dieu bleu* (pr. 1912), for the coronation of George V, it was not successful. Believing that the score rather than his scenario was at fault, Cocteau began to associate with composer Igor Stravinsky, even moving in with him for a while. During this period, Henri Ghéon of *La Nouvelle Revue Française* accused Cocteau of being an entirely derivative poet. Stung by the validity of the review (perhaps coauthored by André Gide), Cocteau began a search for himself as an artist. He underwent what he called a "molting" around 1914, rebelling against older writers who had influenced him, such as Rostand and the Comtesse de Noailles, and moving in the direction of poets such as Max Jacob and Guillaume Apollinaire. *Le Potomak*, with its radical mixture of prose, drawings, and verse, was completed while Cocteau was living with Gide and Stravinsky and is the first important, truly original expression of Cocteau's personality.

Cocteau's attempted enlistment at the outset of World War I was rejected because of his health. He nevertheless became an ambulance driver on the Belgian front (albeit illegally). He was discovered and ordered back to Paris immediately before the group to which he had attached himself was decimated in an attack. These experiences formed the basis for his novel and film *Thomas the Impostor*. As the war continued, Cocteau met artists Amedeo Modigliani and Pablo Picasso in Paris. The latter he introduced to Diaghilev, who put him to work on Satie's ballet *Parade*; the scenario was written by Cocteau, the costumes and set were by Picasso, and the ballet was choreographed by Léonide Massine. The ballet's atonal music and radical set and costumes caused a near riot in the theater. Apollinaire, wearing his uniform and a dressing over his wounded head, barely managed to keep the spectators from assaulting the stage. Cocteau responded in the press, vigorously attacking the musical influence of Claude Debussy, Richard Wagner, and, surprisingly, Stravinsky, and aligning himself with the radical group called Les Six (Georges Auric, Louis Durey, Arthur Honegger, Darius Milhaud, Francis Poulenc, and Germaine Tailleferre).

Raymond Radiguet was fifteen, handsome, and a poetic genius, Cocteau believed, when he met and fell in love with him in 1919. Radiguet was a major influence in moving Cocteau toward a simpler, more classical style. Cocteau's energy revived, and he produced several new works, including *The Grand Écart* and the volume of poems *Plain-Chant*. When in December, 1923, Radiguet died of typhoid, Cocteau was devastated. Diaghilev took Cocteau to Monte Carlo to help him recover, but the discovery of opium there was Cocteau's only comfort. His friends and family were forced to persuade him to enter a sanatorium in 1925, when his addiction had become serious. Jacques Maritain, the Catholic philosopher, briefly restored Cocteau's faith in religion during the cure. The faith waned, but works such as *L'Ange Heurtebise*, *Orpheus*, and *Children of the Game* followed. Patching up his friendship with Stravinsky, Cocteau wrote the libretto for the oratorio *Oedipus-Rex*.

Though Cocteau contracted typhoid in 1931, his artistic output in the 1930's was astonishing. He wrote plays, poems, songs, ballets, art criticism, and a column for the newspaper *Ce Soir*. He published a journal chronicling a trip taken in imitation of Jules Verne's *Le Tour du monde en quatre-vingt jours* (1873; *Around the World in Eighty Days*, 1873). He also became the manager of bantamweight boxer Alphonse Theo Brown. His first attempt at *poésie cinématographique* (poetry of the film), however, was probably his most important activity. He wrote and directed the film *The Blood of a Poet*, which became a classic. His abilities in the visual arts and in visual imagery expressed themselves well in cinema, and he became responsible for a number of major films, including *Beauty and the Beast*, *Intimate Relations*, *The Testament of Orpheus*, and *Les Enfants terribles*.

During the German occupation of France, Cocteau was constantly vilified by the press. His play *The Typewriter* was banned. At one point, he was beaten by a group of French Nazis for not saluting their flag. He testified in court for thief, novelist, and Resistance fighter Jean Genet in 1942, despite much advice to the contrary. Cocteau gained respect for his courage and, after the war, found himself a "grand old man" of the artistic world.

His muse, however, would not let him retire. He traveled, made recordings, and wrote plays, journals, and films. His frescoes for the city hall at Menton, the Chapel of Saint Pierre at Villefranche-sur-Mer, the Chapel of Notre Dame in London, the Church of Saint Blaise-des-Simples in Milly-la-Fôret, and the Chapel at Fréjus, Notre-Dame-de-

Jérusalem created controversy among art critics. He also designed fabrics, plates, and posters. In 1955, he was elected to the Royal Belgian Academy and to the Académie Française. In 1956, he was awarded an honorary doctorate of letters from Oxford University. He died on October 11, 1963, distressed at hearing of the death of his friend Edith Piaf earlier in the day.

ANALYSIS

Le Potomak was a crucial work in Jean Cocteau's development, as he used it to break free of former influences and find an individual voice. Highly experimental, it is, however, not of compelling interest for any other reason, consisting as it does of an exploration of the subconscious through a hodgepodge of verse, prose, and drawings, all of which reveal Cocteau's talents but mostly demonstrate rebellion rather than a mature concept of the novelistic art. Its writing was interrupted by World War I, and the influence of the war is apparent in the revised edition. Under the influence of Radiguet, Cocteau wrote *The Grand Écart* and *Thomas the Impostor*. Mythologizing memories of his childhood, Cocteau based *The Grand Écart* on a childhood visit to Venice and his recollections of boarding school. One of his recurrent images appears indistinctly in this novel in the form of the Englishman Stopwell. Like Dargelos and the Angel Heurtebise, Stopwell is an angel in the form of a tempter who brings about annihilation or metamorphosis. *Thomas the Impostor* was based largely on Cocteau's own experiences during the war. Rejected for service, he posed as an ambulance driver on the Belgian front and was "adopted" by a group of Fusiliers Marins. When discovered by a superior officer, he was arrested and taken from the front. A day later, most of his comrades were killed. Rather than portraying the war as a horror, however, the novel turns it into a ghastly joke, a reflection of humanity's chaotic mind, a cruel trick played by a Euripidean god. Being an impostor is likened to being a poet, and reality and impostorship merge only when Thomas the Impostor is shot in the Waste Land. The "Prince of Frivolity," as Cocteau was known, uses flippant, humorous, outlandish imagery that accentuates the horror. The book is clearly one of his better novels, though not nearly equal to his next.

CHILDREN OF THE GAME

Children of the Game is considered to be Cocteau's most successful novel by far. In addition to being beautifully written, it is an extraordinary evocation of adolescent hopes, fears, dreams, and obsessions; it is said to have been regarded by French teenagers as capturing their alienation from adult society in the same way that J. D. Salinger articulated teen alienation in American culture. Perhaps because Cocteau, as an artist and a man, always held himself as a kind of alien visitor to the realms of the establishment from the world of subjectivity and irrationality, his sensitivity to adolescent alienation was enhanced. *Children of the Game* is not a realistic portrayal of adolescence, however. It is sensitive, but it is so overlaid with dream imagery and mythological overtones that whatever autobiographical elements and psychological truths it might contain are submerged.

Fragments from many mythological sources are identifiable upon even a cursory reading of the work. Cocteau was fascinated with mythology and at various times in his career wrote works dealing with Antigone, Orpheus, Bacchus, and the "Beauty and the Beast" motif. Cocteau wrote *Children of the Game* very rapidly—at the rate of seventeen pages a day for three weeks—while he was undergoing treatment for opium addiction, as if he were trying to let archetypal and subconscious elements flow freely onto the page. Too careful an artist to practice automatic writing without aesthetically manipulating the result, he nevertheless refused to make later changes in the text for fear of destroying the fabric of the book. Characters in *Children of the Game* quite often suggest beings from mythology, as Cocteau imbues people and events from his own life and imagination with a supernatural or divine aura.

Dargelos, for example, whose name is taken from a real boy whom Cocteau admired in his school days, takes on the characteristics of a god. Early in the book, Paul seeks Dargelos among the snowball wars in the Cité Monthiers. Paul's love for Dargelos is described as "sexless and purposeless," and his seeking him in order to fight beside him, defend him, and prove what he can do takes on religious overtones. Paul, however, is silenced by a snowball from one of his idol's acolytes, condemning him to Dargelos's wrath. Dargelos rises up in an immense gesture, his cheeks on fire and his hair in disorder, like a statue of Dionysus. Paul feels the blow of the snowball on his chest—a dark blow, the blow of a marble fist. As Paul loses consciousness, he imagines Dargelos upon a dais, in a supernatural light. Dargelos has struck Paul in the heart, with a snowball like Thor's hammer or Zeus's thunderbolt. Dargelos, throughout the rest of the book, is hardly mentioned; his presence, however, seems to loom over all subsequent events. As Wallace Fowlie has observed, he "grows into the figure of a dark angel who haunts the dreams and thoughts of the protagonist."

Eden is evoked when Paul, his sister Elisabeth, and Gérard find themselves alone without adult supervision. In "the Room," they are free of conventional worries about food and seem innocent of evil. Their childhood seems to be prolonged. Although the situation appears to be fraught with incestuous overtones—Paul and Elisabeth sleep in the same room and bathe together—there is instead a matter-of-fact sexlessness, a lack of shame. When a ball of poison (associated with Dargelos's snowball) causes the cold, outside world of snow and death to blow into their Eden, one may see an analogy to the expulsion from Eden, the coming of mortality into Eden.

One must not, however, treat *Children of the Game* as allegory. Cocteau is weaving a fugue of implications and mythological elements. One critic has found the novel to be about the impossibility of escaping bourgeois ideology; another has found it to be the playing out of fate in the form of Eros-Thanatos. There is certainly a hint of inevitability in the sequence of events. Tragedy is suggested from the beginning, and the classical structure and sparkling sentences help convey this impression. The characters are in the grip of forces beyond their control. When Michael, the rich American Jew, is killed, it seems as if the Room reaches out to protect itself. When Dargelos gives Paul the fist-sized ball of poison, one is reminded of the marble-hard snowball and the apple that destroyed Eden. A reddish gash in the ball is reminiscent of both a wound and female genitalia, suggesting an association between mortality and the loss of innocence. The end is destined, and nothing can hold it back. Childhood is doomed. As Cocteau himself wrote in *The Difficulty of Being:* "Childhood knows what it wants. It wants to emerge from childhood. The trouble starts when it does emerge. For youth knows what it does not want before it knows what it does want. But what it does not want is what we do want." Thus are the "holy terrors" doomed.

LA FIN DU POTOMAK

Le Fantôme de Marseille is a slight work containing associations and local color that Cocteau recalled from his running away to Marseilles at the age of fifteen. Later, in Le Picquey, in a hotel where he had stayed with Radiguet in 1923, Cocteau watched over the convalescence of a new love, actor Jean Marais, and returned to the inspiration of *Le Potomak* for his last novel. *La Fin du Potomak* is a curious mixture of fairy tales, aphorisms, riddles, and true stories recalling Cocteau's experiences after 1913. A revival of Cocteau's classicism has been seen in the work, but most often it is regarded as a mere shadow of *Le Potomak*, as if the author's creative interests had shifted away from *poésie de roman* (poetry of the novel). Brooding over the entire work is a disappointment with human nature and recurrent imagery of death, perhaps evoked by Marais's illness and the memory of Radiguet's sudden death. There is also an acceptance of the author's own death (which was many years in the future), indicated by some lines of poetry at the end: "Death, don't be clever/ . . . You see, I wait standing still/ I even offer you my hand/ . . . What does it matter? I leave behind a book/ That you will not take from me."

J. Madison Davis

OTHER MAJOR WORKS

PLAYS: *Antigone*, pr. 1922 (libretto; English translation, 1961); *Orphée*, pr. 1926 (*Orpheus*, 1933); *Oedipus-Rex*, pr. 1927 (libretto; English translation, 1961); *La Voix humaine*, pr., pb. 1930 (*The Human Voice*, 1951); *La Machine infernale*, pr., pb. 1934 (*The Infernal Machine*, 1936); *L'École des veuves*, pr., pb. 1936; *Les Chevaliers de la table ronde*, pr., pb. 1937 (*The Knights of the Round Table*, 1955); *Les Parents terribles*, pr., pb. 1938 (*Intimate Relations*, 1952); *Les Monstres sacrés*, pr., pb. 1940 (*The Holy Terrors*, 1953); *La Machine à écrire*, pr., pb. 1941 (*The Typewriter*, 1948); *Renaud et Armide*, pr., pb. 1943; *L'Aigle à deux têtes*, pr., pb. 1946 (*The Eagle Has Two Heads*, 1946); *Bacchus*, pr. 1951 (English translation, 1955); *Théâtre complet*, pb. 1957 (2 volumes); *Five Plays*, pb. 1961; *L'Impromptu du Palais-Royal*, pr., pb. 1962; *The Infernal Machine, and Other Plays*, 1964.

POETRY: *La Lampe d'Aladin*, 1909; *Le Prince frivole*, 1910; *La Danse de Sophocle*, 1912; *Le Cap de Bonne-Espérance*, 1919; *L'Ode à Picasso*, 1919; *Escales*, 1920; *Poésies, 1917-1920*, 1920; *Discours du grand sommeil*, 1922; *Vocabulaire*, 1922; *Plain-Chant*, 1923; *Poésie, 1916-1923*, 1924; *Cri écrit*, 1925; *L'Ange Heurtebise*, 1925; *Prière mutilée*, 1925; *Opéra*, 1927; *Morceaux choisis*, 1932; *Mythologie*, 1934; *Allégories*, 1941; *Léone*, 1945; *Poèmes*, 1945; *La Crucifixion*, 1946; *Anthologie poétique*, 1951; *Le Chiffre sept*, 1952; *Appogiatures*, 1953; *Clair-obscur*, 1954; *Poèmes, 1916-1955*, 1956; *Gondole des morts*, 1959; *Cérémonial espagnol du phénix*, 1961; *Le Requiem*, 1962.

SCREENPLAYS: *Le Sang d'un poète*, 1930 (*The Blood of a Poet*, 1949); *L'Éternel Retour*, 1943 (*The Eternal Return*, 1948); *Le Baron fantôme*, 1943; *L'Aigle à deux têtes*, 1946; *La Belle et la bête*, 1946 (*Beauty and the Beast*, 1947); *Ruy Blas*, 1947; *Les Parents terribles*, 1948 (*Intimate Relations*, 1952); *Les Enfants terribles*, 1950; *Orphée*, 1950 (*Orpheus*, 1950); *Le Testament d'Orphée*, 1959 (*The Testament of Orpheus*, 1968); *Thomas l'Imposteur*, 1965.

NONFICTION: *Le Coq et l'Arlequin*, 1918 (*Cock and Harlequin*, 1921); *Le Secret professionnel*, 1922; *Lettre à Jacques Maritain*, 1926 (*Art and Faith*, 1948); *Le Rappel à l'ordre*, 1926 (*A Call to Order*, 1926); *Opium: Journal d'une désintoxication*, 1930 (*Opium: Diary of a Cure*, 1932); *Essai de la critique indirecte*, 1932 (*The Lais Mystery: An Essay of Indirect Criticism*, 1936); *Portraits-souvenir, 1900-1914*, 1935 (*Paris Album*, 1956); *"La Belle et la bête": Journal d'un film*, 1946 (*"Beauty and the Beast": Journal of a Film*, 1950); *La Difficulté d'être*, 1947 (*The Difficulty of Being*, 1966); *Journal d'un inconnu*, 1952 (*The Hand of a Stranger*, 1956; also known as *Diary of an Unknown*, 1988); *The Journals of Jean Cocteau*, 1956; *Poésie critique*, 1960.

BALLET SCENARIOS: *Le Dieu bleu*, pr. 1912 (with Frédéric de Madrazo); *Parade*, pr. 1917 (music by Erik Satie, scenery by Pablo Picasso); *Le Boeuf sur le toit*, pr. 1920 (music by Darius Milhaud, scenery by Raoul Dufy); *Le Gendarme incompris*, pr. 1921 (with Raymond Radiguet; music by Francis Poulenc); *Les Mariés de la tour Eiffel*, pr. 1921 (music by Les Six; *The Wedding on the Eiffel Tower*, 1937); *Les Biches*, pr. 1924 (music by Poulenc); *Les Fâcheux*, pr. 1924 (music by Georges Auric); *Le Jeune Homme et la mort*, pr. 1946 (music by Johann Sebastian Bach); *Phèdre*, pr. 1950 (music by Auric).

TRANSLATION: *Roméo et Juliette*, 1926 (of William Shakespeare's play).

BIBLIOGRAPHY

Brown, Frederick. *An Impersonation of Angels: A Biography of Jean Cocteau*. New York: Viking Press, 1968. Study of the life and work of Cocteau focuses on his artistic milieu and his collaborators and sources of inspiration, such as poet Guillaume Apollinaire, artist Pablo Picasso, novelist André Gide, and filmmaker Jean Marais. Includes illustrations and bibliography.

Crosland, Margaret. *Jean Cocteau: A Biography*. New York: Alfred A. Knopf, 1956. Charming biography written with the help and encouragement of Cocteau himself.

The goal is to relate Cocteau's work to his life and to relate the different aspects of his work to one another. Offers lively comments by fellow artists as well as discussion and interpretation of individual works by Cocteau. Includes excerpts from letters of Cocteau and numerous illustrations.

Crowson, Lydia. *The Esthetic of Jean Cocteau*. Hanover: University of New Hampshire Press, 1978. Scholarly work devotes chapters to Cocteau's milieu, the nature of the real, and the roles of myth, consciousness, and power. Includes introduction and bibliography.

Fowlie, Wallace. *Jean Cocteau: The History of a Poet's Age*. Bloomington: Indiana University Press, 1966. General study defines Cocteau's originality by comparing him with other French writers and film directors of his lifetime. Proposes a very sensible evaluation of Cocteau's real accomplishments.

Knapp, Bettina L. *Jean Cocteau*. Updated ed. Boston: Twayne, 1989. Thorough study pursues both psychological and literary views of Cocteau's work, with chapters following a chronological approach. Includes chronology, notes, bibliography, and index.

Lowe, Romana N. *The Fictional Female: Sacrificial Rituals and Spectacles of Writing in Baudelaire, Zola, and Cocteau*. New York: Peter Lang, 1997. Highlights the sacrificial victim common in nineteenth and twentieth century French texts: woman. Traces structures and images of female sacrifice in the genres of poetry, novel, and theater with close readings of the works of Charles Baudelaire, Émile Zola, and Cocteau.

Mauriès, Patrick. *Jean Cocteau*. Translated by Jane Brenton. London: Thames and Hudson, 1998. Brief but excellent biography provides information that places Cocteau's works within the context of his life. Illustrated with many photographs.

Selous, Trista. *Cocteau*. Paris: Centre Pompidou, 2003. Retrospective catalog compiled by the Centre Pompidou and the Montreal Museum offers an illustrated review of Cocteau's creative output along with seventeen essays on his life and work.

Steegmuller, Francis. *Cocteau*. Boston: D. R. Godine, 1986. Major biography discusses Cocteau's childhood, the influence of his mother, and fellow poets. Defines Cocteau as a "quick-change artist" with a propensity for constant self-invention, discarding old views and activities and assuming new roles or guises with remarkable facility. Includes illustrations, twelve informative appendixes, bibliography, and index.

Williams, James S. *Jean Cocteau*. London: Reaktion Books, 2008. Biography chronicles the development of Cocteau's aesthetic and his work as a novelist, poet, dramatist, filmmaker, and designer. Concludes that Cocteau's oeuvre is characterized by a continual self-questioning.

JOSÉ DONOSO

Born: Santiago, Chile; October 5, 1924
Died: Santiago, Chile; December 7, 1996
Also known as: José Donoso Yañez

PRINCIPAL LONG FICTION

Coronación, 1957 (*Coronation*, 1965)
Este domingo, 1965 (*This Sunday*, 1967)
El lugar sin límites, 1966 (*Hell Has No Limits*, 1972)
El obsceno pájaro de la noche, 1970 (*The Obscene Bird of Night*, 1973)
Tres novelitas burguesas, 1973 (novellas; *Sacred Families*, 1977)
Casa de campo, 1978 (*A House in the Country*, 1984)
La misteriosa desaparición de la Marquesita de Loria, 1980
El jardín de al lado, 1981
La desesperanza, 1986 (*Curfew*, 1988)
Taratuta; Naturaleza muerta con cachimba, 1990 (novellas; *"Taratuta" and "Still Life with Pipe,"* 1993)
Donde van a morir los elefantes, 1995
El Mocho, 1997

OTHER LITERARY FORMS

José Donoso (doh-NOH-soh) was a superb storyteller, and his first literary efforts were in the area of the short story (curiously, his first stories were written in English and published in the Princeton University literary review *MSS*). His collections of stories include *Veraneo, y otros cuentos* (1955; summer vacation, and other stories); *Dos cuentos* (1956; two stories); *El Charlestón* (1960; abridged as *Cuentos*, 1971; *Charleston, and Other Stories*, 1977); and *Los mejores cuentos de José Donoso* (1965; the best stories of José Donoso). Little if any significant thematic or technical distinction can be drawn between Donoso's novels and shorter fiction, other than those imposed by the limits of the genres themselves. Regardless of length, all are superb blends of sociological observation and psychological analysis, in which realism never quite manages to eliminate fantasy, where madness, the supernatural, and the unknown hover just beyond the bounds of consciousness and reason.

Donoso also wrote essays of literary criticism and attracted attention with *Historia personal del "boom"* (1972; *The Boom in Spanish American Literature: A Personal History*, 1977). His *Poemas de un novelista* (1981) is a collection of thirty poems with a twelve-page authorial introduction explaining the personal circumstances that occasioned the verse.

ACHIEVEMENTS

Each of José Donoso's novels had its special success, and the writer's prestige grew with each stage of his career. Despite a slow beginning (he came to the novel at age thirty-three), Donoso published no novel that could be classed a failure by critics or the public, and several of his works have received awards, the most acclaimed being *The Obscene Bird of Night* (a favorite of reviewers and literary critics) and *A House in the Country*, which received the Spanish Critics' Prize, a coveted award despite its lack of endowment, since it reflects the esteem of the country's professional critics as a whole. Donoso was the recipient of two grants from the Guggenheim Foundation for the furthering of works in progress and served as writer-in-residence at various American universities, with stints at the University of Iowa Writers' Workshop (1965-1967) and teaching positions at Princeton University and Dartmouth College. In demand as a distinguished lecturer, he also held a number of editorial posts. His powers of sociopsychological penetration and his marvelous irony and skillful use of allegory, together with his masterful handling of existential themes and the abnormal or psychotic narrative perspective, place Donoso in the forefront of international fiction.

BIOGRAPHY

José Donoso is one of Chile's most widely known writers of prose fiction and one of the most outstanding and prestigious figures of his generation of narrators in Latin America. He was born José Donoso Yañez into an upper-middle-class family of Spanish and Italian descent in Santiago on October 5, 1924. His father (for whom Donoso was named) was a physician; his mother, Alicia Yáñez, came from a prominent Chilean family. It was she who, with the couple's servant, Teresa Vergara, reared Donoso and his two brothers. Until her death in 1976, Donoso's mother continued to live in the spacious home where the future novelist was born, and the atmosphere of decrepitude and decay in the labyrinthine mansion (property of Dr. Donoso's three elderly great-aunts) haunts his fiction.

When Donoso was seven years old, his father hired an English governess, the foundation of his excellent knowledge of the language, which he continued to study at the Grange, an English school in Santiago, from 1932 to 1942. During this period, Donoso's maternal grandmother returned from Europe to make her home with the family, an event that (together with her deteriorating mental and physical condition) left a mark on the future writer's development. A teenage rebel who disliked school and his father's imposition of the British sports ethic (personified in a boxing instructor), Donoso began feigning stomachaches, which led to a real appendectomy and subsequently an equally real ulcer.

Never serious about religion, Donoso proclaimed himself an atheist at the age of twelve. Equally cavalier about classes, he cared only for reading, and in 1943, he dropped out of school. After two years, during which he had not managed to hold a job for more than a few months, he set out for Magallanes at the southern tip of Chile, where he worked as a sheepherder on the pampas for about a year, subsequently hitchhiking through

Patagonia to Buenos Aires, where he lived as a dockhand until he contracted measles, which obliged him to return home. He finished high school in 1947, enrolling in the University of Chile with a major in English and completing his bachelor of arts degree at Princeton in 1951. His study with Allen Tate and his discovery of Henry James, as well as his introduction to the great paintings of the world, would all influence his future writings.

Returning to Chile, Donoso worked as a teacher, journalist, and literary critic but found himself estranged from his homeland and dissatisfied with his work. His ulcer returned, and he began psychoanalysis. He collaborated in launching the newsmagazine *Ercilla*, which he edited, and in 1954, his first short story written in Spanish ("China") was included in an anthology of Chilean short fiction. The following year, his first book, the collection *Veraneo, y otros cuentos*, was published and had a favorable critical reception, winning the Santiago Municipal Short Story Prize. This success and that of his first novel notwithstanding, Donoso found Chilean society oppressive and moved on to Buenos Aires, where he met his future wife and stayed for two years. He published his second collection of short stories upon his return to Santiago, and he became a leading literary critic, which led to teaching in the Writers' Workshop at the University of Iowa; he abandoned this position in order to move to Spain and finish a novel begun years before, which would become *The Obscene Bird of Night*.

Donoso and his wife, Mará del Pilar Serrano, whom he had married in 1961, adopted an infant daughter in Madrid and settled in Mallorca in 1967. Donoso's first Guggenheim award (1966) was followed by a lectureship at Colorado State University (1969). While in Colorado, his hemorrhaging ulcer required surgery; because of his inability to tolerate painkilling drugs, he subsequently went through a period marked by hallucinations, schizophrenia, and paranoia that resulted in suicide attempts. He returned to Mallorca, moved his family to Barcelona, and began to rewrite his novel, incorporating his nightmarish illness. Subsequently, still recuperating, he bought a seventeenth century home in Calaceite, remodeled it, and in 1971 moved to this village of some two thousand inhabitants in the center of Spain. Both his critical history, *The Boom in Spanish American Literature*, and his novellas in *Sacred Families* were published in Spain.

Donoso's second Guggenheim Fellowship, in 1973, enabled him to work on *A House in the Country*. His first trip to Chile in some nine years had to be canceled because of the military coup there (an event that colors both *A House in the Country* and *El jardín de al lado*). His next move, to the Mediterranean fishing and resort village of Sitges (1976), has obvious resonances in *El jardín de al lado*, which, like all of the author's fiction, has a strong autobiographical substratum. Donoso returned to Chile in 1980, winning the Chilean Premio National de Literatura in 1990. He died in Santiago in 1996.

ANALYSIS

José Donoso's first two novels are similar in a number of ways, which makes it convenient to consider them together, despite significant and perhaps fundamental differences in the level of style and technique. Both involve upper-class, traditional Chilean families, a decaying mansion, and the problem of the generation gap; both treat psychological abnormalities in a rigidly stratified society where a rich, decadent minority is contrasted with an impoverished lower class; and in both, members of the aristocracy become emotionally involved with members of the lower class. In *This Sunday*, however, there is a more adroit utilization of innovative techniques and more subtle thematic development, a contrapuntal effect and stream-of-consciousness narration rather than the omniscient narrator of *Coronation*, who summarizes events and describes places and people in photographic fashion, sharpening the narrative perspective and involving the reader's collaborative effort, using secondary characters as third-person reflectors.

Time in *Coronation* is treated in a linear, chronological manner, but in *This Sunday* it is subjected to a more fluid handling, reflecting the philosophical and literary theories of Henri Bergson and Marcel Proust while intensifying the latent Freudian and existential concepts of the first effort, with the result that the aesthetic and intellectual density of *This Sunday* is considerably greater.

CORONATION

Misiá Elisa Grey de Abalos in *Coronation* is a wealthy, demented nonagenarian who lives with her fiftyish bachelor grandson, Andrés, an asexual aesthete whose life is a prime example of abulia and existential inauthenticity, a man addicted to French history and collecting canes (possibly symbolic of his not standing on his own in life). Andrés's world, like that of his grandmother, is hermetic, monotonous, isolated from the "real" workaday world; virtually his only human contact is his lifelong friend, Dr. Carlos Gros. The two aging servants, Rosario and Lourdes, have devoted their lives to the service of the Abalos family but become unable to cope with and care for the bedridden Misiá Elisa; Estela, a sensual country wench, is brought in to care for her, introducing a new element into the previously closed system. Estela is something of a catalyst, awakening Andrés's dormant sexuality and introducing the neighboring shantytown's societal dregs into the mansion (and the novel) via her affair with Mario (whose older half brother, René, is a link with the criminal element).

Coronation is traditional in its technique and employs an almost naturalistic cause-and-effect sequence, portraying most of the characters as products of their environment, although Donoso's interest in psychological analysis transcends the usual naturalistic characterization. Social determinism underlies the formation both of Andrés, who studied law in his youth because it was the thing for young men of his class to do, and of Misiá Elisa, who is pathologically repressed, molded by the religious education and bourgeois puritanism of her family. A similar social determinism is responsible for Mario's fear of entrapment (partly cultural, partly based on his brother's unhappy marriage); Estela's pregnancy thus inspires in Mario panic and instinctive flight.

Following Freudian psychology, Donoso stresses the importance of early-childhood experiences, the power of the unconscious, and the central role of sexuality in other areas of human life, with much of the characters' conduct being irrational, neurotic, or motivated by repressed erotic urges. In her senile dementia, Misiá Elisa becomes overpoweringly obsessed with sexuality, which she suppressed during most of her life, and gives way to obscene outbursts. Obsessions are a recurring motif in *Coronation* and in Donoso's fiction as a whole, and often are associated with recurring symbols, false rituals, repetitive or symbolic dreams, existential themes, and rigid daily routines that acquire an unconscious, magical, or supernatural character for the participants. Any break in the routine, therefore, is a transcendent disruption of order—hence the ultimately catastrophic ramifications of bringing Estela, the new servant, into the rigid and ritualistic existence of the mansion.

Misiá Elisa's conversations with Estela include warnings of the dangers of seduction and reveal that she considers all men "pigs" while considering herself a saint (having never let her husband see her naked). Life for the old lady is a gutter, a sewer, a cesspool from which religion is the only escape; thus she is also obsessed with sin, although for her, sexuality and sin are essentially identical. His grandmother's stern warnings and prohibitions and the inculcation of childhood fears and exaggerated taboos fill the boy Andrés with dread and apprehension, leading ultimately to his falsifying his first confession and, disappointed that instant fire and brimstone is not the result, to a loss of faith and rejection of religion, without any accompanying loss of inhibitions.

Plagued by a recurring nightmare in which a long bridge over an abyss suddenly ends, precipitating him into the void, Andrés experiences extreme existential anguish as he comes to realize the inability of philosophy or science to replace the security promised by faith and to assuage the fear of death, of the infinite, and of nothingness. Existentially, he is also radically alone, his solitude and loneliness so extreme that his abulia and inability to act are the visible result of the isolation and meaninglessness of his life. More than two decades spent in idle alienation, avoiding any engagement with life, end abruptly for Andrés when the terror inspired by his grandmother's approaching death is combined with the disturbing attraction of Estela's presence, bringing the realization that he has never really lived (in contrast with his friend, Carlos Gros, who represents an acceptance of life and love, believes both in science and religion, and exemplifies an existential exercise of free will). Where Misiá Elisa sees life as a sewer, Andrés sees it as chaos, terror, absurdity, a mad trick played upon humankind by an unjust or insane god. Both grandmother and grandson thus exemplify alienation so extreme that it borders upon the psychotic, their fragile equilibrium maintained by a series of obsessive routines and rituals—as in the case of Andrés limiting his cane collection to ten.

Donoso employs an indirect, third-person narration or monologue (comparable to the procedure of James) to plumb the psychological depths of his characters and thereby provide a multiplicity of perspectives, augment dramatic intensity, and allow the reader to identify more directly with a given character's viewpoint. The novel raises serious psychological, social, and philosophical issues, often through Andrés's very avoidance of them (an ironic technique that requires the reader to face the conclusions that Andrés has refused to contemplate), but Donoso also employs humor and numerous aesthetic ingredients. Incongruity is essential to many moments of humor, with the best examples involving Misiá Elisa, who, in her madness, swings like a pendulum from prudishness to obscenities to exaggerated religiosity. Similarly, the ironic contrast between Andrés's adolescent ignorance (in flashbacks to his childhood and youth) and the mature knowledge of narrator and reader provides much black comedy; for example, the young Andrés imagined that there was some connection between hell and the school restroom because the latter was a filthy place, and it was there that he first overheard a conversation about sex.

One of the recurring symbols or images of Donoso's fiction is the decaying mansion, often a Victorian monstrosity replete with gables and turrets, balconies whose only function is decorative, passages leading nowhere, closed or walled-up rooms, and other elements representative of a decadent or outmoded lifestyle. The mansion in *Coronation*, similarly constructed, also exemplifies Donoso's fascination with Art Nouveau—with its opulence of detail, decorative floral borders, and curving lines—while the depictions of the grandmother, her "coronation" and death (amid rococo bows, streamers, and billowing folds of cloth), function to complement and emphasize the theme of conspicuous consumption. The decadent mansion is a transparent allegory of a decadent upper class, while on an individual, psychological level, it also frequently symbolizes existential or emotional emptiness, isolation or alienation, and lack of contact with reality.

Another important symbol in *Coronation* is Andrés's collection of canes, rigidly limited to ten to exteriorize or make visible the rigid, self-imposed limits on his sterile, monotonous, routine existence. When the existential crisis provoked by confrontation with two of life's most powerful forces—love and death, both of which he has previously avoided—obliges Andrés to take radical measures, the one step he is able to visualize is raising the limit on his cane collection. He visits the home of an antique dealer whose wife—with her pink shawl and naked palms, evoking a powerful subconscious association with Estela—profoundly disturbs him; thus brought to an awareness of his desire for Estela, he resolves to win her, a decision that, if carried out, would constitute his first step toward existential engagement and authenticity. As he returns home, however, an accidental glimpse of the girl with her lover beneath a streetlight mortifies him and brings realization of his own absurdity and that of his situation; unable to return to his once-comfortable abulia and solitude, he gradually retreats into madness (a denouement that, in naturalistic terms, might be implicit in his heredity), succumbing to the pernicious influence of his grandmother, whose pervasive madness has gradually undermined his own rationality.

Similarly, Mario's fear of becoming a criminal, arising from his brother's criminal nature, the family's increasingly desperate financial straits, and the injustices of society, presages his fall into crime: He is induced to participate in the theft of the Abalos family silver, thereby setting the stage for the grotesque denouement that combines the frustrated robbery attempt, Andrés's madness, and Misiá Elisa's death.

THIS SUNDAY

The themes of alienation and existential anguish reappear in *This Sunday*, but Donoso's interest in abnormal psychology and the exploration of the unconscious of each of his protagonists are much more visible than in the earlier novel. Don Alvaro Vives and his wife, Chepa, a wealthy, middle-aged couple, live in another of Donoso's mansions, where they are visited by their five grandchildren (one of whom narrates portions of the novel). Other characters include Violeta, a retired former servant of the Vives household and onetime mistress of Alvaro; Maya, a lower-class psychopath who has been convicted of murder; Marujita, a peddler; Mirella, Violeta's illegitimate daughter; and her husband, Fausto.

In brief, the plot revolves around the activities of Chepa, a volunteer welfare worker, and her infatuation with Maya and use of the family's influence to obtain his parole. Settled by Chepa in Violeta's house, Maya is both attracted to his benefactor and fearful of her, and his pathology determines a path of escape through violence once again—this time through the murder of Violeta, which allows him to return to the comfortable alienation of prison, where no existential decisions are required. Rather than a straightforward narrative, *This Sunday* employs an ironic alternation between the naïve or limited vision of characters—first-person narrators who are participants in the action—and the occasional interventions of an omniscient narrator, thereby stressing the characters' ingenuousness, self-deception, or unawareness.

Much of the narrative is retrospective, via the use of Proustian flashbacks (for example, Alvaro's recollections of the beginning of his affair with Violeta are stimulated by the smell of meat pastries, experienced years previously when he had gone to her house). Free association and indirect third-person, stream-of-consciousness narrative are combined in reconstructing Alvaro's life as a weak young man whose social position enabled him to exploit Violeta without assuming responsibilities, avoiding the threats represented by both university girls and prostitutes while preventing the servant girl from living an authentic existence of her own. A victim of the social conventions by which "decent" girls of his own class were sacred, meant only for marriage, Alvaro is unable to truly love Chepa and other upper-class girls, although on the basis of established mores, he assumes that he will love her; actually, he manages to consummate the marriage only by closing his eyes and imagining that he is making love to Violeta.

In their fifties, Alvaro and Chepa have ceased sleeping together, and both live behind masks, maintaining a facade that serves as a substitute for authentic relationships as well as an escape from unpleasant reality. Alvaro's inability to love having become more pronounced with time, he appears narcissistic, withdrawn, and slightly ridiculous—aspects emphasized by his grandchildren's nicknaming him the Doll, his interminable games of chess and solitaire, his deafness, his lack of concern for things other than his health, and his rituals. Chepa, a victim of a loveless marriage that has increased her basic insecurity, provides a self-portrait in a number of interior monologues, most of them precipitated by contact with Maya. As a lonely, aging woman whose children have left home, she seeks to give some meaning to her existence by works of charity—by helping the poor and through her work at the prison—in an attempt to compensate for the knowledge that for Alvaro she is an object devoid of significance.

A good deal of sadomasochism inheres in Chepa's relationships with "her" poor; she imagines herself as "a littered bitch" with a compulsive need to feed the hungry mouths fastened to her. Her philanthropy is a substitute for the normal human relationships that are lacking in her life as well as a mask for less admirable motivations of her own, the desire to dominate or control, and to indulge her more (or less) than maternal interest in Maya. She helps him to set up a leather-goods shop, but her vigilance arouses his resentment and desire to escape; despite his derangement, Maya intuits in Chepa the devouring female, the Jungian evil mother.

Seeking Maya at Violeta's house, Chepa learns both that he has become Violeta's lover and that Violeta had an affair with Alvaro before his marriage to Chepa, provoking the latter's decision to throw off convention and look for Maya in the shantytown. Unfamiliar with the sprawling slums, she becomes lost in the twilight maze of alleys, but she fortuitously encounters Maya's mistress, Marujita, whose revelations of Maya's mixed emotions concerning Chepa inflame her and bring on a surrealistic, nightmarish experience as she is set upon by slum children who rob her of her furs and purse and leave her exhausted, on a trash heap. The inferno of the slums into which Chepa descends is a symbolic, expressionistic representation of her own subconscious with its hidden, conflicting sexual desires. Maya's murder of Violeta has been seen by critics as an instance of transferring his repressed aggression for Chepa to one socially weaker; the murder frees him from his obligations to her as benefactor, and to society.

The differences between Alvaro and Chepa are not so marked as the grandchildren imagine; their inability to communicate with Alvaro leads them to see him as cold, absurd, and slightly grotesque, while the grandmother is perceived in an unrealistically positive fashion as generous and loving (perhaps a result of her own altruistic self-image), a participant in the children's games of fantasy. Actually, both Alvaro and Chepa suffer from inauthenticity, solitude, and unfulfilled emotions, but Chepa is close to achieving authenticity when she recognizes and accepts her desire for Maya and determines to seek him, while Alvaro has lived so long in egotistic aloofness, exploiting without giving, that no self-redemption appears possible.

The novel's title refers to the family's habitual Sunday gatherings for dinner at the grandparents' residence, highlighting an incident of one specific Sunday, when Chepa searches for Maya, returning from the slums so traumatized that her subsequent life is almost that of a catatonic. Maya's murder of Violeta, who is vicariously Chepa, symbolically signals Chepa's death, and although she lives for many years, she spends them in isolation, essentially as dead to her grandchildren as if she were deceased. The rituals in the lives of adults are paralleled by the children's games, and additional parallels and contrasts throughout the novel lend symmetry: Alvaro's relationship with Violeta is socially similar to that of Chepa with Maya (a superior-inferior involvement); Alvaro and Violeta are passive, inert, making no effort to change their lives, while Chepa and Maya are active, attempting to improve their situations or to change them. *This Sunday* explores more complicated relationships, with more tragic repercussions, than those plumbed in *Coronation*, and it does so in a more objective fashion, given the lessening of authorial intervention. Both novels, however, re-create the surrealistic and nightmarish effects of subconscious, irrational, or instinctive forces, achieving especially memorable portraits in the matriarchs (Misiá Elisa and Chepa), who undoubtedly hark back to the mental deterioration of Donoso's own maternal grandmother.

HELL HAS NO LIMITS

Hell Has No Limits, which was published one year after *This Sunday*, provides a departure from the novelist's previous urban settings, being set in a somber, sordid brothel in a backwater rural winegrowing area. Although the existential issues of authenticity and alienation, solitude, and a lack of communication found in the earlier novels are again present to some degree, there is an increased emphasis on absurdity and the grotesque, and Donoso begins to employ mythic elements and ambiguity, symbolically alluding to biblical myths of the Creation and the Fall in depicting the results of a failed economic experiment by a local politician, Don Alejo, who is a sort of local god, even said to resemble the Lord.

The village, Estación El Olivo, created by Don Alejo, a wealthy landowner and area boss, was touted as an earthly paradise at its inception, but some twenty years later, during the novel's present, it has become a caricature of itself, where physical and moral stagnation make it something of a hell on earth. Don Alejo had originally owned the brothel, but as the result of a bet between himself and the madam, Big Japonesa, he signed the property over to her (the wager involved Japonesa's managing to seduce Manuela, a gay cross-dresser who imagines that he is a flamenco dancer). Japonesa won, thanks to her astuteness in manipulating Manuela's erotic fantasy and a promise to make him her partner in the brothel, but during the incident she became pregnant and subsequently gave birth to an unattractive girl, Japonesita, who operated the brothel business following her mother's death. Japonesita, at the age of twenty still a virgin despite her managing a house of prostitution, is a rival of her gay father in a subliminal competition for the affections of Pancho Vega, a truck driver, bully, and closeted gay man whose return precipitates the novel's climax.

Although Don Alejo, as "creator" of Estación El Olivo, is a benign god figure, he is ambiguous by reason of being politically and morally corrupt (he also plots the destruction of the town, since he has decided to convert the whole area to vineyards). His wager, the precipitating factor that brings Manuela's family into being, is a parodic perversion of the concept of Christian marriage, and his association with the powers of evil is symbolized by four vicious black dogs that accompany him (similar dogs appear in *The Obscene Bird of Night*). The ambiguity of Manuela is primarily sexual, for he desires ardently to be a woman; some similar ambiguity appears in Pancho, who is muscular and seemingly virile but in reality is cowardly and in the closet. The ambiguity of Japonesita, virgin madam of the bordello, is underlined by her lack of sexual maturity, her exaggerated thrift, and illusions that hinge on her buying a phonograph—a pathetically unrealistic hope, given the reality of her economic situation.

The catalyst in *Hell Has No Limits* is Pancho, who decides after a meeting with Don Alejo that he will enjoy one last spree at the brothel. He makes sexual advances toward Japonesita, but having aroused her (all the while thinking of his truck—both a Freudian sexual symbol and an instrument of suicidal escape), he sadistically rejects her for Manuela, whose dance provokes him, not so much to sexual desire as to murderous fantasies of disemboweling and leaving her lifeless.

The novel's brutal climax resolves Manuela's existential identity crisis (brought on by age and the depressing material situation). Leaving the brothel with Pancho and his brother-in-law, Octavio, after the flamenco performance, Manuela makes the mistake of kissing Pancho, who fears exposure of his homosexuality; this unleashes a nightmarish flight-and-pursuit sequence in which Manuela is beaten and attempts to seek refuge in the home of Don Alejo. Caught and beaten again, Manuela is sodomized by Pancho and Octavio and left nearly dead by the river. Whether this episode is fatal is also ambiguous; the novel ends on a note of pessimism as Japonesita extinguishes the brothel light and retires to the howling of Don Alejo's dogs and the sobs of a prostitute's child, traditional motifs of doom that combine with the blackness of night to underscore the impression of impending death and oblivion. Because of his psychological complexity, existential revolt, and commitment to ideals of art and beauty, Manuela is one of Donoso's most memorable characters.

The Obscene Bird of Night

The Obscene Bird of Night, considered by critics an antinovel because of Donoso's abandonment of traditional plot, character, and thematic development in favor of a more spontaneous depiction of reality and a virtuosic display of stylistic artistry, is the author's most complex work. Filled with grotesque fantasies, characters with multiple and fluctuating identities or protean, disintegrating personalities, the novel does away with conventions of logic and of mimetic literature, discarding any portrayal of objective reality to present the dilemma of humanity before the existential void.

Humberto Peñaloza, narrator and protagonist, begins as an incipient or would-be writer whose poverty obliges him to accept the job of secretary to Don Jerónimo Azcoitía, a wealthy aristocrat and influential politician. Jerónimo's wife, Inés, inspires Humberto's erotic fantasies, although her witchlike old servant, Peta Ponce, intrudes upon many of them, preventing the consummation—even in his mind—of Humberto's desire. When

Jerónimo and Inés fail to have a son to carry on the family's distinguished name, Peta Ponce supposedly arranges for Humberto to have intercourse with Inés, who conceives and gives birth to Boy, a repugnant little monster, deformed to such an extreme that Jerónimo has him reared on an isolated, distant estate that is placed under the direction of Humberto. Whether Humberto fathers Boy is highly questionable; it may be only another fantasy, as are many other incidents in the novel (the ultimate reality of Boy is also questionable).

The distant estate, La Rinconada, peopled by monsters—gathered by Jerónimo so that Boy will not believe himself abnormal—is a grotesque, absurd mirror image of the Azcoitía estate and a possible expressionist allegory of Chilean society. Years later, after surgery for an ulcer, Humberto becomes obsessed with the notion that his physician, Dr. Azula, has removed eighty percent of his organs; Humberto abandons La Rinconada to take refuge in La Casa—a former convent that has become a domicile for retired female servants—where he retreats into silence and is called Mudito (mute).

Inés, now aging and frustrated in her aspirations to maternity, fails in a mission to the Vatican in which she seeks symbolic perpetuity, via the quest for beatification of a homonymic forebear, and also takes refuge in La Casa, where she spends her time despoiling the grotesque old inmates of their few miserable belongings in a dog-racing game that she always wins. Or does she? The visionary and phantasmagoric world of the protagonist-narrator is so fluctuating, so surrealistic and ambiguous, that the reader assumes the narrative consciousness to be schizophrenic or psychotic and mistrusts his representation of events. Humberto's schizophrenic symptoms include withdrawal from reality, hallucinations, living in a world of fantasy, systems of false selves, masks or personas, fear or terror of engulfment by others or the world, a feeling of imprisonment, and the imagining of himself as an infant. Donoso's uncanny capturing of the schizophrenic's perceptions undoubtedly owes something to his own experience of mental illness, with transient schizophrenia and paranoia induced by his inability to tolerate the painkillers given him after his operation. It is possible—and even plausible—that most of the novel's characters are phantoms generated by Humberto's deteriorating mind, and that the two worlds of the Azcoitía estate and the isolation of La Rinconada respectively represent the rational world of visible reality and the dangers of the invisible world of the unconscious.

A HOUSE IN THE COUNTRY

Although the labyrinthine, dilapidated casa has been seen as an archetypal Jungian symbol of terror, it may also be related to Donoso's use of the decaying mansion throughout his fiction as a symbol of Chilean society with its archaic social structures and decadence. Yet another such house, a seemingly limitless labyrinth with miles of underground passages, secret rooms, false or hollow walls, and hidden doors, appears in *A House in the Country*, seen by some as an allegory of Chilean politics and referring concretely to the military coup of 1973, following in the wake of other novels about Latin American dictators, such as Alejo Carpentier's *El recurso del método* (1974; *Reasons of State*, 1976), Augusto Roa Bastos's *Yo el Supremo* (1974), and Gabriel García Márquez's *El otoño del patriarca* (1975; *The Autumn of the Patriarch*, 1975). If this is true, Donoso's novel does not present the biography of a dictator so much as the ideological configurations of a historical event, alluding to the opponents, victims and villains, the personal concentration of power and attendant aspiration to perpetuity, physical and intellectual repression, official rhetoric, and external intervention, with the house or mansion and its surrounding outbuildings constituting a metaphor for the totalitarian state, especially for the political prison, concentration camp, or detention center.

Beyond allusions to specific concepts or historically recognizable persons, *A House in the Country* is significant for its portrayal of a general problem in Latin America, a vast complex transcending geographical and political boundaries and involving the unholy alliance between oligarchies and foreign interests, militarism and dictatorships, the exploitation of the lower class and the lack of freedom of speech and of the press. It is an abstract political allegory of the abuse of power based on bureaucratic structures, the novel of a family dynasty whose fortune is based on mining in a remote rural area of lush vegetation and unreal, stylized geography, with significant subthemes such as adolescent rebellion, the conflict between idealism and materialism, the generation gap, psychosexual repression, conformism and hypocrisy, inauthentic values and lifestyles, and radical solitude and the inability to communicate.

Set in an imaginary country whose flora and fauna appear to be drawn from all of South America, *A House in the Country* employs a vague chronology, as befits its mythic and ahistorical nature. As something of a dystopia with strong existentialist undercurrents, it portrays a Kafkaesque world where utopia has gone awry via the symbolic narration of a "revolution": Children who take advantage of their elders' absence on an extended and unexplained trip take over the estate and set up their own regime, instituting some reforms among the natives but eventually quarreling among themselves and finally being discovered and chastised after a parental display of force involving the use of troops. *A House in the Country* is thus no more a realistic portrayal of recognizable reality than is *The Obscene Bird of Night*, although powerful realities of another order are captured and conveyed with forceful impact.

Donoso's later novels also display vanguardist tendencies, employing variants of the metanovel and self-conscious fiction, the purpose of which is to erase the boundaries between the real and fictitious worlds, with the author being simultaneously creator and novelistic character, the novel both that which the reader peruses and another work whose genesis is subject or problem of the text at hand. The problem of the relationships among author, text, and reader is a leitmotif in *The Obscene Bird of Night*, *A House in the Country*, and *El jardín de al lado*, where it assumes preponderant proportions. In an encounter between the novelist and one of the Ventura dynasty in *A House in the Country*, the character criticizes many details of the narrative, a situation elaborated in *El jardín de al lado*; in both works, Donoso presents his literary theories or comments upon them, burlesques the expectations of the reader of conventional novels, parodies literary convention, and repeatedly destroys the mimetic illusion in favor of an investigation into the problems of the novel as genre, thereby further separating his last five novels from those of the 1950's and 1960's. Without ceasing to write of Chile, he became more cosmopolitan in his choice of settings and characters; without abandoning social concerns, he incorporated broader themes and more universal literary preoccupations.

Janet Pérez

OTHER MAJOR WORKS

SHORT FICTION: *Veraneo, y otros cuentos*, 1955; *Dos cuentos*, 1956; *El Charlestón*, 1960 (abridged as *Cuentos*, 1971; *Charleston, and Other Stories*, 1977); *Los mejores cuentos de José Donoso*, 1965; *Cuentos*, 1971; *Seis cuentos para ganar*, 1985.

PLAYS: *Sueños de mala muerte*, pb. 1985; *Este domingo: Versión teatral de la novela homónima*, pb. 1990.

POETRY: *Poemas de un novelista*, 1981.

NONFICTION: *Historia personal del "boom,"* 1972 (*The Boom in Spanish American Literature: A Personal History*, 1977).

BIBLIOGRAPHY

Callan, Richard J. *Jung, Alchemy, and José Donoso's Novel "El obsceno pájaro de la noche."* Lewiston, N.Y.: Edwin Mellen Press, 2000. Examines *The Obscene Bird of Night* from the perspective of Carl Jung's analytical psychology. Callan explains how Donoso created his own literary version of Jungian psychology to focus on themes of imprisonment and disguise.

Carbajal, Brent J. *The Veracity of Disguise in Selected Works of José Donoso: Illusory Deception*. Lewiston, N.Y.: Edwin Mellen Press, 2000. Carbajal discusses the use of masks, both literal and metaphorical, in four of Donoso's novels. One chapter focuses on the role of the double in his lesser-known novel *Donde van a morir los elefantes*.

Finnegan, Pamela May. *The Tension of Paradox: José Donoso's "The Obscene Bird of Night" as Spiritual Exercises*. Athens: Ohio University Press, 1992. Finnegan examines the novel as an expression of humanity's estrangement from the world. A difficult but rewarding study for advanced students. Includes a bibliography.

Friedman, Mary Lusky. *The Self in the Narratives of José Donoso: Chile, 1924-1996*. Lewiston, N.Y.: Edwin Mellen Press, 2004. A detailed examination of a major theme in Donoso's writing: the perils of establishing a self. Friedman focuses on his later works, including the novels *The Garden Next Door*, *Curfew*, and *Donde van a morir los elefantes*, to describe how Donoso's works expressed his conception of selfhood.

González Mandri, Flora. *José Donoso's House of Fiction: A Dramatic Construction of Time and Place*. Detroit, Mich.: Wayne State University Press, 1995. A study of

Donoso's incorporation of masks and houses in his fiction, the latter implicating allusions to Henry James. González Mandri focuses on his novels and the novella *Taratuta* (1990). Includes detailed notes, an extensive bibliography, and an index.

King, Sarah E. *The Magical and the Monstrous: Two Faces of the Child-Figure in the Fiction of Julio Cortázar and José Donoso*. New York: Garland, 1992. Informative, although the short citations in Spanish are not translated into English. Nevertheless, this comparative study of two figures of the Spanish American boom in literature is valuable.

McMurray, George R. *Authorizing Fictions: José Donoso's "Casa de Campo."* London: Tamesis Books, 1992. Chapters on Donoso's handling of voice and time, his narrative strategies (re-presenting characters), and his use of interior duplication and distortion. Includes a bibliography.

_______. *José Donoso*. Boston: Twayne, 1979. An excellent introductory study, with chapters on Donoso's biography, his short stories, *The Obscene Bird of Night*, and *Sacred Families*. Includes a chronology, detailed notes, and an annotated bibliography.

Magnarelli, Sharon. *Understanding José Donoso*. Columbia: University of South Carolina Press, 1993. Thoroughgoing study of Donoso's works. The first chapter, "How to Read José Donoso," offers an introduction to his work. Separate chapters analyze his novels *Coronation*, *This Sunday*, *Hell Has No Limits*, *The Obscene Bird of Night*, *A House in the Country*, and *Curfew*.

IVAN GONCHAROV

Born: Simbirsk, Russia; June 6, 1812
Died: St. Petersburg, Russia; September 15, 1891
Also known as: Ivan Alexandrovich Goncharov

PRINCIPAL LONG FICTION

Obyknovennaya istoriya, 1847 (*A Common Story*, 1890)
Oblomov, 1859 (English translation, 1915)
Obryv, 1869 (*The Precipice*, 1916)

OTHER LITERARY FORMS

The early stories and poems of Ivan Goncharov (gon-chah-RAHF) were considered mediocre by the author himself as well as the public and have long been out of print. Goncharov's first significant piece was the sketch "Ivan Savich Podzhabrin," available in *Sobranie sochinenii* (1883, 1888, 1952; collected works). Still widely published and read is the travelogue *Fregat Pallada* (1858; *The Voyage of the Frigate Pallada*, 1965). During the final two decades of his life, Goncharov concentrated on critical essays, reminiscences, and polemical articles. "Mil'yon terzaniy" (1872), his analysis of Alexander Griboyedov's *Gore ot uma* (1825, 1831; English translation, 1857), and his autobiographical memoir "Luchshe pozdno, chem nikogda" (1879; better late than never) have limited circulation, even among literary specialists.

ACHIEVEMENTS

Ivan Goncharov's novels mark the transition from Russian Romanticism to a much more realistic worldview. They appeared at a time when sociological criteria dominated analysis and when authors were expected to address the injustices of Russian life. The critic Nikolay Dobrolyubov derived the term *Oblomovism* from Goncharov's most famous novel, using it to denote the physical and mental sluggishness of Russia's backward country gentry. Thus, Goncharov is credited with exposing a harmful national type: the spendthrift serf-holding landowner who contributed nothing to the national economy and resisted progress for fear of destroying his carefree existence.

By presenting this type in his rather ordinary surroundings and endeavors, stripped of the Romantic aura with which Alexander Pushkin's classical and Mikhail Lermontov's Romantic verse had imbued him, Goncharov gained renown as a critical realist. While all three of his novels remain popular classics in his homeland, only *Oblomov* has found a wide readership and critical acclaim abroad. Emphasis on that work has caused modern Western scholars to value Goncharov as highly for his artful psychological portraits of stunted adults adrift in a changing world as for his sociological contribution.

Oblomov's "return to the womb" predates Sigmund Freud by several decades. On the artistic level, Goncharov far transcends the realistic label often applied to him. His talent for transforming an endlessly mundane provincial existence into a delicate poetic network of pre-Petrine Russian values set standards for the budding Russian novel; his stream-of-consciousness approach points ahead to James Joyce and Marcel Proust. Goncharov has firmly established a place for himself within the genre of the modern psychological novel.

Biography

Ivan Goncharov was born Ivan Alexandrovich Goncharov on June 18, 1812, in remote Simbirsk (now Ulyanovsk) on a country estate of the type featured in his novels. After losing his merchant father at age seven, he was reared in the old tradition by his strong-willed mother and her landowning companion. This heritage of easygoing manor life and progressive mercantile activity characterizes Goncharov's own outlook and that of his major fictional characters. Encouraged to follow in his father's footsteps, he languished for eight years in a school of commerce without graduating. From 1831 to 1834, he attended Moscow University, without taking an active part in the famous philosophical student circles of the time. Instead, he entered the literary world as a tutor in the culturally sophisticated Maikov family, using this experience to produce his first poems and stories.

Goncharov's rise to fame was slow, and he was trapped in a civil service career spanning more than thirty years, almost half of which was spent uneventfully as a translator in the finance ministry. Goncharov's private existence turned out to be equally monotonous. Although he was attracted to a number of women, his courtships were not successful, and he never married. The frustrations of his relationships with women are prominently mirrored in all three novels.

The success of his first novel, *A Common Story*, did not alleviate Goncharov's self-doubt, and he remained fettered to extraliterary activity. A worldwide sailing tour on behalf of the trade ministry in the 1850's yielded material for his travel sketches. The same period brought an appointment to the literary censorship board, a result of Czar Alexander II's relaxed attitude. Goncharov followed a middle-of-the-road philosophy in this post, often enraging progressive writers, whose harsh judgments of conservative ideals he would not accept. He secured his own literary fame with *Oblomov* but felt too insecure to devote himself exclusively to literature. After a brief try at editing the official newspaper *Severnaya pchela* in the 1860's, he returned to a censorial post in the influential Press Council. His civic duties earned for him the Order of Vladimir, third class, prior to retirement in 1868.

Meanwhile, Goncharov's mental state had gradually deteriorated. Ivan Turgenev's literary success easily eclipsed that of Goncharov, and when Turgenev's *Dvoryanskoe gnezdo* (1859; *Liza: Or, "A Nest of Nobles,"* 1869; better known as *A Nest of Gentlefolk*, 1959) superseded *Oblomov* in critical acclaim, Goncharov accused his rival of plagiarism. Arbitration found Turgenev innocent, and the writers reconciled, but in private, the increasingly neurotic Goncharov continued the accusations, venting on Turgenev all the frustrations of his own unsatisfactory existence. Philosophically, Goncharov moved from a modestly progressive stance to a firm defense of the traditional values of the landed gentry. These sentiments found expression in *The Precipice*, in which moral regeneration is embedded in the unchanging order of provincial Russia.

Goncharov died on September 15, 1891, a stranger to the swiftly moving social currents of the latter part of the century. His later published works chronicle his artistic decline. A complete recluse, he burned his letters and manuscripts. He spent his final days not unlike his major hero, Oblomov, in a St. Petersburg flat, looked after by a kindly woman and her children.

Analysis

"My life began flickering out from the very first moment I became conscious of myself." Thus, Ilya Oblomov explains his arrested development to his successful business friend, Stolz, who is making a last try to rouse Oblomov from his fatal lethargy, and thus Goncharov points the reader to the cause of Oblomov's inertia: his childhood in a sleepy, backward manor house, attended by an army of serfs, every moment structured to reinforce an existence of indolently blissful inactivity, a paradise to which the adult strives all of his life to return. Oblomov's failure as a man and his search for a surrogate childhood in a simple St. Petersburg family fit perfectly the scheme of the psychological novel. From this perspective, the seemingly typical Russian landowner Oblomov becomes a universal figure, and the old-fashioned Russian village becomes merely background.

Such a perspective, however, has its drawbacks. If one considers *Oblomov* apart from Goncharov's other novels, as is often the case in the West, the wider artistic sweep of his fiction is neglected. Each of his novels gives expression to a different facet of the contradictions encountered by the Russian patriarchal order as it confronted sociopolitical reform. Goncharov's characters can be said to embody the two warring dominant philosophies of nineteenth century Russia: Slavophilism and Westernization. The author's own struggle between these two opposing forces is cast into sharp focus in the novels, as his progress-oriented mind gradually loses ground to his tradition-loving, Slavophile heart.

Neither Goncharov's personal dissatisfactions nor his conservative turn impair his stature as an accomplished novelist. The expert use of several literary devices contributes to this renown. There is, first of all, his power of observation, the ability to create such a lifelike image of an ordinary event through accumulation of detail that his scenes are compared to Flemish interiors. Authorial ambiguity also enriches the narrative. The first two novels conceptually demonstrate the advantages of a progressive economy and the futility of perpetuating serfdom, but Goncharov presents a dying way of life with such a wealth of attractive imagery that social indifference, indeed exploitation, infantilism, and stagnation, are turned into a languidly cozy, almost noble way of life, feeding on nostalgia and winning sympathy for its prejudices.

No less impressive is Goncharov's skill in suggesting the delusions of the regressive personality. Oblomov's insecure psyche reshapes his ordinary village into a harmless, safe refuge, smoothing craggy mountains into gentle hillocks, swift rivers into murmuring brooks, extremes of climate into eternally pleasant weather, passions into lethargy. Readers are scarcely aware that the descriptions are no longer objective, but the distortions of a frightened mind.

Finally, Goncharov excels in drawing exquisite female portraits; his women also symbolize the synthesis between the old and new. In *A Common Story*, Lizaveta is able to balance the contradictory forces that pull the male characters into adversary position; in *Oblomov*, Olga combines the best of old Russia, its cultural heritage, with an inquisitive mind and an active personality; in *The Precipice*, Vera eventually unites the positive features of her patriarchal upbringing with the progressive forces of a commercially enterprising spouse.

In his final novel, Goncharov's moralizing instincts undermine his mastery of style, as didactic elements intrude too explicitly. The author's own estrangement from the present and his nostalgia for a less complex existence color his perceptions. His slow-paced upbringing, his later insecurities, his realization that progress was necessary, his struggle between old and new, and his final withdrawal from society are the building blocks of all of his works. He delicately managed to balance these elements before yielding to his own preferences.

A COMMON STORY

The unstinting praise of Russia's foremost social critic, Vissarion Belinsky, assured the success of *A Common Story* the moment it appeared in the literary journal *Sovremennik*. Ironically, the work was hailed as an exposé of the degenerate gentry class and a call for modernization. Critics and readers alike noted only the main character Alexander Aduev's final acceptance of St. Petersburg's progressive lifestyle, not his mentor-uncle's disillusionment with it. They also overlooked the author's cautious suggestion that the city's competitive utilitarianism was no more satisfying than the monotony of the backward village.

This misperception attests Goncharov's balancing skill. Alexander is lured from his peaceful, idyllic estate, lovingly presented in the fragrance of its lilacs, berries, bushes, and forests, by visions of cosmopolitan dazzle. Once he is taken in hand by a "new man," his coldly efficient, philistine uncle, Peter, one disappointment succeeds another. Like an early Oblomov, Alexander adjusts only superficially, never able to integrate his rustic values with St. Petersburg's diverse phenomena. Like a young Goncharov, Alexander blunders from one unsuccessful love affair to another. His literary endeavors, characterized by overblown sentimental clichés, are equally fruitless. Despite all efforts by Peter, he turns into a rather ridiculous figure, an out-of-place relic in the bustling city. Goncharov's ambiguous attitude, however, gives enough scope to elicit a measure of pity from the reader, to mark the young man's discomforts and his inability to cope.

Peter's young wife, Lizaveta, compassionately brings out Alexander's positive traits.

When all attempts at acclimatization end in failure, he returns to his quiet country home and recovers his bearings. yet the lessons of the city are not lost. At a distance, its hectic multiplicity develops into a fair alternative to the boring idyll of the placid province. In the end, Alexander sets out for St. Petersburg once more, cured of his romantic expectations, determined to copy his uncle's career through realistic adaptation and lowered sights. His success is presented in the epilogue. He parallels Peter faithfully: fat and balding, engaged to a young heiress, adjusted, mature, eager for progressive endeavors.

While this conclusion heartened liberal critics, Goncharov's reservations are apparent in the incompletely dramatized and therefore unconvincing psychological transformation of Alexander. The artistically unmotivated ending causes a change of focus. The carefully developed juxtaposition of old versus new, village versus city, Slavophile versus Westernizer assumes the outline of a bildungsroman. Peter and Alexander represent two stages of identical development. Alexander's romantic striving mirrors Peter's own youthful immaturity, while Peter's rational, mature stage serves as a marker for Alexander's similar destiny. At the moment of Alexander's arrival at that stage, Peter's dry and joyless stance casts doubt on the wisdom of these very accomplishments, foreshadowing eventual disillusionment for his nephew. The general inattention to this downbeat element is a result of the shortage of bourgeois heroes in Russian literature.

The Romantic characters of Pushkin, Lermontov, and the early Turgenev are immobile, purposeless, and contemptuous of practical activity. Liberal critics had long called for a positively depicted, businesslike nobleman, and they accepted Alexander in his final guise enthusiastically as such. The careful reader is left questioning both men's aspirations and sharing Lizaveta's wistful awareness that St. Petersburg's progress is far from ideal. The alternative of seeking that ideal in Russia's past surfaces only in Goncharov's later works, although the absence of a critical stand against serfdom and landowner privileges already serves to modify the seeming victory of Westernization.

OBLOMOV

Turgenev's popular *A Nest of Gentlefolk* threatened to overshadow *Oblomov*, which was first printed in *Otechestvennye zapiski*, until critic Dobrolyubov's 1859 article "Chto takoyo Oblomovshchina?" ("What Is Oblomovism?") swiftly drew national attention to the work. Following Dobrolyubov's cue, most readers and succeeding generations saw in *Oblomov* the hero's inertia the psychological consequence of total dependence on serf labor. By lavishing endless pages on the harmful effects of Oblomovism and the virtues of Stolz, a Western-influenced business type, Goncharov seemed to strike a forceful blow at the roots of Russia's economic and social evils.

Oblomov appears as the epitome of the superfluous nobleman, the lazy, alienated dreamer who cannot adjust to change or find a place for himself in the present. Different embodiments of this type exist in Pushkin's Onegin, Lermontov's Pechorin, and Turgenev's Rudin. Oblomov differs from these characters in that he rejects even the search for an alternative, preferring instead the never-changing ways of his childhood Oblomovka. The location of this estate on the Asian border aptly suggests the Asian fatalism and circular philosophy that represent Oblomov's and, by extension, Russia's Eastern Tartar heritage. The hero's Asian dressing gown, serving as his security blanket and finally his shroud, is an equally fitting symbol.

The reader is initiated into all the details of Russian provincial backwardness through Oblomov's lengthy dream of his sleepy backwater. The dream, a thematic outline of the work and its centerpiece, had been published separately as a sort of overture as early as 1849. The finished novel shows the deadening effect of this "blessed spot" on those who cannot free themselves from the dependencies it fosters. Little Ilya was born a normal child, willing to experiment, to rough it, to develop. The atmosphere of Oblomovka snuffed out all of these inclinations. Tradition stipulates that a Russian gentleman sit, surrounded by hordes of serfs who attend to his every whim, that he eat and doze most of the day, phlegmatically observe the seasonal and ecclesiastical rituals, ignore any attempt at change, be it literacy or postal service, and hope that the waves of Peter the Great's Westernizing reforms never reach his quiet hamlet. Inevitably, they do reach Oblomovka, and the product of its upbringing must serve his term in St. Petersburg.

The innumerable ways in which the transplanted Oblomov manages to ignore the city's reality take up a good portion of the narrative. Each failure on the realistic plane is paralleled by a success on the imaginary level, which always features a happy Oblomov in a paradisiacal Oblomovka. Eventually, Oblomov gains a questionable victory. A motherly widow's shabby lodging transforms itself into a blissful surrogate of Oblomovka for the by-now infantile hero. He has returned to the womb and lives out a short but happy span, until mental stagnation and greedy overeating end his life.

Two people try their best to save Oblomov. First Stolz, the half-German entrepreneur, as lean as an English racehorse where Oblomov is fat and flabby, uses reason and intellectual appeal to convince Oblomov to change. Then Olga, already adapted to a modern intelligentsia but preserving a deep love for Russia's cultural past, lures him with promises of selfless love. Sexually aroused, Oblomov briefly responds to her, but when he finds that Olga also demands intellectual arousal, constant mental awareness, he takes flight. The equally dull-witted widow offers both maternal and mistress services without the necessity of mental effort.

Stolz and Olga, who eventually marry, represent the best of traditional Russia fused with the best of imported progressive behavior. Stolz is an improved version of Peter Aduev. The latter's negative traits and final pessimistic outlook have been replaced by Stolz's cheerfulness and compassion. Even here, however, the author's descriptive talents hover lovingly over the blubbery Oblomov—over his dreams, his reflections, his blunders—while Stolz comes across as artificial and wooden, the victim of uninspired portrayal. Olga, who loves and appreciates Oblomov's values, is a more credible figure, and it is she who embodies and carries into the future the reconciliation of the conflict. In some respects, she acts as Goncharov's mouthpiece. Her dissatisfactions, even with the faultless Stolz, echo the author's own inability to believe fully in the spiritual benefits of a forward-moving Russia. Goncharov had no such reservations when it came to praising the charms of Oblomovka. Its oneness with nature renders each inhabitant a paragon of virtue. No passionate outbursts or personal animosities mar the peacefulness. Serfs are not slaves, but content to be reflections of their masters. Their sloth and their ample participation in all the feasting, indulged by benevolent owners, help to deplete Oblomovka's reserves. When this slothful behavior is transplanted to St. Petersburg in the person of Oblomov's loyal valet Zakhar, it loses much of its bucolic enchantment, yet the touching interdependence of master and servant redeems the ineptness. It was simply impossible for Goncharov to carry to its logical conclusion his commonsense understanding that radical Slavophilism would result in national stagnation and regression.

THE PRECIPICE

Goncharov's unwillingness to endow his progressive characters with the vitality necessary to make them convincing and interesting asserts itself more fully in his last major work, *The Precipice*. It appeared in *Vestnik Evropy* at a time when emancipation was a fact, when Alexander II's liberalism gave wide scope to social commentators, when literature closely echoed the zeitgeist of reform. Goncharov's liberal representative is the political exile Volokhov, who, like Turgenev's nihilist Bazarov, spreads unrest in a deeply conservative village. Volokhov's positive qualities are quickly neutralized by his seduction of a virtuous country woman, Vera, who naïvely tries to straighten him out. Vera is also a link to the other male principal, Raisky, a St. Petersburg intellectual, who has failed to find a purpose in life and returns to his country estate in search of a footing. It is easy to see in him yet another embodiment of Goncharov's favorite type: the neurotic male whose interests, convictions, and common sense pull him toward reform but whose temperament and deep-seated impulses chain him to the past. In each of these split personalities, Goncharov's own schism finds expression. As before, he reserves the best of his descriptive talents for the backwoods, symbolized by the figure of the grandmother. It is in this traditional setting that the abused Vera finds regeneration and mental recovery; it is the rural past that bequeaths stability, sanity, and direction for the future.

Goncharov had once again drawn an exquisite cameo of old Russia, once again contrasted the conflicting values of old and new, once again pictured an artistically masterful "homecoming." Despite the popularity of the somewhat meandering work, Goncharov's point of view drew heavy moral indignation. Liberal critics were quick to point out that Goncharov had come down on the side of rural conservatism, that he favored the Slavophiles. Obviously and painfully out of step with the tenor of the time, and psychologically unable and unwilling to recapture his artistic independence, Goncharov withdrew. His subsequent writings did not approach the stature of his novels.

Goncharov's significance in the development of the Russian novel and Russian intellectual history remains great. He brought to life the characters of old Russia, with a style peculiarly his own, at a time when that patriarchal order began to disintegrate. In his portraits of Slavophiles and Westernizers, he elaborated on the dominant conflict of mid-century Russia. He was the first Russian author to integrate psychological complexities successfully and expertly into his plots, and thereby he created universal types.

Margot K. Frank

OTHER MAJOR WORKS

SHORT FICTION: "Ivan Savich Podzhabrin," 1848; "Slugi starogo veka," 1888.

NONFICTION: *Fregat Pallada*, 1858 (*The Voyage of the Frigate Pallada*, 1965); "Mil'yon terzaniy," 1872; "Luchshe pozdno, chem nikogda," 1879; "V universitete," 1887; "Na rodine," 1888; "Neobyknovennaya istoriya," 1924.

MISCELLANEOUS: *Sobranie sochinenii*, 1883, 1888, 1952 (8 volumes).

BIBLIOGRAPHY

Diment, Galya. "The Two Faces of Ivan Goncharov: Autobiography and Duality in *Obyknovennaia Istorija*." *Slavic and East European Journal* 32 (Fall, 1988). Diment discusses Goncharov's use of autobiographical facts in his writings, focusing on his novel *A Common Story*.

_______, ed. *Goncharov's "Oblomov": A Critical Companion*. Evanston, Ill.: Northwestern University Press, American Association of Teachers of Slavic and East European Languages, 1998. Collection of essays analyzing various aspects of the novel, including its questions of heroism; themes of mistaken identities and "food, eating, and the search for communion"; and its Freudian perspectives.

Ehre, Milton. *Oblomov and His Creator: The Life and Art of Ivan Goncharov*. Princeton, N.J.: Princeton University Press, 1973. A literary biography and a deep analysis of Goncharov's works. An excellent starting point for research.

Frank, Joseph. "Being and Laziness." *The New Republic*, January 29, 2007. Frank, a professor of comparative literature and Slavic languages and literature at Stanford University, provides a detailed discussion of both Goncharov's life and the novel *Oblomov* in response to the publication of a new translation of the work.

Lyngstad, Alexandra, and Sverre Lyngstad. *Ivan Goncharov*. New York: Twayne, 1971. A psychological sketch of the author and a discussion of his literary works, including separate chapters analyzing *Oblomov* and "The Art of Goncharov." Includes notes, references, and an index.

Maguire, Robert A. "The City." In *The Cambridge Companion to the Classic Russian Novel*, edited by Malcolm V. Jones and Robin Feuer Miller. New York: Cambridge University Press, 1998. Maguire's essay about the theme of the city in *Oblomov* and novels by other authors places Goncharov's work within the broader context of the development of the Russian novel.

Platonov, Rachel S. "Remapping Arcadia: 'Pastoral Space' in Nineteenth-Century Russian Prose." *Modern Language Review* 102, no. 4 (October, 2007): 1105-1121. An examination of the role of space and spatiality in *Oblomov* and three other Russian prose pastorals. Platonov argues that Russian culture gives a particular significance to the notion of boundaries, which explains, in part, why Russian writers' depictions of pastoral paradises are "particularly prone to disintegration and self-destruction."

SHIRLEY ANN GRAU

Born: New Orleans, Louisiana; July 8, 1929

PRINCIPAL LONG FICTION

The Hard Blue Sky, 1958
The House on Coliseum Street, 1961
The Keepers of the House, 1964
The Condor Passes, 1971
Evidence of Love, 1977
Roadwalkers, 1994

OTHER LITERARY FORMS

Although Shirley Ann Grau (grow) has written introductions and occasional essays for magazines, two forms—the novel and the short story—have dominated her literary career. The enthusiastic reception that greeted her first collection of short stories, *The Black Prince, and Other Stories* (1955), has assured her reputation in the genre. Scarcely any anthology of American short fiction excludes her work. In spite of her initial success critically, her second collection of stories, *The Wind Shifting West* (1973), was not so warmly received. *Nine Women*, which appeared in 1985, restored Grau's critical acclaim as a short-story writer. Grau also contributed a chapter to *Haunter of the Ruins* (1997), a book on America's foremost surrealist photographer, fellow Louisianian Clarence John Laughlin.

ACHIEVEMENTS

The most obvious testimony to Grau's success is the Pulitzer Prize for fiction that she received in 1965 for *The Keepers of the House*. Significantly enough, the same novel appeared in condensed form in *Ladies' Home Journal*. Thus, one sees evidence of one of the distinguishing characteristics of much of Grau's fiction: the ability to appeal simultaneously to two often opposed audiences, the person looking for the "good read" and the literary sophisticate. Not many contemporary writers have published stories in both *McCall's* and *The New Yorker*. In *Evidence of Love*, Grau seems to have made an attempt to shed any vestige of her image as a "housewife writer" or yet another southern regionalist. While *Evidence of Love* is rather straightforward, even in its effective use of three overlapping narratives, it nevertheless makes few concessions to a reader looking for the conventional melodramatic staples of sex or violence. *Evidence of Love* also silences the critics who, after the disappointment of *The Condor Passes*, sought to dismiss Grau as a one-novel writer. The one recurring criticism of Grau's later work—that her characters seem bloodless—seems less relevant after the success of other novelists with similar ironic visions—Joan Didion, for example.

As is true of all but a handful of contemporary writers, Grau's achievement cannot yet be fully measured. *Evidence of Love* suggests that she has shifted her emphasis away from the engaging plot to the creation of a cool, ironic vision of psychological intensity. While *Roadwalkers* contains all the ironic vision of Grau's earlier novels and emphasizes the psychological, it represents another technical feat for Grau in a reemphasis on and experimentation with plot. Here Grau interweaves the impressionistic tale of Mary Woods with the separate histories of Charles Tucker and Rita Landry but ends the novel with the rather straightforward narrative of Nanda Woods. In the process, she has kept those elements of style—the brilliant sensory images, the directness of language, the complex heroines—that have given vitality to all her work.

BIOGRAPHY

At the age of forty-five, Katherine Grau and her husband, Adolphe, had a baby girl. Although Shirley Ann Grau's parents were well into middle age, she has described her childhood as free of unhappiness or social alienation. Her Protestant family, with roots in both New England and the South, moved back and forth from Montgomery, Alabama, to New Orleans. Grau attended a girls' finishing school in the Alabama capital until her senior year, when she transferred to an accredited high school in New Orleans, the Ursuline Academy—the institution that one of her heroines remembers as a place to knit, chant, and crochet.

Grau's first experiences with writing came while attending Sophie Newcomb College in New Orleans. Her stories appeared in the campus literary magazine, *Carnival*. After she graduated Phi Beta Kappa, Grau lived in the French Quarter of New Orleans and abandoned her graduate studies for a writing career. Success came quickly. In 1955, her volume of short stories, *The Black Prince, and Other Stories*, received exceptionally fine reviews, and her work was compared favorably with that of other southern writers such as Eudora Welty, Flannery O'Connor, and Carson McCullers.

In the same year, Grau married James K. Feibleman, a remarkable professor of philosophy at Tulane University. Many years her senior, Feibleman had become chair of his department even though he himself had attended college for only two months. He had published numerous books and was acquainted with such luminaries as William Faulkner. Grau has described her life as a "conventional upper middle class" one, divided between summers at Martha's Vineyard and school years in New Orleans.

As she reared her children, Grau continued to write. The novels *The Hard Blue Sky* (1958) and *The House on Coliseum Street* (1961) were published. While both works received considerable notice, it seemed as if Grau might be categorized as a regionalist who had mastered local color. Her selection as the Pulitzer Prize winner for fiction in 1965, however, did much to squelch such categorization. *The Keepers of the House*, a novel that attracted attention for its candid treatment of racial themes, brought her national attention; in fact, U.S. president Lyndon B. Johnson appointed her to the Commission on Presidential Scholars in the same year. In spite of this recognition, the rhythm of Grau's life remained largely unchanged, and she did not rush to bring out her next novel. Instead, she taught creative writing at the University of New Orleans, wrote an occasional story, and gave birth to her fourth child. When her next novel, *The Condor Passes*, appeared in 1971, its sales surpassed the combined total of all her previous works. Its critical reception, however, was at best mixed. After that, Grau published only a few more works.

In many ways validating her comment in an interview with John Canfield that writers are "just very inefficient computers," Grau returned to the novel form with *Roadwalkers* in 1994 after an absence of seventeen years. Despite the span of time separating it from Grau's previous novel, *Roadwalkers* received much critical attention, garnering mixed reviews in a rather unique way. Most critics have been extremely favorable to the first half of the novel, which deals primarily with the "feral" child Mary Woods. They have been puzzled by the second half, which centers on her daughter, Nanda, whom they see as bloodless and arrogant, a criticism that has followed Grau's heroines off and on throughout her career.

Grau worked on a piece of nonfiction, *Haunter of the Ruins*, in 1997. Her interest in and perhaps unjustified identification with the southern grotesque made Grau the perfect writer to include in a collection of essays that accompany the photographs of Laughlin, one of America's earliest surrealist photographers. Rather than dealing specifically with Laughlin's photographs, Grau's essay is a set piece that evokes the haunting imagery that pervades his work.

ANALYSIS

Shirley Ann Grau shares a fate common to many contemporary writers not yet admitted to the pantheon. They are the object of a handful of critical studies, often short and incomplete, that make only a slight effort to detect what vision, if any, gives continuity to the writers' works. At first glance, Grau's novels do seem to defy any attempt to find even a connecting thread. Until the publication of *Evidence of Love*, the label of "southern regionalist" gave some of Grau's reviewers comfort. Readers familiar only with her last three novels could not avoid the recurrence of semilegendary patriarchs in possession of great wealth.

Revenge at one time or another consumes such heroines as Joan Mitchell in *The House on Coliseum Street* and Abigail Mason Tolliver in *The Keepers of the House*, but an equally strong woman such as Lucy Henley in *Evidence of Love* possesses no such motive. Alwyn Berland (in his essay "The Fiction of Shirley Ann Grau") suggests that Grau's heroines favor the hallucinatory over the real, tend to be passive, and have ambivalent responses to sex. Berland's observation is helpful, but the title of Grau's 1977 novel, *Evidence of Love*, gives the clearest clue to the sometimes elusive vision that informs her fictional world. While most of her male characters mechanically pursue money, sex, power, or ironclad order, the heroines seek some evidence of love. Their failure to find it renders both sexes solitary, and their subsequent sense of futility and despair makes their money and power meaningless. What saves the novels from an almost Jamesian pessimism is the possibility of redemption and rebirth. Both Joan Mitchell and Abigail Tolliver are last seen in literal fetal positions, as if awaiting resurrection. Their possibly temporary withdrawal resembles that of the wives of the fishermen in *The Hard Blue Sky*, who passively await the passing of the hurricane that may or may not destroy them.

In the development of her vision, Grau reveals considerable technical skill. Her sense of place is compelling. Equally convincing are such dissimilar scenes as William Howland's atavistic incursion into Honey Island Swamp and Harold Evans's drift into suicide in his meager and bare house in Princeton. As Paul Schlueter has pointed out, few novelists are as successful as Grau in manipulating sensory images, particularly the olfactory. Most satisfying technically is her ability to treat the melodramatic with a cool, analytical detachment. The embattled house that Abigail defends and keeps is above all else a house, not Tara or Sutpen's Hundred. While Edward Milton Henley in *Evidence of Love* is capable of grandiose, operatic gestures and appetites, Grau's sardonic humor and sense of irony keeps him in the orbit of the real. Grau steadfastly refuses to sentimentalize.

Grau's occasional limitations are perhaps most noticeable in characterization. At times her characters lack emotional depth; the rich are not inherently interesting. In spite of lurid, exotic pasts, characters such as the Old Man in *The Condor Passes* lack the complex humanity necessary to be convincing. Further, her characters' motivations are not always clear. Even the sympathetic reader is not entirely sure, for example, why it is that Abigail so intensely dislikes Margaret's children.

THE HARD BLUE SKY

Prior to 1964, Grau published two novels that anticipated her technique and vision in *The Keepers of the House*. The first, *The Hard Blue Sky*, revealed her ability to capture the world of southern Louisiana in stunning detail. Her plot consists of two different but connected stories that take place on islands along the Gulf Coast. The first story concerns the youthful Annie Landry's affair with Inky D'Alfonso. When she ultimately marries Inky, Annie is able to leave the islands for what may be a better life in New Orleans. Annie bears little resemblance to Abigail Tolliver: She has neither the wealth, the sense of family tradition, nor the consuming desire for revenge that drives Abigail.

It is the second story that contains the violence and the revenge motif that will appear in *The Keepers of the House*. Rival groups on two different islands attempt to burn one another out after the disappearance of young lovers from the opposing families. Neither story ends with a clear resolution. It is not clear whether Annie's marriage will be a success, nor does one know if the feud will end, especially since both factions are threatened by a hurricane. Thus, in her first novel, Grau struck what became a crucial and familiar note in her fiction: Her characters are left in a state of uncertainty as they face potential harm or destruction.

THE HOUSE ON COLISEUM STREET

Grau's second novel, *The House on Coliseum Street*, has a much sharper focus than does her first. Joan Mitchell, the protagonist, anticipates Abigail Tolliver in several significant ways. Her relationship with men is disastrous. She is engaged to a businessman named Fred Aleman, whose rather passionless demeanor leaves her vulnerable to a young college professor, Michael Kern; their passionate lovemaking leaves Joan pregnant. After an abortion and Michael's abandonment, a guilt-ridden Joan becomes obsessed with destroying him. She does so by exposing him to his college dean. Like Abigail, Joan brings down her antagonist, but more significantly, she may have destroyed herself emotionally in doing so. That, however, is only a possibility: *The House on Coliseum Street* ends with Joan, having forgotten her key, unable to enter her family house. She is last seen in a fetal position, just as one sees Abigail at the end of *The Keepers of the House*. The possibility of rebirth and redemption is not excluded. Thus, *The House on Coliseum Street*, like *The Hard Blue Sky*, served as a preparation for the greater achievement in *The Keepers of the House*. In both, Grau was able to find sensory images that render the physical world immediate. More important, these early novels introduced Grau's evolving vision of a world with little clear evidence of love or community.

THE KEEPERS OF THE HOUSE

More than forty years after its publication, the reader can see more clearly the truth of Grau's own commentary on *The Keepers of the House*:

> The novel is about the whole human plight of how do you cope with evil? Do you fight back? The people are living in the South but they're just people facing the eternal human problem. I wanted to show the alternation of love and evil, which has always fascinated me. And if there is a moral, it is the self-destructiveness of hatred.

If Grau sees the novel's significance in general moral terms, its popularity nevertheless was rooted in its then explosive characterization of southern racial attitudes.

The novel's narrator, Abigail Tolliver, granddaughter of William Howland, who himself is one of the "keepers of the house," finds herself in almost complete isolation. She and her husband are getting a divorce, two of her children have been forced to go away to school for safety's sake, and she has alienated the citizenry of her hometown, Madison City. Her desolation, mythic in intensity, is tragically linked to the discovery that her grandfather had married his black housekeeper, Margaret Carmichael. While the white community could cavalierly accept a mere sexual liaison, even one that has produced three children, marriage gives legitimacy. Thus, the men of Madison City attempt to burn the Howland estate in retaliation. The discovery of her grandfather's clandestine marriage destroys Abigail's marriage with her amoral, politically ambitious husband. The novel's evil is therefore easy to locate, as is Abigail's vengeful, Medea-like response. She not only burns the cars of the men who come to destroy her house; she also exercises her option to destroy the entire community financially. Yet difficult questions remain when one recalls Grau's own assessment of her work. How convincingly is the love that alternates with evil portrayed? How strongly felt is her "moral"—the self-destructiveness of hate?

Grau will never be accused of sentimentalizing love. Characters rarely, for example, confuse love with sex. When Abigail loses her virginity, she says,

> I found that it wasn't so hard . . . nor painful either. . . . There's only one night like that—ever—where you're filled with wonder and excitement for no other reason but the earth is beautiful and mysterious and your body is young and strong.

Her courtship by and marriage to John Tolliver are presented just as dispassionately. Tolliver, like Stephen Henley in *Evidence of Love* and the Old Man in *The Condor Passes*, subordinates love to ambition. Grau's sexes mate; they rarely love. Neither does there seem to be affection between generations. Abigail bears four children, but they remain abstractions. More mysterious, more horrific is the relation between the black woman, Margaret, and the children she bears William Howland. Half white herself, Margaret sends each child off at the age of eleven to be educated in the North. She refuses to see them thereafter. She is particularly hostile and unyielding toward her oldest daughter, Nina, who returns to the South with her black husband. A certain curiosity exists between these racially mixed children and their mother, but there is no evidence of love.

The possible exception to this bleak vision of human existence is the thirty-year relationship between William Howland and Margaret. After the death of his first wife and the marriage of his daughter, Howland discovers the eighteen-year-old Margaret Carmichael washing clothes at a spring. She comes to him as a housekeeper and ultimately marries him. Both William and Margaret are characterized by Grau in terms larger than life. Howland is heir to the frontier tradition, in which men wrenched a living, indeed an immense fortune, from a hostile environment. Prior to meeting Margaret, he makes a solitary journey into the mystery and danger of Honey Island Swamp, where he at one point strips himself naked and submerges himself into the primordial slime. When he returns to find Margaret at the spring, she appears to him as if she "had folded herself into the earth." Her stride is "a primitive walk, effortless, unassuming, unconscious, old as the earth under her feet." Like gods, apparently, William and Margaret possess the strength and the indifference to violate the most sacrosanct of southern codes. Yet their love, if it exists, is concealed. The only evidence Abigail ever sees of their love is a single embrace.

Until Abigail's epiphany at the novel's end, Margaret is the character most cognizant of evil, particularly the evil inherent in racism. Her own white father abandoned her black mother, who in turn leaves Margaret to search for her missing lover. Margaret further realizes that it is necessary to send her white-appearing children out of the South, a tragic gesture that Abigail alone understands. It is a sacrifice that ends in alienation between parent and child, between white and black.

Grau states that the moral of the novel is the self-destructiveness of hatred. Is she suggesting that the South is destroying itself with its racial hostility? The attack on the Howland farm clearly does not go without destructive retribution. The local bigots have cut their own throats, because Abigail Tolliver owns almost every business in town. Yet her revenge, just as it may be, seems minuscule compared with the sure election of a staunch segregationist as the next governor—the most far-reaching consequence of the exposure of William Howland's marriage.

Of more visceral concern to the reader, however, is the effect of hatred on Abigail. Not only has she decided to destroy Madison City, but she also has chosen to terrorize Margaret's vengeful son, Robert, by threatening to reveal his black origins to his white California wife. Stripped of compassion, devoid of love, Abigail at the conclusion of the novel has not yet taken the step that transcends hate. Her fetal position as she lies weeping in her office offers a possibility of rebirth, but the overriding vision of the novel is one of utter alienation and despair.

THE CONDOR PASSES

In the thirteen years between the publication of Grau's novels *The Keepers of the House* and *Evidence of Love*, one other novel appeared. Ironically, *The Condor Passes* received the worst reviews while posting the highest sales of any of Grau's works. The novel, a family chronicle, depicts the ninety-five years of Thomas Henry Oliver, who during his long life has amassed a huge fortune through such nefarious enterprises as prostitution and bootlegging. The novel bears only superficial resemblance to *The Keepers of the House*. As Grau herself has suggested, it is not concerned with the primitive. Survival is no longer a question. Instead, the characters seek to find a sense of identity in the presence of vast wealth. The novel, however, is wedded thematically to Grau's other works in its despairing vision. One senses that the male figures may have gained the whole world but lost their own souls. The Old Man's daughters are more complex, but their attempts to find enduring love are frustrated. They each have one son, but one dies and the other becomes a priest. The family therefore awaits little more than its own extinction.

EVIDENCE OF LOVE

By contrast, *Evidence of Love* is one of Grau's most successful novels. It, too, is a family chronicle, but its construction is still tight and sharply focused. Again the wealthy patriarch appears, but Edward Milton Henley possesses a sense of irony and self-awareness denied to earlier Grau patriarchs. Set outside the South, *Evidence of Love* frees Grau from often invidious comparisons with William Faulkner and allows her to concentrate on what has been one of the central concerns of all her novels, the need for some sign of love.

While the novel traces the lives of four generations of the Henley family, the voices of Edward Henley; his son, Stephen; and his daughter-in-law, Lucy, dominate the narrative. Paul Schlueter maintains that "nowhere is there any 'evidence of love.'" He sees each character "seeking his own form of satisfaction to the exclusion of others." What in fact gives focus to each of the three stories is the pursuit of some apparently reasonable alternative to love. Because he chooses to relate his story in a satiric, ironic mode, it is not always easy to locate in an exact way Edward's feelings. The evidence of paternal love, he tells the reader, is the wealth his father gave him. If his mother, who is both literally and figuratively distant, did not love him, she at least imparted to him a sense of propriety and morality—which Edward chooses to ignore. These parents were, he says, happy. Himself physically and emotionally transient, Edward rather cavalierly dispenses with wives and male lovers. Yet he never indulges in self-pity. "I prefer to see my life as a pageant. Or a processional. Like that wonderful march in *Aida*." Through the elder Henley, Grau presents her paradox. About this old man, who still dreams of recapturing the drug-induced paradise he once experienced in Mexico, there is a considerable vitality. Edward's audacity, his iconoclasm, and his rather mordant humor do not diminish life. His suicide is neither cowardly nor tragic. His life has been long and in its way full—even without the presence of love.

Edward says of his son, "Stephen was quiet and totally self-contained." Stephen is a Gatsby stripped of illusion and romance. As a young man, he makes a detailed plan of his life, a schedule that he unflinchingly follows. His marriage to Lucy Evans is as rational, as free of either anguish or passion, as is his commitment to the ministry without believing in God. Here is a potential monster, but Grau does not ask the reader to see him as such. He does at least have some awareness of his own condition. For Lucy, he says, "I felt a sudden flood of feeling . . . not lust, not love. Something deeper, something older, something asexually human. The sympathy of blood for blood, of aching chalky bone for aching chalky bone. . . . The visceral sympathy of acquired identity." If what Stephen feels for Lucy is only kinship, it perhaps explains why he is confused by the passionate intensity of his youngest son, Paul.

Quite by chance, Paul discovers, he believes, the identity of Stephen's mother, the young Irish woman Edward had paid to bear him a son sixty years earlier. Stephen wonders, "Was the presence of blood so important to him? What strange evidence of love was this?" The inability of yet another generation of Henleys to understand—or love—another is thus assured. Given Stephen's emotional isolation, one senses the inevitability of Stephen dying alone. Even death cannot shake his detachment. There has been no exhilarating pageant. Knowing he is dying, Stephen thinks, "I hardly cared. It didn't matter. Nothing did."

Although they seek refuge in quite opposing activities, both Stephen and his father rather straightforwardly eschew love. With Lucy, Stephen's wife, the case is more ambiguous, more complex. As in her earlier novels, Grau gives her female character a roundness that her males often lack. When Lucy recalls the sexual pleasure and pain she experienced with her first husband, she remarks that "All that was evidence of love." Because Lucy does not indulge in irony, the reader accepts her assessment. Her openness to physical love is reinforced by her enthusiasm for the lushness of Florida, although Lucy has reservations: When Harold makes love to her, she thinks, "I don't like this. . . . I don't like having feelings I can't control." Perhaps the fear of feeling paradoxically allows her to live comfortably for thirty years with Stephen. After his death, she states that "Old women are supposed to quake with an excess of emotion—perhaps love—and start talking to animals and birds and flowers on the windowsill. I didn't."

At times, she seems even more alienated than either her husband or her father-in-law. When her worried son, Paul, phones her, she thinks to herself that "Love between the generations was a burdensome chore." She hopes to be saved from such love. In her way, Lucy proves as evasive to the reader as she does to her son. Ironically, her last appearance in the novel proves in a perverse way to be evidence of love. She hands Edward Henley the Seconal he wants to end a life grown exceedingly tiresome. Lucy's ambiguous complicity in his death is an appropriate action to close Grau's best work. As Edward's voice dies out, it says, "The taste of paradise, the perfect union. It must be here, Here." Grau teases the reader into thought. Paradoxes abound. Indeed, the novel has presented little if any conventional evidence of love, but one senses the value of the lives presented. In its own characteristically ironic way, *Evidence of Love* is just that. The vision is bleak, but here is her most affirmative work.

ROADWALKERS

Roadwalkers once again chronicles a family, but the family here is very nontraditional and certainly not wealthy, at least not until the end of the novel. Mary Woods and her daughter, Nanda, women of color—Mary is black and Nanda's father was from India—exhibit what Susan S. Kissel calls an "inner strength" unknown to Grau's white heroines, a strength that "empowers and enriches their lives." This strength ironically stems in many ways from Mary's early years as a "roadwalker," a child abandoned by her parents and left to roam the countryside of the South during the Depression years, accompanied first by her sister and brother, then by her brother, and finally, alone. In the description of the early years of Mary, or Baby, as she is then called, Grau produces some of her most poetic writing as she recounts the myriad sensations that make up the small child's life: "Her days were like a hoard of bright-colored beads, their connecting thread broken, lying loose, single, jumbled." The early part of the novel is impressionistic, organically written to mimic the experience that Baby is going through where day follows day unconsciously, and growth is measured only by the alternating cycle of heat and cold and the gradual accumulation of life-sustaining skills.

The progress of the novel itself can be gauged in terms of a symbol that many critics previously have noted to be central to Grau's fiction, the house. From homelessness to a shack built of license plates and Coca-Cola signs to a convent and, finally, to a mansion purchased with the profits of her own talent, Mary Woods's story parallels the rise of displaced African Americans to places of eminence in American society. In her movement from "feral" child to haute-couture designer, Mary encounters hatred, racism, and paternalism, yet somehow comes out of the experience self-assured and happy.

Married at the end of the novel to an alderman who is thinking of running for state representative, Mary spends her days working in her garden, in her own soil, at her own home. The first pages of the novel claim that

> [s]he knew the surface of the earth. Head down, hour after hour, she studied it as she walked. She knew all its forms: dry and blowing with each of her steps; wet and oozing through her toes with a sucking sound. And the grains of the earth: sand fine as sugar; soil black and oily.

At the end, Nanda says of her, "she seems to love the feel of dirt. I've seen her rub light friable soil into dust between her palms and then toss it into the air, solemnly, like a priest dispensing incense." In the meantime the novel recounts the struggle that Mary undergoes to make the world her own from the moment she is ripped from her license-plate shack by the well-meaning Charles Tucker and delivered to the Sister Servants of Mary Home for Children and then focuses on the similarly painful but more typical battle of her own child to excel in a racially charged atmosphere.

Nanda's life resembles her mother's in its struggles. Her struggles are not as much for survival as for acceptance, and they, too, are symbolically mirrored in her places of abode. Unlike the disconnected days of her mother's early life, Nanda recalls her mother's "light high whisper threaded through all my days, linking them tightly together," and her moves are from apartment to apartment and apartment to house rather than on the dusty roads and byways of the roadwalker. "We had passed through a series of lodgings," Nanda says when they move into their first house, "but we had finally gained our castle, the one we had been searching for." She trades this safe haven, however, for a scholarship to the mostly white St. Catherine's and then to college, where she must forge the way for other African Americans. As she returns to her mother's home in the summer, she notices "a change in my mother's world. Black and white were reversing themselves," and she realizes that Mary, a successful clothing designer having "conquered the black kingdom," is now entering "new and dangerous territory on voyages of conquest and discovery."

By the end of the novel the conquest is complete for both Mary and Nanda. Nanda and her husband, Mike, in a happy, if somewhat open, marriage, are free to travel the world at will. Only in the final pages of the book is Nanda settled in a home of her own. Throwing away the basket of toys that had accompanied her through her own nomadic childhood, she says triumphantly, "alone I came into my kingdom. My portion, neither more nor less." The love sought by Grau's previous heroines is found here in mother-child love, in mature husband-wife love, and most significantly and victoriously in Nanda's ability to love herself, thus making *Roadwalkers* the first of Grau's novels to end on an obvious note of triumph and true affirmation.

John K. Saunders
Updated by Jaquelyn W. Walsh

OTHER MAJOR WORKS

SHORT FICTION: *The Black Prince, and Other Stories*, 1955; *The Wind Shifting West*, 1973; *Nine Women*, 1985; *Selected Stories*, 2003.

BIBLIOGRAPHY

Kissel, Susan S. *Moving On: The Heroines of Shirley Ann Grau, Anne Tyler, and Gail Godwin*. Bowling Green, Ohio: Bowling Green State University Popular Press, 1996. Kissel examines the female protagonists in the novels of Grau and two other contemporary women writers, demonstrating how these characters show strength and maturity. Includes bibliographical references and an index.

Oleksy, Elzbieta. "The Keepers of the House: Scarlett O'Hara and Abigail Howland." In *Louisiana Women Writers: New Essays and a Comprehensive Bibliography*, edited by Dorothy H. Brown and Barbara C. Ewell. Baton Rouge: Louisiana State University Press, 1992. Although her essay centers on their heroines, Oleksy nonetheless makes a rather complete comparison of Margaret Mitchell's *Gone with the Wind* and Grau's *The Keepers of the House*.

O'Neal, Susan Hines. "Cultural Catholicism in Shirley Ann Grau's *The Hard Blue Sky*." *Louisiana Folklore Miscellany* 10 (1995): 24-36. O'Neal sees the islanders' attitude in the novel not as an example of their indifference to the mutability of life but rather as a ritual acceptance stemming from their Catholicism and its melding with folk philosophy and worldly truths.

Pearson, Ann. "Shirley Ann Grau: 'Nature Is the Vision.'" *Critique: Studies in Modern Fiction* 17, no. 2 (1975): 47-58. This article deals with Grau's use of nature, which seems to permeate her novels and stories. Pearson suggests that Grau's vision of the world lies in her perception of the ever-present closeness of nature.

Perry, Carolyn, and Mary Louise Weaks, eds. *The History of Southern Women's Literature*. Baton Rouge: Louisiana State University Press, 2002. Grau is included in this comprehensive examination of southern women writers. Part 4, "The Contemporary South, 1960-Present," contains an essay on Grau's work.

Richardson, Thomas J. "Roadwalker in the Magic Kingdom: Shirley Ann Grau." In *Literary New Orleans in the Modern World*, edited by Richard S. Kennedy. Baton Rouge: Louisiana State University Press, 1998. This examination of Grau's work is included in a collection of essays that focus on twentieth century literature about New Orleans and analyze how writers have depicted the city's myths as well as its history and other realities.

Schlueter, Paul. *Shirley Ann Grau*. Boston: Twayne, 1981. The first book-length critical study of Grau's work. Excellent use of details, though it is somewhat short on interpretation. Includes an index and a bibliography.

Wagner-Martin, Linda. "Shirley Ann Grau's Wise Fiction." In *Southern Women Writers: The New Generation*, edited by Tonette Bond Inge. Tuscaloosa: University of Alabama Press, 1990. Wagner-Martin argues that Grau's highly stylized manner of narration in many ways resembles the style of the folktale. Contends that one of Grau's most distinctive traits is her interest in ceremony and ritual, and maintains that Grau's best fiction deals with the nonwhite culture's impingement on the patriarchal matrix that dominates southern life.

Yardley, Jonathan. "Shirley Ann Grau's House, on the Street Where You Live." *The Washington Post*, March 8, 2005. Yardley discusses *The House on Coliseum Street*, recounting his attempts to locate the house in New Orleans. One in an occasional series of articles about notable and neglected authors.

JANE HAMILTON

Born: Oak Park, Illinois; July 13, 1957

PRINCIPAL LONG FICTION

The Book of Ruth, 1988 (also known as *The Frogs Are Still Singing*, 1989)
A Map of the World, 1994
The Short History of a Prince, 1998
Disobedience, 2000
When Madeline Was Young, 2006

OTHER LITERARY FORMS

Jane Hamilton is chiefly a novelist, but she honed her skills writing short fiction. *Harper's* magazine published two of her stories, "Aunt Marji's Happy Ending" and "My Own Earth." Her award-winning *The Book of Ruth* had its origins in a ten-page short story to which the author returned and expanded into a novel.

ACHIEVEMENTS

Jane Hamilton achieved early success with the publication of her first novel. In 1989, *The Book of Ruth* received the Great Lakes College Association New Writers Award, the Banta Award, and the Hemingway Foundation/PEN Award for First Fiction. *The Book of Ruth* and *A Map of the World* were selected for Oprah's Book Club, helping them achieve best-seller status worldwide. Both novels were adapted for film, *A Map of the World* for the cinema in 1999 and *The Book of Ruth* for television in 2004. In 1998, *The Short History of a Prince* received the *Chicago Tribune* Heartland Prize and was short-listed for the Orange Prize. *Disobedience* was named to the *School Library Journal*'s list of the best adult books for high school students in 1991.

BIOGRAPHY

Jane Hamilton was born in 1957 in Oak Park, Illinois, the birthplace also of novelist Carol Shields. Hamilton's father was an engineer and her mother was a theater critic. The fifth and last child in a rambunctious brood, Hamilton was the quiet and introspective daughter who, from an early age, preferred the written word over the spoken. Hamilton's mother and grandmother were writers, too, so writing seemed to be her heritage. She once observed that she thought it only natural that she would grow up to become a writer.

In 1979, Hamilton earned her B.A. in English at Carleton College in Minnesota and then headed east to New York, where she had secured a position in the children's fiction division of a publishing house. En route to New York she took a detour. A brief stop at an apple orchard in Wisconsin that belonged to a friend's family became a permanent relocation. Hamilton never made it to New York nor did she regret her lost career in publishing.

Instead, she became an apple farmer, laboring in the orchards spring through fall and wintering indoors, where she nurtured her writing skills. She applied for but was denied enrollment in the Iowa Writers' Workshop. Undeterred, she continued to submit her short stories for consideration in several publications, but she received rejections. Seeking more formal training in her craft, she spent time at Ragdale in Illinois, a retreat for writers and artists.

In 1982, Hamilton married Robert Willard, one of the owners of the orchard. In 1983, *Harper's* accepted and published two of her short stories, including "Aunt Marji's Happy Ending," launching Hamilton's career as a writer. The couple had a son, Ben, in 1984, the year Hamilton completed the rough draft of what would become *The Book of Ruth*, a novel about the struggles of a poor rural girl whose life rushes toward catastrophe when she marries an emotionally unstable man. The novel was picked up by Ticknor and Fields in 1987, the same year daughter Hannah was born. Published in 1988, the novel received critical and public favor. The next decade proved to be a successful one for Hamilton; she published more novels, and they, too, were embraced by readers and critics.

ANALYSIS

Critics often compare Jane Hamilton favorably to another midwestern author, Pulitzer Prize winner Jane Smiley, whose novels *A Thousand Acres* and *Moo* are set in farm country and explore human resiliency in the face of great obstacles. Hamilton's novels are set in the Midwest, the area where she spent her childhood, attended college, and lived as a full-time writer. Her fiction is populated by rural and small town family members, mothers and fathers, and sons and daughters, who endure life's tragedies with stoicism and frankness, traits often associated with inhabitants of the heartland; Hamilton, though, does not allow her characters to sink into caricature.

Orchards, fields, farmhouses, and main streets provide the backdrop for events that disrupt the quietude of the country environment. The murder of a mother-in-law in *The Book of Ruth*, allegations of child abuse in *A Map of the World*, the closeted life of a gay man in *The Short History of a Prince*, a mother's extramarital affair in *Disobedience*, and a family secret in *When Madeline Was Young* seem drawn from the tabloids, but Hamilton avoids sensationalism. Instead, the challenges and shocks faced by her characters allow her to explore fundamental human values such as forgiveness, reconciliation, acceptance, and loyalty. Like its predecessor, *A Map of the World* is set in a rural community, but it shifts its focus to the lives of middle-class transplants who are viewed by the locals with suspicion after an accidental drowning occurs on their property. *The Short History of a Prince* is a departure from the first two novels in its third-person point of view, its focus on a male character, and its lighter tone. *Disobedience* examines the impact of a parent's affair upon a family when discovered by a child. *When Madeline Was Young* presents an intriguing blended family in which the father's first wife, the Madeline of the title, who has suffered brain injury, passes as his daughter in his second marriage.

THE BOOK OF RUTH

Hamilton's debut novel was a critical success. The book's title alludes to the Old Testament book of the Bible, and biblical passages appear throughout the novel to form a motif, and they are delivered by a preacher in his sermons and reinterpreted ironically by the disbelieving title character, Ruth. The book, too, is named for the story's protagonist; *The Book of Ruth* is Ruth's book. It is the story of her experiences from childhood through her mid-twenties, and it is narrated from her perspective. Additionally, the story tells of the books that provided Ruth a literary education that was denied her in the public school system. Also, a blind neighbor introduces a young Ruth to audio books. The classic stories Ruth reads, tales of men and women who endure and survive, run parallel to her own story. The suffering protagonists of Victorian tomes are her particular favorites. At one point, Ruth imagines entering Charles Dickens's *Bleak House* (1852-1853, serial; 1853, book) to assist the novel's heroine, Esther, with the numerous responsibilities she has in the service of others; ironically, Ruth does not recognize that *she* is the one who requires assistance in the form of rescue. When none arrives, she cheats death and rescues herself.

Ruth grows up marginalized by polite society because she is poor, has a plain physique, and has limited knowledge. Her life was punctuated by abuse from her mother and her husband. Ruth is neglected by relatives who otherwise should protect her. She is abandoned first by her father, who skips out on his family, and later by her brother, who leaves home permanently for higher education. She is kept at a distance from the aunt she idealizes. Though separated by only fifty miles, the two communicate solely through letters.

The larger community is also dismissive of Ruth. Despite being the sister of a gifted brother, Ruth is considered average and expendable by teachers at her school. She is on her own when her drug-addled and emotionally uneven husband, in a fit of fury, attempts to kill her and her mother; he succeeds in the latter and leaves Ruth seriously injured. That Ruth has penned her saga as a form of therapy and forgiveness is revealed on the final page of the novel. Ruth notes, "Perhaps I will write a fiction book when I'm through with this," leaving open the possibility of transformation, at least through writing.

A MAP OF THE WORLD

In *A Map of the World*, Alice Godwin is guilty of a lapse in judgment; in the brief minutes during which she takes a breather from the responsibilities of motherhood, a neighbor child in her care drowns in a pond on her property. The tragedy separates Alice, her husband, Howard, and their daughters from the community, and eventually distances wife from husband and mother from children. The community ostracizes Alice further when an accusation of child abuse surfaces at the school where she is employed as a nurse. Eventually she is cleared of the charge, but not before the life she created, a relatively peaceful secluded existence with her family, is altered irrevocably.

Although written from the first-person perspective, the narrative voice is twofold. *A Map of the World* is divided into three parts; Alice narrates the first and third sections, while Howard voices the middle. He relays the story during the time Alice is in jail and cannot speak for herself, including the daily burden of caring for the farm and his daughters as a single parent. The novel explores the process by which a person, ostracized by her community and estranged from her family, works her way back into these folds. The novel's overarching theme is forgiveness. Alice struggles to forgive those who have transgressed against her, and she can begin to do so only when she forgives herself.

The Short History of a Prince

A coming-of-age story, *The Short History of a Prince* is set in two interwoven decades, the 1970's and the 1990's. In the 1970's, Walter McCloud is a teenage boy whose wish is to be a professional ballet dancer. He is cast as Prince Siegfried in the *Nutcracker* ballet not because he is talented but because he is the sole male dancer in his school old enough for the role. His growing awareness of his limited potential is heightened by adolescent angst, a crush on another boy, and the terminal illness of his older brother.

McCloud in the 1990's is a man recently returned to a small midwestern community to teach English. The interval of the 1980's, during which he worked in New York City in a doll factory, is alluded to but not fully realized. The allusion serves to heighten the contrast between his youthful wishes and his adult responsibilities. A lover of art, music, and books since childhood, McCloud experiences these solaces as a devotee rather than a participant.

Disobedience

Hamilton's fourth novel is about a functioning dysfunctional family, a spying son, and the secrets that family members keep to hold their relationships together. A decade has passed and an older Henry Shaw narrates the events of his senior year of high school, the year of his mother's infidelity. Though troubled by his mother's behavior and his father's apparent ignorance, he imbues his narrative with a sense of humor and compassion. Out of teenage curiosity, he begins to check his mother's e-mail. When he discovers an illicit affair between his mother and a violin maker, his curiosity turns to voyeurism. He begins to feel like an accomplice in the affair because he is the one who set up his mother's e-mail account.

Despite feelings of guilt for snooping, Henry charts the progress of the affair electronically, and wonders how its eventual revelation will impact other family members. His father, a teacher of history, seems blind to events occurring in his own time and in his own family. Henry's sister, Elvira, like her father, prefers past lives, savoring her role as a soldier in Civil War reenactments. Even the mother, in her role as a pianist who performs with a group that plays classics, embraces the past through music. All the members of the Shaw family seem determined to avoid the here and now, even Henry, as he recalls events of ten years prior. The novel's title, *Disobedience*, becomes a reference not only to the mother's betrayal and Henry's invasions of privacy but also to the behavior of an entire family.

Dorothy Dodge Robbins

BIBLIOGRAPHY

Charles, Ron. "A Family Quartet Out of Tune with Itself." *Christian Science Monitor*, November 9, 2000. This review considers the characters in *Disobedience* in terms of their uses of technology, in particular the Internet, and their resultant social behaviors. Classifies the novel as a compelling, but troubling, account of infidelity and its impact on a representative American family.

Hutchings, Vicky. "Boy Talk." *New Statesman* 130 (March 12, 2001). A positive appraisal of *Disobedience* that highlights the gender-role reversals of family members in the novel.

Juhasz, Suzanne. "The Prince Is Wearing a Tutu: Queer Identity and Identificatory Reading in Jane Hamilton's *The Short History of a Prince*." *American Imago: Studies in Psychoanalysis and Culture* 61, no. 2 (Summer, 2004): 134-164. Employs principles of psychology and reader response theory to link reader, author, and character in *The Short History of a Prince*. Also examines Hamilton's portrayals of gender, sexuality, and art.

Neville, Maureen. "*When Madeline Was Young*." Review in *Library Journal* 131, no. 12 (July 1, 2006). Positive appraisal of the novel that highlights its blended family of characters, its Chicago setting, and its decades-spanning time frame. Notes that Hamilton uses world events, such as the Vietnam and Iraq Wars, to provide a larger context for familial events in this domestic novel.

Steinberg, Sybil. "Jane Hamilton: A Kinship with Society's Outcasts." *Publishers Weekly*, February 2, 1998. Explores connections between Hamilton's Walter in *The Short History of a Prince* and similar outcast protagonists in her earlier works: the title character in *The Book of Ruth* and Alice in *A Map of the World*.

Strasser, Judith. "Daily Harvest: At Work with Novelist Jane Hamilton." *Poets and Writers* 26, no. 3 (May/June, 1998): 32-45. This interview focuses on Hamilton's family and career, and the effect of each upon the other. *The Book of Ruth* and *Map of the World* are discussed in terms of their origins and public impact.

Taylor, Pegi. "Jane Hamilton: Good Writing Is in the Details." *Writer* 114, no. 1 (January, 2001): 26-31. Taylor interviews Hamilton about her use of metaphorical language and her creation of characters. The relationship of *Disobedience* to earlier works is discussed. In particular, Hamilton explains how young characters in her other novels are precursors to Henry, the son who discovers his mother's affair in *Disobedience*.

BESSIE HEAD

Born: Pietermaritzburg, South Africa; July 6, 1937
Died: Serowe, Botswana; April 17, 1986
Also known as: Bessie Amelia Emery

PRINCIPAL LONG FICTION

When Rain Clouds Gather, 1968
Maru, 1971
A Question of Power, 1973

OTHER LITERARY FORMS

Bessie Head first published her writing as a journalist in South Africa. In the early 1960's, she also began writing essays and short stories, some of which appear with later work in two posthumous collections of short pieces, *Tales of Tenderness and Power* (1989) and *A Woman Alone: Autobiographical Writings* (1990). The line between fiction and autobiography was always blurred with Head, and critics disagree about the genre of some pieces. In the 1970's, she began studying the history of the Bamangwato people of Botswana. She interviewed many members of the tribe, and the resulting material informed both an oral history, *Serowe: Village of the Rain Wind* (1981), and a collection of short stories, *The Collector of Treasures, and Other Botswana Village Tales* (1977).

ACHIEVEMENTS

In her lifetime, Bessie Head was recognized as one of Africa's greatest writers, although she spent much of her career isolated in Botswana without the papers that would have allowed her to travel and promote her work. She was a featured speaker at the 1976 University of Botswana Writers Workshop, the 1979 Africa Festival in Berlin, and other important events. Her early novel *The Cardinals*, although not published until after her death, is one of the earliest examples of a novel written by an African woman. Her work has been translated into many languages, and *When Rain Clouds Gather* is one of the best-selling volumes in Heinemann's African Writers' series. As a successful writer in Africa in the 1970's and 1980's, she inspired a generation, especially a generation of women.

In 2007, the Bessie Head Heritage Trust and Pentagon Publishers, both in Botswana, announced an annual Bessie Head writing contest to recognize the best creative writing in English by writers in Botswana. That same year, the trust began translating Head's works into Setswana so that they could be used as required readings in Botswana schools.

BIOGRAPHY

Bessie Head was born Bessie Amelia Emery on July 6, 1937, in Pietermaritzburg, South Africa, in the mental hospital where her unmarried white mother, known as Toby, was being treated for schizophrenia. Toby's family had rejected her when they learned that she was pregnant with a mixed-race child. Bessie was placed in foster care, as her father was never identified. At the age of thirteen, she was transferred to an Anglican orphanage in Durban, where she completed high school in 1952 and then studied to become a primary school teacher. After teaching for two years, she moved to Cape Town and then Johannesburg in South Africa, and worked as a journalist for the *Drum* newspapers. In March, 1960, she was briefly arrested, and she attempted suicide in April of that year. In July she met Harold Head, another journalist, and they married that September. She began publishing poetry and short essays in left-wing magazines, using her married name, Bessie Head. Her first novella, *The Cardinals*, was written during this time but was not published until 1993, after her death.

By 1963, Head had a baby son, Howard, but her marriage was over. Her life as a politically aware, biracial woman in white-controlled South Africa was untenable, so she left South Africa for Bechuanaland Protectorate (now Botswana), although she knew she would not be allowed to return to South Africa because of her left-wing political associations. Now an exile, unable to find steady work and unable to obtain a valid passport, she lived with her son in the small village of Serowe and struggled financially until the American publisher Simon and Schuster gave her an eighty-dollar advance to write a novel about the newly independent Botswana. (Editors had read one of her essays, which they liked.) Having depleted the advance, Head wrote what would be her most important work, *When Rain Clouds Gather*, published in 1968. The success of this first novel assured Head's financial stability for a time, but she suffered from periods of mental illness. In 1971, she published *Maru*, her second novel, followed by *A Question of Power* in 1973, an autobiographical novel about a biracial African woman's exile and mental illness.

Since her arrival in Botswana, Head had been studying the history of the Bamanwato tribe, and she produced an oral history and a collection of short stories based on the lives of the people in Serowe. In 1976, she was a featured speaker at the University of Botswana Writers Workshop, and in 1977 and 1978, traveling with documents from the United Nations, she participated in the University of Iowa's International Writing Program. Finally, in 1979, she became a citizen of Botswana, and was free to travel more widely. She gave lectures and readings throughout Africa, Europe, and Australia. In 1984, however, her struggle with mental illness became a struggle with alcohol. Through the last years of her life she was ill and lonely, and she died of hepatitis in 1986 in Serowe at the age of forty-nine. Four of her ten books were published posthumously.

Analysis

Bessie Head's writing occupies a transitional place in African literature between the domestic, village-centered writing of the 1950's and 1960's and the more overtly political and urban writing—much of it written by exiles in Europe and in North America—that came later. Unlike many of her contemporaries who fled South Africa and apartheid, including Es'kia Mphahlele and Lewis Nkosi, Head traveled only as far as Botswana. Her writing focused on life there instead of on the life of problems she had left behind in South Africa.

In addition to village life, Head's great subject was her own life, and the struggle to find a home. She was always "out of place," being a woman in a patriarchal world, a person of mixed race in a racially stratified culture, and a resident of a country that refused to grant her citizenship for fifteen years; she was an exile from a country that would not allow her to return. Her novels and short stories are filled with characters trying to make new homes, trying to fit in, trying to establish community. Frequently, as in *When Rain Clouds Gather*, *Maru*, and shorter works, racism is denounced and harmony is achieved. In addition, she was concerned about the role of capitalism in traditional African agriculture, and a utopian view of communal farming recurs in her work.

Head's fiction, especially *When Rain Clouds Gather* and some of the short stories, is widely read in high school and college classrooms. The qualities that make her work popular with young readers and their teachers—her simple settings and dramatic plots, her optimism, her vivid and sympathetic depictions of African life—have led some critics to call her work immature and naïve. However, her insights into the status of women in African society have made her an important and inspiring early figure in African women's literature.

When Rain Clouds Gather

When Rain Clouds Gather, Head's first and best-known novel, is based in part on the author's own life. It is the story of Makhaya Maseko, a black antiapartheid activist who leaves urban Johannesburg for the small rural village of Golema Mmidi in Botswana in the mid-1960's. Botswana is moving toward independence, and its people are moving toward modern life. Makhaya becomes involved with Gilbert Balfour, a white British agriculturalist, in trying to form a cooperative and teach new farming methods, but they must overcome both the people's hesitation to reject their old ways and the interference of the corrupt subchief Matenge.

Matenge's power is threatened by the egalitarian nature of the project, and he is particularly suspicious of the involvement of women. When he calls out Paulina Sebeso for punishment, the villagers unite against him, and he commits suicide. Makhaya and Paulina marry and begin new lives as nonpolitical farmers in a bucolic village where men and women, blacks and whites, work together for the good of all. Head's descriptions of the landscape and of the harsh Botswana climate are powerful and beautiful. Later in life, though, Head would remark on the inexperience she demonstrated in *When Rain Clouds Gather*. She came to feel, as have many critics, that the dialogue is stilted, and that the novel's central characters lack complexity—that Makhaya and Matenge are rather two-dimensional representations of good and evil. Still, the novel introduces themes that she would continue to explore throughout her career. The conflict of old and new ways is a common theme in African literature, explored perhaps most famously in Chinua Achebe's *Things Fall Apart* (1958). Head's Matenge, however, is treated much less sympathetically than Achebe's Okonkwo. Makhaya finds peace and hope for the future by settling into a humble rural life—a fate that ultimately evaded Head herself.

A Question of Power

A Question of Power, the most autobiographical of Head's novels, is considered her greatest work. The protagonist is Elizabeth, the child of an unmarried mentally ill white woman and a black man in South Africa under apartheid. With her young son, Elizabeth leaves South Africa for the village of Motabeng in Botswana, but finds no peace there as she tries to adjust to rural living and to find acceptance as an independent-minded woman of mixed race. The only person with whom she shares intellectual interests is Tom, a white American Peace Corps volunteer. Elizabeth suffers from delusions and terrifying dreams and is hospitalized twice with mental breakdowns. Only her responsibility to her son and her tenuous friendship with Tom keep her from falling completely into insanity. Ultimately, she recovers and finds contentment in humble village life.

When she was writing *A Question of Power*, Head was recovering from a mental breakdown that led to her hospitalization. That she was able to create such a powerful and controlled description of mental instability is a testament to her mature skills as a writer and to her strength as a person. The novel revisits several of her recurring themes: the possibility of interracial cooperation; the conflict between old ways and news, especially as played out in agriculture and communal farming; the oppressive power of colonialists and of corrupt Africans; and the values of love, compassion, and generosity. Unlike the more linear *When Rain Clouds Gather*, *A Question of Power* alternates narrative and descriptive passages of village life with vivid scenes from Elizabeth's hallucinations and dreams.

Cynthia A. Bily

Other major works

SHORT FICTION: *The Collector of Treasures, and Other Botswana Village Tales*, 1977; *Tales of Tenderness and Power*, 1989; *The Cardinals, with Meditations and Short Stories*, 1993.

NONFICTION: *Serowe: Village of the Rain Wind*, 1981; *A Bewitched Crossroad: An African Saga*, 1984; *A Woman Alone: Autobiographical Writings*, 1990 (Craig Mackenzie, editor); *A Gesture of Belonging: Letters from Bessie Head, 1965-1979*, 1991 (Randolf Vigne, editor).

Bibliography

Brown, Coreen. *The Creative Vision of Bessie Head*. Madison, N.J.: Fairleigh Dickinson University Press, 2003. Brown examines how Head's fiction arose from her experiences with oppression and mental illness. Includes previously unpublished letters.

Eilersen, Gillian Stead. *Bessie Head: Thunder Behind Her Ears—Her Life and Writing*. Portsmouth, N.H.: Heinemann, 1995. The first full-length biography of the author, this book is both thorough and accessible.

Ibrahim, Huma. *Emerging Perspectives on Bessie Head*. Trenton, N.J.: Africa World Press, 2004. Thirteen essays that include examinations of Head's short stories, her reception outside Africa, and her uses of autobiography.

Johnson, Joyce. *Bessie Head: The Road of Peace of Mind—A Critical Appreciation*. Newark: University of Delaware Press, 2008. Examines how Head's reading, writing, and use of oral literature all informed one another and how they shaped Head's understanding of writing as a political art.

MacKenzie, Craig. *Bessie Head*. New York: Twayne, 1999. Part of the Twayne World Authors series. Includes a critical biography, chronology, and annotated bibliography.

Ola, Virginia Uzoma. *The Life and Works of Bessie Head*. Lewiston, N.Y.: Edwin Mellen Press, 1994. A feminist reading of Head's philosophical approaches to power, racism, love, and exploitation.

Olaussen, Maria. *Forceful Creation in Harsh Terrain: Place and Identity in Three Novels by Bessie Head*. New York: Peter Lang, 1997. Focuses on women's identity in *When Rain Clouds Gather*, *Maru*, and *A Question of Power*.

Sample, Maxine, ed. *Critical Essays on Bessie Head*. Westport, Conn.: Praeger, 2003. Eight essays by female critics examine Head's biography, individual novels, and themes of agriculture, power, and gender in her writings. Includes a bibliographic essay.

FRANZ KAFKA

Born: Prague, Bohemia, Austro-Hungarian Empire (now in Czech Republic); July 3, 1883

Died: Kierling, Klosterneuburg, near Vienna, Austria; June 3, 1924

PRINCIPAL LONG FICTION

Der Prozess, 1925 (*The Trial*, 1937)

Das Schloss, 1926 (*The Castle*, 1930)

Amerika, 1927 (*America*, 1938; better known as *Amerika*, 1946)

OTHER LITERARY FORMS

In addition to long fiction, Franz Kafka (KAHF-kah) wrote numerous stories, the most famous of which are *Die Verwandlung* (1915; *The Metamorphosis*, 1936), *Ein Hungerkünstler: Vier Geschichten* (1924; *A Hunger Artist*, 1948), and *The Penal Colony: Stories and Short Pieces* (1948). He also left behind extensive diaries and letters.

ACHIEVEMENTS

What W. H. Auden wrote of Sigmund Freud—that he had become less a person than a climate of opinion—is equally true of Franz Kafka. He is the twentieth century prophet of alienation, his name a household synonym for "angst." His stories—visionary, hallucinatory, yet very controlled artistically—have exerted their powerful influence over modern fiction. Few would dispute the assertion that he is one of the major literary figures of the twentieth century. None of this, however, could have been anticipated of a writer who was not widely known at the time of his death.

Kafka's genius was difficult for him to harness: The fact is that he never completed any of his three novels. Before dying, he left instructions with Max Brod, his friend and executor, to destroy his manuscripts. Reasoning that Kafka was not committed to their destruction as much as he was ambivalent over their fate—could not he have destroyed them had he really wished to do so?—Brod preserved the manuscripts, arranged to have them printed, wrote a biography of his friend, and generously championed his cause. Thus, *The Trial* and *The Castle*, books which so remarkably capture Kafka's paradoxical vision of human existence, came to light.

BIOGRAPHY

Despite the strange occurrences that animate Franz Kafka's fiction, the events of his life are colorless and mundane. Like Emily Dickinson or Henry David Thoreau, however, Kafka could, by sheer imagination, transform the most ordinary life into fascinating reading. Tirelessly, he penned his impressions of his life, recording the nuances of his thoughts and actions in ethical and ontological terms.

Kafka was born on July 3, 1883, in Prague, Bohemia, into a bourgeois German-Jewish family. The Czechs of Kafka's day felt oppressed by the Austrian-Germans and in turn oppressed the Jews, so from his earliest days Kafka was accustomed to the pain of a threefold prejudice—as non-Austrian, as non-Czech, and as a Jew. Franz was the oldest child, the sole surviving son in a family that was later to include three girls. The father, Herrmann Kafka, struggled to achieve financial security for his family, and he succeeded, but the ordeal coarsened him; he became autocratic and irascible. Money and status were his chief passions, and he directed his considerable energy to their acquisition. Nevertheless, he had a zest for life that left its imprint on his son, who could admire though never attain it. Kafka's mother, on the other hand, came from a family of rabbis, scholars, and physicians, and from her Kafka probably inherited his sensitive nature and dreamy tendencies.

As Kafka was heir to divergent traditions in his family, so, too, the city of Prague offered him contrasting traditions. On one hand, Prague, influenced by Austria, looked westward, toward rationalism and the Enlightenment; on the other hand, it gazed eastward, toward Russia with its semimystical fervor. In his Jewish studies, too, Kafka discovered similar tensions: the casuistic flavor of the Talmud straining against the impassioned piety of the mystics. These elements ultimately recombine themselves in Kafka's fiction.

Photographs of Kafka reveal him as dark and slender, respectable in appearance, with an intense and boyish face, delicate and sensitive. He spent his school years in Prague—first at a German elementary school and later at a *gymnasium*; he ultimately graduated from the German Karl-Ferdinand University. For two weeks, he specialized in chemistry but found it uncongenial; soon after, he succumbed to pressure from his friends and family, especially his father, and commenced the study of law. Unhappy, he described it as "living in an intellectual sense, on sawdust, which had, moreover, already been chewed for me in thousands of other people's mouths."

Kafka, however, needed some means to support himself, and the legal profession was an eminently respectable career—especially appealing to Jews. Though he never cared for the practice of law, a major consideration was the hope of winning his father's long-withheld approval. In this, he never succeeded; here was a struggle that allowed neither victory nor retreat.

Much has been written on the subject of Kafka and his father. Are not the fathers in his fiction oversize presences that visit judgment and wrath on their sons? Are not his protagonists accused persons, judged guilty of some undefined transgression against an all-powerful and implacable force that hounds the hero and destroys him? In story after story, in all of his novels, one finds Kafka returning, irresistibly, obsessively, to the theme of the judging father in an effort to exorcise this demon—in vain. Kafka's friend and biographer, Brod, first reported and later released an amazing document penned by the twenty-six-year-old Kafka, the *Brief an den Vater* (1952, wr. 1919; *Letter to His Father*, 1954). The manuscript was given to Kafka's mother for delivery to her spouse. More than one hundred pages long, the document minutely scrutinizes the son's pained relations with his father. Its tone—mingling abjectness and defiance—can be heard in Kafka's fiction as well, where it expresses his protagonists' attitudes toward their parents. One can only speculate how Herrmann Kafka might have responded to the missive: Kafka's mother never delivered the letter.

Completing his studies, Kafka gained legal experience in a district, then in a criminal court, where he observed at first hand the workings of the law, which he later fictionalized in *The Trial*. Soon after, he secured a position with the Workers' Accident Insurance Office, where he remained a respected and admired figure until illness forced his retirement in 1922. There he gained intimate knowledge of the operations of a bureaucracy, which he transferred to his novel *The Castle*.

Though Kafka never married, he did seek romance and the consolation of women. In 1912, he began courting a woman he had met at Brod's house, Felice Bauer. (Her initials are echoed both in *The Trial*, in the name of Fraulein Burstner, and in *The Castle*'s Frieda.) Curiously, Kafka avoided contact with her, although he maintained a voluminous correspondence with her, sometimes writing as many as three letters a day. He feared that marriage would infringe both on his privacy and on his writing, and for three years the relationship waxed and waned; Kafka's ambivalence denied him the domestic peace he so desperately sought. In 1917, soon after their second engagement, Kafka discovered that he had tuberculosis, and once again he and his fiancé were disengaged. After several years of battling this disease, Kafka succumbed in June of 1924.

Though Kafka's life was marked by suffering, both intimates and casual acquaintances testify to the sweetness of his disposition, to his sympathy for others, to his unfailing humor and quiet courage. Brod's biography takes pains to overcome the impression that his friend's character was morbid; indeed, Kafka had a gift for finding wry humor both in his life and in the most dreadful predicaments of his characters. He had a gift for whimsy as well; Brod relates that once, when Kafka was about twenty years old, he came to visit Brod and inadvertently awakened Brod's father, who was napping on the sofa. "Please look upon me as a dream," murmured Kafka as he glided by.

Analysis

The name Franz Kafka conjures up images of a world without a center, of people alienated both from society and from themselves. Kafka lived at the threshold of the modern technological world, and his stories are prophetic of the bewilderment and anxiety that typify modern frustrations and darkest moods: humans increasingly out of touch with their essential nature or, when confronted by totalitarian oppression, out of touch with society. When Eugene O'Neill's hairy ape laments that "I ain't in heaven, and I ain't on oith, but takin' the woist from both woilds," he captured something of the spirit, if not the flavor, of Kafka's tragic vision. For Kafka, humanity has only glimmerings of its formerly blessed state yet desperately attempts to recover it.

With the story *Das Urteil* (1913, 1916; *The Sentence*, 1928; also as *The Judgment*,

1945), Kafka created the kind of fiction that characterizes his maturity, combining the unreality of dream states with images of startling vividness. In this early story, as in *The Trial* and *The Castle*, the protagonist faces a judgment on himself, a fate in which the horrible and the absurd intertwine. In Kafka's fiction, every interpretation begets an alternative—one that may contradict its predecessor. This is partly a result of narrative technique: In limiting the narrative to the protagonist's point of view, Kafka ensures that the reader will share his character's bewilderment without benefit of an omniscient author.

In terms of literary form, Kafka's stories most closely resemble the parable: simple yet enigmatic. His work may be read for its historical and social import as the reflections of a German Jew living in Czech Prague, a city under Austrian influence. Neither Austrian nor Czech but Jewish, he was an outsider. His work may be viewed psychologically, as an anxious son's efforts to deal with an accusing father. (Note that all the novels' protagonists bear the author's initial, *K.*) Finally, his work may be read for its religious content, as Everyman's craving to reconcile the demands of the physical with the yearnings of the spiritual.

Characteristically, Kafka's protagonist is a man going about his normal domestic business when a violent and inexplicable eruption warns him that his life has gone astray. Often he awakens one morning to discover that some incomprehensible change has occurred. In *The Trial*, the protagonist discovers men in his room, mysterious functionaries who announce that he has been arrested on charges they will not explain. In the novella *The Metamorphosis*, Gregor Samsa arises, or attempts to do so, only to discover that during the night he has been transformed into a giant dung beetle. No explanation is forthcoming. Is this a judgment on Gregor from above or from within, or is it caused by some force whose will is unknown and unknowable? Is the transformation a necessary but painful path to enlightenment or a punishment? One reads on, hoping for an explanation, a hint of rational purpose in such mysterious happenings; one watches fascinated as others respond to the protagonist's dilemma; one searches for clues in their responses; and one is disarmed at every turn by paradox piled upon paradox, an infinite regression of possibilities that welcome analysis but will never yield to it. Ultimately, the Kafka protagonist perishes or disappears, but whether he is enlightened remains obscure.

AMERIKA

In 1911, Kafka began a novel that Brod later published as *Amerika*. The first chapter was released during Kafka's lifetime as *Der Heizer* (1913; the stoker), but his journals refer to this chapter as "The Man Who Was Lost Sight Of." The most naturalistic of Kafka's novels, *Amerika* relates the story of an innocent youth, not yet sixteen years old, who is forced to leave home for an indiscretion: He was seduced by an older woman, who conceived a child. Like most of Kafka's fictional parents, Karl Rossmann's, too, harshly judge their loving son, who, despite their punishment of him, yearns to be reunited with them.

Rossmann's first intimation of what the new Eden of America will be like occurs when he sees the Statue of Liberty, holding aloft not a torch but a sword (justice? wrath? expulsion from Eden?). This is not the America of Emma Lazarus's poem "The New Colossus" (1883) but rather a capitalistic/ technological society replete with Mark Twain-like rogues—Robinson and Delemarche—and tycoons à la Frank Norris and Theodore Dreiser.

At first, Rossmann seems blessed: His uncle Jacob, a politician and an industrialist, discovers him aboard a ship and takes the lad under his wing. Rossmann quickly perceives, however, that this highly industrialized state called America degrades all those who come in contact with it—workers, rulers, and politicians. Through the familiar device of the picaresque novel, the hero undergoes a series of adventures loosely strung together—adventures among the rich and poor, insiders and outcasts. Rossmann himself is an innocent, hopelessly entangled in a fallen world, and this is the major problem of the work. Unlike the protagonists of the later novels, Rossmann is not part of the world he observes, merely its victim. The reader can pity Rossmann, impressed with Kafka's diagnosis of a world grown increasingly bureaucratic, but one is not astonished and mesmerized, as readers of the later two novels are. The nightmare in *Amerika* is someone else's nightmare, not the reader's. When Rossmann is vilified and loses his job at the Hotel Occidental for his momentary lapse from duty, the reader is too keenly aware of the injustice, too eager to protest on his behalf.

Compare this, for example, to Kafka's well-known short story *The Metamorphosis*, in which Gregor is transformed into a giant insect. At first, one shares the protagonist's shock—how could such a thing happen, and what does it mean?—but this is quickly succeeded by a more pressing question: How does Gregor know that he is an insect? Not through his senses, for he does not need to look at himself; rather he seems to have intuited the transformation, perhaps invited it. Whether the metamorphosis is a judgment, an injustice, or a signpost to salvation, Gregor's fate, unlike Rossmann's, is part of his character.

Still, in *Amerika* many of Kafka's familiar themes are developed, however embryonically. The theme of justice is manifest in the opening chapter, when Rossmann unsuccessfully attempts to aid the confused stoker in airing his grievances. As in many scenes that follow, Rossmann will be forced to leave those he cares about without succeeding in accomplishing his aims. His departure from the ship with his Uncle Jacob marks the climax of his good fortune. (Indeed, most of Kafka's fiction climaxes in the opening chapter, with the rest of the story exploring the consequences of what proves to be an irreversible judgment.) For ingratitude, Rossmann is promptly disinherited by his uncle, a capitalist and exploiter with overtones of Yahweh (the sort of paradox in which Kafka delighted). The sword that the Statue of Liberty holds aloft adds to the impression that Rossmann is being expelled from his American Eden.

Like the stoker, Rossmann will have difficulties with authority. Soon after departing from his uncle, he is employed at the Hotel Occidental in Rameses—in other words, a symbol of civilization, whether Western or Eastern. Under the patronage of the "Manageress," Rossmann does well at his menial job of elevator operator, but one evening he is caught in a minor infraction. As in the case of the stoker, his efforts to obtain justice—his attempt to justify himself, to minimize his error, to benefit from the help of the Manageress—come to naught, and he is dismissed. The author here creates the kind of nightmarish scene that has become known as Kafkaesque, one in which everything that can go wrong does. The accused cannot stand before authority and state with certainty that he is truly innocent, while the officials on whom his fate depends are blasé, bored, indifferent to petitions, sometimes mocking and malicious.

Leaving the hotel in disgrace (he is even suspected by the police, though no charges have been filed against him), Rossmann is forced once more into the company of the scoundrels Delemarche and Robinson, who have taken up with the former singer Brunelda, a gross embodiment of sensuality who enslaves all three in her love nest. Usually in Kafka's works, the artist points the way to transcendence, but this singer has given up her art to satisfy her lusts. In a memorable scene, she presses her huge body against Rossmann, literally pinning him to the balcony railing while they watch a political demonstration on the streets. The scene reveals humans given over to their appetites: On the balcony, Brunelda pursues carnality; on the streets, the crowd pursues drunkenness. Though this scene is vividly delineated, it reminds the reader once again of the problem Kafka faces here: What has his protagonist to do with the gross bodily appetites which indeed appall him?

At the beginning of the uncompleted final chapter, Rossmann finds himself at the nature theater of Oklahoma. What the author intended here may be inferred from Brod's report that Kafka wished to end the book on a note of reconciliation. Had Kafka realized these intentions, this work would have been unique in his fiction for its promise of hope and transcendence. The extant fragment, however, suggests that Kafka was deviating from his announced plan. The paradoxes continue: The welcoming angels blowing their horns are not angels, or even good musicians, and they are elevated above common humanity with the aid of ladders that can be seen through their gowns. Rossmann does get a job, but again it is a lowly one, far from a profession. At the novel's end, he is on a train, presumably heading westward—to a promising future or, as the title suggests, simply to vanish.

THE TRIAL

"Someone must have denounced Joseph K., for without having done anything wrong he was arrested one morning." Thus begins Kafka's second novel, *The Trial*. What are the charges? K. never learns, though he encounters several functionaries of the court, attends preliminary hearings, and hires a lawyer to defend him. This might have been the opening of a novel of political repression, but one quickly discovers that the law here, unlike its operation in Arthur Koestler's *Darkness at Noon* (1940), for example, does not represent the state judiciary system but a shadow court, one that is paradoxically both loftier and seedier. When Kafka speaks of the law, he means what the Chinese philosopher Laozi (Laotzu) called The Way—that style of living that conduces to right conduct and enlightenment. Kafka's protagonists (and his readers) grope for truth along a path circumscribed by darkness.

Has K. really done nothing "wrong"? He is certainly innocent of civil or criminal wrongdoing. A respected bank official, his conduct has been apparently irreproachable. Yet he is under arrest—a curious form of arrest, in which he is not "prevented from leading [his] ordinary life." Curiously, the "criminal" must not only defend himself but also discover his crime. Critics diverge in their efforts to understand the nature of the charge against him. According to Brod, K. is unable to love; according to another commentator, his mediocrity condemns him. A third argues that his crime lies in his suppression of his guilt. For yet another, K. is one who refuses to act in accordance with his knowledge of good and evil because he lacks the strength for such action. No easy answer emerges. Whether humanity is indeed guilty or is falsely accused by a divinity unable or unwilling to help it comprehend its own essence is never revealed. What is clear is that K. feels guilty even while defending his innocence.

What sort of man is K.? Like most Kafka protagonists, he is a bachelor, uncommitted to others. He dwells in a rooming house, ignoring both his cousin, who lives in town, and his mother, who lodges in the country. His friends are mainly business associates; his lover, a woman visited once a week. No doubt, Kafka, in his diaries, often expressed contempt for such an existence ("My monotonous, empty, mad bachelor's life"), but is this K.'s crime? If so, he could easily have been informed of that by any number of the officials he encounters. Moreover, K. seems to be living a life similar to that of most of the officials of the court. Can the priest denounce him for bachelorhood? The Examining Magistrate or the painter Titorelli for womanizing? The Magistrates for vanity? Lawyer Huld for placing his profession before his personal life? Rather, Joseph K. is a flawed human being, flawed in some fundamental spiritual way, one who lacks self-confidence. The best clue to understanding his situation is the guilt he only halfway acknowledges. He is told, "Our officials never go hunting for guilt in the populace, but, as the Law decrees, are attracted by guilt, and must then send out us warders." The implication is that K. himself lured the warders to him in the interests of self-realization and self-extermination—the two are synonymous in Kafka's fiction.

Joseph K., respectable, even dignified in the world's eyes, experiences a number of humiliations, each of which will signify the hopelessness of his position. Arrested in his own bedroom by intruders who offer to sell his clothing (they confiscate his underwear), observed by a couple across the courtyard as well as by his landlady and three of his subordinates at the bank, K. finds his privacy, self-respect, and professional competence shredded. He has indeed awakened to a nightmare.

What authority has this court? It is independent of the civil judiciary system; K. is notified that his first hearing is to be held on a Sunday, in a shabby part of town. In fact, he discovers, he is being tried in an attic; most of the attics in the city, he learns, house divisions of this omnipresent bureaucracy. Very likely, Kafka is suggesting that most people are under indictment. The hearing is alternately comic and maddening. At the outset, the judge mistakes the chief clerk of a bank for a house painter. Have they arrested the wrong man? Are they incompetent, or are they simply ignorant underlings blindly administering a form of justice they themselves do not comprehend?

K.'s efforts to denounce these outrageous proceedings, however, reveal that he does not grasp the nature or gravity of his situation. However clownish these officials may appear (the Examining Magistrate browses over obscene drawings throughout the hearing), their power should not be underestimated. K.'s speech mocking the court proceedings does not reveal confident self-sufficiency but swaggering ignorance. "I merely wanted to point out" remarked the Examining Magistrate afterward, "that today . . . you have deprived yourself of the advantage an interrogation usually confers on an accused man." Unfortunately, this and all the other bits of information about the court that K. receives, whether valid or invalid (and how is he to distinguish between them?), are equally useless to him.

Of K.'s plight the philosopher Martin Buber remarked that, though men and women have been appointed to this world, they are forever caught in the thick vapors of a mist of absurdity. Is divinity unwilling to reveal itself? Possibly. "The highest court . . . is quite inaccessible to you, to me, and to all of us," K. is told. It is equally possible, though, that it reveals itself every moment but that people either blind themselves or are simply ill-equipped to internalize the message. Near the novel's conclusion, the priest shrieks out to him, "Can't you even see two inches in front of your nose?" K. both can and cannot: Indeed, the tragedy of human relations with divinity is the near-impossibility of communication between them.

K. can never get beyond dealing with underlings; humans lack the spiritual strength and the understanding necessary for their quest. In the often excerpted passage of the doorkeeper of the Law, the priest suggests that the petitioner might have merely stepped through the first door of justice had he the temerity and the wisdom. Presumably, the same applies to K., but all of his efforts to assert himself—to demonstrate that he is innocent or that the Law is in error—come to naught. Even the women from whom he has sought comfort have misled him. He has made many errors, and now, the priest informs him, his guilt is all but proved.

Earlier, K. had met another functionary of the court, the painter Titorelli. The name itself is a pseudonym, an amalgam of the names of famous Italian artists. In reality, he is a hack court painter, as degenerate as another artist, Brunelda, in Kafka's *Amerika*. Efforts that artists once dedicated to the glory of God, during an age of worship, Titorelli now dedicates to cynical aggrandizement of petty officials. From the painter, K. learns of the three possible directions for his case: definite acquittal, ostensible acquittal, and indefinite postponement. Even this, however, may be merely a joke: Definite acquittals do not occur. "I have never heard of one case," avers the artist. Ostensible acquittal grants provisional freedom, which may last for years or only for an hour, followed by re-arrest. Postponement seems to be the tactic another accused man, Mr. Block, has resolved to follow, but such an approach would deny K. an opportunity to face his creator and accuser; it would reduce him to the status of a beggar, more a cringing beast than a man. Are the courts merely playing with people? Possibly: Titorelli's drawing of Justice makes her look "exactly like the Goddess of the Hunt in full cry."

Exactly one year after K.'s arrest, when K. is thirty-one years old (Kafka's age at the time the novel was written), two men come for him. Garbed in black, K. is prepared for his executioners. Somber as this scene is, however, it has comically grotesque elements. "Tenth rate old actors they send for me," he muses. "Perhaps they are tenors." Joseph K. is led through the streets; at times he even does the leading, indicating acceptance of his fate. The final scene is richly textured and enigmatic. His executioners require that he lie down on the ground and intimate that he is to reach for the knife and execute himself. Wordlessly, K. refuses. Is this further evidence of his rebellious nature or his own judgment of the shameful justice rendered by the court? He is stabbed and dies "like a dog, it was as if the shame should survive him." As one critic has asked, whose shame, that of the man or of the court? On this ambiguous and troubling note, Kafka's unfinished novel ceases.

THE CASTLE

Sometime in 1922, less than two years before his death, Kafka began his final novel, the longest and most thematically complex of his narratives. In *The Castle*, Kafka's settings grow even sparer than those of his earlier works, reinforcing the parablelike nature of the tale. *The Castle* is the story of K., a land surveyor, who leaves his village to live and work near the castle. Unlike Joseph K., who is summoned to trial, K. seeks out the castle of his own volition: He wishes to be the castle's land surveyor. Unable to enter the castle, he attempts to secure an interview with the Court Official in charge of land surveyors, Klamm. Like the petitioner who has come to the Law in *The Trial*, K. finds his way barred. No matter what he attempts, he is no nearer the castle at the novel's end than he was on the first day. His quest wears him out, and though Kafka never concluded this novel, he did make it clear that K. was to die, exhausted by his efforts.

Again, Kafka's enigmatic art has kindled various interpretations. Brod interprets the castle theologically, as the attempt to secure Divine Law and Divine Grace. Others assert that Kafka's novels describe human efforts to overcome limitations as physical beings to grapple with the spiritual self in a vain effort to unify the two sides. Another group perceives this novel as a denunciation of the bureaucracy that ruled Kafka's country. All sides can adduce strong arguments—more testimony to the paradoxical and allegorical nature of Kafka's art.

K. is an outsider, an Everyman attempting to find a meaningful life in a world that has lost its spiritual moorings. In doing so, he looks toward the castle, but whether the castle is even occupied, whether it has corporeal existence or is the inward world the narrator yearns to reach, must remain a mystery: At the novel's opening, K. stands "for a long time gazing into the apparent emptiness above him." This emptiness echoes and amplifies the spirit of T. S. Eliot's *The Waste Land* (1922) and Oswald Spengler's *Der Untergang des Abendlandes* (1918-1922; *The Decline of the West*, 1926-1928). The never seen owner of the castle is named Count Westwest.

Like many of Kafka's protagonists, K. is aroused from a deep sleep to face an identity crisis. He claims at the inn where he is staying that he has been summoned by the castle, but a telephone call to the castle brings a hasty denial; then, before K. can be ejected from the inn, another call reverses the first judgment. The issue of K.'s status is further complicated when he observes that the castle "was accepting battle with a smile." The castle accepts the intruder's invasion but its smile is not easily decipherable. Much suggests that it is mocking. The assistants assigned to him are childish and troublesome, very likely dispatched as spies. The messages he receives are so ambiguous in language, so ill-informed regarding his activities, that he despairs after receiving them, despite the fact that he wants nothing more than to be acknowledged. One official, Bürgel, even informs him that the present moment holds the key to his hopes, implying that if he were to present his petition at once, it would be accepted. Alas, K. has fallen asleep.

As in *The Trial*, the protagonist's efforts to justify himself before officialdom prove fruitless. His superior, Klamm, is perceived by K. through a peephole, but all attempts to speak to him are rebuffed. To K.'s request for an interview comes the reply "Never. Under no conditions!" Resolutely, K. determines to intercept Klamm at his carriage, but the official will not venture forth. Stalemated, K. feels he

> had won a freedom such as hardly anybody else had ever succeeded in winning, as if nobody could . . . drive him away . . . [but] at the same time there was nothing more senseless, nothing more hopeless, than this freedom.

K. cannot be driven away, but he will never be recognized.

By means of subplots, mainly involving the family of K.'s messenger, Kafka reinforces his theme that humans are alienated from their society, their inner self, their God. The reader who is familiar with the Aristotelian formula of a protagonist who successfully completes an action will be disarmed by Kafka's novel, in which developments serve only to clarify the impossibility of a successful completion of the goal.

Like Joseph K. of *The Trial*, K. discovers some respite in women. Frieda (peace), the mistress of Klamm, represents domestic pleasure, the highest Earth has to offer. Although she agrees to leave Klamm for K., his Faustian spirit is not satisfied. Forsaking the sensual and domestic comforts, K. continually leaves Frieda in pursuit of his goal, transcendence of the merely mundane, while maintaining that he does so in part for her. This paradoxical attitude probably mirrors Kafka's own relationship with Felice Bauer. Kafka was torn between committing himself to his fiancé and freeing himself for his art, an ambivalence reflected in K.'s inconsistent behavior with Frieda. After losing her, K. remarks that though he "would be happy if she were to come back to me . . . I should at once begin to neglect her all over again. This is how it is." Thus, the reader sees why K. can never know peace, why he is doomed to wear himself out.

In addition to Frieda, K. is intimate with Olga, Barnabas's sister. Like K., she is desperate to reach the castle to redress a wrong done to her family by one of its officials. Olga's sister, Amalia, has been grossly propositioned by one of the castle officials. Her family has worn itself out, as K. is doing, in a fruitless attempt to justify themselves before the authorities, to gain access to the Law; even the villagers find the authorities inaccessible. From K.'s perspective, the authorities seem impersonal, aloof. In ruling, they are attentive to trivial detail but bureaucratically indifferent to human considerations. Though Kafka did not complete *The Castle*, his intended ending was communicated to Brod. Around K.'s

> deathbed the community assembles and from the castle comes this decision: that K. has no claim to live in the castle by right—yet taking certain auxiliary circumstances into account, it is permitted him to live and work there.

With remarkable prescience, Kafka had sketched his own epitaph. Consider the treatment accorded his memory: Czech authorities placed signs in five languages to mark his grave, yet for more than twenty years they forbade sale of his works.

Stan Sulkes

OTHER MAJOR WORKS

SHORT FICTION: *Betrachtung*, 1913 (*Meditation*, 1948); *Das Urteil*, 1913, 1916 (*The Sentence*, 1928; also known as *The Judgment*, 1945); *Die Verwandlung*, 1915 (*The Metamorphosis*, 1936); "In der Strafkolonie," 1919 ("In the Penal Colony," 1941); *Ein Hungerkünstler: Vier Geschichten*, 1924 (*A Hunger Artist*, 1948); *Beim Bau der Chinesischen Mauer: Ungedruckte Erzählungen und Prosa aus dem Nachlass*, 1931 (*The Great Wall of China, and Other Pieces*, 1933); *Erzählungen*, 1946 (*The Complete Stories*, 1971); *The Penal Colony: Stories and Short Pieces*, 1948; *Selected Short Stories*, 1952.

NONFICTION: *The Diaries of Franz Kafka*, 1948-1949; *Tagebücher, 1910-1923*, 1951; *Brief an den Vater*, 1952 (wr. 1919; *Letter to His Father*, 1954); *Briefe an Milena*, 1952 (*Letters to Milena*, 1953); *Briefe, 1902-1924*, 1958; *Briefe an Felice*, 1967 (*Letters to Felice*, 1974); *Briefe an Ottla und die Familie*, 1974 (*Letters to Ottla and the Family*, 1982); *I Am a Memory Come Alive: Autobiographical Writings*, 1974 (Nahum N. Glatzer, editor); *Franz Kafka: The Office Writings*, 2009.

MISCELLANEOUS: *Hochzeitsvorbereitungen auf dem Lande und andere Prosa aus dem Nachlass*, 1953 (*Dearest Father: Stories, and Other Writings*, 1954; also known as *Wedding Preparations in the Country, and Other Posthumous Prose Writings*, 1954).

BIBLIOGRAPHY

Anderson, Mark, ed. *Reading Kafka: Prague, Politics, and the Fin de Siecle.* New York: Schocken Books, 1989. Collection of essays presents a good sampling from the enormous body of contemporary scholarship, in both English and German, on Kafka's writings.

Bloom, Harold, ed. *Franz Kafka.* New York: Chelsea House, 2005. Essays in this collection provide good, readable general introductions to several contemporary approaches to Kafka's work.

Gray, Richard T., Ruth V. Gross, Rolf J. Goebel, and Clayton Koelb. *A Franz Kafka Encyclopedia.* Westport, Conn.: Greenwood Press, 2005. Comprehensive volume contains alphabetized entries that discuss all aspects of Kafka's life and work, including characters, places, and events.

Gray, Ronald. *Franz Kafka.* New York: Cambridge University Press, 1973. Concise study by a renowned Kafka scholar. Still one of the best overviews of his work available in English.

Hayman, Ronald. *K: A Biography of Kafka.* New ed. London: Phoenix, 2001. Presents a solid and readable account of Kafka's life, intended for the general reader. Includes a chronology and an extensive bibliography. First published 1981.

Karl, Frederick. *Franz Kafka: Representative Man—Prague, Germans, Jews, and the Crisis of Modernism.* New York: Ticknor & Fields, 1991. Massive study is perhaps the most comprehensive attempt to place Kafka within the context of his own time and to study his writings as central to the modernist movement in twentieth century literature.

Pawel, Ernst. *The Nightmare of Reason: A Life of Franz Kafka.* New York: Farrar, Straus and Giroux, 1984. Revisionist work places Kafka in historical context and attempts to dispel the myths of the author as a helpless neurasthenic clerk. Describes him as an effective executive who was in many ways typical of his age and class.

Preese, Julian, ed. *Cambridge Companion to Kafka.* New York: Cambridge University Press, 2002. Collection of essays presents various approaches to Kafka's work. Part of Cambridge's respected companion series.

Robertson, Ritchie. *Kafka: Judaism, Politics, and Literature.* Oxford, England: Clarendon Press, 1985. Discusses a wide variety of Kafka's works in the context of his politics and his interest in Judaism.

MADAME DE LA FAYETTE

Born: Paris, France; March 18, 1634 (baptized)
Died: Paris, France; May 25, 1693
Also known as: Marie-Madeleine Pioche de la Vergne; Mademoiselle de la Vergne; Segrais

PRINCIPAL LONG FICTION

La Princesse de Montpensier, 1662 (novella; as Segrais; *The Princess of Montpensier*, 1666)
Zayde, 1670-1671 (2 volumes; as *Segrais*; also known as *Zaïde*; English translation, 1678)
La Princesse de Clèves, 1678 (published anonymously; *The Princess of Clèves*, 1679)
La Comtesse de Tende, 1724 (novella; as Segrais)

OTHER LITERARY FORMS

In addition to her novels, Madame de La Fayette (lah-fah-YEHT) wrote the following historical works: *Histoire de Madame Henriette d'Angleterre* (1720; *Fatal Gallantry*, 1722) and *Mémoires de la cour de France pour les années 1688 et 1689* (1731).

ACHIEVEMENTS

Madame de La Fayette is frequently described as the first person to write a modern novel (as opposed to a romance) in French. *The Princess of Clèves* is considerably briefer than the pastoral and chivalric prose romances, often filling thousands of pages, which were fashionable earlier in the seventeenth century. La Fayette's plot construction clearly distinguishes between the main characters and those involved in the many subplots. The resultant concentration on the heroine allows readers to follow the development of her character and her motivations. Because the reader's attention is not dispersed over many plots, as in the romances, suspense and empathy are more intense. In fact, the public's identification with the novel's heroine reached such proportions that a torrent of letters and pamphlets appeared, taking passionately held positions on the rightness or error of the heroine's conduct. It is said that engagements were broken off because couples could not agree about the conduct of the princess of Clèves.

In purely literary terms, *The Princess of Clèves* constitutes a major change in the way fiction relates to history in French literature. Instead of placing her story in the distant past or in an exotic Asian or African country, La Fayette blended real historical persons, well known to her readers, with purely imaginary characters. This proximity of the story to the life of the reader awakened an expectation of verisimilitude or realism that made the reader compare him- or herself with the characters. Reading thus became a critical activity of a new sort, for the reader could claim that a character behaved in an unlikely way or, on the contrary, could decide to identify with the character and try to model real-life action on the fictitious pattern. The so-called quarrel of *The Princess of Clèves* marks the historical beginning of the attempt to use the novel as a serious tool of social examination, an attempt that culminated two centuries later with Émile Zola.

BIOGRAPHY

Born in Paris and baptized on March 18, 1634, as Marie-Madeleine Pioche de la Vergne, Madame de La Fayette was well connected with the royal court. Her mother, Isabelle Pena, was the daughter of the physician of King Louis XIII. La Fayette's father had an honorable career in the royal army until his death in 1649. Her mother's second husband, Renaud-René de Sévigné, was involved in the aristocratic rebellion known as the Fronde and was exiled from the court in 1652. Three years later, La Fayette married François, Comte de La Fayette.

Madame de La Fayette spent less than four years at her husband's estate in the Auvergne. By 1659, the couple was back in Paris, where their second son was born. In 1661, the count returned to the Auvergne, leaving Madame de La Fayette to live in the house built by her father and to participate in the life of the court. She was close to Madame de Sévigné and to Princess Henrietta of England, wife of Philippe d'Orléans, brother of the king. She frequented the salon of the literary Du Plessis-Guénégauds, held at the Hôtel de Nevers. In 1665, she began a long friendship with the Duc de La Rochefoucauld, a former leader of the Fronde and author of the well-known *Maximes* (1665-1678; *The Maxims*, 1670, 1706). After his death in 1680 and her husband's death in 1683, she renewed her friendship with the active literary figure Gilles Ménage. In the later 1670's, she was active in secret diplomatic negotiations with the duchy of Savoy. After 1689, she turned toward religion under the direction of the Abbé de Rancé.

ANALYSIS

Although it is frequently neglected by readers because of its exaggerated reputation as a difficult and complex novel, Madame de La Fayette's *Zayde* (often spelled *Zaïde*) is a highly polished, thoughtful work, containing many of the elements of La Fayette's undoubted masterpiece, *The Princess of Clèves*. Like the latter, *Zayde* contains a principal plot interrupted with less important plots appearing in inserted tales—that is, stories told by the characters. The inserted tales in *Zayde* are longer than those in *The Princess of Clèves* and differ also in that the characters in *Zayde* tell their own stories and not stories about other people. This constant changing of narrative voice and of character does make *Zayde* somewhat harder to follow than the later novel, but *Zayde* is simple and clear by comparison to such earlier works as Honoré d'Urfé's *L'Astrée* (1607-1628; *Astraea*, 1657-1658).

Thematically, *Zayde* is closely linked to *The Princess of Clèves* by the characters' probing of the nature of reality in contrast to their presuppositions and fears about it. The heroes are their own worst enemies. They are paralyzed by assumptions about life and other people that simply do not match experience. In *Zayde*, La Fayette's hero, Consalve, is literally afraid of himself, for the novelist has used a banal motif of Baroque literature—the lost portrait—and has treated it as a metaphor for a person's division from himself (or herself), his alienation, in his fears and desires.

ZAYDE

At the beginning of *Zayde*, Consalve, a younger courtier from one of the two most powerful families of the court of León, leaves the court to seek utter solitude on the Spanish coast. There he meets another gentleman, Alphonse, who offers him a place to stay. The two exchange their stories of disenchantment. Consalve's story concerns his betrayal by his two best friends, the Prince Don Garcie and Ramir. The three of them had discussed whether love arises most strongly in a man for a woman he knows well or for someone he does not know until the moment of surprise, when he finds himself totally and irrationally attracted. Consalve claimed that he could not love a woman he did not know well, adding that he would prefer that she not have any prior sentiment for another. His two friends argued that acquaintance defeats love, and Ramir added that the desirability of the loved object increases if she already is attached to another. When Consalve tells Alphonse this story, he demonstrates the illusory character of the knowledge of his beloved, because he did not know that she had the capacity to leave him for Ramir, and of the knowledge of other people in general, since he was betrayed by his two best friends as well.

Alphonse's story follows the pattern of Consalve's, for Alphonse, too, had developed a general concept of human conduct that subsequently failed him. He had decided that he would not marry a beautiful woman, because women in general are faithless and because a beautiful woman, having more temptation to infidelity, would make him unhappy by making him jealous of his rivals. In spite of this resolve, Alphonse had fallen in love and become jealous—to such an extent that he killed his best friend and drove his beloved into a convent. Yet no one was at fault except Alphonse, whose ideas about women were so rooted in his mind that he did not need any real reason to be jealous. In many ways, Consalve's and Alphonse's stories are symmetrical. Consalve was betrayed by others in whom he placed excessive trust; Alphonse killed his best friend and ruined the life of his beloved because of an excessive lack of trust. Consalve believed that he knew Nugna Bella well enough to love her; Alphonse did not believe that he knew Bélasire well enough and, indeed, could never be satisfied, no matter how great a quantity of information was supplied to him.

If the vanity of trying to guide one's life by preconceived notions is not already clear, it becomes abundantly evident in the course of the novel, which is largely devoted to Consalve's love for Zayde. She is a young woman whom Consalve finds washed up on the beach after a violent storm. Only Zayde and her woman companion have survived a shipwreck. Although they are dressed in Moorish costumes, the hero, accustomed to Arabic because of his frequent military encounters with the foe, does not recognize their tongue. For months, he tries to converse with Zayde and fails, except by using gestures and paintings. He intuits that Zayde finds in his face the likeness of someone else she has loved. Because Consalve is in love, by now, with this person of whom he knows only the name and the "fact" that she has loved someone else, he is jealous when Zayde looks at him with tenderness. He thinks that she sees him only as the image of her absent lover.

The hero has, of course, proved that his initial assumptions about the relationship of love and knowledge are entirely wrong. His "maxim" of conduct does not correspond to his experience. Knowledge and love are, however, related in *Zayde*, but it takes many adventures and many more inserted tales before Consalve discovers what the relationship is. At the end of the novel, when he and Zayde meet after a long separation, they are able to speak to each other. She has learned Spanish, and he has discovered that her language is Greek and has learned it. He finds that she recognized in him the face from a portrait that had been identified for her as that of the prince of Fez, to whom she had been promised in marriage. This resemblance explains her emotion on seeing Consalve. The portrait, however, is actually a lost portrait of Consalve.

La Fayette concludes her novel with this trite mechanism for undoing complicated plots, but she uses the lost portrait for a specific reason that is quite original. One aspect of love, one that has afflicted both Consalve and Alphonse, is the attempt to impose on the outside world a conception of the way things are or ought to be. In a sense, both Consalve and Alphonse are seeking in love someone who will mirror themselves. Alphonse is punished by his inability to see that Bélasire is not the mirror of his jealousy. Her actions and his jealousy are unrelated. Consalve's purgatory is the long quest to discover that it is his own image that stands in the way of his love for Zayde.

THE PRINCESS OF CLÈVES

Although *The Princess of Clèves* is briefer than *Zayde* and has a less difficult plot, this acknowledged masterpiece addresses problems that are fully as complex as those in *Zayde*. In her second novel, La Fayette also treats the relationship between general assumptions and individual experience, but she does so by tracing the life of a woman, Mademoiselle de Chartres (the heroine has no first name), who comes to the court as an adolescent with her mother, who wants to arrange a good and prestigious marriage for her daughter. Although the setting of this story gives La Fayette the opportunity to analyze the political intrigues of the French court, a milieu she knew intimately, the principal focus in *The Princess of Clèves*, as in *Zayde*, is on the relationship between knowledge and experience. Since Mademoiselle de Chartres arrives at the court with neither opinions about nor acquaintance with its ways, she relies entirely on her mother to form her.

In her educational endeavor, the mother uses two approaches: plain assertion and illustrative narration. The problem, however, is that the mother's assertions about the way a woman can be happy (the sole means of obtaining feminine happiness, she says, is to love one's husband and to be loved by him) and the story she tells about Madame de Valentinois (Diane de Poitiers), the mistress of King Henry II, do not coincide. The king's mistress is the most powerful woman at the court. She is faithful neither to her husband nor to her lovers, yet there is no indication of unhappiness on her part. There is a further contradiction between the mother's claim about happiness and her struggle, largely out of personal vanity it seems, to arrange a marriage that will show the whole court that she and her family are important.

This contradictory maternal pedagogy is the starting point for one of the structural problems of the novel, a problem that was noted shortly after publication. Valincour, one of the earliest critics of *The Princess of Clèves*, felt that the internal narratives told by various characters to the heroine simply did not hold together. Surely, if the novelist wanted simply to create local color, she would not have needed to interrupt her narrative repeatedly to have characters fill in the gaps in the heroine's knowledge of court intrigue. The heroine could learn about these things without the reader of the novel having to listen verbatim to all the accounts given of the life of Mary Stuart or of Madame de Tournon, among others. It is more probable that the act of listening to such stories and trying to apply them to one's own life as models of conduct is a matter of interest in its own right. The heroine is trying to fit her general ideas about life—including such notions as that men are never faithful—to these stories in search of confirmation of her expectations. Even when she does not find her assumptions borne out, she clings to the instructions given to her by her mother.

The heroine's marriage to the prince of Clèves does not give her happiness, but it does give her someone to talk to after her mother dies. This is not a small matter in this novel, nor indeed in the court milieu that La Fayette knew. Her friend La Rochefoucauld wrote, "Nothing flatters us so much as the confidences of the great, since we see them as the consequence of our merit, without considering that they usually come only from vanity or from the inability to keep a secret." The "inability to keep a secret" is a frequent problem in *The Princess of Clèves*, as several of the internal stories show. The princess, however, has a special reason for not being able, or not wanting, to keep a secret. She has learned to seek guidance by using stories as examples of conduct and is accustomed to telling her own life, as a story, to her mother. When the princess falls in love with the duke of Nemours, she fails to tell her mother, who nevertheless notices her daughter's infatuation and is mortally grieved by the silence that covers this one event in her daughter's life. The princess's husband becomes the only person in whom she can confide. After trying to keep her love for Nemours secret, even from Nemours, the princess believes that she must either yield to her passion or tell it to someone. The confession scene at Coulommiers, where she tells her husband that she is in love with someone else, is therefore a logical consequence of the mother's (and the novel's) insistence on telling stories.

One of La Fayette's contemporaries, the count of Bussy-Rabutin, wrote, "The wife's confession to her husband is extravagant and can only be told in a true story." His opinion was widespread, for the readers of the novel generally thought that no woman would ever make such a confession. On one hand, their opinion was based on the social mores of the time. Women were generally married very young (often to older men) by their parents. Love and marriage were therefore strictly separate, despite the teachings of the Catholic Church and the somewhat utopian doctrine presented by the princess's mother that women should love their husbands. Husband and wife frequently had little to do with each other, living separate lives, as did Madame de La Fayette and her husband, the count. Under these circumstances, it would be either superfluous or imprudent for a wife to tell her husband about a love affair.

Beyond the sociological aspect, the confession raises the specifically literary problem to which Bussy-Rabutin alluded when he claimed that it could be told only in a true story. Here a distinction is being made between "true" and "verisimilar." Seventeenth century French classical theory distinguished these two categories (in an application of Aristotle's *Poetics*). Many things could happen in real life, it was thought, that were so improbable as to render a story suspect. Therefore, unlikely events could be recounted only in authentic historical narratives, whereas fiction should limit itself to the probable.

To make matters worse, from both the sociological and the literary standpoints, La Fayette multiplied the improbabilities of her novel. If the confession is in itself unlikely, how likely is it that Nemours, the object of the wife's adulterous passion, should be hidden in the trees, listening to everything she says? If his presence there is already stretching one's capacity to suspend disbelief, Nemours's secret return to the Clèves estate to spy on the princess another time is certainly hard to credit. Finally, in the list of improbabilities detected by the early readers, the princess's refusal to marry or to have an affair with Nemours after her husband's death (caused by a broken heart) raised numerous objections.

La Fayette seems to be playing with the reader's assumptions about what is normal. She can do so only by locating her novel in a time and space sufficiently close to the reader's own for the reader to apply the same standards to both book and world. If the princess had been a figure in a romance such as Ludovico Ariosto's *Orlando furioso* (widely read in France at the time), readers would probably have accepted anything she did as no less credible than the flying steed and the magic palace of Ariosto's work. In *The Princess of Clèves*, however, there is a real tension between what Bussy-Rabutin, Valincour, and other readers found unbelievable and the historical accuracy of most of the setting. La Fayette herself, in a celebrated letter, denied her authorship of *The Princess of Clèves*, adding that

> what I find in it is a perfect imitation of the world of the court and of the way in which one lives there. There is nothing novelistic [Romanesque] and high-flown about it; thus it is not a novel [*roman*]: it is rather a book of memoirs.

Whatever one thinks of the author's sincerity in this letter, the tension between the novelistic and the realistic, or "perfect imitation," is evidently maintained.

The key to this puzzle may very well lie in the last sentence of *The Princess of Clèves*, when, after having left the court for a remote country house, the widowed princess dies and leaves the world "inimitable examples of virtue." The notion of example belongs both to literary or rhetorical theory and to everyday assumptions about life. The many inserted stories of this novel are used by the heroine as examples of conduct at the court. As such, they must be supposed in some way representative of general truths, and they must be useful as guides to conduct. La Fayette has clearly used the inserted stories as a counterpoint to the heroine's own behavior. Despite the apparent educational value for the young woman in these stories, they serve a strictly negative function, showing her, if anything, what kind of conduct does not conform to her mother's precepts about feminine happiness. Furthermore, throughout the novel—the confession is only the most notable instance—the princess is described by her husband, by her mother, and even by herself as being unlike others. La Fayette squarely poses the problem of the usefulness of examples by confronting exemplary stories of the court with a heroine who is unique and who leaves behind examples that cannot be imitated.

The Princess of Clèves has been described as the first novel of psychological analysis. Although this description is in some ways a projection into the seventeenth century of late nineteenth century approaches, it does have the merit of emphasizing the heroine's role in seeking to understand her own desires and the conduct of those around her. She does this by talking about it, and this verbal approach does have similarities to the "talking cure" of modern psychotherapies. Yet there are considerable areas of the mind and emotions of the principal characters that remain ambiguous. Even the heroine's decision to leave the court and not to marry Nemours remains a subject of great controversy. Some critics claim that she follows a basically religious impulse that leads her to flee from the man who led her to the brink of sin and, in doing so, apparently precipitates the death of her husband. Others see this ultimate refusal of love as a utilitarian flight from unhappiness in view of her conviction (based on her mother's teaching) that men are never faithful when they are satisfied both emotionally and sexually.

Perhaps in trying to find a single reason for her actions, readers are being too simplistically psychological, forgetting that the heroine does not really have a psyche because she is entirely a fictive creation. Perhaps, too, readers forget the seventeenth century discovery of the dispersion of the self as it unfolds in La Rochefoucauld's work, particularly in reflections such as the one that was first in the original edition of *The Maxims*, where self-love is described as multiform and so contradictory that it can even effect self-hatred. One of the intercalated stories in *The Princess of Clèves*, the one about Madame de Tournon and her lover, Sancerre, portrays a character whose conduct is composed of layers of actions and motivations so dissimilar that no one seems to be able to seize the totality of her personality.

The persistence of mystery in the self is a link between *The Princess of Clèves* and *Zayde*. For all of their attempts to compress human conduct into clear definitions and rules, Consalve, Alphonse, and the princess are never really certain what will happen or even precisely what passes through their own minds.

John D. Lyons

OTHER MAJOR WORKS

NONFICTION: *Histoire de Madame Henriette d'Angleterre*, 1720 (*Fatal Gallantry*, 1722); *Mémoires de la cour de France pour les années 1688 et 1689*, 1731.

BIBLIOGRAPHY

Beasley, Faith. "The Voices of Shadows: Lafayette's *Zaïde*." In *Going Public: Women and Publishing in Early-Modern France*, edited by Elizabeth C. Goldsmith and Dena Goodman. Ithaca, N.Y.: Cornell University Press, 1995. Beasley suggests that the multiplicity of narrative voices in *Zayde* reflects the collaborative model of writing practiced in the literary salons of seventeenth century Paris.

Beasley, Faith, and Katherine Ann Jensen, eds. *Approaches to Teaching Lafayette's "The Princess of Clèves."* New York: Modern Language Association of America, 1998. Although this book is aimed at teachers, it also provides useful background material and analysis for students. It places *The Princess of Clèves* within the context of the French novel and of seventeenth century French history, and it discusses the novel's themes, structure, and treatment of masculinity.

François, Anne-Lise. "L'Aveu sans suite: Love's Open Secret in Lafayette's *La Princesse de Clèves*." In *Open Secrets: The Literature of Uncounted Experience*. Stanford, Calif.: Stanford University Press, 2008. François describes La Fayette's novel as a work of "uncounted experience," or literature in which "nothing happens" because the characters reject modernist pressures for self-actualization and self-denial.

Green, Anne. *Privileged Anonymity: The Writings of Madame de Lafayette*. Oxford, England: Legenda, 1996. Green analyzes La Fayette's novels and nonfiction from the perspective of gender studies, arguing that La Fayette was conflicted about being a female writer and she expressed these feelings in her representations of sexual relationships.

Henry, Patrick, ed. *An Inimitable Example: The Case for the Princesse de Clèves*. Washington, D.C.: Catholic University of America Press, 1992. A collection of fourteen essays that provide feminist, psychological, sociocritical, ethical, and religious interpretations of the novel, including discussions of the book's depiction of love and of its eponymous character.

Letts, Janet. *Legendary Lives in "La Princesse de Clèves."* Charlottesville, Va.: Rookwood Press, 1998. Letts focuses on how La Fayette's novel depicts well-known historical figures, including Catherine de Medici, Diane de Poitiers, Mary Stuart, and Henry II. Includes a chronology, a bibliography, and an index.

Paulson, Michael G. *Facets of a Princess: Multiple Readings of Madame de la Fayette's "La Princesse de Cleves."* New York: Peter Lang, 1998. Paulson brings a multifaceted approach to his examination of La Fayette's novel, analyzing the book from political, historical, feminist, and religious perspectives. Includes bibliographical references.

Racevskis, Roland. "Time and Information In and Around *La Princesse de Cleves*: Anteriority, Communication, Interiority." In *Time and Ways of Knowing Under Louis XIV: Molière, Sévigné, Lafayette*. Lewisburg, Pa.: Bucknell University Press, 2003. A unique study in which Racevskis analyzes the representation of time in La Fayette's novel. Part of his study of how the then-new technology of clocks and timepieces was addressed and represented in seventeenth century French literature.

Redhead, Ruth. *Themes and Images in the Fictional Works of Madame de Lafayette*. New York: Peter Lang, 1990. Redhead analyzes La Fayette's fiction, focusing on how her use of imagery enables her to express themes of absence, presence, sincerity, and deception. Includes bibliographical references.

CLARICE LISPECTOR

Born: Chechelnik, Ukraine, Soviet Union (now in Ukraine); December 10, 1925
Died: Rio de Janeiro, Brazil; December 9, 1977

PRINCIPAL LONG FICTION

Perto do coração selvagem, 1944 (*Near to the Wild Heart*, 1990)
O lustre, 1946
A cidade sitiada, 1949
A maçã no escuro, 1961 (*The Apple in the Dark*, 1967)
A paixão segundo G. H., 1964 (*The Passion According to G. H.*, 1988)
Uma aprendizagem: Ou, O livro dos prazeres, 1969 (*An Apprenticeship: Or, The Book of Delights*, 1986)
Água viva, 1973 (*The Stream of Life*, 1989)
A hora da estrela, 1977 (*The Hour of the Star*, 1986)
Um sopro de vida: Pulsações, 1978

OTHER LITERARY FORMS

Clarice Lispector (leh-SPEHKT-ur) was a prominent short-story writer as well as a novelist; among her collections of stories are *Alguns contos* (1952; some stories) and *Laços de família* (1960; *Family Ties*, 1972). *A legião estrangeira* (1964; *The Foreign Legion*, 1986) is a collection of stories and brief miscellaneous prose pieces.

ACHIEVEMENTS

Clarice Lispector is regarded as one of the most influential and important Brazilian fiction writers of the twentieth century. A member of the revisionist school of writers that emerged in the period following World War II, she was a force in the move, in Brazilian fiction, from the regionalism and sociological orientation of the 1930's to an intense interest in subjective experience.

She first achieved general acclaim with *Family Ties*, a collection of inward-looking short stories. *The Apple in the Dark* marked Lispector's major artistic breakthrough. Lengthy and complex, symbolic and mythic, the novel employs an intense, lyrical style that recalls the works of Djuna Barnes, Virginia Woolf, and Katherine Mansfield.

Lispector was the recipient of many literary prizes. In 1944, the publication of *Near to the Wild Heart* won for her the Graça Aranha Prize. She received the Cármen Dolores Barbosa Prize for *The Apple in the Dark* in 1961, a prize from the Campanha Nacional da Criança for a children's story, "O mistério do coelho pensante" (the mystery of the thinking rabbit) in 1967, and the Golfinho de Ouro Prize for *An Apprenticeship* in 1969, and she was awarded first prize in the tenth Concurso Literário Nacional for her overall contribution to Brazilian literature in 1976, one year before her death.

BIOGRAPHY

Clarice Lispector was born in Chechelnik, in the Ukraine, in 1925, of Jewish parents. The family moved to Brazil when she was two months old. Lispector attended school first in Recife, then in Rio de Janeiro. In 1943, she graduated from the Faculty of Law in Rio. She married a diplomat and lived in Italy, Switzerland, Great Britain, and the United States for many years. After she and her husband divorced, she settled permanently in Rio de Janeiro in 1959. She died from cancer in 1977.

ANALYSIS

Most, but not all, of Clarice Lispector's protagonists are female, and the author is keenly aware of women's problems and of the female side of the psyche. Her major works deal with internal guests. An occurrence in the protagonists' lives causes them to move out of their daily routines and enter into new types of relationship with themselves and with the physical world. They live each moment intensely, as if every breath of existence is a major experience, tightly connected to the pulsating rhythm of life itself. The protagonist's quest has no specific goal except to move forward, as in *The Apple in the Dark*:

> Still in his favor was the fact that he knew he should walk in a straight line because it would not be very practical to lose the thread of the maze. In his disfavor there was a danger he was on the lookout for: the fact that there were pleasure and beauty in a person's losing himself.

Lispector's major protagonists are all making their way through the maze of life, lost at times, but always eventually able to resume their journey toward enlightenment.

NEAR TO THE WILD HEART

Near to the Wild Heart, Lispector's first novel, published when she was still a teenager, is considered a breakthrough in Brazilian literature because of its modernistic style. It is the story of Joana, a young orphan who, after an introspective adolescence, lives through a marriage and a subsequent divorce. In part 1, descriptions of Joana's childhood alternate with descriptions of her life as Octavio's wife. Part 2 tells the story of her marriage, her husband's infidelity, her divorce, and her ultimate encounter with herself as a free entity in the world. The epigraph for the novel, "He was alone. He was abandoned, happy, close to the savage heart of life" is taken from James Joyce's *A Portrait of the Artist as a Young Man* (1916).

As a child, Joana is keenly aware of the cycle of life and death. Eating a chicken makes her think of the worm in the earth on which the chicken once nourished itself. Behind all life there is death, and the only thing that distinguishes human beings from other organisms is consciousness. A feeling of being connected with the physical world through a common destiny provides moments of profound pain and profound joy to Joana as well as to most of Lispector's later protagonists. "Oh, pity, that is what I sense then. Pity is my form of love. Of love and of communication."

Marriage proves to be a very disturbing experience for Joana, who as a child quizzed her teacher about the goal of happiness: "Be happy in order to obtain what?" she had wondered. While her need to touch another human being through love nevertheless remained strong, her marriage resulted in a sense of imprisonment. How does one tie oneself to another human being without becoming imprisoned by that person's construction of walls around one's body and soul? How is it possible to possess things without having things possess one? These are questions that will haunt all of Lispector's major protagonists. In her marriage, Joana's quest for self-fulfillment constantly comes into conflict with the bland happiness she finds with Octavio: "Lightly surprised she dilated her eyes, perceived her body plunged into a comfortable happiness. She did not suffer, but where was she?"

Part 2 describes Joana's long struggle to free herself from Octavio: "His presence, and more than his presence: knowing that he existed left her without liberty." Her time is no longer her own: "Now all her time was handed over to him and the minutes that were hers, she felt them allotted, distributed in small cubes of ice that she must swallow rapidly, before they melted." Marriage, she believes, is betrayal of herself and of the vision of life that she developed during adolescence. For Octavio, on the other hand, Joana's restlessness, which originally attracted him to her, proves too disturbing, and he seeks refuge in his former fiancé, Lidia, a woman whose dream is to create a conventional family. Victimized by irrational jealousy, Joana, too, takes a lover, at the same time attempting to retain Octavio. The drive toward self-fulfillment, however, proves stronger than the forces that link her to either her husband or her lover, and in the novel's last chapter Joana is alone. Her only goal now is to walk humbly down the road of life, without fear, receptive to the world and to death. Finally in harmony with the fluidity of life itself, Joana experiences within herself a burst of creative energy.

THE APPLE IN THE DARK

The Apple in the Dark is considered Lispector's most important novel. Martim, the protagonist, is fleeing a crime. At the beginning of the novel, he is in bed in a womblike hotel room. The balcony outside his room overlooks a garden bathed in darkness. Still half asleep, Martim walks out onto the balcony, observes that a car that has been parked in front of the hotel has disappeared, and suspects that a German who lives in the hotel has gone to turn him in to the police. Totally awake now, Martim jumps from the balcony into the garden and begins a long, slow walk into the dark.

The Apple in the Dark is a dreamlike narrative of Martim's quest for a side of the self with which he has lost contact while living as a married man in a conventional social setting. Unsure of where he is going, his only goal is to move in a straight line so as to avoid a circular return to the walls of the hotel. Martim's quest ends on an ambiguous note, since at the end of the novel he appears to have given up and is ready to be captured and returned to the world he left behind.

Nevertheless, Martim's journey has provided him with experiences and insights that he did not possess at the beginning of the book. "We don't know where we came from and we don't know where we're going; but we just experience things, we experience! And that's what we have, Ermelinda." Surrounded by stones and plants, Martim experiences exquisite moments of connection with the mystery of the natural world, as all of his senses open and his mind abdicates its power and accepts being merely a part of life "with the nakedness of his lack of understanding." He makes the surprising discovery that "the more stupid he was the more face to face with things he was." In his new state of consciousness, Martim replaces understanding with awareness. He senses the air he breathes with the delicate tension of a plant and attempts to adopt the patient rhythm of grazing cows.

The Apple in the Dark is a novel about love, both for the world itself and for other human beings. A significant part of the book describes Martim's stay at a farm and his encounter with two women, Ermelinda and Vitória. Ermelinda seeks, in her love for Martim, protection against her obsessive fear of death, only to discover that physical love, on the contrary, brings her closer to an experience of dying than does any other emotion. This newly won insight finally enables Ermelinda to accept her own mortality. Martim's encounter with Vitória is different, a communion of souls rather than bodies. In a moving description, Lispector shows how Martim's resistance to intimate contact with another person is gradually broken down, as Vitória for the first time in her life gives expression to her innermost thoughts and emotions. While communication does not last, the experience proves crucial to Martim, who is finally able to look upon himself with love and respect: "The man was loving himself for the first time, which meant that he was ready to love others." Martim no longer needs to flee, and he willingly consents to cut short his quest and return to society.

The title of the novel is important. *The Apple in the Dark* can be read as a commentary on the biblical myth on the tree of knowledge. The understanding of the world that Martim achieves is intuitive rather than rational. He never actually eats the apple, he merely reaches out for it in the dark, hoping that he will be able to hold on to the fruit: "And I have that clumsy way of reaching for an apple in the dark—and trying not to drop it."

THE PASSION ACCORDING TO G. H.

The quest for identity continues in *The Passion According to G. H.* While Martim's quest took the form of a voyage through external space, G. H.'s quest is wholly internal. The killing of a cockroach triggers in the protagonist an extensive and painful meditation on life, death, and writing, and on her own place within the order of things. Toward the end of the novel, G. H., like Martim, will emerge from her introspection with an increased awareness that will enable her to live her daily life in a more productive way than before.

AN APPRENTICESHIP

An Apprenticeship, written five years later, is Lispector's most optimistic novel. The novel has two protagonists, a woman and a man, engaged in an extensive dialogue. Lori, a physically attractive young teacher, lives an empty, nonreflective life until she falls in love with Ulysses, a professor of philosophy. Although Lori has had several affairs, Ulysses refuses to consummate their love until she has completed her "apprenticeship" and learned the secret meaning of life. Only then, he believes, is a permanent union of two people possible. Lori, feeling frustrated and rejected, reluctantly starts her slow, painful route toward self-discovery under his guidance.

Until the meeting with Ulysses, Lori had eliminated pain from her life, but she had also cut off any potential for meaningful contact with herself, with other people, or with life itself: "Without pain, she had been left without anything, lost in her own world and that of others without any means of contact." Love, reduced to sex, failed to connect her to anything outside herself. Ulysses realizes this and decides that Lori must reestablish contact with her own body and soul before she will be able to love him or anybody else: "I could have possessed you already with my body and my soul, but I will wait even though it takes years, for you, too, to have a body and a soul to love with," he tells her.

During her apprenticeship, Lori experiences an increased sense of awareness of the world around her and of the silence of death that lurks perpetually behind the bustling noises of life. Lori discovers that pain and pleasure, life and death, are inextricably linked. By attempting to escape from pain she has excluded pleasure from her life as well. Consequently, her new receptivity to pain will restore her ability to experience pleasure. It is only after having accepted the pain of death that she can start to feel a genuine joy of living.

The pleasure results from her growing ability to strip away facades and protective mechanisms and dare finally to be herself. Lori soon experiences flashes of communication and insights accompanied by a keen sense of genuinely existing. During this period of profound introspection, Lori needs to distance herself from society and from Ulysses as well, in order to be more fully with herself. Her ultimate goal, however, is connection, not isolation. First, she must be reattached to the earth itself. Then, she hopes to reestablish the link between herself and other people.

In an episode typical of Lispector's fiction, Lori is walking slowly and wearily down the street. She notices a girl waiting for the bus, and her heart begins to throb—she has decided to try to make contact with another person. After the brief encounter, Lori realizes that what she is looking for is more profound. She returns home and calls Ulysses. She bites into an apple and discovers that the eating of the fruit leads her to a state of grace rather than exile: "Unlike Eve, when she bit into the apple she entered paradise. . . . It was the beginning . . . of a state of grace." The state of grace is the state of someone who does not have to guess any longer, according to the narrator, someone who simply knows. The world around her acquires a kind of halo that radiates almost perfectly from things and people, a kind of energy consisting of very fine particles of light. Lori, at the same time, realizes that she does not want to experience grace often; she does not want to become addicted to it, because it would distance her from the struggle, from the perplexity and joy of an ordinary human destiny: "It was important not to forget that the state of grace was merely a small opening to the world which was like paradise—it was neither an entrance into it nor did it give one the right to eat from the fruits of its orchards."

Lori, then, does not stay in paradise but emerges from her experience of grace as a better human being. Ulysses, in the following chapter, tells her that she is now ready for love. Before leaving her apartment to join him, Lori stands by her window, watching the rain. She feels neither pain nor pleasure, only a keen sense of connection and release: "She and the rain were busy with their violent outpouring." She intuitively knows that she will be able to transfer her newly won intimacy with the world to her relationship with Ulysses, leaves her apartment without putting on her customary makeup, and takes a taxi to his place. Somehow, living and loving have finally become simple, as Lori has discovered that it is possible for her to give herself without losing herself. After a period of passionate lovemaking, she sees in a vision the fruit of the world, "And it was in midair that she placed her mouth on the fruit and managed to bite into it, yet leaving it intact gleaming in space." Ulysses is no longer a teacher to Lori. The two of them are equal, united through mutual love.

THE STREAM OF LIFE

An Apprenticeship, with its vision of a mature, passionate, conscious relationship between a man and a woman, is an exception within Lispector's total work, a pleasant detour along the road. In *The Stream of Life*, written four years later, the author returns once again to a solitary, questing protagonist. The novel is an intense, fluid monologue addressed to an absent *you*, a person with whom the narrator was once intimately involved. In the novel's first paragraph, the narrator bursts out in a cry of joy upon realizing that she is once again free. It is a joy mixed with the sadness of separation and the fear of an unknown future. Nevertheless, she wants to capture the present moment, to connect with the spirit of life, and to sing out the joy she experiences from being in the world: "And I sing hallelujah in the air like the bird does."

The Stream of Life is a glorification of the self alone in the world, detached from material possessions and from other people. The prevailing emotion in the book is one of being intensely alive, bought at the price of separation from the person she loves. Her new lover is nature, a feminine principle both soothing and ferocious. This love affair with life itself is for the narrator a way of approaching God. Such a radical break is necessary for Lispector's narrator in order to escape from a society that flattens out emotional lives and turns people into automatons, unable ever to grasp the present moment. Separation, thus, becomes a gift of life that she, through her writing, wants to bestow on her former lover as well. Separation is seen as a birth trauma, painful but necessary for the lover to experience the exquisite joy of liberty: "I give you liberty. First I break the waterbag. Then I cut the umbilical cord. And you are alive in your own right." On the book's final page, she addresses the lover for the last time: "Look at me and love me. No: you look at yourself and love you. And that is what is just."

The Stream of Life is a long meditation on love, separation, life, death, and God, seemingly inspired by Asian mysticism: "Profound prayer is a meditation on nothingness," according to the narrator. Faced with the pain of separation, analogous to the pain of dying, the narrator chooses to respond with joy, "because it is too cruel, so I respond by the purity of indomitable joy. I refuse to be sad. Let us be joyous." The style of *The Stream of Life* is fluid and poetic, each sentence giving birth to the next with no preconceived structure, as Lispector attempts to capture the rhythm of her own respiration.

LAST NOVELS

The Hour of the Star is also a detour. It is different from Lispector's other novels in that it focuses on a social rather than a metaphysical problem. Macabéa, the protagonist, is a young woman who moves from the poor northeast part of Brazil to the city. The novel deals with the problems of the rural North versus the urban South, of poverty and the dream of a better life, and, finally, of an uneducated woman's struggle to survive in a sexist society.

In her final novel, *Um sopro de vida* (a breath of life), Lispector returns for the last time to an intensely personal inquiry into the problems of life, death, and writing. Completed shortly before the author's own death, the novel is the ultimate statement of an artist whose own road has come to an end, for whom reality has caught up with her life's vision, and for whom each breath now literally encapsulates the essence of life itself. The novel was published posthumously.

Randi Birn

OTHER MAJOR WORKS

SHORT FICTION: *Alguns contos*, 1952; *Laços de família*, 1960 (*Family Ties*, 1972); *A legião estrangeira*, 1964 (*The Foreign Legion*, 1986); *Felicidade clandestina: Contos*, 1971; *A imitação da rosa*, 1973; *Onde estivestes de noite*, 1974; *A via crucis do corpo*, 1974; *A bela e a fera*, 1979; *Soulstorm*, 1989 (includes stories from *Onde estivestes de noite* and *A via crucis do corpo*).

NONFICTION: *Para não esquecer*, 1978; *A descoberta do mundo*, 1984 (*Discovering the World*, 1992); *Correio feminino*, 2006.

CHILDREN'S LITERATURE: *O mistério do coelho pensante*, 1967; *A mulher que matou os peixes*, 1968 (*The Woman Who Killed the Fish*, 1982).

MISCELLANEOUS: *Seleta de Clarice Lispector*, 1975.

BIBLIOGRAPHY

Alonso, Cláudia Pazos, and Claire Williams, eds. *Closer to the Wild Heart: Essays on Clarice Lispector*. Oxford, England: Legenda and European Humanities Research Centre, 2002. Collection of twelve essays includes discussion of Lispector's critical reception in the United States; analysis of Lispector's representations of urban poverty, feminism, and the question of nation; and examinations of the novels *An Apprenticeship* and *The Passion According to G. H.*

Barbosa, Maria José Somerlate. *Clarice Lispector: Spinning the Webs of Passion*. New Orleans: University Press of the South, 1997. Examines Lispector's work from a feminine perspective, demonstrating how the author subverts authority and uses language to empower women as both authors and subjects within Brazilian literature.

Cixous, Hélène. *Reading with Clarice Lispector.* Minneapolis: University of Minnesota Press, 1990. Provides a deconstructionist reading of Lispector's work, including her novels *The Stream of Life*, *The Apple in the Dark*, and *The Hour of the Star.* Recommended for advanced students.

Fitz, Earl E. *Clarice Lispector.* New York: Twayne, 1985. Excellent study of Lispector's writings by the foremost authority on her work. Devotes separate chapters to biography and background; Lispector's place in the history of Brazilian literature; discussion of her literary style, structure, and point of view; and analysis of her novels and short stories.

_______. *Sexuality and Being in the Poststructuralist Universe of Clarice Lispector: The Difference of Desire*. Austin: University of Texas Press, 2001. Examines how Lispector's protagonists, who are driven by a desire for the unattainable and indefinable "other," exemplify many of the issues that are crucial to poststructuralist literary theory.

Peixoto, Marta. *Passionate Fictions: Gender, Narrative, and Violence in Clarice Lispector.* Minneapolis: University of Minnesota Press, 1994. Analyzes, from a decidedly feminist perspective, Lispector's frequently violent subject matter, juxtaposing it with her strange and original use of language. Pays special attention to the autobiographical elements of her novel *The Stream of Life* and her short story collection *A via crucis do corpo*.

Trigo, Benigno. "Transformative Witnessing: Clarice Lispector's Dark Ties." In *Remembering Maternal Bodies: Melancholy in Latina and Latin American Women's Writing*. New York: Palgrave Macmillan, 2006. Chapter devoted to discussion of Lispector's work is part of a larger study of the writings of Latin American female authors whose works challenge traditional ideas about motherhood and maternity and who seek to eliminate their women readers' melancholy and depression.

Williams, Claire. "*The Passion According to G. H.* by Clarice Lispector." In *The Cambridge Companion to the Latin American Novel*, edited by Efraín Kristal. New York: Cambridge University Press, 2005. Analysis of Lispector's novel is included in a historical overview of Latin American literature. Williams has written extensively about Lispector.

MALCOLM LOWRY

Born: Liscard, England; July 28, 1909
Died: Ripe, Sussex, England; June 27, 1957
Also known as: Clarence Malcolm Lowry

PRINCIPAL LONG FICTION

Ultramarine, 1933 (revised 1962)
Under the Volcano, 1947
Dark as the Grave Wherein My Friend Is Laid, 1968
Lunar Caustic, 1968 (novella)
October Ferry to Gabriola, 1970

OTHER LITERARY FORMS

All but two of the volumes now attributed to Malcolm Lowry were published after his death at the age of forty-seven. During the last decade of his life, after the publication of *Under the Volcano*, Lowry worked more or less concurrently on numerous projects but was unable to finish any of them before his death. The one closest to completion when he died was *Hear Us O Lord from Heaven Thy Dwelling Place* (1961), a collection of seven interrelated tales. Additional short fiction has been collected in *Malcolm Lowry: Psalms and Songs* (1975), edited by Margerie Bonner Lowry. A selection of poems, edited by Earle Birney, appeared in 1962. *Lunar Caustic*, a novella edited from two earlier versions by Birney and Margerie Bonner Lowry, was published in 1968.

Throughout his career, Lowry elaborated and reelaborated a massive scheme of interlocking narratives called, collectively, "The Voyage That Never Ends," which, had he lived to complete it, would have included all of his longer works, with *Under the Volcano* at the center of the "bolus," as he called it. *Selected Letters of Malcolm Lowry*, edited by Harvey Breit and Margerie Bonner Lowry, appeared in 1965 and played a large part in the revival of interest in Lowry during the 1960's and 1970's. Lowry was also much interested in the cinema and, in collaboration with his second wife, Margerie Bonner (herself a published novelist), prepared a screenplay for an adaptation of F. Scott Fitzgerald's *Tender Is the Night* (1934); the film was never produced, but Lowrys' notes for the film script were published in 1976. Malcolm Lowry's life is the subject of the film *Volcano: An Inquiry into the Life and Death of Malcolm Lowry* (1977), directed by Donald Brittain.

Given that so many of Lowry's works were left unfinished at his death, and that even the works published posthumously are selections from numerous versions Lowry left behind, selections made and pieced together by editors, the authenticity of the texts published after 1957 is at least questionable. The special collection of Lowry manuscripts housed at the University of British Columbia Library in Vancouver is, therefore, very important.

ACHIEVEMENTS

The only Malcolm Lowry novel to attract any notable attention during the author's lifetime was *Under the Volcano*, which was in general very warmly received (in France and the United States at any rate, though curiously it was all but ignored in England) upon its appearance in 1947. During the ten years following, however, no extended works of fiction by Lowry appeared in English, and by the time of his death, even *Under the Volcano* was out of print. Nevertheless, an underground following quietly persisted in admiration for what must then have seemed, to most, a cometlike blaze of genius revealed in that one novel, appearing out of nowhere and as suddenly disappearing from sight.

The situation altered with the posthumous publication of other Lowry works in the 1960's, beginning with *Hear Us O Lord from Heaven Thy Dwelling Place*. By 1965, a selection of poems had appeared, *Ultramarine* and *Under the Volcano* had been reissued, *The Paris Review* offered a new edition (the first to appear in English) of *Lunar Caustic*, and *Selected Letters of Malcolm Lowry* was published to largely favorable reviews. Lowry was belatedly "discovered" in England, and Philip Toynbee hailed *Under the Volcano* as "one of the great English novels of this century." With the appearance at the end of the decade of the heavily edited, fragmentary novels *Dark as the Grave Wherein My Friend Is Laid* and *October Ferry to Gabriola*, however, a reaction set in. Both books were widely regarded as failures, and Lowry's tendency toward solipsism was judged to have gotten the better of him in his abortive later works. This view probably does an injustice to Lowry. First, works never brought to completion by Lowry cannot be justly measured against a fully realized work on which the author lavished almost ten years of concerted labor. Even so, Douglas Day's long-awaited authorized biography, published to nearly universal acclaim in 1973, seemed to legitimate the view of Lowry as an artist manqué whose single triumph amounted to a kind of fluke accomplished despite its author's compulsive tendencies to self-destruction and willed failure. In the late twentieth century, there were salutary signs of a reassessment of the Lowry canon as a whole, with such critics as Muriel C. Bradbrook, Ronald Binns, and Sherrill Grace arguing persuasively against the distortions of the "one-book author" label.

BIOGRAPHY

The youngest of four brothers, Clarence Malcolm Lowry was born at Warren Crest, North Drive, Liscard, Cheshire, England, on July 28, 1909. His father, Arthur O. Lowry, was a wealthy cotton broker of sturdy Victorian probity; his mother, Evelyn Boden, was the daughter of Captain Lyon Boden of Liverpool. A prominent shipowner and mariner, Captain Boden had died of cholera while homeward bound from Calcutta (now known as Kolkata), India, in 1880. This part of the family legacy, so unlike that of the paternal side, would provide Malcolm Lowry with the doom-tinged romantic yearning for the sea much in evidence in his fiction.

At fourteen, Lowry was sent to a public school, The Leys, from which he was expected to proceed to Cambridge University, as his brothers had done. It was during his four years at The Leys, however, that he began to engage in what amounted to a subtle subterfuge of the respectable middle-class life that his father had prescribed for him. He became infatuated with jazz and took up playing the "taropatch," or tenor ukulele. Enthusiastic readings of Herman Melville, Joseph Conrad, Jack London, and the early Eugene O'Neill fed his dreams of adventure at sea. Meanwhile, encouraged by one of his schoolmasters (the model for James Hilton's "Mr. Chips"), he began to write his own stories for the school's literary magazine. At this time, too, he began, surreptitiously at first, what would become another of his lifelong infatuations: alcohol.

By 1927, the conflict with his father had become overt, but Lowry finally agreed to go to Cambridge—after going to sea. In May, he shipped out as deckboy aboard the SS *Pyrrhus*, bound for the Far East. This experience, which lasted about six months and was to provide the raw material for *Ultramarine*, punctured at least some of his youthful illusions about the sea. It was followed, in the summer of 1928, by another pilgrimage, this time to New England, where he went to pay homage to Conrad Aiken. The American writer's experimental novel of the sea, *Blue Voyage* (1927), was the catalyst of a kind of private tutorial (Lowry being already engaged in the writing of *Ultramarine*). The two got on famously, beginning a literary kinship—and, later a competition—as of father and son, which would last in one form or another for thirty years.

At Cambridge, Lowry scarcely applied himself to his formal studies. Instead, he plumped the role of the loutish yet brilliant sailor, took up jazz again, became a connoisseur of avant-garde German silent films, drank, ran with an "advanced" circle of friends, and continued to work on *Ultramarine*. In November, 1929, one of his friends, Paul Fitte, committed suicide. The circumstances remain uncertain, but it is clear from the obsessive references to this event in his later fiction that Lowry felt partly responsible for it. The other significant occurrence of this time came in the summer of 1930, when Lowry again shipped out, this time as fireman on a Norwegian tramp steamer bound for Archangel in the White Sea. His purpose was to pay a visit to Norwegian author Nordahl Grieg, whose novel *Skibet går videre* (1924; *The Ship Sails On*, 1927) seemed to Lowry as important a precursor as Aiken's *Blue Voyage*. This journey and the eventual meeting between the two men gave Lowry the idea for another novel, to be titled "In Ballast to the White Sea," on which he worked intermittently for the next fourteen years until the manuscript (running to some one thousand pages) was destroyed in a fire at his home in Canada in 1944.

After graduating with third-class honors in English, Lowry traveled on the Continent, meeting Aiken in Spain in the spring of 1933. There he also met and soon married Jan Gabrial, formerly a stuntwoman in Hollywood films. It was an unhappy match, and Jan left him only a few weeks after their marriage in January, 1934. She returned to the United States, Lowry following her by ship the next autumn. In June, 1935, after a particularly severe bout of drinking, he was admitted to the psychiatric ward of Bellevue Hospital in

New York. Upon his release ten days later, he began, between further drinking marathons, to write the first draft of *Lunar Caustic*. When an attempt to find a job in Hollywood proved fruitless, Jan and Lowry sailed to Mexico in November, 1936, settling soon after in Cuernavaca, where he began to write *Under the Volcano*. In December of the following year, Jan, who had never been faithful to the unstable Lowry, left him permanently. He drifted south to Oaxaca, where he spent some days in jail and formed an important friendship with a Mexican named Juan Fernando Márquez. Almost continually drunk, Lowry, with the assistance of "agents" sent by his father, was at length put on a train out of the country in July, 1938.

Back in California, Lowry met and fell in love with another American, Margerie Bonner. By the end of 1940, divorced from Jan and remarried to Margerie, Lowry had moved with Margerie into a squatter's shack in Dollarton, on Burrard Inlet, British Columbia. Here they would remain, with occasional trips to Mexico, Haiti, and Europe, for the next fourteen years. It was by far the happiest, most sober (comparatively speaking), and most productive period of Lowry's life. By December, 1944, he had completed the fourth and final version of *Under the Volcano*. A five-month return visit to Mexico between 1944 and 1945 had nearly disastrous consequences—a suicide attempt, more drinking, the discovery that his Mexican friend, Juan Fernando Márquez, had been killed, trouble with the Mexican authorities, and finally deportation—but from these experiences Lowry gained most of the materials for *Dark as the Grave Wherein My Friend Is Laid* and the unpublished fragment "La Mordida." By 1950, he was working, as it were, simultaneously on these novels, the stories to be collected in *Hear Us O Lord from Heaven Thy Dwelling Place*, the film script for *Tender Is the Night*, his poems, and *October Ferry to Gabriola*.

This period of intense creative effort came to an end in 1954, when Lowry's American publisher, out of patience with his proliferating but seemingly unproductive schemes for his "bolus," severed their contract. Another severance occurred when the Lowrys left their "northern paradise" in Dollarton. After a final, brief reunion with Aiken in New York, they sailed for Italy. In late 1955, Lowry was admitted to a hospital in London for psychiatric treatment. Released in February, 1956, he settled with Margerie in the village of Ripe, Sussex, where he resumed his work. His sudden death, on June 27, 1957, caused by a fatal combination of alcohol and barbiturates, was officially termed "death by misadventure." Not surprisingly, Lowry had long since arrived at his own verdict:

> Malcolm Lowry
> Late of the Bowery
> His prose was flowery
> And often glowery
> He lived, nightly, and drank, daily,
> And died playing the ukulele.

Analysis

Like most artists, Malcolm Lowry was always fascinated by the mystery of the creative process. Unlike many other modern writers, however, he was little inclined to the explicit formulation of aesthetic theories. Still, his attitudes toward art, particularly his own art, are frequently embodied in his fiction. In the opening chapter of *Under the Volcano*, for example, one of the main characters, a film director named Jacques Laruelle, sees a drunken horseman "sprawling all over his mount, his stirrups lost, . . . barely managing to hold on by the reins, though not once . . . [grasping] the pommel to steady himself." Hurtling at breakneck speed through the narrow, winding streets of a Mexican village, the rider slips to one side, nearly falls, rights himself, almost slides off backward, and barely regains his balance, "just saving himself each time, but always with the reins, never the pommel." A closer look reveals a machete in one of the rider's hands, used to beat the horse's flanks furiously. It is, as M. Laruelle reflects, a "maniacal vision of senseless frenzy, but controlled, not quite uncontrolled, somehow almost admirable." This image serves, mutatis mutandis, as an epitome of Lowry's art: full of high risk, willfully unstable, disdainful of conventional controls, precariously balanced—but balanced all the same.

Obviously, such balance is achieved, when it is achieved, with great difficulty. This was particularly true for Lowry, whose inclination was always to follow the minutest divagations of the mind. His is an art of excess, in several senses. The composition of a novel, for him, meant continual amplification and expansion, patiently adding layer after layer of meaningful reference and telling detail, until the structure of the whole fairly exploded with a rich profusion of reverberating meanings. Such "overloading," to use Lowry's own word describing his technique, is felt at every level. His prose style, for example, is characterized by wheeling complex sentences, rife with qualifications, suspensions, and parentheses. Brian O'Kill has aptly described this style as "expansive" and "centrifugal," persistently "avoiding the closed unit of the periodic sentence in favor of an open form with an almost infinite capacity for addition and reduplication."

Lowry's range of tone is also wide and varied. As Robert B. Heilman has observed,

> In recording a disaster of personality that is on the very edge of the tragic, [Lowry] has an extravagant comic sense that creates an almost unique tension among moods. Desperation, the ludicrous, nightmare, the vulgar, the appalling, the fantastic, the nonsensical, and the painfully pathetic coexist in an incongruous melange that is still a unity.

In a famous letter defending *Under the Volcano* against various suggestions for further revision, Lowry argued that the book could be regarded as a symphony, an opera, a jazz break, a poem, a tragedy, a comedy, a farce, a Churrigueresque cathedral, a wheel, a cryptogram, a prophecy, a film, and a kind of machine. If this claim sounds extravagant, it should be remembered that Lowry believed, with Charles Baudelaire, that "life is a forest of symbols." Virtually everything in this novel—from a theater marquee to items on a menu, newspaper advertisements, an armadillo digging a hole, a cat chasing a dragonfly, amusement park rides, a travel brochure, a urinal—signifies. Appearing amid profuse allusions to the Bible, Christopher Marlowe, Dante, the Cabbala, John Bunyan, Sophocles, William Shakespeare, Herman Melville, and T. S. Eliot, among many others, these "found objects" in the setting gradually develop into a vast network of the protagonist's plight, elevating it to the level of a modern myth, indeed a tragedy for modern times.

In these respects, as in many others, Lowry resembles no one so much as Melville. Lowry once admitted, characteristically with irony at his own expense, that he identified himself with the American novelist for several reasons but "mostly because of his failure as a writer and his whole outlook generally." Both novelists were acutely aware of the monstrous potencies of the human imagination, which could envision—and proceed resolutely to enact—apocalyptic destruction as readily as it could create life-serving works of art. Both knew well the dangers involved in unleashing those potencies, particularly in the service of a narcissistic quest for what Melville's Ishmael calls "the ungraspable phantom of life," the self.

Such a view of the imagination, overtly Romantic and possessed by the seductive demon of an artistic ego of leviathan, of volcanic, proportions, is clearly fraught with risk. Lowry, like Melville, accepted the risks involved, not the least of which was the gamble that the reader would go along, entertaining the terms of the risk. There are times when, inevitably, the gamble fails. "Overloading"—the Melvillian tendency in Lowry to pile on six portents or allusions or symbols to evoke something that another writer would either summarize in a simple declarative sentence or else not attempt to say at all—sometimes threatens to sink the vessel. Reading the work of both writers requires the granting of far more than the usual share of indulgences before the bountiful aesthetic rewards can be reaped.

Some readers, however, do not find such tolerance of unevenness to their taste, and *Under the Volcano* is on the way to becoming one of the least read of great novels, in company with *Moby Dick* (1851). Lowry's other works (like Melville's *Pierre: Or, The Ambiguities*, 1852, and *The Confidence Man: His Masquerade*, 1857) are so much the more neglected, despite the efforts of later critics to call attention to their worth. One can only regret this aesthetic stinginess, along with the more commonplace preference for readily accessible, streamlined fictions. In Lowry's case, the reader who gives him- or herself to the experience proffered, accepting the terms of risk including the excesses involved, and the occasional failings, is likely to find that the gamble more than justifies itself. For, as Matthew Corrigan has aptly observed, when such "writing works for us, it does so . . . because it entails a vision of a higher order of creative existence altogether than we ordinarily get in modern literature."

UNDER THE VOLCANO

Under the Volcano is a book of wonders, a grand testament to the undiminished plentitude of the English language and the prodigious powers—both creative and destructive—of the human imagination. Not the least of its wonders is that Malcolm Lowry began writing it while he was in Mexico suffering through the personal anguish of a failed marriage, chronic alcoholism, and a terror of life so pervasive that it is a minor miracle he survived at all, much less that he was able to write. The novel went through at least four complete drafts in nine years (the third draft having been rejected by thirteen publishers) and was finally completed in December, 1944. By that time, Lowry, from the far more stable perspective provided by living simply on the beach in Dollarton with his second wife, Margerie, had succeeded in sufficiently harnessing his inner demons so as to transform his earlier sufferings into art. He described the work in an important letter to his British publisher, Jonathan Cape, as a "drama of . . . man's struggle between the powers of darkness and light," but it would be more precise to call it a "Bible of Hell" written by one who had been a member of the Devil's party and knew it well.

One index of Lowry's ability to amplify his experience, transmuting it into a pattern with universal implications, is his management of setting. While the fictional village of Quauhnahuac is loosely modeled on Cuernavaca, where Lowry lived between 1936 and 1938, there is no attempt at documentary realism. To be sure, Lowry selects elements from the real town—the surrounding mountains dominated by the great volcano, Popocatepetl; the Cortes palace, with its revolutionary frescoes; the Hotel Casino de la Selva; the dilapidated Borda Gardens of Maximilian and Carlota; the winding cobbled streets; the quaintly named cantinas; the fetid barranca, or ravine, winding through the town—but his rendering of them emphasizes not mere local color but the power of the mind to metamorphose external reality into an interlocking set of correspondences to the inner life. One of Lowry's strongest convictions was that life is, as Baudelaire said, a forest of symbols. Thus, Hernando Cortes's palace and the Diego Rivera frescoes adorning it suggest the Spanish Conquest and the Mexican Revolution of 1910-1920, which in turn suggest both the endless internecine conflicts of history and the perpetual battle of the individual human soul against the powers of darkness. The Borda Gardens embody similar meanings, along with the aura of doomed love.

The volcano literally looms large over the entire novel, its snowy summit serving as a symbol of the characters' spiritual aspiration toward ascent, while at its base winds the ubiquitous barranca, suggestive of an alternative destination awaiting the wayward soul. The proximity of the barranca to the totemic volcano and to the many gardens in the novel (most of them, like the Borda Gardens, overgrown, untended, and ruined) calls attention to one of Lowry's central themes: the "infernal paradise" that is the essence of Mexico and, by extension, the modern world itself. This oxymoronic image owes something to D. H. Lawrence, whose novel *The Plumed Serpent* (1926) similarly links the contradictions endemic to revolutionary Mexico with the struggle of his protagonist to undergo a kind of rebirth of spirit. In Lowry, however, the allure of the infernal paradise does not liberate his protagonist from the despoiled garden of life and propel him toward redemption; rather, it arrests him in a state of prolonged inertia, a paralysis of will that renders him finally incapable of actively pursuing the spiritual ascent he so often imagines for himself. In Lowry's version of the myth, at least in *Under the Volcano*, humans are condemned to inhabit a garden gone to seed, bereft of its creator: Paradise, surviving only as an image of longing, is irretrievably lost. Solipsistic dreams of ascent succeed only in preventing the upward progress of the soul and, indeed, in promoting its gradual descent into the infernal abyss.

Lowry's narrative, like his setting, is designed to encourage the reader to view the events in broadly symbolic terms. Apart from the opening chapter, which is set one year to the day after the events recounted in the rest of the novel, the narrative's present action is confined to the events of a single day, November 2, 1938, the last day in the life of the protagonist, Geoffrey Firmin, a former British consul and an alcoholic's alcoholic. It is also the last day in the life of his wife, Yvonne. The Firmins have been divorced for nearly a year, but on this holiday, known to all in Mexico as the Day of the Dead (All Soul's Day), Yvonne has returned to try to reconcile with Geoffrey. He realizes, however, that such a reconciliation—which he himself has desperately longed for during her absence—would require that he give up drinking, and this he cannot bring himself to do. They quarrel, fail at making love, and part for a time, the Consul to the company of a bottle, Yvonne to that of Geoffrey's half brother Hugh, formerly her lover. Later, the threesome make a day trip "downhill" by bus to Tomalín, where, as Hugh makes a spectacle of himself at an event called a "bull-throwing," Yvonne fervently proposes to Geoffrey that they leave Mexico and try to make a new life together in some "northern paradise" (clearly a reference to Dollarton).

At length, after more drinking and more quarreling, the Consul emphatically refuses and runs off alone, claiming that he prefers "hell" to her offer of a "sober" northern paradise. Pursuing Geoffrey in the darkness through the woods, Yvonne encounters a spooked horse and is trampled to death. The Consul, meanwhile, has gone to the lurid Farolito cantina in Parián, where, after a series of misunderstandings and mescal-inspired blunders—culminating in his freeing of a tethered horse (the same animal that tramples Yvonne in the forest), an act of fuddled yet genuine protest—he is accused of being a communist spy and is shot to death by fascist "irregular police." His body is thrown down into the barranca along with that of a dead dog. In the novel's opening chapter, these tragic events, along with many earlier incidents in the lives of the doomed Firmins, are recollected on the Day of the Dead one year later by Jacques Laruelle, a retired French film director who had once been the Consul's closest friend as well as another of Yvonne's lovers.

Such a summary is inevitably misleading, for *Under the Volcano*, like most of Lowry's fiction, really offers little in the way of conventional plot. For one thing, the story is deliberately deprived of any ordinary sort of suspense by the disclosure of its tragic outcome in the first chapter. What this curiously epilogue-like prologue accomplishes, among other things, is a displacement of emphasis away from the sequence of events themselves to their causes and, in the grief of M. Laruelle, some of their effects. Other disruptions of the superficial story interest stem from the frequent use of flashbacks (although strictly speaking, the entire novel after the first chapter is a flashback), as the characters brood on their past lives leading up to this day of crisis; from ellipses caused by the Consul's passing out or hallucinating; and from the constantly shifting narrative viewpoint. Five of the novel's twelve chapters are presented from the Consul's perspective, three from Yvonne's, three from Hugh's, and one from Laruelle's. The focus is thus chiefly inward, on the embattled consciousness of the characters.

Even the characters' surroundings in the external world—Laruelle's bizarre mosque-like house with the oracular inscription on one of the towers (*no se puede vivir sin amar*—"one cannot live without loving"); the municipal garden with its equally oracular warning sign (*¿Le gusta este jardín que es suyo? ¡Evite que sus hijos lo destruyan!*—"Do you like this garden that is yours? See that your children do not destroy it!"); the amusement park rides, including a loop-the-loop contraption called (after a play by Jean Cocteau) *La Máquina Infernal* and a "luminous wheel" that is as much time or fortune as a Ferris wheel; the advertisements for a horror film, *The Hands of Orlac*, about an artist-turned-murderer; a cantina called *La Sepultura* and another called *Salón Ofelia*; the forest around Quauhnahuac and Parián equated repeatedly with Dante's dark wood—all of these external places or objects (and there are many other examples) are essentially coordinates on the map of the mind that the novel traces. Indeed, so densely overgrown is Lowry's "forest of symbols" that one can sometimes lose sight of the immediate or human level of the story. At such junctures, time seems to be arrested or abolished by the self-reflexive play of images and motifs, just as it does in T. S. Eliot's *The Waste Land* (1922) and other great "spatializing" works in the modernist tradition. In *Under the Volcano*, however, the force of time is powerfully affirmed at the bottom of the reeking barranca.

Despite the novel's inward focus, Lowry manages to achieve an ironic detachment from his characters. This is no mean feat, not only because of the autobiographical origins of the story but also because the Consul himself lays claim to ironic detachment even as he observes his own downfall. Lowry's detachment is achieved precisely through the form of the novel, an exceedingly complex design that includes but is finally larger than even the Consul and his remarkably resourceful capacity to transform his life into species of "quixotic oral fiction." Even though the Consul's tragedy in a moral sense is of his own making, it is made by Lowry to resonate like a central melodic pattern within an enormous surrounding symphonic structure. In part, this resonance derives from the novel's frequent echoing of its own infernal music—the leitmotifs mentioned previously. Equally important are the allusive echoes to literature, myth, and history.

The novel teems with allusions direct and implicit to the Bible, the Kabbala, Sophocles, Ovid, Dante, Christopher Marlowe, William Shakespeare, Johann Wolfgang von Goethe, William Blake, Percy Bysshe Shelley, Edgar Allan Poe, Herman Melville, Joseph Conrad, and T. S. Eliot, among others. Persistently, the Consul's situation is compared (often by the Consul himself) with that of Oedipus, Prometheus, Adam, Christ, Judas, the Fisher King, Faust, and Hamlet. These allusions, moreover, are not gratuitous. Individually and collectively, they amount to a kind of running commentary on the pattern of heroism to which the Consul, and sometimes the other characters, aspire, and against which his downfall may be measured. What is one to make, for example, of a hero who, at one moment, proclaims in impressive Promethean tones that "the will of man is unconquerable. Even God cannot conquer it," and who collapses "with a crash," unconscious, the next?

Even more tellingly ironic are the historical analogues that Lowry draws between the Consul and such figures as Cortes, William Blackstone the explorer, Maximilian, and General Victoriano Huerta. All of the latter were men of action, which the Consul emphatically is not; yet, like him, they all became involved, sooner or later, in nefarious political intrigues whose result—sometimes unwittingly—was the exploitation of a subject people, usually of another nation or race. During World War I, Geoffrey, then lieutenant commander of a Q-boat, the SS *Samaritan*, was obscurely implicated in the murder of captured German officers; and as Lowry wrote to Cape, "you can even see the German submarine officers taking revenge on the Consul in the form of the *sinarquistas* and semi-fascist *brutos* at the end." However absurd on the face of it, the political pretexts for the murder of the Consul by the pro-Fascists carry a certain underlying truth.

In an important episode in chapter 8, a wounded Mexican Indian is found by the roadside. Because of a Mexican law prohibiting any interference in a crime, even after the fact, the Consul prevents Hugh from attempting to help the dying man. *"Compañero,"* the Indian says, appealing to them, but all they can do is ruminate on the horror of it all, even as another traveler on the bus to Tomalín openly steals the dying man's money. Clearly, there is but a small difference between this sin of commission, the theft, and the Consul's sin of omission, so that in the last chapter, it is fitting that he should be "the one dying by the wayside and no good Samaritan would halt." "We evict those who destroy," warns the terrible sign in the garden (as meaningfully mistranslated by the Consul) and, like Cortes, Huerta, and no doubt every other person, in one diluted way or another, Geoffrey Firmin stands guilty at heart: "*No se puede vivir sin amar.*"

While Lowry more than encourages the reader to see his characters against this elaborate backdrop of interrelated allusions, symbols, and motifs, however, it would be a mistake to overemphasize the backdrop at the expense of the foreground figures. The Consul, Hugh, Yvonne, and Laruelle are the cynosures through whose eyes the reader is allowed to glimpse the "massive interests" of a world sliding into the abyss beneath the volcano. At the same time, there is admittedly a deficiency in Lowry's portrayal of character, if by "portrayal" one has in mind the conventions of realistic characterization such as found in Henry James. Lowry was well aware of this deficiency. "The truth is," he wrote to Jonathan Cape, "that the character drawing [in *Under the Volcano*] is not only weak but virtually nonexistent, save with certain minor characters, the four main characters being intended, in one of the book's meanings, to be aspects of the same man, or of the human spirit." Lowry seems almost to be opting for a kind of allegorist's stance when he adds that there "are a thousand writers who can draw adequate characters till all is blue for one who can tell you something new about hell fire. And I am telling you something new about hell fire." This is, as it were, Lowry's *donnée*. He is not particularly interested in his characters as fully realized individuals whose development over the course of time is gradually presented.

The four main characters are all, as he said to Cape, "aspects of the same man." Hugh is "Everyman tightened up a screw . . . the youth of Everyman"; Yvonne is "the eternal woman," the anima principle; Laruelle is the Consul's doppelgänger, a surrogate for the artist/betrayer with blood on his hands. Although Lowry has provided glimpses into these characters' past lives, his purpose is less to trace the etiology of, for example, the Consul's alcoholism, than it is to locate key moments that chime with the present situation or offer ironic contrast to it. As Terence Wright has noted,

> Lowry is not concerned with the Consul's fall as a *process*, nor with the attempts to save him as a thing which may or may not be accomplished, but with the *contemplation* of a state of affairs—the state of affairs being that a man is in Hell.

Notwithstanding the Consul's grandiose gestures toward Promethean rebellion, what is really most remarkable about him is his readiness to embrace his own death and damnation. This is perhaps what Lowry was referring to when he claimed to be teaching the world "something new about hell fire." The Consul knows, as his very utterance indicates ("A corpse will be transported by express!"), that his "glorious" descent is nearing its conclusion and that death is imminent, just as the reader knows, from the opening chapter, that Geoffrey has already succeeded in finding the disaster he has so ardently courted. This curious sense that everything has already happened conditions the whole feeling of the book and makes possible a range of effects—including moments of wild comedy and soaring lyricism—that one would not ordinarily expect to find in a tragic tale. It is as if the Consul, having resigned himself to the inevitability of his downfall, having indeed long since chosen the "hell" of addiction, solipsism, and despair represented for him by the Farolito, can undergo his descent and simultaneously observe himself descending, even deriving a certain amusement from the spectacle. The Consul's semidetachment from his own suffering derives in part from his very awareness of the paradigms of tragic downfall in literature, above all Marlowe's Doctor Faustus, whose despairing quest for forbidden knowledge he deliberately emulates. At the same time, indulging in this "heroic" despair, he seems to harbor the illusion (derived this time from Blake) that "right through hell there is a path" leading to a "new life" beyond: By sinking as low as it is possible for a man to sink, giving himself over to complete damnation, he will somehow be saved in the end.

Salvation, however, will come, if it comes, not in the form of a loving union with Yvonne in some sober northern paradise but in the form of mystical vision—a state of mind for which, he believes, alcohol is "*absolutamente necesario*." The Consul regards his drinking as a religious exercise comparable to the partaking of an eternal sacrament. His determination to resist the meddling "salvage operations" of Hugh and Yvonne takes on the significance of a kind of holy war, an anticrusade, so to speak. As he tells Jacques

Laruelle, he is fighting for nothing less than "the survival of the human consciousness." The fact that these are, on one level, an alcoholic's rationalizations does not alter the issue. Drink, as the principal means of access to the visionary state, has become an integral part of his quest for occult knowledge and, as such, is immutably associated with a peculiar kind of fulfillment that the Consul has actually known: "How, unless you drink as I do, can you hope to understand the beauty of an old woman from Tarasco who plays dominoes [in the cantina] at seven o'clock in the morning?"

This mixture of attitudes accounts for the "tragic joy" that, for a time, mitigates the gathering darkness of *Under the Volcano*. The Consul's vision at such moments is of genuinely heroic proportions, for he succeeds not merely in embracing Faustian despair but in transcending it, albeit fleetingly. The Consul is a man of awesome imaginative energies and tremendous resources of humor and intelligence, so that when he dies, the reader experiences that sense of immense waste that accompanies the deaths of great tragic heroes such as Doctor Faustus. The very qualities that set him apart, however, contribute directly to his downfall. The ultimate irony here is that even though he succeeds in finding at the Farolito the "hell" he has sought all along, he succeeds "in a manner somewhat outside his calculations." He finds that damnation is not so ennobling—much less is it an amusing object for detached contemplation—after all. Knocked flat on his face by the shots of a Chief of Rostrums (of all people), the Consul is disappointed, as he was bound to be: "Christ . . . this is a dingy way to die," he tells himself. At this point, the Consul in effect sloughs off the trappings of a borrowed literary heroism and achieves his own "autochthonous" stature as a hero. He dies not as a modern-day Faustus but as Geoffrey Firmin, self-evicted from the potential satisfaction of living in even an infernal paradise. Nevertheless, as he lies dying, shorn of all vestiges of grandiosity, he recognizes what, in his solipsism, he has become. He acknowledges the tragic error of attempting to live without loving—faces, that is, his own essential humanity—though, as his final vision of climbing the volcano only to find himself hurtling down into it makes clear, it is too late for him to act on this new awareness. Moreover, even if he could somehow act, Yvonne is no longer attainable, thanks to his last defiant gesture of releasing the horse.

The novel closes with the Consul's final vision (chorically echoed by the oracular warning sign in the ruined garden), at once the culminating comment on his life of solipsistic denial and a vision of apocalyptic destruction:

> The world itself was bursting, bursting into black spouts of villages catapulted into space, with himself falling through it all, through the inconceivable pandemonium of a million tanks, through the blazing of ten million burning bodies, falling, into a forest, falling.

LATER WORKS

Although *Under the Volcano* is Lowry's best and most highly regarded work, his other pieces have received more sympathetic treatment. Muriel C. Bradbrook was the first to call attention to Lowry's early experiences on the Wirral Peninsula, in public school, and at Cambridge as in many ways the crucial source of his mature vision, an emphasis that nicely balances Douglas Day's excessive dwelling on the last, doom-haunted years.

Ronald Binns is one of several critics to examine Lowry's fiction after *Under the Volcano* both seriously and sympathetically, finding in it evidence of a new direction toward the metafictional mode of such postmodernists as Samuel Beckett, Vladimir Nabokov, and Jorge Luis Borges, rather than mere failed attempts to repeat the "high modernist" performance that links *Under the Volcano* with the older tradition of James Joyce and Marcel Proust. For her part, Sherrill Grace maintains that *Under the Volcano* is "best viewed as the magnificent Popocatepetl among lesser, but by no means uninteresting, peaks." In short, although *Under the Volcano* still stands as Lowry's undisputed masterpiece, an adequate appreciation of his complex achievement finally depends on a firm understanding of his "bolus" as a whole. When this understanding occurs, there is reason to believe that Lowry will be recognized as one of the greatest of modern visionary artists.

Ronald G. Walker

OTHER MAJOR WORKS

SHORT FICTION: *Hear Us O Lord from Heaven Thy Dwelling Place*, 1961; *Malcolm Lowry: Psalms and Songs*, 1975 (Margerie Bonner Lowry, editor).

POETRY: *Selected Poems*, 1962 (Earle Birney, editor); *The Collected Poetry of Malcolm Lowry*, 1992 (Kathleen Scherf, editor).

NONFICTION: *Selected Letters of Malcolm Lowry*, 1965 (Harvey Breit and Margerie Bonner Lowry, editors); *Sursum corda! The Collected Letters of Malcolm Lowry*, 1995-1997 (2 volumes; Sherrill E. Grace, editor).

MISCELLANEOUS: *Notes on a Screenplay for F. Scott Fitzgerald's "Tender Is the Night,"* 1976 (with Margerie Bonner Lowry); *The Voyage That Never Ends: Malcolm Lowry in His Own Words, Fictions, Poems, Fragments and Letters*, 2007 (Michael Hofmann, editor).

BIBLIOGRAPHY

Asals, Frederick. *The Making of Malcolm Lowry's "Under the Volcano."* Athens: University of Georgia Press, 1997. Charts the slow development of the novel, examining the various manuscripts Lowry produced between 1940 and 1947 and analyzing the implications of the novel's revisions. Includes bibliography and index.

Asals, Frederick, and Paul Tiessen, eds. *A Darkness That Murmured: Essays on Malcolm Lowry and the Twentieth Century*. Toronto, Ont.: University of Toronto Press, 2000. Collection of essays features contributions by the best-known Lowry scholars as well as by people who knew the author, including his first wife. Essays cover biographical material as well as criticism and interpretation of Lowry's work. Includes bibliography and index.

Binns, Ronald. *Malcolm Lowry.* New York: Methuen, 1984. Brief work discusses the Lowry "myth," with emphasis given to *Under the Volcano* and the autobiographical elements in Lowry's writing. The chapter on metafiction is a particularly useful survey of Lowry's late experimental novels and stories. A valuable guide for the beginning reader of Lowry.

Bowker, Gordon. *Malcolm Lowry Remembered.* London: British Broadcasting Corporation, 1985. Readable collection of reminiscences that attempt to "penetrate the myth and reach the man." Includes interviews with Lowry's two former wives and many of his friends and admirers.

_______. *Pursued by Furies: A Life of Malcolm Lowry.* New York: St. Martin's Press, 1995. Comprehensive, scholarly biography includes a preface that provides pithy comments on the relationship between Lowry's life and his fiction. Argues that Lowry's life after the publication of *Under the Volcano* grew so chaotic that he was unable to devote his attention to writing a comparable novel.

Costa, Richard Hauer. *Malcolm Lowry.* New York: Twayne, 1972. Approaches the study of Lowry's work from a Jungian perspective, looking at the author's "mystical-messianic aspects." The second half of this volume deals with Lowry's work during his fifteen years in Canada.

Gabrial, Jan. *Inside the Volcano: My Life with Malcolm Lowry.* New York: St. Martin's Press, 2000. Lowry's first wife presents a very personal view of the author. Includes photographs and index.

Grace, Sherrill, ed. *Swinging the Maelstrom: New Perspectives on Malcolm Lowry.* Montreal: McGill-Queen's University Press, 1992. Collection of essays begins with an editor's introduction that serves as a useful guide to Lowry's reputation. Part 1 contains essays on the relationship between Lowry's life and his fiction, part 2 concentrates on *Under the Volcano*, part 3 examines Lowry's subsequent fiction, and part 4 presents assessments of his body of work.

McCarthy, Patrick A. *Forests of Symbols: World, Text, and Self in Malcolm Lowry's Fiction.* Athens: University of Georgia Press, 1994. Presents a critical interpretation of Lowry's work, his use of symbols, and his emphasis on the nature of self and psychology in his work. Includes bibliography and index.

Markson, David. *Malcolm Lowry's Volcano: Myth, Symbol, Meaning.* New York: Times Books, 1978. Critical study examines Lowry's *Under the Volcano*, considered his masterpiece and recognized by many critics as a major novel of the twentieth century. Indispensable to the serious scholar of Lowry.

Woodcock, George, ed. *Malcolm Lowry: The Man and His Work.* Tonawanda, N.Y.: Black Rose Books, 2007. Collection of essays provides analysis of all of Lowry's fiction as well as discussion of the influences on Lowry's writings, including his life experiences and his love of jazz and films.

HUGH MACLENNAN

Born: Glace Bay, Nova Scotia, Canada; March 20, 1907
Died: Montreal, Quebec, Canada; November 7, 1990
Also known as: John Hugh MacLennan

PRINCIPAL LONG FICTION

Barometer Rising, 1941
Two Solitudes, 1945
The Precipice, 1948
Each Man's Son, 1951
The Watch That Ends the Night, 1959
Return of the Sphinx, 1967
Voices in Time, 1980

OTHER LITERARY FORMS

Throughout his career, Hugh MacLennan was a prolific writer of nonfiction. Following his youthful attempts at poetry and the publication of his dissertation on a Roman colonial settlement in Egypt, *Oxyrhynchus: An Economic and Social Study* (1935, 1968), MacLennan began writing articles, reviews, autobiographical pieces, travel notes, and essays, publishing in a variety of magazines, including *The Montrealer*, *Maclean's*, and *Holiday*. Journalism sometimes served as a necessary supplement to his income and occasionally was used to try out material later incorporated into his novels. It has been claimed that his talent finds truer expression in his essays than in his novels; while this may be a questionable judgment, there is no denying the excellence of much of his nonfiction. Selections from the more than four hundred essays that he wrote have been collected in four books, the first two of which won Canada's Governor-General's Award: *Cross-Country* (1949), *Thirty and Three* (1954), *Scotchman's Return, and Other Essays* (1960), and *The Other Side of Hugh MacLennan: Selected Essays Old and New* (1978, Elspeth Cameron, editor). Additionally, his concern for Canada's history and geography found expression in his *Seven Rivers of Canada* (1961; revised as *Rivers of Canada*, 1974) and *The Colour of Canada* (1967). *Rivers of Canada*, in which MacLennan provided the text to accompany the beautiful photography of John de Visser, contains some of his best writing.

ACHIEVEMENTS

Hugh MacLennan, as his biographer, Elspeth Cameron, has observed, "set out to be a writer, not a 'Canadian' writer," yet it was as a Canadian "nationalist" that he was first recognized, and in spite of his intermittent attempts to renounce this label, it was as a distinctively Canadian writer that his career and his reputation developed. He held a solid place as something like the dean of Canadian letters; for many years he was a public figure in

Canada, appearing on radio and television, frequently being asked to comment not only on Canadian writing but also on culture generally and on politics. He made continual attempts to tap the American market (with some success, especially with *The Watch That Ends the Night*), his works have been translated into many languages, and his last novel, *Voices in Time*, is international in setting, yet MacLennan was thought of both in his own country and elsewhere as a, perhaps *the*, Canadian novelist.

Having written two unpublished novels with international settings, MacLennan turned to his own Halifax, Nova Scotia, when writing *Barometer Rising*. This first published novel was immediately successful and was praised for its Canadian nationalism. His next novel, *Two Solitudes*, treated the divisions between the English and French cultures in Quebec; the book's title, taken from Rainer Maria Rilke, entered popular usage as a convenient phrase to sum up this cultural schism. MacLennan continued to be hailed for his contributions to defining a Canadian identity. When his third novel, *The Precipice*, attempted to develop an international theme, presenting the love between a Canadian woman and an American man, he met with less critical acceptance. He returned to writing about Nova Scotia in *Each Man's Son* and followed this with a novel set primarily in Montreal, *The Watch That Ends the Night*. This work was both a critical success and a best seller, not only in Canada but also throughout the English-speaking world; it also sold well in translation. MacLennan's reputation as a major novelist was assured; it was bolstered by Edmund Wilson's lavish praise in *O Canada* (1965). Even the many unfavorable reviews of MacLennan's subsequent novel, *Return of the Sphinx*, which treated the Quebec independence movement, did not call into question his importance in Canadian writing. Those who thought this importance was only historical and that his novelistic powers had passed their peak were proven wrong by his subsequent and last novel, *Voices in Time*, which was well received even though it clearly transcended Canadian national issues.

As *Voices in Time* suggests, seeing MacLennan in the narrow focus of Canadian nationalism is too limiting. It is certainly true that his work was informed by his nationality and that younger Canadian writers owe a debt to his pioneering treatment of Canadian themes. It is also true that his achievement must be primarily judged thematically. While he was competent in plotting and occasionally excellent in characterization, these were not his strong points. He was a conservative novelist in craft, contributing no new forms to the genre, although his own technique did develop, especially in his use of point of view and manipulation of time.

Granting that MacLennan emphasized theme and wrote out of his Canadian experience, his relationship to Canada can be best understood, however, if he is seen not as a nationalist or a local colorist, but rather as a writer who used his Canadian background to put into perspective his political, social, and psychological ideas and to reinforce his sense of history. It is essentially as a creator of novels of ideas that MacLennan bids fair to appeal to future generations of readers around the world.

Biography

John Hugh MacLennan was born in Glace Bay, Cape Breton, Nova Scotia, on March 20, 1907. He drew on his memories of this birthplace, a coal-mining company town set at the edge of the Atlantic, explicitly in *Each Man's Son*, but his impressions of the seagirt land, a topography appropriate to the Scottish Highland character that was his heritage, entered, less directly, into much of his work. In this setting, his father practiced medicine among the miners. A dominating figure, "the Doctor" was to become the prototype of a number of characters in his son's novels.

In 1915, when MacLennan was eight, the family moved to Halifax, a venerable but lively port that fascinated the boy. The small city, with its sense of community, became a lifelong ideal for MacLennan, as did the contrasting beauty of the Cape Breton countryside where the family spent time in the summer, prefiguring the thematic retreat to the woods of many of MacLennan's fictional characters. As recounted in *Barometer Rising*, much of Halifax was destroyed by an explosion in 1917, but the city was rebuilt, and MacLennan was reared there, doing well in both studies and sports, and graduated from Dalhousie University in 1928.

Later in that year, a Rhodes scholarship allowed him to attend Oxford. While there he played rugby and tennis; an excellent athlete, MacLennan, as a novelist, frequently used sports to reveal character. At Oxford, he also wrote poetry and traveled extensively, during vacations, on the Continent. These holidays, especially those to Germany, were drawn upon in his first two, unpublished, novels and returned to in *Voices in Time*, and some of his own experiences from this time were used in creating those of his character, Paul, in *Two Solitudes*.

MacLennan also studied at Oxford, quite diligently in fact, and graduated in 1932, proceeding to graduate studies at Princeton. Returning to England, he met, on the ship, an American, Dorothy Duncan, who was to become his first wife. His developing love and his new devotion to becoming a novelist absorbed more of his attention than did his studies. While he did not find Princeton congenial, he completed his Ph.D. in history, with a dissertation discussing the Roman colonial settlement at Oxyrhynchus in Egypt.

In 1935, in the midst of the Depression, MacLennan's degree was not able to secure for him the university teaching position he desired; he accepted a job teaching at Lower Canada College, a boys' school in Montreal. (He was to give a fictionalized satiric portrait of the school in *The Watch That Ends the Night*.) After a year at the school, he married Dorothy Duncan and settled into a life of working as a schoolmaster during the day and writing at night, sinking in roots as a Montrealer, which he was to remain.

His first novel, *So All Their Praises*, had been completed while MacLennan was at Princeton; it was accepted by a publisher that ceased operation before the book was published. His second novel, *A Man Should Rejoice*, suffered a similar fate in 1938; its publication was postponed and finally dropped. These novels, the first owing a debt to Ernest Hemingway, the second to John Dos Passos, although never published, have their virtues.

They both present comments on the political situation preceding World War II and employ international settings.

For his next novel, MacLennan turned, at his wife's suggestion, to Canada. *Barometer Rising* is set in Halifax in 1917. It was an immediate success. MacLennan continued his teaching and writing career in Montreal; an ear problem kept him out of the war. After the success of his second published novel, *Two Solitudes*, and the establishment, additionally, of his wife's successful career as a writer (Dorothy Duncan published nonfiction; one of her books, *Partner in Three Worlds*, 1944, won the Governor-General's Award for nonfiction), he resigned from Lower Canada College in 1945. Following a period of journalism and broadcasting and the publication of *The Precipice*, in 1951 he took a part-time position teaching in the English department at McGill University; he assumed a full-time post in 1964, becoming professor emeritus in 1979.

During the years in which he was establishing himself as a writer in Montreal, publishing *Cross-Country*, *Each Man's Son*, and *Thirty and Three* (a period described in *The Watch That Ends the Night*), his wife's declining health—she suffered a series of embolisms—added greatly to the pressures he experienced. Dorothy Duncan died in 1957. MacLennan dedicated *The Watch That Ends the Night* to her; the novel, originally titled *Requiem*, has as its heroine a figure whose characterization owes much to Dorothy Duncan. MacLennan married Frances Walker in 1959 and after a period of producing nonfiction—*Scotchman's Return, and Other Essays* and *Seven Rivers of Canada*—wrote *Return of the Sphinx*. This novel was unfavorably reviewed by a number of Canadian critics, but MacLennan continued to receive numerous honorary degrees and public recognition. He began consideration of another novel, but interrupted work on it to write *Rivers of Canada*. His last novel, *Voices in Time*, appeared to favorable reviews in 1980. In 1982, MacLennan retired from McGill, after more than thirty years of teaching there. He died in Montreal on November 7, 1990, at the age of eighty-three.

ANALYSIS

Hugh MacLennan began as a historian, and, in a sense, he remained one throughout his long writing career. His doctoral dissertation, *Oxyrhynchus*, discussing the history of an area in Egypt during the seven hundred years that it was subject to the Roman Empire, foreshadowed such major themes in his novels as colonialism, the wanderer, the town-country antithesis, and geographical determinism. Underlying both the dissertation and the novels is a view of historical causality.

As Erich Auerbach has remarked, "Basically, the way in which we view human life and society is the same whether we are concerned with things of the past or things of the present"; a corollary of this may be that when a writer is, like MacLennan, both a historian and a novelist, his or her narratives of individual human lives will be shaped by larger forces that transcend the concerns of the psychological novelist. In MacLennan's fiction, geography is preeminently such a force.

In both his fiction and his nonfiction, MacLennan had a continual concern for the impact of geography on character, and thus, as people make history, on action, fictive or historical. That a Canadian, living in a frequently harsh terrain and climate, would appreciate the significance of geography is hardly surprising, but MacLennan went further, adopting a geographical theory of history. His sense of geography's interaction with psychology and history provides the ideological framework that, more than any other single factor, gives his work its distinctive character. This framework is especially useful to MacLennan as a way of putting into perspective his personal experience, for he drew less on "pure" invention than do many novelists. His method, in both his essays and his novels, was to use personal experience to support general and philosophical concepts.

This means that, fundamentally, MacLennan wrote novels of ideas; it does not mean, however, that his ideas were necessarily free from self-contradiction or that they remained entirely consistent throughout his career. His ideology, complex but ultimately growing from a sense of the fundamental importance of geography, is most explicit in his first three published novels, in which he worked toward a definition of Canadian identity by first contrasting Canada to England (*Barometer Rising*), then dealing with the potentials of Canadian unity (*Two Solitudes*), and finally differentiating Canada from the United States (*The Precipice*). The next novel, *Each Man's Son*, is transitional in that it conveys a strong sense of the land, Cape Breton in this case, while anticipating the greater interest in psychology that characterized his subsequent novels. Even in these later novels, however, history as geography remains a basic concept. While psychological concepts became more important to MacLennan, he employed topographical images to express this interest.

Character, then, in a MacLennan novel is closely related to theme, as is plot, and the theme is tied to setting. While he created a fairly wide range of characters, including some minor figures that are presented with Dickensian humor, the central focus in his characterization was either on the "love interest" or on a conflict of generations. Both of these recurring motifs are normally subservient to theme in that the characters, whether they come together in love, as, for example, Paul and Heather in *Two Solitudes*, or stand apart in years, as do Alan Ainslie and his son in *Return of the Sphinx*, represent different value systems or cultures. Their psychology, which motivates their interactions, is seen in terms of their conditioning by history and, ultimately, by geography.

Admittedly, this emphasis is modified, especially in the later novels, by MacLennan's concern with various ideological factors, such as Calvinism in *Each Man's Son*, and by his interest in psychological theories, especially Freudianism, particularly notable in *Return of the Sphinx*. Nevertheless, similar imagery and recurring motifs, reflecting a sense of historical causation, run through both his earlier and later works. One finds, for example, the antithesis between the city and the country; the retreat into the woods; the theme of the wanderer, exiled from his or her roots; frequent references to weather; and imagery of trees, gardens, and water, in all of his novels.

MacLennan's novelistic techniques did change, however, as he developed his craft, as can be seen in his plotting, use of point of view, and style. In plotting, as in many aspects of his craft, MacLennan was old-fashioned; he kept the reader interested in how the story will come out. MacLennan was by nature given to relatively happy endings, but after the upbeat conclusions characterizing his first three novels, his optimism became tempered, appearing more as a coda following climactic elements of tragedy in *Each Man's Son, The Watch That Ends the Night*, and *Return of the Sphinx. Voices in Time* has a series of climaxes occurring at different points in the novel and producing different effects on the reader. That MacLennan was able to unify the various narratives included in this, the most complex of his works in its plotting, is an indication of the development of his craftsmanship.

His ability to manipulate increasingly complex narrative patterns is closely related to his mastery of point of view. Although none of MacLennan's novels approaches a Jamesian concern for this aspect of the art of fiction, with *The Watch That Ends the Night*, as he moved away from straightforward chronological sequences, he slipped skillfully between first- and third-person narration. *Return of the Sphinx* uses third-person narration but with a shifting between the viewpoints of different characters. This novel, however, lacks what Henry James called "a fine central intelligence." Alan Ainslie does not provide this unifying quality as effectively as does John Wellfleet in *Voices in Time*; Wellfleet's perspective gives coherence to the novel's varied narrative strands.

As MacLennan's ability to structure his novels developed, slowly and within a fairly conventional framework, yet with increasing skill in his craft, so did his style mature. His earlier novels exhibited some tendency toward overwriting: *Barometer Rising* has "set pieces" that skirt the borders of sentimentality, *Two Solitudes* is sometimes verbose, and *The Precipice* is not free from clichéd expression. In *Each Man's Son*, the style, reflecting the dramatic structure, is tightened. *The Watch That Ends the Night* contains superior passages of description, although the dialogue (never one of MacLennan's strengths) occasionally shows some of the stilted qualities of the earlier novels. *Return of the Sphinx* is notable for its economy of style and in this respect prepares for *Voices in Time*, in which MacLennan's style is the most fully unselfconscious and "organic."

MacLennan, then, is a novelist whose works may be read for the pleasure to be found in an interesting story well told, but he remains a writer less likely to be remembered as a storyteller or fictional craftsperson than as a man of ideas, a dramatizer of history.

BAROMETER RISING

When, following his wife's advice to write about what he knew best, MacLennan turned to his hometown, Halifax; he used it not only as the novel's setting but also as its subject. In *Barometer Rising*, he was also writing of Canada; Halifax, with its colonial attitudes overlaying social and ideological divisions, is a microcosm of a new Canada. The book's title is in large part explained in a subsequent essay, in which MacLennan describes Halifax as a barometer for the whole country.

What goes up must have been down; if the barometer rises—if, by implication, Canada faces a halcyon future—it does so only after a great storm and a particularly violent stroke of lightning. The action of *Barometer Rising* is centered on an actual historical event, the blast that occurred when a munitions ship exploded in Halifax harbor on December 6, 1917. The largest single human-made explosion before the use of the atomic bomb at Hiroshima, it destroyed a major portion of the town and killed some two thousand people.

A result of Halifax's role in World War I, the explosion is also symbolically related to Canada's involvement in that bloody conflict. While the concurrent destruction of life, property, and outworn colonial beliefs—the old world dying with a monstrous bang—constitutes the core of the book, a number of other motifs are woven into its thematic patterns. The conflict of generations, the return of the wanderer and the Odysseus theme, the psychological aspects of technological change—these are all important elements of the novel that continued to reverberate in MacLennan's subsequent work. Underlying all the thematic strands is the author's view of historical process, a view that puts a strong emphasis on the conditioning significance of physical geography.

It is Halifax's geographical situation that underlies the book's basic contrast, that between old and new Canada, colony and country. The harbor gives the town its meaning; facing away from the rest of Canada, Halifax looks toward Britain and the Continent, in both a literal and a figurative sense. From the topographical facts, carefully elaborated at the beginning of the novel, derive the prevailing attitudes of the Haligonians: it is the preservation of England that motivates all of what happens in Halifax; the colonial mentality prevails. Had the geography been different, the town's development and activity would have been different, and, consequently, its people would have been different.

If geography is destiny, however, there is no rigid determinism in MacLennan's view of that destiny. Halifax, although pointed toward Britain physically and thus psychologically as well, is part of the New World and has, therefore, the potential for a different orientation. This reorientation follows from the book's central event, the explosion, an event that, while the result of accident, is influenced by topography in both cause and effect. The explosion is a result of the collision, in Halifax harbor, of a munitions ship with a Norwegian freighter; the crash occurs because the physical nature of the harbor limits visibility. As a result of the destruction, new values arise from the rubble of the old; Halifax is no longer dominated by the rigid ideas of its old colonial aristocracy.

While the story has this allegorical quality, with a message made explicit in a concluding passage on what might be termed Canada's "manifest destiny," its allegory is fleshed out with particular, three-dimensional characters, conditioned by geography and history, but living out their private lives within the interstices of that conditioning framework.

Neil Macrae, the book's hero, is, like Odysseus, a soldier returned from the war, bearing an assumed identity acquired after he was falsely accused of disobeying an order during an attack in which he was thought to have been killed. His accuser is the novel's villain, Colonel Wain, representative of the old order and father of Penelope—whose Homeric name is intentional—the heroine with whom Neil is in love. The cast is completed by a number of skillfully drawn secondary characters derived from MacLennan's memories, including Penny's younger brother Roddie, modeled on MacLennan himself, and Angus Murray, also in love with Penny, the first in a series of heroic doctors who appear in MacLennan's novels.

Following the explosion and the vindication of Neil's conduct during the attack in France (the outcome of the battle depending, just as does the collision in the harbor, on terrain), Neil and Penelope are finally united; the storm is over, and the future is bright. While the novel is marred by this rather facile happy ending and by its general didacticism, the basic interest in both action and character, reinforced with symbolism, makes *Barometer Rising* artistically satisfying. Although MacLennan was to write more subtly in future novels, *Barometer Rising*, representing clearly his basic approach, fiction as dramatized history, remains one of his best achievements.

TWO SOLITUDES *and* THE PRECIPICE

MacLennan's next two novels also use love stories to express theme and continue to demonstrate his interest in the impact of geography on the character of a people. *Two Solitudes*, centered on the romance between Paul Tallard and Heather Methuen, begins with a description of the landscape of Quebec; throughout, the symbolism of the river, the forest, and the town reinforces the theme of the relationship of the English and French in Quebec.

The Precipice, with its love affair between a Canadian woman and an American man, contrasts Canada and the United States by relating the characters of the peoples to their respective terrains. Set primarily in Ontario, the novel uses Lake Ontario as a dominant symbol, reinforced by references to weather, gardens, the city, and other imagery prevalent in MacLennan's fiction.

EACH MAN'S SON

Similar imagery informs *Each Man's Son*; thematic conflicts are drawn between two sides of the Scottish Highland character, between religion as a sense of sin and religion as inspiration, and between science and superstition, particularly focused through the contrast between the mines and the sea of Cape Breton. A major turning point in the plot occurs when Dr. Ainslie (whose name is taken from a Cape Breton place-name) gives his to-be-adopted son, Alan, a lesson in history, followed by one in geography.

THE WATCH THAT ENDS THE NIGHT

Arguably MacLennan's best novel, *The Watch That Ends the Night* demonstrates a significant advance in his technique. The didactic quality of his earlier novels is reduced; the imagery becomes more involved, as does the handling of time; characters take on more interest, not as symbols, but in their own right. Concurrently, the sense of the formative power of geography on character is moved more to the background, as though Canada, having been conditioned by geography, is able to go beyond this conditioning. Nevertheless, in this, as in all his novels, MacLennan writes from essentially the same perspective on history and employs many of the same patterns in fictional construction.

Again, just as in the earlier novels, the book is based on a strong sense of place, in this case Montreal, described in memorable, often loving detail. Again, the plot centers on a love interest, a triangle involving George Stewart, who has autobiographical connections with MacLennan; Jerome Martell, a doctor with mythic qualities; and Catherine Carey, a remarkable woman (who takes on, for Canada, some of the symbolism Kathleen ni Houlihan does for Ireland) whose portrait owes something to MacLennan's wife Dorothy. George loves Catherine, but she marries Martell. After Martell is thought to have been killed by the Nazis, Catherine and George eventually marry, but, much later, Martell reappears. (The story begins at this point, and is told primarily through flashbacks.) Although Catherine stays with George, suffering a heart condition, she has little time left to live.

Within this framework, MacLennan presents a rich picture, with numerous well-realized minor characters, of Montreal during the Depression and during the time of the Korean War. For all his interest in psychology in this work, it is, as are all his novels, less a "novel of character" than a working out, through characters, of ideas, and a dramatization of social-historical processes. While the plot (except in the New Brunswick section) does not hinge on terrain, the imagery does. Images derived from nature control much of the book's tone, with references to rivers and oceans particularly important. In *The Watch That Ends the Night*, MacLennan moved beyond any mechanistic application of historical theory to the novel; he did not, however, change his fundamental view of the forces underlying human events.

Return of the Sphinx

His next novel, *Return of the Sphinx*, reintroduced Alan, from *Each Man's Son*, now a grown man with his own son. Dealing, on the surface, with events of the Quebec liberation movement in the 1960's, it is set mainly in Montreal and Ottawa but contains a "retreat to the woods" section and begins with an explicit statement of the impact of geography and weather on culture; it ends with images of the land. Beneath the political action lies a deeper psychological theme, in essence that of the Oedipus complex, as MacLennan extends in this novel his interest in psychological theory, begun in *Each Man's Son* and continued in *The Watch That Ends the Night*; he also extends his use of imagery derived from nature and geography to express psychological states.

Voices in Time

In MacLennan's final novel, *Voices in Time*, his lifelong interest in the perspective provided by history is obvious and central to the book's structure. Indeed, the direct, albeit complicated manner in which this interest informs the novel may be a key to its success. MacLennan's focus on history was always essentially pragmatic—to use the past to understand the present and anticipate the future; this is what *Voices in Time* undertakes.

The book intertwines the story of three men from three different generations: Conrad

Dehmel, born in Germany in 1910, a concentration camp survivor; Timothy Wellfleet, a Canadian born in 1938 who becomes a television interviewer; and John Wellfleet, another Canadian, born in 1964. John Wellfleet is the central narrator. He is one of the few humans who has lived through the "destructions" of atomic explosions, and when the novel opens in 2039, he is approached by the young André Gervais, who has found materials related to Wellfleet's family and wants the old man to use them to reconstruct the past that has, in effect, been destroyed for Gervais and his friends. Wellfleet works out Dehmel's story, involving opposition to Hitler and love for a Jewish woman, and finds it subsequently connecting to Dehmel's stepson Timothy, who interviews Dehmel on television in 1970. As a result of the interview, during which Timothy accuses Dehmel of having been a Nazi, Dehmel is assassinated.

Obviously, the presentation of this material, these voices from different times, calls for a complicated structure: Timothy's story is told by John Wellfleet; Dehmel's is told both by Wellfleet and, through diaries, by himself; and Wellfleet's own story is concluded by Gervais. The time scheme moves from 2039, to the late 1960's, to 1909, to 1918-1919, to 1932-1945, to a climax in 1970, and finally to 2044.

Like the time scheme, MacLennan's view of causation that underlies this historical presentation is intricate, especially compared with *Barometer Rising* and his earlier novels. Nevertheless, his belief in the significance of geography, nature, and landscape in motivating character can still be seen, even though the landscape has become primarily urban, and character may be formed, or deformed, by *separation* from fundamental geography. Nature continues to provide MacLennan with a thematic contrast to the urban, technological environment and to be a source of much of his imagery. Timothy is cut off, in his technological world, from natural geography; at nineteen thousand feet, he flies over the woods his father's generation had known intimately. Dehmel finds a temporary salvation, in both the world wars, in Germany's Black Forest. John Wellfleet lives on the outskirts of what was once Montreal, with trees, flowers, and birds. Drawing on Walt Whitman, MacLennan uses lilacs and a star to make a contrast with urban technology and its sense of time; he has Wellfleet think of the "time-clocks" of plants and birds. In one key passage, civilization is compared to a garden. Most significantly, perhaps, when compared to the thoughts about civilization, its rise and fall, and time, which MacLennan presents in *Rivers of Canada*, is the mentioning of rivers, as when, for example, the cautious optimism that tempers the tragic events narrated in *Voices in Time* is symbolized by the return of salmon to the St. Lawrence River.

Voices in Time was MacLennan's final novel and was a fitting climax to a successful career. It indicated that although he assuredly has a major position in the history of Canadian letters, he was one of those novelists who, although solidly rooted in time and place, transcended both. His ability to dramatize his geographical sense of history suggests that MacLennan is a writer who will continue to speak to future generations.

William B. Stone

Other major works

nonfiction: *Oxyrhynchus: An Economic and Social Study*, 1935, 1968; *Cross-Country*, 1949; *Thirty and Three*, 1954; *Scotchman's Return, and Other Essays*, 1960; *Seven Rivers of Canada*, 1961 (revised as *Rivers of Canada*, 1974); *The Colour of Canada*, 1967; *The Other Side of Hugh MacLennan: Selected Essays Old and New*, 1978 (Elspeth Cameron, editor); *On Being a Maritime Writer*, 1984; *Dear Marian, Dear Hugh: The MacLennan-Engel Correspondence*, 1995 (Christl Verduyn, editor).

edited text: *McGill: The Story of a University*, 1960.

miscellaneous: *Hugh MacLennan's Best*, 1991 (Douglas M. Gibson, editor).

Bibliography

Bach, Susanne. "The Geography of Perception in Hugh MacLennan's Maritime Novels." In *Down East: Critical Essays on Contemporary Maritime Canadian Literature*, edited by Wolfgang Hochbruck and James O. Taylor. Trier, Germany: Wissenschaftlicher, 1996. Informative analysis of MacLennan's work is included in a collection of essays that analyze novels and dramatic works by authors from the Maritime Provinces of Canada. Includes bibliography.

Buitenhuis, Peter. *Hugh MacLennan*. Edited by William French. Toronto, Ont.: Forum House, 1969. Biography of MacLennan is accompanied by critical analyses of his first six novels and his nonfiction. Supports MacLennan's preoccupation with Canadian nationhood and provides an evenhanded, although somewhat academic, assessment of MacLennan's strengths and weaknesses. Includes bibliography.

Cameron, Elspeth. *Hugh MacLennan: A Writer's Life*. Toronto, Ont.: University of Toronto Press, 1981. Critical biography was written with MacLennan's cooperation. Presents assessments of MacLennan's work in addition to providing facts about his life, devoting a separate chapter to each of his seven novels.

Leith, Linda. *Introducing Hugh MacLennan's "Two Solitudes": A Reader's Guide*. Toronto, Ont.: ECW Press, 1990. Excellent resource for students includes an analysis of *Two Solitudes*, a chronology of MacLennan's life, information about the book's critical reception, a bibliography, and an index.

Lucas, Alec. *Hugh MacLennan*. Toronto, Ont.: McClelland & Stewart, 1970. Provides clear analysis of MacLennan's fiction and essays. Each chapter addresses a different component of MacLennan's vision in general and social morality in particular. Includes bibliography.

MacLennan, Hugh. Interview by Alan Twigg. In *Strong Voices: Conversations with Fifty Canadian Authors*. Madeira Park, B.C.: Harbour, 1988. In this absorbing interview conducted in 1979, MacLennan focuses mainly on his lifelong interest in Canadian nationhood and how that interest influenced his writing.

Pell, Barbara. *Faith and Fiction: A Theological Critique of the Narrative Strategies of Hugh MacLennan and Morley Callaghan*. Waterloo, Ont.: Wilfrid Laurier University

Press, 1998. Analyzes MacLennan's works from a theological perspective. Demonstrates how the author's novels, particularly *The Watch That Ends the Night*, chart his journey from Calvinism to Christian existentialism.

Tierney, Frank M., ed. *Hugh MacLennan*. Ottawa, Ont.: University of Ottawa Press, 1994. Solid critical study addresses MacLennan's works, personality, and character. Includes bibliographical references.

Woodcock, George. *Introducing Hugh MacLennan's "Barometer Rising": A Reader's Guide*. Toronto, Ont.: ECW Press, 1989. Offers careful, instructive methodology for reading the novel. Also includes a chronology of MacLennan's life and publications, biographical details, and an assessment of MacLennan's place in Canadian literature.

_______. "Surrogate Fathers and Orphan Sons: The Novels of Hugh MacLennan." In *Northern Spring: The Flowering of Canadian Literature*. Vancouver, B.C.: Douglas & McIntyre, 1987. Essay included in a two-part book on Canadian prose writers and poets examines what Woodcock perceives as MacLennan's central metaphor for the definition of "Canadian" nation: a generational theme. Also discusses the strongly didactic element that pervades MacLennan's works.

KATE O'BRIEN

Born: Limerick, Ireland; December 3, 1897
Died: Canterbury, England; August 13, 1974

PRINCIPAL LONG FICTION

Without My Cloak, 1931
Mary Lavelle, 1936
Pray for the Wanderer, 1938
The Land of Spices, 1941
The Last of Summer, 1943
That Lady, 1946 (also known as *For One Sweet Grape*)
The Flower of May, 1953
As Music and Splendour, 1958

OTHER LITERARY FORMS

Kate O'Brien's first success was a play, *Distinguished Villa*, which had a three-month run in London's West End in 1926. She successfully dramatized her novel *That Lady* for a Broadway production (1949) in which Katherine Cornell played the title role. O'Brien was also the author of two travel books, *Farewell, Spain* (1937) and *My Ireland* (1962). Her *English Diaries and Journals* was published in 1943 and a biography, *Teresa of Avila*, in 1951. Her last major published work was a book of reminiscences, *Presentation Parlour* (1963).

ACHIEVEMENTS

While Kate O'Brien's first novel, *Without My Cloak*, received two of the English literary establishment's most prestigious awards, the Hawthornden Prize and the James Tait Black Memorial Prize, her most notable achievement may best be assessed in the context of contemporary Irish literature. In this context, she remains—together with, though in a much more culturally significant manner than, her perhaps better-known contemporary Elizabeth Bowen—an exemplary representative not only of women's writing but also, through her works and career, of women's potential, broadly considered. Partial recognition of her achievement came in 1947 with her election to the Irish Academy of Letters.

BIOGRAPHY

Kate O'Brien was born in the city of Limerick, Ireland, on December 3, 1897, to a comfortable, middle-class family. Educated at a local convent, she went on to attend University College, Dublin, at a time when Ireland's capital was witnessing the consolidation of the Irish Literary Revival, though the cultural enthusiasm of the time left little or no mark either on O'Brien's student days or on her writing.

The years immediately following graduation seem to have been marked by a degree of uncertainty. She first worked in England as a journalist for the (then) *Manchester Guardian* and as a teacher. A brief period in Washington, D.C., as a diplomatic aide was followed by a sojourn in Bilbao, Spain, as a governess. Returning to London in 1924, she married Gustav Renier; the marriage was not a success. Spain soon became her second home, though for more than ten years after the completion of her World War II service at the ministry of information in London she was refused admission to Spain, her depiction of King Philip II in *That Lady* having rendered her persona non grata.

By this time, O'Brien was no stranger to controversy arising out of her fiction: Her 1941 novel, *The Land of Spices*, was notoriously banned by the Irish censorship board for alleged sexual impropriety. In 1950, she took up residence again in Ireland and lived there until 1961, when she returned to England. She died on August 13, 1974.

Analysis

Kate O'Brien's career emerged and developed during a difficult time for Irish writing; indeed, models of Irish women novelists who might have provided her with beneficial influence and nurturing were virtually nonexistent. Despite these unpromising cultural origins, and despite the obvious struggle O'Brien experienced in order to express herself and command a responsive and sustaining audience, her career can be seen in historical retrospect to be marked with notable integrity, independence of mind and action, and devotion to her art.

In a literary culture where women have not always received sufficient critical attention and have not had their works readily incorporated into the canon of a given generation's achievements, critical responses to O'Brien's life and work have belatedly been seen as manifestations of unwarranted narrowness. The belatedness of this view is perhaps a result of the author's long years of exile, along with the fact that her one major popular success, *That Lady*, published when a fresh audience was ready for her work, is a historical romance rather than another in her sequence of novels about Irish family life. Yet the republication of many of her works during the 1980's not only facilitated a reappraisal of her literary achievements but also had the effect of redrawing the map of Irish literary culture at a crucial period in its development.

The generation of Irish writers to which O'Brien belongs had the unenviable task of following in the pathbreaking footsteps of the principal artists of the Irish Literary Revival—the novelist George Moore, the poet William Butler Yeats, and the playwright John Millington Synge. O'Brien's generation was as different in background and outlook from these three illustrious avatars as it is possible to be. Provincial in upbringing, nationalist in politics, unexperimental in art, and Catholic in cultural formation, this generation had at once a greater intimacy with the actual life of its fellow citizens and a more actively critical perception of the society in whose name it had elected to speak. It also had the not inconsiderable disadvantage of attempting to assert its cultural and artistic validity and vi-

Kate O'Brien
(Library of Congress)

ability while the star of the revival had not yet entirely waned, and while Yeats, for example, was willing to co-opt new voices to articulate the agenda of his cultural politics.

The most important writers of this generation—those who went on to establish a somewhat more populist orientation for Irish literature, or at least a more populist role for the Irish writer—have long been considered to be Seán O'Faoláin, Frank O'Connor, and Liam O'Flaherty. The different orientation that they represent may be initially discerned in the fact that they each espoused a form largely neglected by the revival—namely, prose fiction, in particular the short story—and implicitly rejected the formal and ideological explorations of their more modernist forebears. O'Brien is a member of this generation not merely by virtue of her provincial background and conventional education but also because her works reflect this generation's concerns, a reflection that receives added point and importance from the fact of its feminist—or, to be historically accurate, protofeminist—perspectives.

The disillusion and disorientation that emerge as a resonant theme in Irish fiction during the 1930's, the problematized rendering of the independence that the country secured in the late twentieth century in juridical and political terms, and the conflicts between tradition and individuality as the culture seeks not merely aesthetic but moral renewal, far from being neglected by O'Brien, are all the more authentically present in her work through being presented from the standpoint of already marginalized female protagonists. (With the exception of *Pray for the Wanderer*, with its protagonist Matt Costello, all of O'Brien's works feature female protagonists.)

WITHOUT MY CLOAK

O'Brien's first novel, *Without My Cloak*, rehearses a number of the problems that arise from her heritage and anticipates the most important of her fiction's preoccupations. A family saga, it brings to awareness, through the use of an essentially nineteenth century model, the social and psychological forces that gave cultural and moral legitimacy to O'Brien's own class and ideological background. The novel traces the development of the Considine family through three generations from the late eighteenth century, plausibly detailing its establishment in an urban, mercantile setting, for which the author uses her native Limerick.

A major motif in the work is the question of security. The Considine ethos consists of a sublimation of development in consolidation, and the emotional claustrophobia that results from this mode of behavior within the family circle is memorably detailed. The security motif is tensely related to its obverse, a quest for independence; the dynamics of the novel enact the struggle familiar from nineteenth century fiction between individual and society, between the assertion of selfhood and institutional constraints, with the emphasis in this instance falling on the power of institutions.

In particular, the social and moral function of the Catholic Church receives special attention in *Without My Cloak* and retains a particularly important place throughout O'Brien's fiction. Because of its status in her first novel, it is possible to refer to the Considine family as embodying an ethos, since the Church operates as a source of moral and social identity, and alternative sources of such security and self-awareness are nowhere to be found. The power of the Church to authorize selfhood as a tissue of constraints makes of it a second, larger, more absolute family, and the matter of the effect of its power on the individual conscience and consciousness, rather than being resolved in *Without My Cloak*, becomes an increasingly emphatic preoccupation in O'Brien's fiction prior to the publication of *That Lady*. (The fact that O'Brien herself seems to have considered the conflicts of her first novel unresolved may be inferred from their reenactment in condensed and more artistically disciplined form in her next work, *The Anteroom*.)

The role and power of the Church is so central to her work that O'Brien has frequently been thought of as a Catholic, more than as an Irish, novelist. Like most Irish writers, however, she is concerned with the culture of Catholicism; its social, personal, and interpersonal influence; and its significance as a generator of a politics of the spirit rather than as a spiritual convalescent home. Indeed, one of her most fundamental fictional preoccupations is with the difficulty of dealing with impersonal authority, whether conceived as institutional or, as in the portrait of Philip II in *That Lady*, monarchical.

MARY LAVELLE

The fact that O'Brien perceived her preoccupations as continuing difficulty rather than as eventual solution is suggested by the regularity with which her protagonists, for all the author's sympathetic dramatization of their intensity of their struggles, typically fail to attain the independence they desire. An exception to this general outcome is the eponymous heroine of *Mary Lavelle*. This novel, which draws more directly on immediate personal experience than does *Without My Cloak*, tells of a young Irish woman working as a governess for a bourgeois Spanish family. In some sense an account of an innocent abroad—Mary seems to be innocence itself—the novel is also a narrative of conflicting loyalties. The heroine is in many respects an ideal employee, fitting into the Areavaga family with the ease of somebody familiar with a culture in which people know their places. It is Mary's very compliance, however, that is responsible for the novel's central drama.

Mary involuntarily falls for Juanito, the married son of the house, a state of affairs that brings her into conflict not only with the outlook in which she had been rigorously brought up in Ireland but also with its powerfully reinforced presence in Doña Consuelo, the commanding head of the household. The conflict between duty and freedom, between individual desire and ethical obligation, in addition to the novelist's welcome transposition of her concerns to a non-Irish locale and the development of a sexual dimension to Mary's struggle for authentic womanhood, contributes to an impressive sense of the novelist's development. Nevertheless, it is not clear what the overall effect of Mary's experiences has been, whether she accepts or rejects the conflict-laden nature of her experiences. "Anguish and anger for everyone and only one little, fantastic, impossible hope," read the closing lines of *Mary Lavelle*, "was the fruit of her journey to Spain." An unexpected fruit of the publication of *Mary Lavelle*, however, was its banning by Irish censors, an act that may be read now as an unintended tribute to O'Brien's insightful presentation of her heroine's moral authenticity but that, at the time, deepened the alienation from her background that her works articulated with increasing conviction.

THE LAND OF SPICES

This alienation reached its highest level when O'Brien's next novel, *The Land of Spices*, met with a similar fate to that of *Mary Lavelle* at the hands of the censors, as a result of which the novel achieved unjust notoriety—and subsequently, when censorship was relaxed in the early 1970's, a certain amount of popular success. The banning of *The Land of Spices* proved instrumental in calling the censorship board's procedures into question and led indirectly to a revision of its mode of operation. It might be argued that the board's very existence was in itself strongly illustrative of the cultural conflicts and repressions that, from a broader, nonbureaucratic, social perspective, form the core of O'Brien's fictional concerns. The pretext for banning *The Land of Spices* was so slender—consisting of a mere handful of words with potentially homosexual implications—

that it came to be seen as a paradigm of the narrow-minded, prurient, and often antifeminist orientation of the official guardians of Irish literary culture.

The Land of Spices can be read as a redeployment and intensification of the mother-and-governess relationship in *Mary Lavelle*, a relationship that is emblematic of relationships conceived throughout O'Brien's work as exercises in power. On this occasion, foreignness of setting and the enclosed nature of the immediate environment are combined to attain a new level of intensity: The action takes place within an Irish convent of a French order of nuns. In addition, this work's animating relationship now has the intimacy of teacher, Mère Marie-Hélène Archer, and pupil, Anna Murphy, with all of its reverberations of nurturing and mastery, the source of which is the overarching presence of Mother Church. The pressures Mary Lavelle felt with regard to her moral development and sense of autonomy are here articulated more dramatically, given how much more difficult it is to escape them, and the sexual component of *Mary Lavelle* is similarly intensified.

The novel, however, has a more meditative than critical tone. Taking its title from the English metaphysical poet George Herbert's "Prayer (1)" ("Church bells beyond the stars heard, the soul's blood,/ The land of spices, something understood"), the emphasis falls on the ritualistic and selfless aspects of the vocational life, on the complexities of agape rather than the challenge of eros, on the willingness to serve rather than the urge to escape, while at the same time remaining crucially sensitive to the urgent presence of humanity and its needs. *The Land of Spices* will seem to many O'Brien's most satisfying production, in which she attains more objective possession of her psychological and spiritual preoccupations without running the risk of compromising them.

THAT LADY

O'Brien's characterization of a woman's fate in the context of power relationships receives its most lavish treatment in her greatest popular success, *That Lady*. As well as being adapted for the stage, *That Lady* was filmed with Olivia de Havilland in the title role in 1955. Set in sixteenth century Spain, the novel tells the story of Ana de Mendoza y de la Cerda, princess of Eboli and duchess of Pastrana; clearly, despite O'Brien's strong Spanish interests, it is an entirely new departure for her as a novelist. Instead of concentrating on the various stages of Ana's life as a woman in an attempt to reconstruct a novel of historical verisimilitude, O'Brien concentrates instead on the years of Ana's unlikely liberation into an experience of womanhood that had hitherto been hidden from her. The reader is explicitly informed in a foreword that this "is not a historical novel"; instead, the imaginative treatment of the material dwells centrally on a dramatization of the psychological and emotional conflicts of the case. Thus, despite a certain amount of costumery, inevitable under the circumstances, *That Lady* achieves an internal consistency with O'Brien's other novels.

That Lady covers the years spent by Ana, now widowed, in state service. To some extent, her work for the Spanish Crown during this brief period recapitulates her early years, when by virtue of her noble birth and excellent marriage she became intimate with affairs of state. Together with the old intimacy, however, there now comes a new, and this development of an additional dimension in Ana's life is at once enhancing and destructive, enriching her personal existence while risking a scandal that would entail the king's serious displeasure. Because of the character of the prevailing power structure, the most significant experience in Ana's personal life—the affair with Don Antonio Pérez—becomes the occasion of her banishment and confinement. The novel's heightened courtly context accentuates rather than dilutes its emphasis on tensions familiar from O'Brien's earlier novels—between passion and form, between desire and responsibility, between a woman's external role and her internal needs. To these tensions and conflicts her work returns again and again, and it is in her identification and negotiation of them that O'Brien's fiction is worthy of the critical attention that, beginning in the late 1980's, it has at length come to receive.

O'Brien's work is noteworthy on two levels. In the first place, it represents significant additions to the history of anglophone women's writing in the period between the two world wars. Her location of her female protagonists in conditions of moral difficulty, emotional complexity, cultural unfamiliarity, and even geographical estrangement provides a comprehensive method of dramatizing women's experience as problematic and unamenable to tidying away by the powers that be. O'Brien's own willingness to live a life as autonomous as that sought by her protagonists testifies to her steadfastness, courage, and integrity. The fact that so much of her writing life was spent in exile is a tribute to both her singularity and her perseverance.

In addition, however, O'Brien's accomplishments become all the more significant when seen in an Irish context. While her novels do not articulate the concerns of her generation as explicitly as the critiques of nationalism and assumption of embattled cultural and ideological positions favored by many of her contemporaries, her work belongs with theirs as part of a concerted effort to render more authentically—that is, with greater respect for individuality and its internal realities—the life of her time. O'Brien's original contributions to this effort make her the first significant female writer of independent Ireland.

George O'Brien

OTHER MAJOR WORKS

PLAYS: *Distinguished Villa*, pr. 1926; *The Bridge*, pr. 1927; *The Schoolroom Window*, pr. 1937; *That Lady*, pr. 1949.

NONFICTION: *Farewell, Spain*, 1937; *English Diaries and Journals*, 1943; *Teresa of Avila*, 1951; *My Ireland*, 1962 (travel); *Presentation Parlour*, 1963 (reminiscence).

BIBLIOGRAPHY

Bloom, Harold, ed. *British Women Fiction Writers, 1900-1960*. 2 vols. Philadelphia: Chelsea House, 1997-1998. Volume 2 includes brief biographies of O'Brien and twelve other authors and critical essays about their work, including analyses of individual books and broader discussions of the authors' place in literary history

Dalsimer, Adele. *Kate O'Brien: A Critical Study*. Dublin: Gill and Macmillan, 1990. The first comprehensive study of O'Brien's entire literary output, with an emphasis on the feminist dimension of her works. Includes a biographical sketch, a bibliography, and an index.

Kiberd, Declan. "Kate O'Brien: *The Ante-Room*." In *Irish Classics*. Cambridge, Mass.: Harvard University Press, 2001. O'Brien's novel is one of the thirty-five greatest works of Irish literature that Kiberd discusses in her book on the classics of the Irish literary tradition.

Kiely, Benedict. "Love and Pain and Parting: The Novels of Kate O'Brien." In *A Raid into Dark Corners: And Other Essays*. Cork, Ireland: Cork University Press, 1999. Kiely, a popular Irish literary critic and a writer for more than fifty years, includes an analysis of O'Brien's novels in this collection of his essays.

O'Brien, Kate. "The Art of Writing." *University Review* 3 (1965): 6-14. Provides valuable insights into the author's thoughts about the writing process.

Reynolds, Lorna. *Kate O'Brien: A Literary Portrait*. Totowa, N.J.: Barnes & Noble Books, 1987. This study is divided into two parts, the first dealing with the major fiction in chronological order and the second surveying O'Brien's treatment of various major themes. Also contains a valuable treatment of O'Brien's family background.

Walshe, Eibhear. *Kate O'Brien: A Writing Life*. Dublin: Irish Academic Press, 2006. A comprehensive chronicle of O'Brien's life. Walshe maintains that O'Brien was a pioneering writer whose novels depicted independent female protagonists and created a literary identity for the Irish middle class.

_______, ed. *Ordinary People Dancing: Essays on Kate O'Brien*. Cork, Ireland: Cork University Press, 1993. This selection of critical essays examines O'Brien's heritage and feminism, describing how her works challenged the religious and social restrictions of the new Irish republic.

AMOS OZ

Born: Jerusalem, British Mandate of Palestine (now in Israel); May 4, 1939
Also known as: Amos Klausner

PRINCIPAL LONG FICTION

Makom aher, 1966 (*Elsewhere, Perhaps*, 1973)
Mikha'el sheli, 1968 (*My Michael*, 1972)
Laga 'at ba-mayim, laga 'at ba-ruah, 1973 (*Touch the Water, Touch the Wind*, 1974)
Menuhah nekhonah, 1982 (*A Perfect Peace*, 1985)
Kufsah shehorah, 1987 (*Black Box*, 1988)
La-da'at ishah, 1989 (*To Know a Woman*, 1991)
Matsav ha-shelishi, 1991 (*Fima*, 1993)
Al tagidi lailah, 1994 (*Don't Call It Night*, 1995)
Panter ba-martef, 1994 (*Panther in the Basement*, 1997)
Oto ha-yam, 1999 (*The Same Sea*, 2001)
Pit'om be-'omek ha-ya'ar, 2005
Haruze ha-hayim veha-mavet, 2007 (*Rhyming Life and Death*, 2009)

OTHER LITERARY FORMS

Amos Oz is a widely regarded and well-known Israeli intellectual and writer. He has published essays on politics, literature, and other topics. His journalistic essays have appeared in the Israeli labor newspaper *Davar* and, beginning in the 1990's, the newspaper *Yedioth Ahronoth*. His nonfiction has been published in *The New York Times* and *The New York Review of Books*, and his political essays are collected in *Po va-sham be-Erets-Yisra'el bi-setav* (1982; *In the Land of Israel*, 1983) and *Israel, Palestine, and Peace: Essays* (1994). He also has published collections of literary essays, *Mathilim sipur* (1996; *The Story Begins: Essays on Literature*, 2000); short stories, *Artsot hatan* (1965; *Where the Jackals Howl, and Other Stories*, 1981); and novellas, *Har ha'etsah ha-ra'ah* (1976; *The Hill of Evil Counsel: Three Stories*, 1978). His remarkable memoir *Sipur 'al ahavah ve-hoshekh* (2002; *A Tale of Love and Darkness*, 2004) tells about coming-of-age in a period of violence.

ACHIEVEMENTS

Amos Oz has written books in Hebrew and hundreds of articles and essays that have been translated into more than thirty-five languages. He was a visiting fellow at St. Cross College, Oxford, and an author-in-residence at Hebrew University of Jerusalem, Colorado Springs College, and Boston, Princeton, Tel Aviv, and Indiana universities. He was named Officer of Arts and Letters in France and honored with the French Prix Femina for best foreign novel published in France. In 1942, he won the German Frankfurt Peace

Prize, and the city of Frankfurt also awarded him the Goethe Prize in 2005 (an award earlier received by Sigmund Freud and Thomas Mann, among others).

In 2007, Oz won the Prince of Asturias Award of Letters, one of a series of annual prizes given in Spain by the Foundation Principe de Asturias since 1981 to individuals or entities who make notable achievements in the sciences, humanities, or public affairs. He earned his country's most prestigious literary prize—the Israel Prize for Literature—in 1998, the fiftieth year of Israel's independence. He received an honorary degree from the University of Antwerp, Belgium, in 2008, and in the same year received the Dan David Prize for Creative Rendering of the Past. Oz has been active in the Israeli peace movement, which works for a two-state solution to the Israeli-Palestinian conflict.

BIOGRAPHY

Amos Oz, born Amos Klausner in 1939, spent his early years in Jerusalem. Until the age of fifteen, he lived at No. 16 Amos Street, a place that plays a prominent part in his memoir *A Tale of Love and Darkness*. Yehuda Klausner and Fania Mussman, his father and mother, were Zionist immigrants from Eastern Europe. Much of his father's family was right-wing Zionist. Yehuda, who had studied history and literature in Lithuania, worked as a librarian and writer in Jerusalem. His maternal family emigrated from Poland to Haifa in 1934.

Although Oz's immediate family was not religious, he attended the community religious school, Tachmoni, instead of the alternative socialistic school because it was antithetical to his family's political views. He then attended the Hebrew high school in Rehavia. Oz's mother, who suffered from depression, committed suicide in 1952.

Oz was fourteen years old when he changed his last name from Klausner to Oz ("Oz" means strength and power in Hebrew). He left his father's home and joined Kibbutz Hulda, where he intended to work as a field laborer and live by the Zionist ideals of labor, equality, and simple living. However, he found himself increasingly drawn to study and writing and took leave from the kibbutz to complete a degree in literature and philosophy at Hebrew University. As time went on, royalties from his writing allowed him to perform less field work. In 1960, Oz married Nily Zuckerman, whose father was the librarian of the kibbutz. Oz completed his service in the Israeli Defense Forces in 1961, but he later fought in the Six Day War of 1967 and the Yom Kippur War of 1973.

Oz remained on the kibbutz until 1986, when he and his wife moved to the drier climate of southern Israel because of his son's asthma. In addition to being a prolific writer, Oz has been a professor of Hebrew literature at Ben-Gurion University of the Negev. Both his life and his writing are deeply rooted in his native land.

ANALYSIS

Amos Oz's fiction is often concerned with domestic relationships, portrayed in a realistic manner. However, within this realistic facade, his characters struggle with internal conflicts between body and spirit, their own desires and social constraints, irrational impulses opposed to stability, and their faith in Israel tinged with skepticism. While they dream of perfection and long for the Messiah, they must navigate the dangerous reality of life in Israel. Most of Oz's novels are serious psychological studies, thoughtful and self-assured, and occasionally lightened by a mordant humor. Many of his characters believe they are living in a dream world, especially when people they believe they know suddenly behave in uncharacteristic ways.

In style, Oz is innovative. His novels take varying shapes, from *Black Box*, an epistolary novel, to the free-flowing lyricism of *The Same Sea*, which is told in poetic paragraphs that intersperse the past and the present, the near and the far. Among the story's extraordinary range of voices, the reader sometimes hears the ghostly voice of the deceased. Some of his novels have a claustrophobic feeling, which mirrors the claustrophobia of the intense familial relationships they portray.

MY MICHAEL

My Michael, published in 1968, became Oz's breakthrough work and made him one of Israel's best young novelists. *My Michael* is the story of its first-person narrator, Hannah Greenbaum, a thirty-year-old native of Jerusalem who is married to Dr. Michael Gonen, a geologist and, in Hannah's own words, a "good-natured man." Unlike traditional plots, this novel is structured by Hannah's slow decline into mental illness during her courtship and marriage.

Michael and Hannah meet when they are both students: he a third-year geology student and she a first-year student at Hebrew University. In the mornings she teaches at a kindergarten. One of the first clues to Hannah's instability is her relationship to her deceased father, whose presence in Hannah's mind is felt from the beginning of the novel, when she interrupts her story of how she and Michael met with the incongruous declaration that she has never loved anyone as much as her father. She also fondly recalls a bout of diphtheria she suffered when a child, from which she recovered reluctantly. Memories and fantasies of childhood are interspersed throughout her narrative.

Michael is an only child, and his family hopes he will be a scholar. After a brief courtship with Hannah, he proposes marriage. Hannah accepts, but she also realizes that Michael bores her. Their son, Yair, is born near the end of their first year of marriage. Hannah gives up her studies in literature at Hebrew University and Michael passes his exams, but money is still scarce. Hannah has a nervous breakdown, and when she is ill, Michael is called up for military duty in the 1956 war, giving Hannah new fantasies of military excursions mixed with news from the front. Eventually, her mental condition improves, and Michael returns from military duty. Their days settle down to routine: Michael finishes his thesis and Hannah is once again pregnant, yet she remains lost in fantasy and Michael remains unable to enter her interior world. *My Michael* is distinguished by the remarkable integration of Hannah's inner and outer worlds and its pattern of significant motifs woven delicately throughout the narrative.

BLACK BOX

Black Box is written as a series of letters among Alex Gideon, his former wife Ilana, her new husband Michael, and Alex and Ilana's son Boaz. Interspersed with these letters are communications from Alex's lawyer Zakheim and from Ilana's sister Rahel, whose calm common sense is in direct contrast to Ilana's passionate temperament, which is still in thrall to her first husband. The novel is further enriched by Michael's constant quoting of scripture; reviews of Alex's new book, *The Desperate Violence: A Study in Comparative Fanaticism*; court records; and reports from a private investigator.

The sixteen-year-old Boaz is the apparent instigator of the plot. Ilana first writes to Alex, who is now a university professor in Chicago, to help her find Boaz, who has a penchant for physical violence and is often in trouble. A boy who deeply resents both his parents and Ilana's second husband (Michael), Boaz is gradually won over by Michael's ability to get his son out of trouble by using his vast network of relatives. Slowly, the reader recognizes that each character is a fanatic: Alex is a hardened officer with the Israel Defense Forces who is obsessed with terrorism, Ilana is a slave to masochistic sex, Michael is driven by his absolute religious devotion, and Boaz is ruled by his thirst for independence.

A "black box" is a term used to describe an airplane's recorders of flight data and cockpit communications. In the case of an airplane crash, for example, recorders are useful for the data they might reveal about the cause of that crash. The black box and its functions are apt metaphors for the novel, which centers on the correspondence between Alex and Ilana as they rehash their troubled marriage and divorce of seven years earlier, as well as their courtship. As the correspondence continues over the course of a year, Alex and Ilana gradually get over their bitterness toward each other. The wealthy Alex establishes Boaz in his own childhood home in Israel. Slowly, Boaz "finds" himself there, establishes a commune, and pursues farming and astronomy while rehabilitating his house. He remains an idealist and perhaps the truest embodiment of the Zionist tradition.

In the second half of the novel, the reader discovers that Alex is dying of cancer. He returns to his old home in Israel, where Boaz cares for him; Ilana and her young daughter also nurse him. Michael, at first outraged that Ilana has rejoined Alex, relents and gives both Ilana and Alex his blessing when Alex informs him that he has but a few months to live. Only in the proximity of death are these four strong characters able to find true reconciliation.

TO KNOW A WOMAN

To Know a Woman is the story of Yoel Ravid, told in the omniscient third person but confined to the viewpoint of this tired, recently widowed and retired, forty-seven-year-old man. Employed for twenty-three years with the Israeli secret service, he was on an assignment in Helsinki, Finland, when his wife had a fatal accident. Perhaps because of his wife's death and the responsibility of taking care of his sixteen-year-old daughter, or perhaps because, as he says, his concentration is failing, he retires from his job and rents a house near Tel Aviv to live with his mother, mother-in-law, and daughter.

Yoel starts to fill the void first by tinkering around the house compulsively, performing small repairs. He expands his reach to the garden, while his mind is taken up with the past and attempts to understand his deceased wife and slightly impaired daughter. Recurrent images fill his mind, particularly of a paraplegic he saw on a street in Helsinki. He has an affair with an American neighbor who lives with her brother, his daughter finds a boyfriend, and he resists the efforts of the secret service to woo him into one last mission, one that would have been fatal. Occasionally, he gives in to paranoia; he has joyous moments when the sheer beauty of the landscape overwhelms him. His daughter moves out to live with her boyfriend, and although he has deep qualms about it, he heeds the advice of his friends and lets her set out on a life of her own.

Most important in this obsessive, claustrophobic novel, Yoel gives in to his real estate agent's suggestion to volunteer at the local hospital, and there he finds his true calling. Surrounded by bloodstains, filth, and odors of urine, excrement, and sweat, he finds these elements bring him a certain joy; he knows he is alive, removed from the empty life he had lived since his wife's death. He also discovers new powers in himself: He has the power to allay pain, soothe the distraught, and pacify the terrified. He is able to summon a mixture of compassion and firmness that the hospital patients need, and he is often called by doctors to calm a patient impervious to injections. The reader leaves this former spy using his trained ability of concentration to stare into the blackness of disease, trauma, and death, hoping for an occasional flicker of light.

Sheila Golburgh Johnson

OTHER MAJOR WORKS

SHORT FICTION: *Artsot hatan*, 1965 (revised 1976; *Where the Jackals Howl, and Other Stories*, 1981); *Ahavah me'uheret*, 1971 (*Unto Death*, 1975); *Har ha'etsah ha-ra'ah*, 1976 (*The Hill of Evil Counsel: Three Stories*, 1978).

NONFICTION: *Be-or ha-tekhelet ha-'azah: Ma'amarim u-reshimot*, 1979 (*Under This Blazing Light: Essays*, 1995); *Po va-sham be-Erets-Yisra'el bi-setav*, 1982 (*In the Land of Israel*, 1983); *Mi-mordot ha-Levanon: Ma'amarim u-reshimot*, 1987 (*The Slopes of Lebanon*, 1989); *Shetikat ha-shamayim*, 1993 (*The Silence of Heaven: Agnon's Fear of God*, 2000); *Israel, Palestine, and Peace: Essays*, 1994; *Mathilim sipur*, 1996 (*The Story Begins: Essays on Literature*, 2000); *Kol ha-tikvot: Mahashavot 'al zehut Yisre'elit*, 1998; *Sipur 'al ahavah ve-hoshekh*, 2002 (*A Tale of Love and Darkness*, 2004); *How to Cure a Fanatic*, 2006.

CHILDREN'S LITERATURE: *Sumkhi*, 1978 (*Soumchi*, 1980).

BIBLIOGRAPHY

Coetzee, J. M. "Whither Dost Thou Hasten." *The New York Review*, March 5, 1998. A review of Oz's novel *Panther in the Basement* that explores a repeated theme in his work:

A young boy is at a crossroads in his life, which coincides with a crossroads in the life of his nation.

Cohen, Joseph. *Essays and Interviews with Yehuda Amichai, A. B. Yehoshua, T. Carmi, Aharon Appelfeld, and Amos Oz.* Albany: State University of New York Press, 1990. Each chapter provides a critical look at the English translations of these Israeli writers. Each critique is rounded out by interviews with the five authors. Discusses the relationship of politics to literature, the responsibility of the writer, and the relationship between literature and life.

Mayot, Yair. *Somber Lust: The Art of Amos Oz.* Translated by Margaret Weinberger. Albany: State University of New York Press, 2002. Excellent critical study of Oz's fictional work. Part of the Modern Jewish Literature and Culture series.

WALKER PERCY

Born: Birmingham, Alabama; May 28, 1916
Died: Covington, Louisiana; May 10, 1990

PRINCIPAL LONG FICTION

The Moviegoer, 1961
The Last Gentleman, 1966
Love in the Ruins: The Adventures of a Bad Catholic at a Time Near the End of the World, 1971
Lancelot, 1977
The Second Coming, 1980
The Thanatos Syndrome, 1987

OTHER LITERARY FORMS

As a writer of imaginative literature, Walker Percy devoted himself exclusively to the novel. However, he also wrote more than fifty reviews and essays on many of the same topics that inform his novels: existential philosophy, language theory, modern scientific method, contemporary American culture, the South, and literature. With one or two exceptions, the most important of these essays are collected in *The Message in the Bottle* (1975), which has as its peculiarly Percyean subtitle *How Queer Man Is, How Queer Language Is, and What One Has to Do with the Other.* An indispensable book, *The Message in the Bottle* not only clarifies the author's major concerns as well as his commitment to that most basic philosophical question, "What is man?" but also details the formidable intellectual foundation on which his fiction so unpretentiously rests. That unpretentiousness is especially evident in *Lost in the Cosmos* (1983), ironically subtitled *The Last Self-Help Book*, in which Percy employs satire and semiotics in an effort to clarify the human being's social and more especially spiritual predicament as a uniquely "lost" creature needing the good news of the gospels but all too often willing to settle for the insights of scientists and talk-show hosts.

ACHIEVEMENTS

Walker Percy is perhaps most easily described as a Catholic-existentialist-American-southern novelist, a baggy phrase that at least has the virtue of identifying the various currents that are blended together in his distinctive works. In Percy's fiction, Mark Twain's Huck Finn from the novel *Adventures of Huckleberry Finn* (1884) and Jean-Paul Sartre's Antoine Roquentin from the play *Nausea* (1938) meet in a single character adrift in a world where, despite the formless sprawl of mass society, the possibility of grace still exists. Percy's fiction is readily identifiable by its distinctive narrative voice. That voice—laconic yet disarmingly honest and filled with wonder—gained for Percy both critical respect and a dedicated readership. Percy received the National Book Award for *The Moviegoer*, the Los Angeles Times Book Prize for *The Second Coming*, and the St. Louis Literary Award for *Lost in the Cosmos*. Among his other literary honors were memberships in the National Institute of Arts and Letters and the American Academy of Arts and Sciences.

BIOGRAPHY

Walker Percy was born in Birmingham, Alabama, on May 28, 1916. When his father, lawyer Leroy Percy, committed suicide in 1929, the young Percy, his two brothers, and their mother moved to Greenville, Mississippi, where they lived with Leroy's bachelor cousin, William Alexander Percy. William adopted the boys in 1931, following their mother's death in an automobile accident. The Greenville home served as something of a local cultural center; the uncle, the author of several works, including an autobiographical memoir of the South titled *Lanterns on the Levee* (1941), entertained such house guests as William Faulkner, Carl Sandburg, Langston Hughes, David Cohn, and Harry Stack Sullivan.

In the early 1930's, Percy attended Greenville High School, where he wrote a gossip column and became the close friend of Shelby Foote, who was by then already committed to a literary career. At the University of North Carolina, which was noted for its school of behaviorism, Percy majored in chemistry and received a bachelor of science degree in 1937. He then enrolled in Columbia's College of Physicians and Surgeons and received his medical degree in 1941. In addition to his studies, Percy underwent psychoanalysis and became a frequent filmgoer. The turning point in his life came in early 1942 when, as a medical resident at Bellevue Hospital in New York, Percy contracted tuberculosis. During his two-year convalescence at Saranac Lake, he began reading extensively in philosophy and literature (Sartre, Albert Camus, Søren Kierkegaard, Gabriel Marcel, Fyodor Dostoevski, Nikolai Gogol, Leo Tolstoy, Franz Kafka). What he discovered was that as a medical doctor he knew much about people but had no idea how to define a human.

Following a relapse and further convalescence in 1944, Percy seemed sure of only two things: He was a doctor who did not wish to practice medicine; he was literally as well as existentially homeless (his uncle having died in 1942). In 1945, he traveled with Foote to New Mexico and then stayed on alone for a time. On November 7, 1946, he married Mary Bernice Townsend, and less than a year later they both converted to Catholicism. (The decision to convert was, Percy said, in large measure the result of their reading of Kierkegaard's essay, "The Difference Between a Genius and an Apostle.") Soon after, the Percys moved from Sewanee, Tennessee, to New Orleans, Louisiana, where Percy continued his contemplative life. Financially secure—thanks to his uncle's estate—and intellectually rich, his landlord, Julius Friend, a professor of philosophy, introduced him to the writings of Charles Saunders Peirce, whose triadic theory of language formed the basis of Percy's own linguistic speculations. (Percy's interest in language had another and more personal source: The younger of his two daughters was born deaf.) In 1950, the Percys moved to Covington, Louisiana, "a pleasant non-place," Percy said, where it is possible to live as a stranger in one's own land; it is neither the "anyplace" that characterizes mass society nor the "someplace" of New Orleans or a Richmond, where the past haunts the present.

In the 1950's, Percy began publishing essays in such journals as *Thought*, *Commonweal*, and *Philosophy and Phenomenological Research*. After discarding two early novels, he began writing *The Moviegoer* in 1959, revising it four times before its publication two years later. Until his death on May 10, 1990, Percy lived quietly in Covington, a serious and meditative novelist pondering the world in thought, fiction, and an occasional essay.

Analysis

Walker Percy acknowledged that Kierkegaard's writings provided him with "a theoretical frame of reference," and one of the most important ideas that he adapted from this frame is Kierkegaard's rejection of Hegelian rationalism in favor of a subjective and intensely passionate commitment on the part of the individual. In Percy's view, modern science in general and the social sciences in particular have mistakenly and indiscriminately adopted the behaviorist, or biological, method and have consequently defined the human being reductively and abstractly.

Existentialism, including the existential novel, on the other hand, presents an alternative to behaviorism: a concrete phenomenological approach whose aim is the recovery of humankind's uniqueness. Percy admits that the behaviorist method is valid to a point; ultimately, however, it must fail because, in classifying the human as a biological organism acting in accordance with rules applicable to all biological organisms, it fails to deal with what is distinctly human, the nonbiological goals. Concerned solely with sameness, the scientific method cannot account for Dostoevski's "underground man" except as a deviation from the norm. Existentialism, Percy believes, does account for this, as does Christianity, which acknowledges the Fall of Man and his distance from God, and defines existence as "the journey of a wayfarer along life's way." Denying the Fall, modern science makes the Gnostic mistake; it attempts to build Eden, the secular city, where human guilt and anxiety are conditioned away, where all biological needs are met, and where existence is certified by experts.

Percy rejects this "brave new world" and calls instead for a radical anthropology that can account for the ontological as well as the biological aspects of human existence. Guilt and anxiety, he points out, are not symptoms of maladjustment to be gotten rid of so that the individual (as human organism) can live the life of the satisfied consumer; rather, these signs of estrangement serve to summon a person not to self-fulfillment but to authentic existence. Humanity is on earth not to have needs met, Percy says, not to surrender sovereignty to the theories of experts (a view raised again by Christopher Lasch in his controversial book *The Culture of Narcissism*, 1979), but to be saved, and that necessitates consciousness of the human situation.

It is important to realize that Percy's sovereign wayfarer, or castaway, is not entirely identifiable with Kierkegaard's knight of faith. In place of Kierkegaard's extreme subjectivity, Percy posits the intersubjectivity of Gabriel Marcel, a Christian existentialist whose *we are* stands in stark contrast with both Kierkegaard's *I choose* and René Descartes's *I think*. We know we exist, Marcel says, by participating in the world. He does not think of being as experience, however, but as a presence within experience that is to be understood as simultaneously transcendent and immanent. To separate the two components of being is to pervert them and to transmogrify the individual as sovereign wayfarer into either angel—the abstract knower, the objective consciousness—or beast—a culture organism satisfying its needs. (The terms are Percy's, borrowed from Blaise Pascal.)

Marcel's quest for being, which is the quest for salvation as well, manifests itself in Percy's theory of language as intersubjective communication, where *we name* implies the same religious affirmation as Marcel's *we are* and Martin Buber's *I-Thou*. Percy originally turned to language theory to answer the question "What is man?" because the answer provided by the behaviorist method was reductive and because the old theological view, along with the words in which it was couched, has been rendered ineffective by the general acceptance of the scientific method, which predisposed modern humanity to view itself as the behaviorists had defined it. Percy then set himself the task of finding "the delta factor": that which makes the human what it is and not something else.

According to the old theological view, humankind's singularity is its "soul," a meaningless word in a scientific age that demands empirical proof. For soul, Percy substitutes language, which he defines not as a sign system (the behaviorist position) but as the uniquely human process of symbolization. At the heart of language (and therefore at the heart of humanity as well) is something mysterious (compare Marcel's "mystery of being"). The mystery is explained by what Percy calls the "coupling process," the intersubjective human context by which people name, or symbolize, the world and in this way come both to know it and to share it. Language is, therefore, an attempt to bridge the gap between self and other, or, considered in the religious context of the Fall of Man, between self and God. What complicates the situation is the fact that in the late twentieth century, Percy believed, language became as meaningless, as clichéd, as the old theology. Before there can be intersubjective communication, humankind must again learn how to speak.

To learn to name and therefore to know and share that knowledge with another is the basic plot of a Percy novel. As Robert Coles has pointed out, Percy's novels trace the protagonist's movement from lofty observation to active participation in the openness of life—its possibilities and the necessity of making choices. Each of his major characters feels estranged

> from being, from his own being, from the being of other creatures in the world, from the transcendent being. He has lost something, but what he does not know; he only knows that he is sick to death with the loss of it.

Since this quest for being is a quest for God, it involves the hero's progress through Kierkegaard's three stages: the aesthetic (the pursuit of pleasure; the self becomes an uncommitted ironic spectator detached from him- or herself and from others); the ethical (living within a general human code, such as marriage); the religious (requiring an entirely personal and—Kierkegaard would say—absurd leap of faith). The hero's search for being begins only when he or she becomes conscious of his or her despair and tries either to understand it or to alleviate it in one of two ways: rotation or repetition.

Rotation—the quest for new experiences to offset everydayness—makes up the comic substance of Percy's novels. Repetition—the return to the past—may be rendered comically, but more often it serves a darker purpose, for Percy's heroes are, like those of William Faulkner, haunted by the past; as a result, they do not live fully in the present. Only when they confront the past directly and become conscious of it can they break its spell and become sovereign wayfarers.

Frequently, Percy equates the past with the southern stoicism his uncle espoused, which, in Percy's judgment, leads only to pessimism, obsession with death, and "the wintry kingdom of self"; in short, it is the very antithesis of Percy's Christian existentialism. Rotation and repetition provide only temporary relief from the malaise that prevails within the aesthetic stage. The only escape from "aesthetic damnation" is through ordeal, especially the death of a loved one. Ordeal brings heroes face-to-face with mortality and enables them to see their world and themselves as if for the first time. The search they then begin is in effect a rejection of the absurdist position of aesthetic existentialists such as Camus and Sartre. The world is not absurd; it is a world to be named, known, and shared by the authentic self and the other in a mode of existence that is not so much religious *or* ethical as a synthesis of the two.

There are analogues for Walker Percy's religious-phenomenological conception of the human search for being in his method of composition and in his prose style. The author's search for narrative form parallels the hero's search for being. Beginning with a situation rather than a plot or set of characters, Percy wrote with no fixed purpose or end in mind. As he explained, the writing, while not "haphazard," involved "many false starts, many blind detours, many blind passages, many goings ahead and backing up." Stylistically, his elegantly and precisely written novels suggest wonder, humor, and forbearance rather than the ponderous solemnity of other existential novelists such as Sartre. Moreover, his prose is richly and sensuously detailed; like two other converts to Catholicism, Marcel and even more particularly Gerard Manley Hopkins, he took pleasure in a natural and human world that is, although marred by evil, essentially sacramental.

THE MOVIEGOER

John Bickerson Bolling—Binx—is the narrator and main character of *The Moviegoer* and the first of Percy's spiritually "sick" protagonists. At age twenty-nine, he is a successful broker in a modern world where the church has been replaced by the brokerage house. Although financially secure, Binx feels uneasy; although adept at planning his client's futures, he has trouble living his own life from day to day, fearful that he may at any moment succumb to that worst of all plagues, the malaise of everydayness. To counter its effects, Binx becomes a moviegoer, partly because films project a "heightened . . . resplendent reality," albeit temporarily, and partly because films provide Binx with accepted role models: thus his impersonations of such canonized figures as Gregory Peck, Clark Gable, Dana Andrews, and Rory Calhoun (who also serves as his confidant). The impersonation can never fully satisfy the moviegoer, however, who must eventually face the fact that the reality of his own life can never attain the heightened illusion of the star's gestural perfection. Moviegoing serves Binx in two additional ways: It enables him to view his world through the perspective of the films he has seen and, more important, to observe the world as if it were itself a film and he the passive audience.

Binx's detachment is both a virtue and a vice. As the detached spectator, he observes those around him closely and accurately, thus exposing the roles they have unknowingly adopted. Appropriately, the novel's temporal setting is the week before Mardi Gras, the period of rehearsals for New Orleans' citywide impersonation. Instead of recognizing their situation as castaways, these others feel serenely at home in the world, whereas in fact they are, as Binx understands, dead. Neither virtuous nor sinful, they are merely "nice"; they speak, but in clichés; they ask questions, but neither expect nor desire answers. Binx, who fears becoming invisible—losing his identity—is right to keep his distance from these shadowy others. At the same time, however, he longs to be like them, to have his identity certified for him by such spurious means as films, identity cards, *Consumer Reports*, newspaper advice columns, and radio shows such as "This I Believe," which broadcasts the meaningless affirmations of abstracted religionists to a half-believing, half-skeptical Binx.

If it is his ironic detachment that saves Binx from the unreflective life of mass humanity, then it is his search that most clearly characterizes his longing for authenticity and being. "To become aware of the possibility of the search is to be onto something," Binx says. "Not to be onto something is to be in despair." Binx distinguishes two kinds of search. The "vertical" leads to abstraction: theories that explain the world but fail to explain what humankind is. (One alternative to such abstraction is the romanticism that killed Binx's father and that the son wisely rejects.) The other is the "horizontal" or phenomenological search that Percy himself counsels in *The Message in the Bottle*. While Binx is indeed "onto something," his search is different from Percy's; it constitutes a "debased" form of the religious search because, as Percy explained, Binx, like Sartre, "has already ruled God out." His search takes a purely aesthetic form. To ease "the pain of loss," he pursues money and women, but the pursuit leads only to boredom and depression because the novelty of his possessions quickly wears off and everydayness inevitably returns to remind him of his inauthenticity and his position as a castaway.

Fortunately, Binx's yearning has a deeper current. As a college student, he found himself "lost in the mystery of being alive at such a time and place"; upon his return from the Korean War, he began his eight-year "exile" in the New Orleans suburb of Gentilly, which, like Covington, is a nonplace; as a broker he has taken to reading *Arabia Deserta*, by the self-styled "God's pilgrim," Charles Montagu Doughty, concealed inside a Standard & Poor's binder.

Binx's search begins with the fact of his own "invincible apathy" and eventually leads, after many wrong turns, to authenticity and intersubjective relationships with his fourteen-year-old half brother, Lonnie Smith, and his twenty-five-year-old cousin, Kate Cutrer. There exists a complicity between Binx and the dying Lonnie, who faces life with true serenity because he understands it religiously. Like the other dying children in Percy's novels, Lonnie represents the paradox of unmerited suffering in a world ruled by a supposedly benevolent God, a paradox Percy resolves by depicting their spiritual victory in a "world full of God's grace where sorrow and death do not have the final word." Binx attends to the "good news" that Lonnie embodies because, in part, Lonnie's monotonous way of talking makes his words fresh and therefore meaningful, "like a code tapped through a wall."

Kate, unlike Lonnie, lives in pure anxiety, swinging wildly between various extremes, especially the longing to be free and the desire "to be an anyone who is anywhere." Although she lacks Binx's degree of awareness as well as his ironic detachment and is more prone to impersonation than he, Kate, like Binx, is aware of her disease, which others can only understand in psychological terms. (Thus, the novel's epigraph, taken from Kierkegaard: "the specific character of despair is precisely this: it is unaware of being despair.") Binx and Kate neatly complement each other: His childlike "simplemindedness" allows her to feel secure enough to speak honestly, while she correctly points out that in his search Binx may be overlooking something "obvious." Her request that Binx be her God—by which she means he is to tell her what to do—is not at all absurd given Marcel's brand of Christian existentialism. Significantly, her other suitors play the part of intersubjective God rather badly: One wants to send her to a high-priced psychoanalyst; the other promises an interminable vista of "niceness" and everydayness.

Binx's leap from nominal Catholic existing in despair to sovereign wayfarer and authentic being occurs very late in the novel and is effected by what, in a parallel context, Percy calls "some dim dazzling trick of grace." In fact, only a few pages from the end Binx laments that, having but one gift, "a good nose for merde," the only course for him to follow is "to fall prey to desire." There is even some justice to his Aunt Emily's judgment of him: In crucial situations, Binx invariably chooses to "default," to exit. Yet, in the final pages, it is clear that Binx will do so no longer. Neither, however, will he play the part his aunt has chosen for him—southern stoic. He will go to medical school, not because she wants him to but because now he knows what to do: to observe *and* to serve others.

Binx's leap is reflected in the very texture of Percy's prose. Until the epilogue, which takes place one year later, Binx has narrated his tale chiefly in what may be termed his detached, matter-of-fact, moviegoer style, against which the very few lyrical passages, used to underscore Binx's wonder and the gracefulness of his world, stand in vivid contrast. In the epilogue, Binx drops the moviegoer style (and the references to films) entirely; instead, he speaks easily, authentically, authoritatively. The man who earlier had been cousin, half brother, and ironic impersonator, now is husband, brother, and sovereign wayfarer.

THE LAST GENTLEMAN

Williston Bibb Barrett, or Billy Barrett, the protagonist of Percy's second novel, *The Last Gentleman*, is a modern-day version of Dostoevski's Prince Myshkin in *The Idiot* (1868). Although far less ironic than Binx Bolling, Barrett is far more disturbed, as his periodic fugue states and bouts of amnesia and déjà vu attest. Existing in a state of pure possibility, he is incapable of making any one decisive act or choice. He has tried and failed both to live the therapeutic life and to engineer his own destiny. Knowing something is missing in his life, Barrett seeks to recover reality and find his being in the "gap" between self and other. Specifically, these others are the members of the Vaught family, and his search is a spiritual odyssey, modeled on Twain's *Adventures of Huckleberry Finn*, which takes him from New York to his native Ithaca, then on to Mississippi, and finally to Santa Fe (Holy Faith), New Mexico, and the Sangre de Cristo (Blood of Christ) mountains.

The search begins when Barrett accidentally discovers Kitty Vaught and her sister-in-law, Rita, in Central Park. Rita, a secular humanist and advocate of self-fulfillment, quickly realizes she will not be able either to control or to convert Barrett and tries unsuccessfully to get rid of him. Barrett, however, has already fallen in love with Kitty, a rather pale version of Kate Cutrer—less anxiety-ridden, more successful in her impersonations. Barrett's love affair is both furthered and complicated by Kitty's younger brother, Jamie, whose traveling companion he becomes. The fact that Jamie is dying establishes definite limits to the pure possibility of his and Barrett's lives and causes Barrett to consider his search more profoundly when he meets another sister, Val, and brother, Sutter, the two "absentee experts" (as Barrett calls them) who force him to make his existential choice. Val, a convert to Catholicism and a nun, has dedicated herself to teaching mute children to speak and to believe the Catholic religion. (All people are like her children, she claims; they are waiting to be told what to do.) Whereas she is hopeful and apostolic, Sutter, a diagnostician and pathologist, is suicidal and ironically quixotic. He rejects her belief in the human as wayfarer, claiming "We are doomed to the transcendence of abstraction and I choose the only reentry into the world which remains to us": cynicism, lewdness, and detachment.

Sutter's mistake, as Barrett well understands, is the positing of extreme alternatives such as God or no God, transcendence or immanence. Moreover, Sutter's concern for Jamie betrays his basically religious nature, and it is this, more than his medical expertise, that has led Barrett to look to him for answers. At Jamie's baptism, it is Sutter who comprehends what is happening. Barrett, although he acts as interpreter between Jamie and the priest, misses the religious significance. He does understand that something has happened, however, and to discover what that something is he tracks down Sutter, who has decided to commit suicide. Barrett's search for an answer is, as Percy noted, a search for a father, ultimately for the Father, God; his own father, Barrett finally realizes, had looked for his answer in all the wrong places—solitude, "old sad poetry," and the music of Johannes Brahms. The son's "wait" did not keep the father from killing himself, but it does save Sutter, who appears in the final tableau less as an oracle than as Barrett's self-chosen—and therefore sovereign—responsibility.

LOVE IN THE RUINS

Subtitled *The Adventures of a Bad Catholic at a Time Near the End of the World*, Percy's *Love in the Ruins* is a broad satire on the state of the modern world—in particular, its behaviorist assumptions and political absurdities. The novel may be flawed, as some reviewers have contended, by the author's insistent and at times rather heavy-handed social criticism; there is, however, a comic vitality in this novel that seems to offset such reservations about it as literary art. This comic vitality, quite unlike the irony and understatement that characterize Percy's earlier novels, is appropriate to a work that has the topics of community and reconciliation as two of its major concerns. As Percy explained in his essay "Notes for a Novel about the End of the World," the apocalyptic novelist serves two purposes: As prophet, or canary in the coal mine, he cries out in order to avert disaster; and as coupling agent, he connects humankind with reality. It is by means of the coupling process that disaster is averted, as Percy quietly suggests in the novel's closing image of a couple "twined about each other as the ivy twineth," in which what has been a sign of ruin (the ivy) is transformed into a symbol of intersubjective love.

The story, which is spoken into a pocket tape recorder by the hero, Tom More, as he keeps watch for snipers, follows a five-part structure (July Fourth, First, Second, Third, Fourth) that progressively becomes more chaotic until, in the epilogue ("Five Years Later"), peace and order are restored. The time of the novel is a not too distant future that bears a clear, if comically exaggerated, resemblance to the American 1960's: The fifteen-year war in Ecuador continues, racial tensions and Bantu uprisings are increasing, and the Catholic Church has split into three factions. In short, "the center did not hold." The physical setting is just as perverse as the social-political: Paradise Estates, home of the well-to-do and the spiritually impoverished; Fedville, a sprawling compound that includes a Masters and Johnson Love Clinic, where former priest Kev Kevin reads *Commonweal* and presides over the vaginal console; Honey Island Swamp, a counterculture retreat; and the golf course, where a banner proclaims "Jesus Christ, the Greatest Pro of Them All."

Percy's hero is as troubled as his society but in a different way. Forty-five years old and a collateral descendant of Sir/Saint Thomas, he is at once a doctor and a mental patient, a diagnostician but also a metaphysician in a world of behaviorists ready and willing to condition away any remaining feelings of guilt he may have. He is of the type that Kierkegaard termed aesthetic damnation, as he loves, in descending order of importance, women, music, science, God, and, "hardly at all," his fellow human. He has lost that thread in the world labyrinth that, until the death of his daughter, Samantha, made the world seem sensible and holy. His faith gone, Tom More has his own messianic ambition, a plan to "save" America with More's Qualitative Quantitative Ontological Lapsometer. His invention—"the stethoscope of the spirit . . . the first caliper of the soul"—is designed to measure the gap between the outer, social self and true, inner being; he hopes to modify the lapsometer so that it can cure as well as diagnose humankind's fall from being, to put together what Descartes tore apart. Like Percy and, to a degree, like Sutter Vaught, More is troubled by the modern world's indifference to being and people's willingness to define themselves in half measures: the angel that, falling prey to abstraction, is unable to "reenter the lovely ordinary world," or the beast that adapts to its environment and so becomes the organism behaviorists say the human is.

Art Immelmann (Mephistopheles to More's Faust) tempts him with spurious "good news": a multimillion dollar development grant and the Nobel Prize. The price is, of course, More's soul—his being, his sense of personal responsibility. More resists the devil and so escapes aesthetic damnation; by not committing the unpardonable sin (refusing God's grace), he puts an end to the "feasting on death" that has preoccupied him since the onset of his daughter's illness and begins to live in the "lovely ordinary world" once again. Instead of an apocalypse, the novel ends with a new beginning, a Christmas morning. Reborn, Tom More no longer loves abstractly or bestially; he has married his former nurse, Ellen Oglethorpe, a Georgia Presbyterian, whose belief takes the form of charity. Equally important, More now knows what it is he wants: not prizes or women, but

> just to figure out what I've hit on. Some day a man will walk into my office as ghost or beast or ghost-beast and walk out as a man, which is to say sovereign wayfarer, lordly exile, worker and waiter and watcher.

LANCELOT

Percy's fourth novel, *Lancelot*, is by far his most troubling. Structurally, it follows the odd dialogue form of Camus's *The Fall* (1956); until the last two pages, only the voice of the protagonist is heard, addressing a "you" whose responses are not given. More disturbing is that, as Joyce Carol Oates has pointed out, the views of the main character, a self-righteous and unrepentant murderer, are strikingly similar to those of the author. Readers must recognize, as Percy surely does, the nature of the protagonist's grotesque mistake—the sources from which it derives and the ends to which it leads.

Lancelot Andrewes Lamar speaks his Poe-like tale from the Center for Aberrant Behavior in New Orleans, where he has been confined for one year. Although in the course of his apologia/confession Lance identifies his wife Margot's infidelity as the immediate cause of his murdering her and the members of the film company with whom she was involved, the actual causes go much further back and have less to do with Margot than with his own wasted life and his position as the last in a fallen line of southern aristocrats. As a Lamar, Lance has inherited not only the family homestead, Belle Isle, but also a way of judging humankind in absolute terms. His first wife, Lucy, was (or so Lance remembers her) an angel, whereas Margot, who for a time he turned into a goddess, became beast or devil.

Dividing his life into two parts—before he discovered his wife's adultery and after—he proclaims that the past is "absolutely dead" and the future will be "absolutely new." This penchant for absolutes suggests Lance's inability or unwillingness to confront the ambiguity and mystery of human existence and is related to the way the Lamars view human life in terms of individual, historically significant events. Thus, Lance's life is reduced to his 110-yard touchdown run against Alabama and his destruction of Belle Isle and everyone in it. Lance does understand that performing such feats is actually less difficult than living an ordinary life, but when he turns Margot's infidelity into a quest for the "unholy grail," he in effect sidesteps the ordinary life that is far "more complicated and ambiguous" than either the historical events venerated by the Lamars or the clichéd films of Margot and her friends.

Like their film, Lance's quest is superficial and derivative (it is cast in the mold of the Raymond Chandler detective novels he has been reading). Moreover, it leads Lance, as Cleanth Brooks has demonstrated, to commit a modern version of the Gnostic heresy. Claiming that the original sin was something God did to humans and judging Christianity as much a failure as southern stoicism, Lance determines to destroy the present age, which he cannot tolerate, and start over in a new Eden with his new Eve, a fellow patient named Anna who, he believes, as the victim of a brutal gang rape, has been restored to innocence. Lance is wrong about Anna, however; she never lost her innocence. He also is wrong about Christianity, if one distinguishes, as Kierkegaard did, between Christianity (as embodied in Percival, Lance's listener to whom the novel is spoken) and Christendom, which Lance is right to reject as a viable alternative to his intolerable age.

Lance's confession, as well as his predicament, brings his friend Percival's spiritual ambivalence into sharp focus; Percival, the Prince Hal of their early manhood who has since been ordained Father John, is torn between two roles—priest and psychiatrist—and two approaches to human existence—the religious and the behavioral. It is Percival's fellow psychiatrists who certify Lance as sane, even though both Lance and Percival know there is still something wrong, something missing. As a psychiatrist, Percival cannot help Lance, whose problem is ontological and spiritual rather than psychological, and whose self-righteous ranting masks his deeper uncertainty and longing. When, at the very end of the novel, Lance asks, "Is there anything I can do for you before I leave?" Percival's "Yes" identifies him as the apostolic Father John, the bearer of the good news for which Lance has been waiting. Against such grand gestures as blowing up Belle Isle, Percy offers the power of a small, ordinary word freshly heard.

THE SECOND COMING

The Second Coming was, as Percy noted, his "first unalienated novel." Instead of the ambiguity that characterizes the endings of his earlier novels, here the author celebrates the unequivocal victory of love over death. While such a conclusion did not please all reviewers, many of whom found it unconvincing or even sentimental, it is consistent with Percy's religious vision and his flexible aesthetic with its various tones and broad range of narrative structures: the novelist's version of God's plenty.

The novel picks up the life of Will Barrett some twenty years after *The Last Gentleman*. At the age of forty-three, Will is a retired lawyer, a wealthy widower living in Linwood, North Carolina, and a recent recipient of the Rotary's man-of-the-year award; yet, he is still a sick man, subject to dizzy spells and tricks of memory. What troubles Will is not the loss of his wife, Marion, but the sudden realization that he has wasted his life and been "only technically alive." At the brink of the abyss, he sees himself as a stranger; only two percent of himself, he sets out to find the missing ninety-eight percent. His search takes him in a number of directions. One is back to his father, or more specifically to the only "event" in his life. This is a hunting accident that he comes to realize was no accident at all but instead the father's attempt to kill his son and then himself and so free them both from lives not worth living.

Like his father, Will rejects the "death in life" that characterizes modern believers as well as unbelievers; Will also rejects his father's solution, suicide, because it proves nothing. Instead, he devises the "ultimate scientific experiment" that will, he believes, provide conclusive proof of either God's existence or His nonexistence/noninvolvement. As the narrator points out, Will is mad; moreover, his plan (to starve himself and so force God either to save or abandon him) is badly flawed in two important ways. The language Will uses to define his experiment (actually more a "covenant") betrays his egotism as well as his legalistic frame of reference; to his "huge" bequest (his life), he attaches a "huge" condition (God's appearing to him). Not until much later in the novel does he learn "the economy of giving and getting" and the superiority of ordinary existence to his own ultimate experiments or his father's extraordinary "events."

In addition, Will is looking for God in the wrong place. While waiting in the cave for "a clear yes [or] no," he misses the unambiguous beauty of Indian summer; and while he assails God's "unavailability," his own "fade outs," such as the cave experiment, preclude the very intersubjective relationships through which God manifests Himself to humankind. The sign he does receive, a toothache, is "a muddy maybe" that cuts short the experiment and sends Will howling in pain out of the wilderness of self and into a world that, while not physically new, can be seen in an original way.

The person who changes Will's angle of vision is Allison Huger (Kitty Vaught's daughter), who has just escaped her own cave, a mental hospital, and begun a new life in an abandoned greenhouse. She resembles Will in that she feels uncomfortable around other people, as well she should, for the Allison they see is the mentally disturbed organism for whom they can imagine nothing better than "the best-structured environment money can buy." Although she wants to live an entirely self-reliant life, each afternoon about four o'clock she experiences a sense of loss or emptiness. What she feels is identical to one of the symptoms of Will's disease (Hausmann's syndrome), which the doctors call "inappropriate longing." There is a pill to control Will's disease, but there is only one way to satisfy the longing, and that is by loving Allison, by finding his being in her just as she finds hers in him. As Allison explains in her characteristically melodic way, "Our lapses are not due to synapses." Percy's love story is not, therefore, simply romantic; rather, it is religious in the Christian existential sense. Their love is, to quote Allison again, "be-all" but not "end-all." When, in the novel's concluding scene, Will confronts Father Weatherbee, an old priest, Will's

> heart leapt with joy. What is it I want from her and him, he wondered, not only want but must have? Is she a gift and therefore a sign of the giver? Could it be that the Lord is here, masquerading behind this simple holy face? Am I crazy to want both, her and Him? No, not want, must have. And will have.

Here, as in the four earlier novels, one finds what Sartre called humanity's useless passion, but for Percy this passionate longing is not useless at all because the world is not absurd. Percy's search is not one of Sartre's purely arbitrary projects; rather it is a thoroughly modern and, for many readers, an entirely convincing rendition of John Bunyan's *The Pilgrim's Progress* (1678, 1684) in an age mired in the slough of behaviorism and unbelief.

THE THANATOS SYNDROME

The Thanatos Syndrome, Percy's sixth and last novel, ends a bit differently, which is to say less insistently. Narrator-protagonist Dr. Tom More's "well well well" befits the smaller scale of his latter-day desires, yet this fit proves ironic, given the novel's overgrand, at times messianic ambitions (of the kind More himself had in *Love in the Ruins*). Similarities between the two novels are obvious (they share a number of the same characters and the same futurist-fantasy approach), but both the strengths and the weaknesses of *The Thanatos Syndrome* owe far more to *Lost in the Cosmos* than to *Love in the Ruins*: the satirizing of contemporary absurdities (inauthenticity in some of its craziest manifestations) and, unfortunately, the hardening of that spiritual need, which characterizes Will Barrett and Binx Bolling, into religious dogma. What was a translation of Christian belief into psychological, cultural, and semiotic terms inthe earlier novels has begun to sound here like a propounding of conservative Catholic teachings, which undermines a novel that otherwise effectively mixes Sir Thomas More's 1516 *Utopia*, medieval romance, Dostoevski, and Robin Cook.

The novel picks up the life and times of Tom More in the mid-1990's, a short while after his release from federal prison, where he has served a two-year term for illegally selling drugs. A brilliant diagnostician, More describes himself as "a psyche-iatrist, an old-fashioned physician of the soul" who believes that it is better, psychologically and spiritually speaking, to be sick (anxious, even terrified) than well, for disease is the natural state of the prelapsarian human being. Many of the people around him are, he realizes, anything but anxious. They are, instead, content: without inhibitions, without anxiety, without anything more than rudimentary language skills, and, most important, without a sense of self. With the help of his epidemiologist cousin Lucy Lipscomb, More discovers Blue Boy, a clandestinely funded pilot project that involves introducing heavy sodium into the local water supply in order to stem the tide of social deterioration (crime, teenage pregnancy, even acquired immunodeficiency syndrome).

The ironically "graceful" Bob Comeaux (née Robert D'Angelo Como), who calls Blue Boy "our Manhattan Project," is the director of Blue Boy and indeed of the entire "Fedville" complex (including an Equalitarian Center with facilities for "pedeuthanasia" and "gereuthanasia" and a propensity for obfuscating acronyms). He tries to cajole, seduce, bribe, and threaten More into complicity, all to no avail. Although he remains a lapsed Catholic throughout, the doctor nevertheless sides with the enigmatic, certainly depressed, previously alcoholic, perhaps mad Father Simon (as in Simeon Stylites and Simon Peter) Smith. Father Simon spends all of his time in a fire tower silently triangulating the positions of forest fires, atoning for his sins, and, on one notable occasion, claiming that all tenderness inevitably leads to the gas chamber (or to the Equalitarian Center, which may be the same thing in a different, more socially acceptable, guise). Comeaux would make everyone happy, at the cost of his or her freedom as well as awareness of him- or herself as a distinctly human being: a creature caught in the malaise, lost in the cosmos, in need of something other than heavy sodium or self-help.

As in Saul Bellow's *The Dean's December* (1982), *The Thanatos Syndrome* expresses More's faith (in there being "more" than Comeaux allows) in the form of a doubt concerning the modern belief that the causes and cures of humankind's problems are invariably physical. To the extent that *The Thanatos Syndrome* articulates this doubt, it, like Percy's other novels, succeeds extraordinarily well. To the extent that it propounds Catholic dogma in response to a host of topical issues (abortion, quality of life, sexual freedom, child abuse, bio- and behavioral engineering, among others), it fails according to the very terms that Percy himself adopted at the time of his conversion, turning the triadic mystery of Kierkegaard's apostle into dyadic pronouncement, sign into signal, and spiritual predicament into position paper.

Robert A. Morace

OTHER MAJOR WORKS

NONFICTION: *The Message in the Bottle*, 1975; *Lost in the Cosmos: The Last Self-Help Book*, 1983; *Conversations with Walker Percy*, 1985 (Lewis A. Lawson and Victor A.

Kramer, editors); *The State of the Novel: Dying Art or New Science?*, 1987; *Signposts in a Strange Land*, 1991 (Patrick Samway, editor); *More Conversations with Walker Percy*, 1993 (Lawson and Kramer, editors); *A Thief of Peirce: The Letters of Kenneth Laine Ketner and Walker Percy*, 1995 (Samway, editor); *The Correspondence of Shelby Foote and Walker Percy*, 1997 (Jay Tolson, editor).

BIBLIOGRAPHY

Allen, William Rodney. *Walker Percy: A Southern Wayfarer.* Jackson: University Press of Mississippi, 1986. Allen reads Percy as a distinctly American, particularly Southern writer, claiming that the formative event in Percy's life was his father's suicide, not his reading of existentialist writers or conversion to Roman Catholicism.

Coles, Robert. *Walker Percy: An American Search.* Boston: Little, Brown, 1978. An early but always intelligent and certainly sensitive reading of Percy's novels and essays by a leading psychiatrist whose main contention is that Percy's work speaks directly to modern humanity.

Desmond, John F. *Walker Percy's Search for Community.* Athens: University of Georgia Press, 2004. Desmond examines Percy's six published novels to analyze his concerns about community. Discusses how Percy formed his own ideas about community from the ideas of philosophers and from his Catholic beliefs.

Dupuy, Edward J. *Autobiography in Walker Percy: Repetition, Recovery, and Redemption.* Baton Rouge: Louisiana State University Press, 1996. Discusses Percy's autobiographical novels as psychological fiction. Includes bibliographical references and an index.

Hardy, John Edward. *The Fiction of Walker Percy.* Urbana: University of Illinois Press, 1987. The originality of this book derives from Hardy's choosing to read the novels in terms of internal formal matters rather than, as is usually the case, in terms of Percy's essays, existentialism, Catholicism, or Southern background.

Kobre, Michael. *Walker Percy's Voices.* Athens: University of Georgia Press, 2000. Analyzes Percy's novels from the theoretical perspective of Russian theorist Mikhail Bakhtin. Kobre is especially interested in Percy's characters, who must sort out the conflicting inner voices of friends, therapists, family, and others until they eventually determine their own identities.

Lawson, Lewis A. *Following Percy: Essays on Walker Percy's Work.* Troy, N.Y.: Whitston, 1988. A collection of essays originally published between 1969 and 1984 by one of Percy's most dedicated, prolific, and knowledgeable commentators. Discussions of *The Moviegoer* and *Lancelot* predominate.

Pridgen, Allen. *Walker Percy's Sacramental Landscapes: The Search in the Desert.* Selingsgrove, Pa.: Susquehanna University Press, 2000. An examination of the imagery, themes, and other elements of literary technique in four of Percy's novels—*The Last Gentleman*, *Love in the Ruins*, *The Second Coming*, and *The Thanatos Syndrome*.

Quinlan, Kieran. *Walker Percy: The Last Catholic Novelist*. Baton Rouge: Louisiana State University Press, 1996. Features chapters on Percy as novelist and philosopher, existentialist, and explorer of modern science. Recommended for the advanced student who already has some knowledge of the religious themes in Percy's writing. Includes notes and a bibliography.

Samway, Patrick H. *Walker Percy: A Life*. New York: Farrar, Straus and Giroux, 1997. The authorized biography, written with Percy's approval and assistance. Samway portrays Percy, whom he met in a writing program, as a writer of great intellect and passion.

Tolson, Jay. *Pilgrim in the Ruins: A Life of Walker Percy*. New York: Simon & Schuster, 1992. A comprehensive account of Percy's life and work, written with Percy's assistance. Tolson describes how Percy was guided by his religious faith; he maintains that Percy's life was a heroic contrast to that of his ancestors, including his father and grandfather, who committed suicide.

Wyatt-Brown, Bertram. *The Literary Percys: Family History, Gender, and the Southern Imagination*. Athens: University of Georgia Press, 1994. Wyatt-Brown explores Percy within the context of his nineteenth century ancestors, including women, who were writers, and analyzes the melancholy that pervades the family.

DOROTHY RICHARDSON

Born: Abingdon, Berkshire (now in Oxfordshire), England; May 17, 1873
Died: Beckenham, Kent, England; June 17, 1957
Also known as: Dorothy Odle; Dorothy Miller Richardson

Principal long fiction

Pointed Roofs, 1915
Backwater, 1916
Honeycomb, 1917
Interim, 1919
The Tunnel, 1919
Deadlock, 1921
Revolving Lights, 1923
The Trap, 1925
Oberland, 1927
Dawn's Left Hand, 1931
Clear Horizon, 1935
Dimple Hill, 1938
March Moonlight, 1967
Pilgrimage, 1938, 1967 (includes all previous titles)

Other literary forms

Dorothy Richardson's literary reputation rests on the single long novel *Pilgrimage*. She referred to the parts published under separate titles as "chapters," and they were the primary focus of her energy throughout her creative life. The first appeared in 1915; the last—unfinished and unrevised—was printed ten years after her death. Before 1915, she wrote some essays and reviews for obscure periodicals edited by friends and also two books growing out of her interest in the Quakers. She contributed descriptive sketches on Sussex life to the *Saturday Review* between 1908 and 1914. During the years writing *Pilgrimage*, Richardson did an enormous amount of miscellaneous writing to earn money—columns and essays in the *Dental Record* (1912-1922), film criticism and translations as well as articles on various subjects for periodicals including *Vanity Fair*, *Adelphi*, *Little Review*, and *Fortnightly Review*. She also wrote a few short stories, chiefly during the 1940's. None of this material has been collected. A detailed bibliography is included in *Dorothy Richardson: A Biography* by Gloria G. Fromm (1977).

Achievements

The term "stream of consciousness," adapted from psychology, was first applied to literature in a 1918 review of Dorothy Richardson's *Pointed Roofs*, *Backwater*, and *Honey-*

comb. In the twentieth century, novels moved from outward experience to inner reality. The experiments that marked the change were made almost simultaneously by three writers unaware of one another's work: The first volume of Marcel Proust's *À la recherche du temps perdu* (1913-1927; *Remembrance of Things Past*, 1922-1931) appeared in 1913, James Joyce's *Portrait of the Artist as a Young Man* began serial publication in 1914, and Richardson's manuscript of *Pointed Roofs* was finished in 1913.

Richardson was the first novelist in England to restrict the point of view entirely to the protagonist's consciousness, to take for content the experience of life at the moment of perception, and to record the development of a single character's mind and emotions without imposing any plot or structural pattern. Her place in literature (as opposed to literary history) has been less certain; some critics feel that her work is interesting only because it dates the emergence of a new technique. The absence of story and explanation make heavy demands on the reader. Since the protagonist's own limited understanding controls every word of the narrative, readers must also do the work of evaluating the experience in order to create meaning.

Richardson wrote what Virginia Woolf called "the psychological sentence of the feminine gender"; a sentence that expanded its limits and tampered with punctuation to convey the multiple nuances of a single moment. She deliberately rejected the description of events, which she thought was typical of male literature, in order to convey the subjective understanding that she believed was the reality of experience. The autobiographical basis of *Pilgrimage* was not known until 1963. Richardson, like her protagonist and like other women of her period, broke with the conventions of the past, sought to create her own being through self-awareness, and struggled to invent a form that would communicate a woman's expanding conscious life.

Biography

Dorothy Richardson, born on May 17, 1873, was the third of four daughters. Her father, Charles Richardson, worked in the prosperous grocery business that his father had established, but he wanted to be a gentleman. He abandoned Nonconformity for the Church of England and, in 1874, sold the family business to live on investments. During Dorothy's childhood, periods of upper-middle-class luxury (a large house, servants, gardens, membership in a tennis club) alternated with moves arising from temporarily reduced circumstances.

Charles had hoped for a son, and he took Dorothy with him to lectures in Oxford and meetings of scientific associations. She was sent at age eleven to a private day school for the daughters of gentlemen. It was late enough in the century for the curriculum to emphasize academic subjects; her studies included logic and psychology. In 1890, realizing that her family's financial condition had become seriously straitened, Dorothy looked to the example of Charlotte Brontë and *Villette* (1853) and applied for a post as pupil-teacher in a German school. Six months in Hanover were followed by two years teaching in a North

London private school and a brief spell as governess for a wealthy suburban family.

By the end of 1893, Richardson's father was declared bankrupt; in 1895, two of her sisters married. Her mother, Mary Richardson, was troubled by an unusually severe bout of the depression that had gripped her for several years. Richardson took her mother to stay in lodgings near the sea and found that she required almost constant companionship and supervision. On November 30, 1895, while her daughter was out for a short walk in the fresh air, Mary committed suicide.

At the age of twenty-two, responsible for her own support and severely shaken by the past two years' events, Richardson moved to an attic room in a London lodging house and took a job as secretary and assistant to three Harley Street dentists. For young women at that time, such a step was unusual; by taking it Richardson evaded the restraint, protection, and religious supervision that made teaching an acceptable profession for young women of good family. The nineteenth century was drawing to a close and London was alive with new ideas. Richardson explored the city, made friends with women who worked in business offices, and lived on eggs and toast so that she could afford concert tickets.

Soon after moving to London, she was invited for a Saturday in the country by an old school friend, Amy Catherine Robbins, who had married her science instructor at London University: That instructor's name was H. G. Wells. He had just published *The Time Machine* (1895). Richardson was fascinated by Wells and by the people and ideas she encountered at his house but angered by his way of telling her what to do. She was aware that she stood outside the class system and between the Victorian and modern worlds. She was drawn both to picnics with cousins at Cambridge and to anarchist and Fabian meetings. She sampled various churches (including Unitarian and Quaker) but refrained from committing herself to any group or cause.

In 1902, Richardson began contributing occasional articles and reviews to *Crank* and other magazines edited by a vegetarian friend. She refused a proposal from a respectable physician and broke her engagement to a Russian Jew, Benjamin Grad. Her friendship with Wells passed at some point into physical intimacy, but she continued to struggle against being overwhelmed by his ideas and personality. In 1906, finding herself pregnant, she brought the affair to an end; she looked forward to raising the child on her own and was distressed when she suffered a miscarriage.

Exhausted physically and mentally, Richardson left her dental job and went to Sussex to recover and think. In 1908, she began writing sketches for the *Saturday Review*. Then, as her fortieth year approached, she began deliberately searching for the form that would allow her to create what she called "a feminine equivalent of the current masculine realism."

Pointed Roofs was at first rejected by publishers. When it was published in 1915 it puzzled readers, distressed some reviewers, and failed to make money. Richardson persisted, however, on the course she had set, even while living an unsettled life in YWCA hostels and borrowed rooms and earning a minimal income by proofreading and by writing a monthly column for the *Dental Record*. In 1917, she married artist Alan Odle, who was fifteen years younger than she and had been rejected for military service by a doctor who told him he had six months to live.

Richardson's books attracted some critical recognition in the years after World War I, but they never earned money; she was usually in debt to her publishers. She supported herself and Odle (who lived until 1948) and also coped with all the practical details of their life—housekeeping, paying taxes, writing checks, doing his business with publishers and exhibitors. The couple moved frequently, spending the off-season (when lodgings were less expensive) in Cornwall and going to rooms in London for the summer. During the early 1930's, Richardson took on the burden of five full-length translations from French and German. Returning to *Pilgrimage* and the state of mind in which it was begun became increasingly difficult for Richardson; the later volumes were weakened by extraliterary distractions and also by the psychological difficulty for the author in concluding the work that was based on her own life. The final segment, *March Moonlight*, was found unfinished among her papers after she died on June 17, 1957, at the age of eighty-four.

ANALYSIS

Pilgrimage is a quest. The novel's protagonist, Miriam Henderson, seeks her self and, rejecting the old guideposts, makes her own path through life. The book remains a problem for many readers, although since 1915 most of Dorothy Richardson's technical devices have become familiar: unannounced transitions from third-person narration to the first person for interior monologue, shifts between present and past as experience evokes memory, and disconnected phrases and images and fragmentary impressions representing the continuous nonverbal operations of the mind.

Looking back on the period when she was trying to find a way to embody Miriam Henderson's experience, Richardson described her breakthrough as the realization that no one was "*there* to *describe* her." Impressed by Henry James's control of viewpoint, she went one step further. The narrator and the protagonist merge; the narrator knows, perceives, and expresses only what comes to Miriam's consciousness. Furthermore, the narrator does not speak to any imagined reader and therefore does not provide helpful explanations. The scenes and people are presented as they impinge on Miriam's awareness—thus the most familiar circumstances are likely to be undescribed and the most important people identified only by name, without the phrases that would place them or reveal their relationship to Miriam.

Many readers are discouraged by the attempt to follow the book and make meaning of it; some are tempted to use Richardson's biography to find out what "really" happened and others prefer to read isolated sections without regard to sequence, responding to the feeling and imagery as if it were poetry. Because there is no narrative guidance, meaning is continually modified by the reader's own consciousness and by the extent of identification.

Miriam Henderson novels

The first three titles show Miriam Henderson in the last stages of her girlhood and form the prelude to her London life. *Pointed Roofs* covers her experience in Hanover; in *Backwater*, she is resident teacher in a North London school and still drawn to the possibility of romance with a young man from her suburban circle; in *Honeycomb*, she briefly holds a post as governess before her sisters' weddings and her mother's death complete the disintegration of her girlhood family.

The Tunnel begins Miriam's years in London and introduces situations and characters that reappear in the next several volumes: the dental job; the room at Mrs. Bailey's lodging house; the new women, Mag and Jan; and the dependent woman, Eleanor Dear; and a visit to her school friend, Alma, who has married the writer Hypo Wilson. In *Interim*, Miriam perceives the difficulty of communicating her current thoughts and experiences to her sister and other old friends. *Deadlock* treats her acquaintance—growing into an engagement—with Michael Shatov. In *Revolving Lights*, she has decided not to marry Shatov and becomes increasingly involved with Wilson.

The Trap shows her sharing a cramped flat with a spinster social worker and growing despondent about the isolation that, she realizes, she imposes on herself to avoid emotional entanglements. *Oberland* is a lyrical interlude about a holiday in Switzerland. In *Dawn's Left Hand*, Miriam has an affair with Wilson and an intense friendship with a young woman (Amabel) who becomes a radical suffragist. *Clear Horizon* concludes much of the practical and emotional business that has occupied Miriam for several years; she disentangles herself from Wilson, Shatov, and Amabel and prepares to leave London. In *Dimple Hill*, she lives on a farm owned by a Quaker family, absorbs their calm, and works at writing. *March Moonlight* rather hastily takes Miriam up to the point of meeting the artist who would become her husband and to the beginning of her work on a novel.

This summary of events is the barest framework. Life, for Miriam Henderson, exists not in events but in the responses that create her sense of awareness. The books are made up of relatively independent sections, each treating a single segment of experience or reflection. Because of the depth with which single moments are recorded, the overall narrative line is fragmentary. Despite *Pilgrimage*'s length, it embodies isolated spots of time. Frequently, neither narration nor the memories evoked by subsequent experience indicate what events may have taken place in the gaps between. Furthermore, the book concentrates on those moments important to Miriam's interior experience, and it leaves out the times when she acts without self-awareness—which may include significant actions that take place when Miriam is so engrossed by events that she does not engage in thought or reflection.

Richardson disliked the phrase "stream of consciousness" because it implies constant movement and change. She preferred the image of a pool—new impressions are added, and sometimes create ripples that spread over the previously accumulated consciousness. Thus, Miriam's interior monologue becomes steadily more complex as she grows older.

Her consciousness widens and deepens; fragmentary phrases show her making connections with her earlier experiences and perceptions; her understanding of past events alters with later awareness. The earlier volumes have more sensory impression and direct emotion; later, as Miriam grows more self-aware, she has greater verbal skill and is more likely to analyze her responses. Because of her more sophisticated self-awareness, however, she also grows adept, in the later volumes, at suppressing impressions or fragments of self-knowledge that she does not want to admit to consciousness.

In many ways, Miriam is not likable—readers are sometimes put off by the need to share her mind for two thousand pages. In the early books, she is a self-preoccupied, narrow-minded adolescent, oppressively conscious of people's appearance and social class, annoyingly absorbed in wondering what they think about her, defensively judgmental. The wild swings in mood and the ebb and flow of her energies during the day appear to have little cause and to be unworthy of the attention she gives them. Most people, however, would appear unpleasantly selfish if their minds were open for inspection. Miriam creates her self by deliberate consciousness. The danger is that she tends to withdraw from experience in order to contemplate feeling.

Pilgrimage

The events of *Pilgrimage* span the decades at the turn of the century but, because of the interior focus, there is relatively little physical detail or explicit social history to create an objective picture of the era. Women's developing self-awareness, however, must be seen as one of the period's significant events. Miriam reflects the mental life of her times in her range of responses to religion, the books she reads, and the people, ideas, and movements she encounters.

A good deal of life's texture and even its choices take place at levels that are not verbalized. Richardson's first publisher described her work as "female imagism." Miriam responds particularly and constantly to the quality of light. Readers are also aware of her reaction to places, objects, and physical surroundings; ultimately, it is through mastering the emotional content of this response that she is able to discover what she needs to have in her life.

Another continuing thread is created by Miriam's thoughts about men, about men and women together, and about the roles of women in society. Her basic animosity toward men gives shape to a series of statements on their personal, emotional, social, and intellectual peculiarities that falls just short of a formal feminist analysis. Each possible romance, each rejected or forestalled proposal amounts to a choice of a way of life. The matter is, however, complicated by Miriam's sexual reticence. Even though she can talk about free love, she is not conscious—or perhaps will not permit herself to become conscious—of overt sexual urges or of physical attraction to men or to women. She struggles not to let her feeling for certain women lead her to be absorbed by their lives or roles. In *Backwater*, Miss Perne's religion is dangerously comfortable; Eleanor Dear's passive feminine helplessness forces Miriam to become her protector; Amabel's possessiveness is as stifling as Hypo Wilson's. At the end—in *March Moonlight*—there is a hint of emotional involvement with the unidentified Jane. Struggling to know herself, Miriam is constantly faced with the problem of knowing other women.

Pointed Roofs

Pointed Roofs comes close to being a structural whole—it begins with Miriam Henderson's journey to Hanover and ends with her return home six months later. She is on her first trip away from home, looking at new scenes, anxious about her ability to do her job and earn her wages, having her first taste of independence. Since Miriam is seventeen years old—and, as a Victorian daughter, a relatively innocent and sheltered seventeen—the reader often understands more than Miriam does and can interpret the incidents that develop her sense of who she is and where she fits in the world. Some of Miriam's reactions are cast in the form of mental letters home or imaginary conversations with her sisters, which provide a structured way to verbalize mental processes. Miriam pays attention to the sights and sounds and smells of Hanover because they are new, giving readers a sense of the physical setting absent in many of the later books.

Miriam's moods are typically adolescent. An incident or object can set off a homesick reverie or a bout of self-recrimination; the sound of music or the sight of rain on paving stones can create an inexpressible transport of joy. She is alternately rebellious and anxious for approval; she is glad to learn that her French roommate is Protestant (because she could not bear living with a Catholic), proud of the skill in logic that allows her to criticize the premises of a sermon, moved by the sound of hymns in German. She worries about her plainness, her intellectual deficiencies, her inability to get close to people. Observing class and cultural differences lets her begin to understand that she has unthinkingly absorbed many of her tastes and ideas; she starts to grow more deliberate. This portrait of Miriam at the age of seventeen—which forms the essential background for the rest of *Pilgrimage*—is also interesting for its own sake.

Because the narrative is limited to Miriam's consciousness, the reader is able to supply interpretation. In one key scene, the middle-aged Pastor Lahmann, chaplain to the school, quotes a verse describing his ambition for "A little land, well-tilled,/ A little wife, well-willed" and then asks Miriam to take off her glasses so that he can see how nearsighted her eyes really are. Miriam, who is both furious at being "regarded as one of a world of little tame things to be summoned by little man to be well-willed wives" and warmed by the personal attention that makes her forget, for a moment, that she is a governess, is oblivious to the sexual implications of Pastor Lahmann's behavior, and she cannot understand why the headmistress is angry when she walks in upon the scene. Although Miriam's consciousness will develop in subsequent volumes, her combination of receptivity to male attention, anger at male assumptions, and blindness to sexual nuance will remain.

DEADLOCK

Deadlock contains a greater proportion of direct internal monologue than the earlier books. Miriam has grown more articulate; she interprets her emotional states and examines the premises underlying her conflicts. During her first years in London, she had cherished the city for the independence it gave her. By such acts as smoking, eating alone in restaurants, and dressing without regard to fashion, she deliberately rejected Victorian womanhood. In *Honeycomb*, she refused a marriage that would have satisfied her craving for luxuries because she could not accept a subordinate role. In *Deadlock*, Miriam is faced by the loneliness that seems inextricably linked to independence. Her work has become drudgery because she no longer has the sense of a social relationship with her employer. A Christmas visit to her married sister reveals the distance that has grown between them; Miriam had not even realized that Harriet's marriage was unhappy.

Deadlock is shaped by the course of Miriam's relationship with Michael Shatov. The romance forces her conflicts to the surface. Shatov is a young Jew recently arrived from Russia; a lodger at Mrs. Bailey's arranges for Miriam to tutor him in English. As she shows Shatov London, tired scenes recapture their original freshness. Miriam is excited by her ability to formulate ideas when she argues about philosophy or works on a translation. Yet, although Miriam is buoyed by the joy of sharing her thoughts with another person, Shatov's continual presence comes between her and the life that was her own. Her love has a maternal quality: Though Shatov is only three years younger than Miriam, he is a foreigner and also, Miriam finds, rather impractical; she feels protective. She is also sexually reticent: Because she has despised traditional femininity, she does not know how to behave as the object of a courtship. The romance ends when Miriam deliberately engages Shatov in an argument that reveals his views of woman's limited nature. (The final scene restates the problem more concretely when Miriam visits an Englishwoman married to a Jewish man.)

Beneath these specific difficulties lies the friction between Miriam's individualism and Shatov's tendency to see problems in the abstract—she talks about herself, he dwells on the future of the race. For Richardson, the conflict reflects the irreconcilable difference between masculine objectivity (or materialism) and feminine subjectivity. The images of darkness accumulate as Miriam realizes the extent of her deadlock; unable to be a woman in the sense that men see women, she seems to have no path out of loneliness and alienation.

DAWN'S LEFT HAND

Dawn's Left Hand is a prelude to the deliberate detachment and observation that would turn Miriam into a writer. *Oberland* (the preceding book) vibrates with the sensory detail of a two-week holiday in Switzerland that makes London complications seem far away; returning, Miriam sees people objectively even when she is with them. The transitions between third-person narrative and internal monologue are less noticeable; Miriam and the narrator have virtually merged. The visual content of scenes reveals their meaning. Miriam looks at pictorial relationships and examines gesture and tone for the nonverbal communications that, to women, are often more meaningful than words. (During the years that she worked on *Dawn's Left Hand*, Richardson wrote regularly about films—which were still silent—for the magazine *Close Up*.)

Images of light carry emotional and symbolic content throughout *Pilgrimage*. When Miriam visits Densley's medical office early in *Dawn's Left Hand*, the drawn shades are keeping out the light; she refuses his proposal—one last offer of conventional marriage—with a momentary wistfulness that is immediately replaced by a great sense of relief. She is increasingly aware of herself as an actor in the scenes of her life. Self-observation allows physical compositions to reveal power relationships: When Wilson comes into Miriam's room, she notices that he stands over her like a doctor, and when he embarks on a program of seduction to the music of Richard Wagner, she disputes his control by rearranging the chairs. On another occasion, in a hotel room, Miriam looks in the mirror to observe herself and Wilson. Her own position blocks the light and thus the scene is chilled even before she begins to see him as a pathetic naked male.

During the final stages of the Wilson affair, Miriam is increasingly preoccupied by a beautiful young woman—soon to be a radical suffragist—who pursues her ardently and pays homage to her as a woman in ways that bring home to Miriam the impossibility of real communion with men. Yet the deep commitment demanded by Amabel is frightening; her intense adoration forces Miriam into a role that threatens her independence more crucially than Wilson's overt attempts at domination. The advantage of being with people who interact only on superficial levels, Miriam realizes, is that she can retain her freedom.

MARCH MOONLIGHT

Although Richardson struggled to bring the events in *March Moonlight* up to 1912, the year that she began writing *Pilgrimage*, her form and subject virtually required the book to remain without conclusion. The narrative techniques of *March Moonlight* grow more deliberate; when Miriam begins to write, she thinks and sees differently and is aware of selecting and arranging details. Thus, the book's ending is only a middle: Miriam's sense of self would inevitably change as she reexamined and re-created her experiences in order to write novels. Once traditional formulas are rejected and *being* itself becomes the subject, there can be no ending; there is no epiphany, no coming-of-age, no final truth but rather a continuous process of self-making through self-awareness.

Sally Mitchell

OTHER MAJOR WORKS

NONFICTION: *Gleanings from the Works of George Fox*, 1914; *The Quakers Past and Present*, 1914; *John Austen and the Inseparables*, 1930.

Bibliography

Bloom, Harold, ed. *British Women Fiction Writers, 1900-1960*. 2 vols. Philadelphia: Chelsea House, 1997. A brief biography and critical essays about Richardson's work and place in literary history is included in volume 2 of this survey of British women writers.

Bluemel, Kristin. *Experimenting on the Borders of Modernism: Dorothy Richardson's "Pilgrimage."* Athens: University of Georgia Press, 1997. The first chapter assesses Richardson and previous studies of her. Subsequent chapters explore Richardson's handling of gender, the problems of the body, science in *Pilgrimage*, and the author's quest for an ending to this long work. Includes notes and a bibliography.

Fromm, Gloria G. *Dorothy Richardson: A Biography*. Champaign: University of Illinois Press, 1977. An objective biography, which carefully draws distinctions between the events of Richardson's life and those of her fictional characters, but also identifies clear correlations between the two. Extensively researched and well written and supplemented by illustrations, chapter endnotes, a comprehensive bibliography, and an index.

Garrity, Jane. "'Neither English nor Civilized': Dorothy Richardson's Spectatrix and the Feminine Crusade for Global Intervention." In *Step-Daughters of England: British Women Modernists and the National Imaginary*. New York: St. Martin's Press, 2003. Garrity examines works by Richardson and three other modernist women writers to demonstrate how these works express the writers' ambivalent and complex feelings about English national culture.

Gevirtz, Susan. *Narrative's Journey: The Fiction and Film Writing of Dorothy Richardson*. New York: Peter Lang, 1996. A probing discussion of Richardson's aesthetic. This is a challenging study for advanced students. *Pilgrimage* receives detailed discussion throughout the book. Includes an extensive bibliography not only on Richardson but also on feminist theory, literary and cultural theory, poetics and phenomenology, theology and spirituality, travel and travel theories, and narrative.

McCracken, Scott. "Editorial." *Pilgrimages: The Journal of Dorothy Richardson Studies* 1, no. 1 (2008). Richardson scholar Scott McCracken introduces the first issue of a new academic journal focusing on Richardson's life and works.

Parsons, Deborah L. *Theorists of the Modernist Novel: James Joyce, Dorothy Richardson, Virginia Woolf*. New York: Routledge, 2007. A study of the aesthetic theories of Richardson and two other modernist writers. Parsons examines realism, characterization, gender representation, and other elements of Richardson's work.

Radford, Jean. *Dorothy Richardson*. Bloomington: Indiana University Press, 1991. An excellent introductory study, with chapters on reading in *Pilgrimage*, the author's quest for form, London as a space for women, and Richardson as a feminist writer. Includes notes and a bibliography.

Randall, Bryony. "Dailiness in Dorothy Richardson's *Pilgrimage*." In *Modernism, Daily*

Time, and Everyday Life. New York: Cambridge University Press, 2007. Argues that the temporal notion of "the day" partly structures Richardson's fiction. Also examines Richardson's attempts at rendering time without beginnings and endings.

Rosenberg, John. *Dorothy Richardson, the Genius They Forgot: A Critical Biography*. New York: Alfred A. Knopf, 1973. The strength of Rosenberg's biography lies in his scholarly credibility, as he aptly parallels events in *Pilgrimage* to Richardson's life. His concluding analysis of Richardson's pioneering impact upon the development of the novel, however, lacks the impact of his earlier writing but is still perceptive. Includes an index and a bibliography.

Winning, Joanne. *The Pilgrimage of Dorothy Richardson*. Madison: University of Wisconsin Press, 2000. Winning argues that Richardson's thirteen-volume novel contains a subtext of lesbian desire and sexuality, and she compares this novel to works by other lesbian modernist writers.

LAURENCE STERNE

Born: Clonmel, Ireland; November 24, 1713
Died: London, England; March 18, 1768

PRINCIPAL LONG FICTION

The Life and Opinions of Tristram Shandy, Gent., 1759-1767 (commonly known as *Tristram Shandy*)

A Sentimental Journey Through France and Italy, 1768

OTHER LITERARY FORMS

Laurence Sterne began his literary career with political pieces in the *York-Courant* in 1741. Two years later, he published a poem, "The Unknown World," in *The Gentleman's Magazine* (July, 1743). His song "How Imperfect the Joys of the Soul," written for Kitty Fourmantel, appeared in Joseph Baildon's *Collection of New Songs Sung at Ranelagh* (1765), and a four-line epigram, "On a Lady's Sporting a Somerset," was attributed to Sterne in *Muse's Mirror* (1778). His sermons were published in three installments: two volumes in 1760, another two in 1766, and a final three volumes in 1769. A satire titled *A Political Romance* was published in 1759 but quickly suppressed. After Sterne's death, *Letters from Yorick to Eliza* appeared in 1773, and his daughter arranged for the publication of the three-volume *Letters of the Late Rev. Mr. L. Sterne to His Most Intimate Friends* (1775). These volumes include an autobiographical *Memoir* and the *Fragment in the Manner of Rabelais*. In 1935, Oxford University Press published the definitive edition of Sterne's letters, edited by Lewis Perry Curtis. The *Journal to Eliza*, composed in 1767, was not published until 1904.

ACHIEVEMENTS

When Laurence Sterne went to London in March, 1760, he was an obscure provincial parson. He rode as a guest in Stephen Croft's cart, and he brought with him little more than his "best breeches." Two months later, he returned to York in his own carriage. Robert Dodsley, who the year before had refused the copyright of *The Life and Opinions of Tristram Shandy, Gent.* (commonly known as *Tristram Shandy*) for 50 pounds, now gladly offered Sterne 250 pounds for the first two volumes, 380 pounds for the next two, as yet unwritten, and another 200 pounds for two volumes of sermons. The famous artist William Hogarth agreed to provide a frontispiece to the second edition of volume 1 and another for volume 3; Joshua Reynolds painted Sterne's portrait. Like Lord Byron, Sterne could have said that he awoke to find himself famous. As Sterne did say, in a letter to Catherine Fourmantel, "I assure you my Kitty, that Tristram is the Fashion." Despite the carpings of a few—Horace Walpole thought *Tristram Shandy* "a very insipid and tedious performance," and Samuel Richardson thought it immoral—the novel was the rage of

Laurence Sterne
(Library of Congress)

London, inspiring so many continuations and imitations that Sterne had to sign the later volumes to guarantee their authenticity.

After the novel's initial popularity, sales did drop off. In book 8, Tristram complains that he has "ten cart-loads" of volumes 5 and 6 "still unsold." Dodsley abandoned publication of the work after volume 4, and Sterne's new publisher, Thomas Becket, complained in April, 1763, that he had 991 copies of volumes 5 and 6 unsold (from a printing of 4,000). Samuel Johnson's famous comment, though ultimately incorrect, probably reflected the opinion of the day: "Nothing odd will do long. *Tristram Shandy* did not last." Even Sterne may have tired of the work; the volumes grew slimmer, and volume 9 appeared without its mate, volume 10 having, in Sterne's apt words for an obstetrical novel, "miscarried."

Tristram Shandy has lasted, however. It retains a readership, even if it has continued to justify Sterne's complaint of being "more read than understood." Some modern-day readers have made great, perhaps exaggerated, claims for the novel, seeing it as the harbinger of the works of Marcel Proust, James Joyce, and Albert Camus, who, it is said, derived from Sterne the concept of relative time, the stream of consciousness, and a sense of the absurd. Even if one discounts such assertions, there can be no question of the work's importance in the development of the novel or of *Tristram Shandy*'s place in the first rank of eighteenth century fiction.

Less has been claimed for *A Sentimental Journey Through France and Italy* (commonly known as *A Sentimental Journey*), yet this work, apparently so different from and so much simpler than *Tristram Shandy*, greatly influenced Continental, especially German, literature of the Romantic period. Though critics debate the sincerity of the emotions in the work, eighteenth century readers generally did not question Yorick's sentimentality, which contributed to the rise of the cult of sensibility exemplified by such works as Henry Mackenzie's *The Man of Feeling* (1771). Because of its brevity, its benevolence, and its accessibility, *A Sentimental Journey* has enjoyed continued popularity since its first appearance. Although lacking the stature of *Tristram Shandy*, it remains a classic.

BIOGRAPHY

Laurence Sterne was born in Clonmel, Tipperary, Ireland, on November 24, 1713. On his father's side, he could claim some distinction: His great-grandfather, Richard Sterne, had been Archbishop of York, and his grandfather, Simon Sterne, was a rich Yorkshire country squire. Roger Sterne, Laurence's father, was less distinguished. Sterne described his father as "a little smart man—active to the last degree, in all exercises—most patient of fatigue and disappointments, of which it pleased God to give him full measure." Sterne added that his father was "of a kindly, sweet disposition, void of all design." Many have seen Roger Sterne as the model for Uncle Toby Shandy. At the age of sixteen, Roger joined the Cumberland Regiment of Foot, and on September 25, 1711, he married Agnes Nuttall. Agnes, according to her son, was the daughter of "a noted sutler in Flanders, in Queen Ann's wars," whom Roger married because he was in debt to her father. Actually, she may have been the daughter of a poor but respectable family in Lancashire.

From his birth to the age of ten, Sterne led a nomadic life, wandering from barracks to barracks across Great Britain. During these years, he may have acquired some of the military knowledge that appears throughout *Tristram Shandy*, or at least that fondness for the military that marks the work. When Sterne was ten, his uncle Richard sent him to school near Halifax, in Yorkshire, and in 1733, Sterne's cousin sent him to Jesus College, Cambridge, where his great-grandfather had been a master and where both his uncle Jaques and his cousin had gone. At Cambridge, Sterne met John Hall, who later renamed himself John Hall-Stevenson. Hall-Stevenson was to be one of Sterne's closest friends throughout his life; his library at "Crazy Castle" would furnish much of the abstruse learning in *Tristram Shandy*, and he would himself appear in both that novel and *A Sentimental Journey* as Eugenius, the sober adviser. While at Cambridge, Sterne suffered his first tubercular hemorrhage.

After receiving his bachelor's degree in January, 1737, Sterne had to choose a profession. Because his great-grandfather and uncle had both gone into the clergy, Sterne followed their path. After Sterne served briefly in St. Ives and Catton, his uncle Jaques, by then archdeacon of Cleveland and canon and precentor of the York Cathedral, secured for him the living of Sutton on the Forest, a few miles north of York. A second post soon followed; Sterne received the prebend of Givendale, making him part of the York Cathedral chapter and so allowing him to preach his turn there.

At York, Sterne met Elizabeth Lumley, a woman with a comfortable fortune. Their courtship had a strong sentimental tinge to it. Indeed, if Sterne actually wrote to Elizabeth the letters that his daughter published after his death, his is the first recorded use of the word "sentimental," and the emotions expressed in these letters foreshadow both *A Sentimental Journey* and the *Journal to Eliza*. Even if these letters are spurious, Sterne's description of his courtship in the *Memoirs* is sufficiently lachrymose to rival the death of Le Fever in *Tristram Shandy*. Unfortunately for Sterne, he, unlike Tristram, did go on; on March 30, 1741, he married Elizabeth. The unfavorable portrait of Mrs. Shandy owes much to Sterne's less than sentimental feelings toward his wife, whom he called in March, 1760, the "one Obstacle to my Happiness."

The year 1741 was also important for Sterne because it marked his first appearance in print. His uncle Jaques was a strong Whig, and he recruited his nephew to write in support of the Whig candidate for York in that year's election. Sterne wrote, the Whig won, and Sterne received the prebend of North Newbold as a reward. The Whig success was, however, short-lived. When the Walpole government fell in 1742, Sterne wrote a recantation and apology for his part in "the late contested Election," and thereby earned the enmity of his uncle, an enmity that ended only with Jaques's death in 1759.

For eighteen years, Sterne lived as a typical provincial clergyman, attending to the needs of his parishioners and publishing two sermons. One of these, "For We Trust We Have a Good Conscience," Sterne reprints in its entirety in the second volume of *Tristram Shandy*. In 1751, he received the commissaryship of Pickering and Pocklington, despite his uncle's efforts to secure this position for Dr. Francis Topham. Sterne and Topham collided again in 1758, when Topham attended to include his son in a patent and thus secure for him a post after his own death. When the dean of York Cathedral blocked the inclusion, a pamphlet war ensued. Sterne fired the final shot; his pamphlet *A Political Romance* so squashed Topham that he agreed to abandon the fray if Sterne would withdraw the work. Sterne did withdraw *A Political Romance*, but he was not finished with Topham, who was to appear in *Tristram Shandy* as Phutatorius and Didius.

A Political Romance is little more than a satiric squib, but it shows that Sterne was familiar with the works of Jonathan Swift. In its use of clothes symbolism as well as in its severity it recalls *A Tale of a Tub* (1704), and it shows that Swift's work was running in Sterne's head between 1758 and 1759. He was making other use of Swift, too. On May 23, 1759, Sterne wrote to Robert Dodsley, "With this You will receive the Life & Opinions of

Tristram Shandy, which I choose to offer to You first." By this time, the first volume of the novel was finished. Although Dodsley refused the copyright for the sum of 50 pounds that Sterne requested, Sterne continued to write, completing a second volume and revising the first to remove "all locality" and make "the whole . . . more saleable," as he wrote to Dodsley several months later.

Salable it was. The York edition sold two hundred copies in two days when it appeared in December, 1759, and when Sterne went up to London, he was told that the book was not "to be had in London either for Love or money." Dodsley, who had been unwilling to risk 50 pounds on the copyright, now purchased it for 250 pounds, gave another 380 pounds to publish the still-unwritten volumes 3 and 4, and yet another 200 pounds for two volumes of Sterne's sermons. Sterne was honored by the great. Thomas Gray wrote to Thomas Wharton, "Tristram Shandy is still a greater object of admiration, the Man as well as the Book. One is invited to dinner, where he dines, a fortnight beforehand."

In March, 1760, Sterne also succeeded to the curacy of Coxwold, a better position than his earlier one at Sutton. In May, 1760, he therefore settled at Coxwold, renting Shandy Hall from Earl Fauconberg. Here he worked on the next two volumes of *Tristram Shandy*, which he brought to London at the end of the year. In 1761, he repeated this pattern, but he did not return to Yorkshire after delivering the manuscript of volumes 5 and 6. Having suffered a tubercular hemorrhage, he set off for the warmer, milder air of France.

There he repeated his earlier triumph in London, and he incidentally acquired materials for book 7 of *Tristram Shandy* and *A Sentimental Journey*. Sterne remained in France for almost two years; when he returned to England, he hastily wrote the next two volumes of *Tristram Shandy*, which appeared in January, 1765. In October of that year, he brought twelve sermons to London rather than more of his novel. After leaving the manuscript with his publisher, he again set off for the Continent; he would combine the adventures of this trip with those of his earlier one in writing *A Sentimental Journey*.

In June, 1766, Sterne was back in Coxwold, where he wrote what proved to be the last installment of *Tristram Shandy*. This he brought with him to London in late December; shortly after his arrival, he met Eliza Draper, the wife of an East India Company clerk twenty years her senior. Though initially unimpressed with her, Sterne was soon madly in love. When Sterne met her, she had already been in England some two years, and she was to return to India less than three months later, yet she was to color Sterne's last year of life. Before she sailed on the *Earl of Chatham* on April 3, 1767, Sterne visited her daily, wrote letters to her, drove with her, and exchanged pictures with her. After their separation, Sterne continued his letters; those he wrote between April 13 and the beginning of August, 1767, constitute the *Journal to Eliza*. When he broke off this journal with the words "I am thine—& thine only, & for ever" to begin *A Sentimental Journey*, her spirit haunted that work, too, as the Eliza upon whom Yorick calls.

By December, Sterne had finished the first half of *A Sentimental Journey* and again set off for London and his publisher. On February 27, 1768, *A Sentimental Journey*, volumes

1 and 2, appeared. Less than a month later, on March 18, Sterne died. He was buried in London on March 22; on June 8, 1769, he was reinterred in the Coxwold churchyard in Yorkshire.

ANALYSIS

Readers may be tempted to see Laurence Sterne's works either as sui generis or as eighteenth century sports that had no mate until Marcel Proust and James Joyce. In fact, Sterne was very much a product of his age. His humor owes much to such earlier writers as François Rabelais, Miguel de Cervantes, Michel Eyquem de Montaigne, Sir Thomas Browne, and Jonathan Swift, all of whom influenced his experimentation with the form of the newly emerged novel. Even this experimentation is typical of the age. Thomas Amory's *The Life and Opinions of John Buncle Esquire* (1756-1766) may have suggested to Sterne his complete title *The Life and Opinions of Tristram Shandy, Gent.* Like *Tristram Shandy*, Amory's book is full of digressions, and its narrator is conceited.

Sterne's experimentation did go beyond the traditional; one need look no farther than the typography, the varying length of the chapters in *Tristram Shandy*—from four lines to sixty pages—or the unusual location of certain conventional elements—for example, the placing of *Tristram Shandy*'s preface after the twentieth chapter of book 3 or Yorick's writing the preface to *A Sentimental Journey* after chapter 6. At the same time, Sterne relied on the conventions of the novel. He is meticulous in his descriptions of clothing, furniture, and gesture. His characters are fully developed: They walk, sometimes with a limp, they cough, they bleed, they dance. From Swift, Daniel Defoe, and Samuel Richardson, Sterne took the first-person narrator. From Richardson, he adopted the technique of writing to the moment; from Henry Fielding, he got the idea of the novel as a comic epic in prose. From numerous sources—Rabelais, Cervantes, and Swift, to name but three—he learned of the satiric potential of the genre.

A Political Romance reveals Sterne's powerful satiric abilities, but this work has little in common with the novels. True, the personal satire of the pamphlet does persist in the novels. Sterne lampoons Dr. Burton (Dr. Slop), Dr. Richard Meade (Dr. Kunastrokius), and Francis Topham (Phutatorius, Didius) in *Tristram Shandy*; Tobias Smollett (Smeldungus) and Samuel Sharp (Mundungus) in *A Sentimental Journey*. For the most part, however, Sterne is after bigger game. As he wrote to Robert Dodsley, the satire is general; and, as he wrote to Robert Foley some years later, it is "a laughing good tempered Satyr," another distinction between the novels and the pamphlet.

The objects of this general satire are several: system-makers of all types, pedants, lawyers, doctors, conceited authors, prudes, and self-deceivers. A common thread uniting all these satiric butts is folly, the folly of believing that life should conform to some preconceived notion, of trying to force facts to fit theories rather than the other way around.

Sterne's insistence on common sense and reason is consistent with the Augustan tradition, which itself is rooted in Anglican beliefs that Sterne emphasized in his sermons as well as in his fiction. Although Sterne's satire is good-tempered, it attacks people's tendency to evil, a tendency noted in Article IX of the Thirty-nine Articles of the Anglican Church. Like his fellow Augustans, Sterne saw this tendency to evil in many spheres. Like them, therefore, he attacked these deviations from the norm as established by religion and reason (which for Sterne are the same), by nature, by tradition, and by authority. The characters in *Tristram Shandy* and Yorick in *A Sentimental Journey* (who is the only sustained character in that work) are laughable because they deviate from the norm and because they refuse to accept their limitations.

Sterne repeatedly reminds the reader of people's finiteness. Thus, death haunts the novels: In *Tristram Shandy*, Toby, Walter, Mrs. Shandy, Yorick, Trim, and Bobby are all dead, and Tristram is dying. In *A Sentimental Journey*, a resurrected Yorick sees death all around him—a dead monk, dead children, a dead ass, dead lovers. Another, less dramatic symbol of the characters' limitation is their inability to complete what they begin. *Tristram Shandy* and *A Sentimental Journey* remain fragments. Trim never finishes his tale of the King of Bohemia and his seven castles. Walter never finishes the *Tristrapaedia*. Obadiah never goes for yeast. Yorick never finishes the story of the notary. Nor can characters communicate effectively with one another: Walter's wife never appreciates his theories, Toby's hobbyhorse causes him to understand all words in a military sense, Dr. Slop falls asleep in the middle of Trim's reading, and Yorick in *A Sentimental Journey* never pauses long enough to develop a lasting friendship.

Death, the prison of the self, the petty and great disappointments of life—these are the stuff of tragedy, yet in Sterne's novels they form the basis of comedy, for the emphasis in these novels is not on the tragic event itself but rather on the cause or the reaction. Bobby's death, for example, is nothing to the reader, not only because one never meets Bobby alive but also because one quickly becomes involved in Walter's oration and Trim's hat. In *A Sentimental Journey*, Sterne focuses on Yorick's reaction to Maria rather than on her poignant tale: Consequently, one laughs at Yorick instead of crying with Maria. The prison of words that traps the characters is not the result of people's inherent isolation but rather of a comic perversity in refusing to accept the plain meaning of a statement. The tragic is further mitigated by its remoteness. Though Tristram writes to the moment, that moment is long past; Tristram's account is being composed some fifty years after the events he describes, and Yorick, too, is recollecting emotions in tranquillity. The curious order of *Tristram Shandy* and the rapid pace of *A Sentimental Journey* further dilute the tragic. Yorick dies in book 1 but cracks the last joke in book 9. Yorick has barely begun a sentimental attachment with a *fille de chambre*, or lady's maid, in Paris when he must set off for Versailles to seek a passport. Though the disappointments, interruptions, failures, and deaths recur, individually they quickly vanish from view. What remains are the characters, who are comic because they refuse to learn from their failures.

Sterne's world is therefore not tragic; neither is it absurd. In the world of the absurd, helpless characters confront a meaningless and chaotic world. For Sterne, the world is reasonable; he shares the Augustan worldview expressed so well by Alexander Pope: "All Nature is but Art, unknown to thee,/ All Chance Direction which thou canst not see." The reasonableness of the world is not, however, to be found in the systematizing of Walter Shandy or the sentimentalism of Yorick. People can live in harmony with the world, Sterne says, only if they use common sense. The comedy of these novels derives in large part from people's failure or laziness to be sensible.

TRISTRAM SHANDY

In *Aspects of the Novel* (1927), E. M. Forster writes: "Obviously a god is hidden in *Tristram Shandy* and his name is Muddle." There is no question that the muddle is present in the novel. Chapters 18 and 19 of book 9 appear as part of chapter 25. The preface does not appear until the third volume. There are black, marbled, and white pages. In book 4, a chapter is torn out and ten pages dropped. Uncle Toby begins knocking the ashes out of his pipe in book 1, chapter 21, and finishes this simple action in book 2, chapter 6. The novel begins in 1718 and ends, if it may be said to end, in 1713. Although called *The Life and Opinions of Tristram Shandy, Gent*., the novel recounts the life of Uncle Toby and the opinions of Walter Shandy.

One must distinguish, however, between the muddle that the narrator, Tristram, creates and the ordered universe that Sterne offers. Theodore Baird has demonstrated that one can construct an orderly sequence of events from the information in *Tristram Shandy*, beginning with the reign of Henry VIII (III, xxxiii) through the wounding of Trim in 1693 (VIII, xix; II, v), the siege of Namur at which Toby is wounded in 1695 (I, xxv), the conception and birth of Tristram Shandy in 1718 (I-III), the death of Bobby (1719; IV, xxxii, and v, ii), the episode of Toby and the fly (1728; II, xii), the death of Yorick (1748; I, xii), and the composition of the novel (1759-1766). Tristram does attempt to impose some order on these events; the first five and a half books trace his life from his conception to his accident with the window sash and his being put into breeches. He then breaks off to recount the amours of Uncle Toby, which again appear essentially in sequence, with the major exception of book 7, Tristram's flight into France.

Although Tristram attempts to order these events, he fails. He fails not because life is inherently random or absurd, but because he is a bad artist. He pointedly rejects the advice of Horace, whose *The Art of Poetry* (c. 17 B.C.E.) was highly respected among eighteenth century writers. He will not pause to check facts and even refuses to look back in his own book to see whether he has already mentioned something; this is writing to the moment with a vengeance. He refuses to impose any order at all on his material, allowing his pen to govern him instead of acting the part of the good writer who governs his pen.

In governing his pen, the good writer carefully selects his material. Many a person has told a plain, unvarnished tale in less space than Tristram, but Tristram cannot decide what is important. Must one know what Mrs. Shandy said to Walter on the night of Tristram's begetting, which, incidentally, may not be the night of Tristram's begetting at all, since the night described is only eight months before Tristram's birth rather than nine—does Tristram realize this fact? Does one need so vivid an account of how Walter falls across the bed upon learning of Tristram's crushed nose? Is it true that one cannot understand Toby's statement, "I think it would not be amiss brother, if we rung the bell," without being dragged halfway across Europe and twenty-three years back in time? Such details serve the purpose of Tristram's creator by highlighting the follies of a bad writer, but they hardly help Tristram proceed with his story.

Tristram's failure to select his material derives in part from laziness. "I have a strong propensity in me to begin this chapter very nonsensically, and I will not balk my fancy," he writes (I, xxiii), for it requires intellectual effort to balk a fancy. In part, too, this failure to select reflects Tristram's belief that everything concerning himself is important. His is a solipsistic rendering of the humanist's credo, "*Homo sum, humani nihil a me alienum puto*"—I am a man, and nothing that relates to man can be foreign to me. He is confident that the more the reader associates with him, the fonder he (the reader) will become. Hence, the reader will want to know about his failure with Jenny, about his aunt Dinah's affair with the coachman, about his attire as he writes, about his casting a fair instead of a foul copy of his manuscript into the fire. Tristram sets out to write a traditional biography, beginning with a genealogy and proceeding to birth, education, youthful deeds that foreshadow later achievements, marriage, children, accomplishments, death, and burial. He becomes so bogged down in details, however, that he cannot get beyond his fifth year. The episode of Toby and the fly must substitute for a volume on education, and the setting up of his top replaces an account of his youthful deeds.

Although Tristram refuses to impose any system on his writing, he is a true son of Walter Shandy in his willingness to impose systems on other aspects of his world. He devises a scale for measuring pleasure and pain, so that if the death of Bobby rates a five and Walter's pleasure at delivering an oration on the occasion rates a ten, Walter proves the gainer by this catastrophe. Tristram has another scale for measuring his own writing; he awards himself a nineteen out of twenty for the design of the novel. Tristram attaches much significance to the way he is conceived, believing that one's conception determines his entire life. His declared method of describing character is similarly reductive, focusing strictly on the individual's hobbyhorse. He has a theory on knots, on window sashes, and on the effect of diet on writing. Tristram thus serves as a satire on systematizers as well as on bad writers.

The more obvious butt of Sterne's satire on system-makers is Walter Shandy. The Augustan Age has also been called the Age of Reason, and Sterne recognizes the importance of reason. At the same time, the Augustans recognized that a person's reason alone is often an insufficient guide because it can be corrupted by a ruling passion, as Yorick's sermon in *Tristram Shandy* reveals. Tristram fails as an author because he trusts exclusively to his own logic instead of following conventional guidelines. Walter Shandy is another example of one who becomes foolish because of his reliance on his own reason. Like Pope's dunces, Walter is well read, and like Pope's dunces, he fails to benefit from his learning because he does not use common sense. He will look in the Institutes of Justinian instead of the more obvious, and more reliable, catechism—part of Sterne's joke here is that the source Walter cites does not contain what he wants. Walter will consult Rubenius rather than a tailor to determine of what cloth Tristram's breeches should be made. From his reading and reasoning he develops a host of theories: that cesarean birth is the best way of bringing a child into the world, that Christian names determine one's life, that auxiliary verbs provide a key to knowledge. Each of these theories rests on a certain logic. Walter is correct that no one would name his child Judas. From this true observation, however, he erects a most absurd theory, proving Tristram's statement that "when a man gives himself up to the government of a ruling passion,—or, in other words, when his Hobby-Horse grows headstrong,—farewell cool reason and fair discretion" (II, v). Neither Walter nor his son will rein in his hobbyhorse, and, as a result, they become ridiculous.

They may also become dangerous. While Walter is busily engaged in composing his *Tristrapaedia* that will codify his theories of child rearing, Tristram grows up without any guidance at all. Walter is willing, indeed eager, to have his wife undergo a cesarean operation because he believes that such an operation will be less harmful to the infant than natural childbirth. That such an operation will cause the death of Mrs. Shandy is a fact that apparently escapes him.

Even the benign and lovable Uncle Toby makes himself ridiculous by yielding to his hobbyhorse. Not only does this hobbyhorse lead him into excessive expense and so deprive him of money he might put to better use, but also it keeps his mind from more worthwhile occupations. Repeatedly, Sterne, through Tristram, likens Toby's garden battlefield to a mistress with whom Toby dallies; the Elizabethan sense of hobbyhorse is precisely this—a woman of easy virtue. As Tristram notes early in the novel, when "one . . . whose principles and conduct are as generous and noble as his blood" is carried off by his hobbyhorse, it is better that "the Hobby-Horse, with all his fraternity, (were) at the Devil" (I, viii). Deluding himself that he is somehow contributing to the defense of England, Toby blinds himself to the real horrors of war. Wrapped up in his military jargon, he isolates himself verbally from those around him; a bridge or a train has only one meaning for him. No less than Tristram, he is betrayed by words, but in his case as in Tristram's the fault lies not with the words but with the individual betrayed.

Nor is Toby's hobbyhorse dangerous to himself alone. It keeps him away from the Widow Wadman and so prevents his fulfilling his legitimate social responsibilities of marrying and begetting children; his hobbyhorse renders him sterile even if his wound has not. This hobbyhorse also comes close to rendering Tristram sterile, for Trim removes the weights from the window sash to make cannon for Toby's campaigns.

Each of the major characters is trapped in a cell of his own making. Tristram can never finish his book because his theory of composition raises insurmountable obstacles. The more he writes, the more he has to write. Walter's and Toby's hobbyhorses blind them to reality and prevent their communicating with each other or anyone else. The Shandy family is well named; "shandy" in Yorkshire means crackbrained. Significantly, the novel begins with an interrupted act of procreation and ends with sterility. As in Pope's *The Dunciad* (1728-1743), the uncreating word triumphs because of human folly.

Sterne's vision is not quite as dark as Pope's, however; the novel ends not with universal darkness but with a joke. Yorick, the voice of reason and moderation, remains to pull the reader back to reality. Yorick is a jester, and the role of the jester is to remind his audience of the just proportion of things as well as to make them laugh. Yorick does not put a fancy saddle on a horse that does not deserve one. He will destroy a sermon because it is too bad (unlike Tristram, who destroys a chapter because it is too good). He makes only modest claims for his sermons and is embarrassed even by these (unlike Tristram, who repeatedly proclaims himself a genius). Yorick thus offers in word and deed an example of living reasonably and happily.

Sterne offers a second consolation as well. Even though characters isolate themselves with their hobbyhorses, even though they cannot or will not understand one another's words, they can and do appreciate one another's feelings. These emotional unions are short-lived, but they are intense and sincere. Walter will continue to make fun of Toby even after promising not to, but at the moment the promise is made, the two are united spiritually and physically. Tristram and Jenny quarrel, but they also have their tender moments. Trim looks for a carriage in a book by shaking the leaves, and he mistakes fiction for reality in a sermon, but he allows his parents three halfpence a day out of his pay when they grow old. The benevolence that Sterne urged in his sermons is capable of bridging self-imposed isolation. Although one laughs at the characters in *Tristram Shandy*, one therefore sympathizes with them as well, seeing their weaknesses but also their underlying virtue. Though they have corrupted that virtue by yielding to a natural tendency to evil, they redeem themselves through their equally natural tendency to kindness.

Tristram Shandy offended many contemporary readers because of its bawdy tales; reviewers much preferred such seemingly sentimental episodes as the death of Le Fever and urged Sterne to refine his humor. *A Sentimental Journey* superficially appears to have been written to satisfy these demands. It is full of touching scenes, of tears, of charity, of little acts of kindness. Moreover, in a letter to Mrs. William James in November, 1767, Sterne describes the novel as dealing with "the gentle passions and affections" and says his intention is "to teach us to love the world and our fellow creatures better than we do." Sterne's letters, and especially his *Journal to Eliza*, reveal him as a man of feeling, and *Tristram Shandy* satirizes all aspects of human life except for benevolence. Sterne's sermons reinforce his image as a believer in the importance of charity. As a Latitudinarian, he believed that the Golden Rule constitutes the essence of religion, that ritual and church doctrine, while important, are less significant than kindness. Because Yorick in *Tristram Shandy* is Sterne's spokesman, it is tempting to see Yorick in *A Sentimental Journey* as having the same normative function. Though the narrator of *Tristram Shandy* is a dunce and a satiric butt, can one not still trust the narrator of *A Sentimental Journey*?

No. In a famous letter to Dr. John Eustace, Sterne thanks Eustace for the gift of a curious walking stick: "Your walking stick is in no sense more shandaic than in that of its having *more handles than one*." Readers could regard *Tristram Shandy* as total nonsense, as a collection of bawdy stories, as a realistic novel, as a satire on the realistic novel, or as a satire on the follies of humankind. Sterne's second novel, too, is "shandaic." The reader can see it as a tribute to the popular spirit of sentimentality or can view it as a satire of that spirit, yet a careful reading of the book will demonstrate why Sterne wrote to the mysterious "Hannah" that this novel "shall make you cry as much as ever it made me laugh." In other words, Sterne is sporting with rather than adopting the sentimental mode.

A Sentimental Journey

The object of Sterne's laughter is Yorick. The Yorick who recounts his travels is not the same normative parson as appears in *Tristram Shandy*. He is by now twice dead—dead in William Shakespeare's *Hamlet* (pr. c. 1600-1601) and dead again in *Tristram Shandy* some fifteen years prior to the events of *A Sentimental Journey*. This second resurrection may itself be a joke on the reader, who should recall Yorick's death in book 1 of the earlier novel.

This revived Yorick bears a great similarity to Tristram. He is, for one thing, a systematizer. He establishes three degrees of curses; he discovers "three epochas in the empire of a French woman" ("Paris"), he is able to create dialogues out of silence, and he derives national character not from "important matters of state" but rather from "nonsensical minutiae" ("The Wig—Paris"). Like Tristram, too, Yorick is vain. He gives a sou to a beggar who calls him "My Lord *Anglois*" and another sou for "*Mon cher et très charitable Monsieur*." He does not worry about being unkind to a monk but is concerned that as a result a pretty woman will think ill of him.

Even his style, though less difficult to follow than Tristram's, bears some similarities to that of Sterne's earlier narrator. In the midst of the account of his adventures in Versailles, Yorick introduces the irrelevant anecdote of Bevoriskius and the mating sparrows, thus combining Tristram's habit of digressing with Walter's love of abstruse learning. Yorick later interpolates an account of the Marquis d'E****, and while telling about Paris he presents a "Fragment" that does nothing to advance the story. Like Tristram, too, Yorick cannot finish his account, breaking off in midsentence. Apparently, he is more governed by his pen than governing.

Yorick also reminds the reader of the narrator in Swift's *A Tale of a Tub*, who believes that happiness is the state of being well deceived. Yorick is disappointed to learn that his small present to Le Fleur has been sufficient only to allow his servant to buy used clothes: "I would rather have imposed upon my fancy with thinking I had bought them new for the fellow, than that they had come out of the *Rue de friperie*" ("Le Dimanche—Paris"). Instead of inquiring about the history of the lady at Calais, he invents a pleasant account of her until he gets "ground enough for the situation which pleased me" ("In the Street—

Calais"). He deceives himself into believing that he is accompanying a pretty *fille de chambre* as far as possible to protect her when actually he wants her company. Even his benevolence is self-deception. He conjures up images to weep over—a swain with a dying lamb, a man in the Bastille, an imaginary recipient of charity. When in this last instance he confronts the reality, his behavior is hardly benevolent, though.

Sterne is not satirizing benevolence as such. In his sermons "The Vindication of Human Nature" and "Philanthropy Recommended" he rejects the notion that people are inherently selfish and stresses his belief in humankind's natural benevolence, yet he had to look no farther than his own nose to discover that benevolence can become a hobbyhorse that can carry a person away from the path of reason. Yorick's hobbyhorse of benevolence is no less dangerous than Uncle Toby's or Walter Shandy's. Yorick will weep over a carriage, over a dead ass, or over a caged starling. He admits that he does not even need an object for his sympathy: "Was I in a desert, I would find out wherewith in it to call forth my affection" ("In the Street—Calais"). Real human misery, however, he cannot understand. He can weep over his imagined prisoner in the Bastille, but he cannot imagine the real suffering there. He can be callous to the poor, but never to a pretty young woman.

Yorick's benevolence is thus a compound of self-deception and lust. He will give no money to the poor monk until he wants to impress a pretty woman. He gives a sou to a beggar with a dislocated hip, but he gives an unsolicited crown to a pretty *fille de chambre*, and he gives three *louis d'or* to a pretty grisette. He imagines that in offering to share his chaise with another pretty young lady, he is fighting off "every dirty passion" such as avarice, pride, meanness, and hypocrisy. Actually, he is yielding to desire.

True benevolence is guided by reason, and it is not a thing of the moment only, as Sterne points out in his sermon on the Good Samaritan. Yorick's benevolence is impulsive and short-lived. The cry of a caged starling moves him greatly: "I never had my affections more tenderly awakened," he says ("The Passport—The Hotel at Paris"). The hyperbole of the language is itself a warning of Yorick's inability to temper emotion with reason. After such a reaction, his attitude changes abruptly; Yorick buys the starling but never frees it. After tiring of it, he gives it away to another as callous as himself. At Namport, he mourns for a dead ass and praises its owner for his kindness, adding, "Shame on the world! . . . Did we love each other, as this poor soul but loved his ass—'twould be something" ("Namport—The Dead Ass"). By the next page, Yorick is sending his postilion to the devil. Yorick goes out of his way to find the mad Maria, whom Sterne had introduced in book 7 of *Tristram Shandy*. He weeps with Maria at Moulines; she makes such an impression on him that her image follows him almost to Lyon—an entire chapter.

Yorick is humorous because, like Tristram, Walter, and Toby, he is the victim of his hobbyhorse. He gallops away from reason, failing to examine his motivation or to temper his sudden fanciful flights. In "Temporal Advantages of Religion," Sterne provides a picture of the ideal Christian traveler. "We may surely be allowed to amuse ourselves with the natural or artificial beauties of the country we are passing through," Sterne notes, but he warns against being drawn aside, as Yorick is, "by the variety of prospects, edifices, and ruins which solicit us." More important, Yorick forgets the chief end of people's earthly sojourn: "Various as our excursions are—that we have still set our faces towards Jerusalem . . . and that the way to get there is not so much to please our hearts, as to improve them in virtue." Yorick has come to France for knowledge, but he learns nothing. His benevolence is much closer to wantonness than to virtue; it is fitting that he ends his account in the dark.

In *A Sentimental Journey*, as in *Tristram Shandy*, Sterne mocks excess. He shows the folly that results from the abdication of reason. Though he introduces norms such as Yorick in *Tristram Shandy* or the old soldier in *A Sentimental Journey*, the ideal emerges most clearly from a depiction of its opposite—perverted learning, bad writing, and unexamined motives. When Sterne arrived in London in 1760, Lord Bathurst embraced him as the heir to the Augustan satirists.

Joseph Rosenblum

OTHER MAJOR WORKS

NONFICTION: *A Political Romance*, 1759; *The Sermons of Mr. Yorick*, 1760 (volumes 1-2), 1766 (volumes 3-4); *Sermons by the Late Rev. Mr. Sterne*, 1769 (volumes 5-7); *Letters from Yorick to Eliza*, 1773; *Letters of the Late Rev. Mr. L. Sterne to His Most Intimate Friends*, 1775 (3 volumes); *Sterne's Letters to His Friends on Various Occasions, to Which Is Added His History of a Watch Coat*, 1775; *In Elegant Epistles*, 1790; *Journal to Eliza*, 1904.

BIBLIOGRAPHY

Bowden, Martha F. *Yorick's Congregation: The Church of England in the Time of Laurence Sterne*. Newark: University of Delaware Press, 2007. Examines the religious environment in which Sterne wrote his novels and sermons, explicating passages from his work to demonstrate how his experience of life in rural parishes informed his novels.

Cash, Arthur Hill. *Laurence Sterne*. 2 vols. London: Methuen, 1975-1986. Considered the definitive biography of the author. The first volume follows Sterne's life to early 1760 and offers many details about his role in the religious and political affairs of York. The second volume treats Sterne the author. Presents a realistic picture, freed from Victorian strictures and romantic glosses. Interesting appendixes provide a series of portraits and letters that were previously unpublished.

Cash, Arthur Hill, and John M. Stedmond, eds. *The Winged Skull: Papers from the Laurence Sterne Bicentenary Conference*. Kent, Ohio: Kent State University Press, 1971. Collection of essays covers a wide range of subjects, including Sterne's style, his reputation outside England, and his fictional devices. Includes some helpful illustrations.

Gerard, W. B. *Laurence Sterne and the Visual Imagination*. Burlington, Vt.: Ashgate, 2006. Study focuses on the illustrations by William Hogarth and other artists that complemented Sterne's work in the original editions. Examines the pictorial quality of Sterne's writing, describing how it inspires the visual imagination, and analyzes some of the illustrations for *Tristram Shandy* and *A Sentimental Journey*.

Keymer, Thomas, ed. *The Cambridge Companion to Laurence Sterne*. New York: Cambridge University Press, 2009. Collection of specially commissioned essays provides analyses of all of Sterne's works and their key issues of sentimentalism, national identity, and gender. Some of the essays consider Sterne's life and milieu, his literary career, and his subsequent influence on modernism; others analyze *Tristram Shandy* and *A Sentimental Journey*.

Kraft, Elizabeth. *Laurence Sterne Revisited*. New York: Twayne, 1996. Provides a short biography and then devotes individual chapters to specific works. Closes with a discussion of Sterne's changing critical reputation. Includes a selected bibliography.

New, Melvin. *"Tristram Shandy": A Book for Free Spirits*. New York: Twayne, 1994. Begins with background on the literary and historical milieu of Stern's most famous work and then explores five different methods of approaching *Tristram Shandy* in sections headed "Satire," "Heads" (viewing the work intellectually), "Hearts" (viewing it emotionally), "Joy," and "Tartuffery" (examining it as a humorous attack on hypocrisy).

Ross, Ian Campbell. *Laurence Sterne: A Life*. New York: Oxford University Press, 2001. Thorough and well-researched biography concentrates on the events of Sterne's life rather than on the analysis of his literary works. Includes bibliography and index.

Stedmond, John M. *The Comic Art of Laurence Sterne: Convention and Innovation in "Tristram Shandy" and "A Sentimental Journey."* Toronto, Ont.: University of Toronto Press, 1967. Provides helpful readings of Sterne's novels and describes how the works highlight the comic distance between aspiration and attainment that is endemic in human existence. Includes an appendix recording Sterne's direct borrowings.

Walsh, Marcus, ed. *Laurence Sterne*. New York: Longman, 2002. Sterne's works are particularly amenable to poststructuralist interpretation; this collection pulls together a stimulating group of essays that take modern theoretical approaches to the work.

AUGUST STRINDBERG

Born: Stockholm, Sweden; January 22, 1849
Died: Stockholm, Sweden; May 14, 1912
Also known as: Johan August Strindberg

PRINCIPAL LONG FICTION

Från Fjärdingen och Svartbäcken, 1877
Röda rummet, 1879 (*The Red Room*, 1913)
Jäsningstiden, 1886 (*The Growth of the Soul*, 1914)
Hemsöborna, 1887 (*The Natives of Hemsö*, 1965)
Tschandala, 1889 (in Danish), 1897 (in Swedish)
I havsbandet, 1890 (*By the Open Sea*, 1913)
Le Plaidoyer d'un fou, 1893 (in German), 1895 (in Swedish; *A Madman's Defense*, 1912; also known as *The Confession of a Fool*)
Inferno, 1897 (English translation, 1912)
Ensam, 1903 (*Alone*, 1968)
Götiska rummen, 1904
Svarta fanor, 1907
Syndabocken, 1907 (*The Scapegoat*, 1967)
Taklagsöl, 1907
Författaren, 1909

OTHER LITERARY FORMS

August Strindberg was an extremely prolific writer whose collected works total fifty-five volumes. Outside Scandinavia, he is known chiefly as a dramatist, and many of his plays—such as *Fadren* (pr., pb. 1887; *The Father*, 1899), *Fröken Julie* (pb. 1888; *Miss Julie*, 1912), and *Ett drömspel* (pb. 1902; *A Dream Play*, 1912)—continue to be performed regularly in many parts of the world. Strindberg also wrote several collections of shorter prose pieces; two volumes of short stories titled *Giftas I* (1884) and *Giftas II* (1886; *Married*, 1913; also known as *Getting Married*, 1973, which includes both *Giftas I* and *Giftas II*) are particularly well known. He also wrote and published poetry throughout his life.

ACHIEVEMENTS

August Strindberg is known throughout the world as one of the fathers of modern drama. In his native Sweden, and increasingly abroad as well, he is also known as a psychological novelist of considerable importance. His second novel, *The Red Room*, is considered the first modern novel in Swedish literature, and another of his novels, *The Natives of Hemsö*, is still one of the best-loved books in Sweden.

Strindberg has also appealed to the smaller audience of the literary establishment. Considered Sweden's greatest writer of belles lettres, he has remained the object of critical attention both in his homeland and abroad. All of his important works have been translated into English, and his reputation has long been securely established.

BIOGRAPHY

Johan August Strindberg was born in Stockholm, Sweden, on January 22, 1849. On the side of his father, a steamship agent, he came from a solid middle-class background; his mother, however, was the daughter of a tailor and had been a waitress before coming to the home of her future husband as his servant girl. Strindberg later somewhat romantically referred to himself as "the son of the maidservant," when in fact he was solidly anchored in the Swedish bourgeoisie. Strindberg grew up around his father's business and early developed an appreciation for matters relating to the sea, especially the Stockholm archipelago. Unlike his several brothers, however, he was not to be prepared for a business career. In 1867, he received his matriculation certificate and soon thereafter took up residence as a student at the University of Uppsala.

Not finding academic life entirely to his liking, Strindberg was only intermittently a full-time student and for a time earned a living as a tutor and as an elementary school teacher. During that time, he wrote several insignificant plays, one of which was performed at Stockholm's Royal Dramatic Theatre in the fall of 1870. After abandoning his studies in 1872, Strindberg began pursuing a career as a writer more aggressively. The first fruit of this activity was the prose version of his drama *Mäster Olof* (pb. 1878; *Master Olof*, 1915), completed in early August of 1872. No theater would accept the play, however, and for the next few years, Strindberg made a living as a journalist and assistant at Stockholm's Royal Library.

In the late spring of 1875, Strindberg was introduced to Siri von Essen, the young wife of Baron Carl Gustaf Wrangel, and a love affair ensued. Siri obtained a divorce in June of 1876, after which she and Strindberg were married in December of 1877. In the same month, Strindberg had a collection of short stories published.

Strindberg's breakthrough as a prose writer came in 1879 with the publication of his novel *The Red Room*. After a period of research into cultural history, he moved with his family to France, where he would spend a considerable portion of his life. In 1884, however, he briefly returned to Sweden to stand trial on the charge of blasphemy; one of the short stories in his just-published collection *Married* was found by the authorities to be disrespectful of the Sacrament of the Lord's Supper. Strindberg was acquitted, but the matter was agonizing for him. A second volume of *Married* stories followed in 1886, however, and the same year saw the publication of the first two volumes of the somewhat fictionalized four-volume autobiography *Tjänstekvinnans son: En s äls utvecklingshistoria* (1886; *The Son of a Servant: The Story of the Evolution of a Human Being*, 1966, volume 1 only).

Strindberg returned to Scandinavia in 1887 after a further stay in France, Switzerland, and Germany. This time he settled in Copenhagen, where his naturalistic drama *The Father* was soon to be performed. In the same year, he published his most popular novel, *The Natives of Hemsö*, utilizing memories from an island in the Stockholm archipelago where he had spent several summers. Before returning to Sweden in 1889, he also had established a short-lived experimental theater; had written two more plays, *Miss Julie* and *Fordringsägare* (pb. 1888; *Creditors*, 1910); and had finished the manuscript, written in French, of his novel *The Confession of a Fool*, for which his marriage to Siri had provided him with the raw material. Annoyances experienced in Denmark in the summer of 1888 formed the basis for *Tschandala*.

During the summer of 1889, Strindberg stayed on one of the islands near Stockholm and began work on another novel arising from the archipelago, *By the Open Sea*. After a break in his labors, this book was finished in the summer of 1890. Marital difficulties, which had been present for several years, led to the beginning of divorce proceedings, and his marriage to Siri was dissolved in 1891. Strindberg did not remain unmarried for long, however; early in 1893, during a visit to Berlin, he met the Austrian Frida Uhl. They were wed the following year but soon separated, and Strindberg again went to Paris.

The next three years, the so-called *Inferno* crisis, was probably the most difficult period in Strindberg's life. He wanted to conquer Paris not only as a writer but also as a scientist, and he carried on a series of chemical experiments. His experiences during this time became material for his autobiographical novel *Inferno*.

This novel inaugurated another great creative period in Strindberg's life, which produced his well-known play *Till Damaskus* (pb. 1898-1904; *To Damascus*, 1913) and, after his final return to Sweden the following year, a series of important historical dramas. In 1901, he married the young Norwegian actor Harriet Bosse; this marriage lasted until 1904. These years saw such great plays as *Dödsdansen* (pb. 1901; *The Dance of Death*, 1912) and *A Dream Play*. In 1907, after the establishment of Stockholm's Intima Teatern (intimate theater), Strindberg published a series of what he called chamber plays, the best known of which is *Spöksonaten* (*The Ghost Sonata*, 1916). He also wrote a number of prose works, including the infamous satiric novel *Svarta fanor.*

Strindberg had lived a stormy life, and his final years were no exception. A series of newspaper articles begun in April, 1910, set off the most intensive debate in Swedish literary history. Nicknamed the "Strindberg Feud," this debate resulted from both personal and philosophical differences and became particularly vicious when it was suggested that Strindberg—who, because of his radical views, had not received the Nobel Prize in Literature—ought to receive an equivalent prize from the Swedish people. The author's difficult financial situation made this particularly appropriate. The prize did not materialize, but Strindberg nevertheless succeeded in obtaining financial security through the sale of the rights to the collected edition of his works. Shortly thereafter, he became seriously ill and died from cancer of the stomach on May 14, 1912.

ANALYSIS

August Strindberg's novels constitute a striking illustration of the dialectical relationship between life and art. Strindberg truly lived for his art; he consciously ordered his life in such a manner that he might obtain material for his fiction, much of which was narrated in the first person. This has led several critics to overemphasize the bizarre aspects of his books and to hold that he was mentally ill when in reality he was only experimenting with his sanity. Such is especially the case with two intensely autobiographical novels, *The Confession of a Fool* and *Inferno*. There can be no doubt, however, that Strindberg's art also profoundly affected his life. Popular successes, such as *The Red Room* and *The Natives of Hemsö*, brought him considerable fame and enabled him to improve his standard of living, while *The Confession of a Fool*, which was a fictionalized account of his marriage to Siri von Essen, did much to seal the destruction of that marriage. In *Inferno*, Strindberg deliberately led the reading public to believe that he, the author, was identical with the novel's vacillating and easily frightened protagonist, who with justice was considered mentally ill. Strindberg thus consciously injured his personal reputation for the sake of his art, for he knew that the aesthetic effect of the book would depend on the reader's identification of author and narrator-protagonist during the reading process. Even the lighthearted *The Natives of Hemsö*, which Strindberg thought to be his sanest book, took its toll on the personal affairs of the author. Strindberg had used as models for some of his characters certain people then living on Kymmendö, an island near Stockholm where he had spent many happy summers. His models were offended, and Strindberg was never again welcome on the island.

An important question, therefore, is what it was that drove Strindberg to exploit so ruthlessly both his own life and the lives of those who were close to him. Part of the answer has been suggested by the American Strindberg scholar Eric O. Johannesson, who has proposed that the fundamental theme of Strindberg's novels is the author's quest for identity. This quest, according to Johannesson, takes the form of an exploration of both the author's own self and the human psyche in general. There is little doubt that Strindberg's desire for truth, along with his need for recognition as a man of letters, was a powerful motivating force behind his artistic activity.

Strindberg's originality as a thinker did not, however, match his quality as an artist, and in his search for truth he relied heavily on ideas that had been generated by others. Constantly in step with the literary and intellectual avant-garde, he tested the validity of the various ideas and standpoints of his age as they became available to him. His development as a novelist thus closely parallels that of European intellectual history. He began as a realist and naturalist who in *The Red Room* criticized social conditions in Sweden. In the stylistically seminaturalistic *The Natives of Hemsö*, the social satire is absent; its humorous and detailed description of life in the skerries has made it one of Strindberg's best-loved books. *The Confession of a Fool* is likewise heavy with naturalistic detail, but there is also a strong interest in individual psychology that manifests itself in the "battle of the brains" that is taking place between Axel, the book's narrator, and his wife, Maria. The same emphasis on psychology is found in *By the Open Sea*, the protagonist of which is virtually a Nietzschean superman who succumbs only because he possesses the one fatal flaw of allowing himself to be influenced by a woman. The novel *Inferno*, with its interest in mysticism, religion, and other aspects of the supernatural, places Strindberg squarely within the neo-Romanticism of the 1890's.

Strindberg's desire for truth in all aspects of life, which also manifested itself in his quest for identity, was in part a function of the uneasiness with which he viewed his social position. The mixture of a middle-class background on his father's side and working-class origins on his mother's side created a strong tension in his life. His instincts were those of the bourgeoisie, but he felt considerable loyalty to the lower classes. At the same time, he desired upward mobility, to which he felt especially entitled because of his intellectual prowess. These tensions account for the sociological perspective present in his works.

The desire for an understanding of the self also explains the prevalence of autobiographical elements in Strindberg's novels. *The Confession of a Fool* and *Inferno* have been viewed as straightforward autobiography by many critics, and *The Red Room*, which tells about a group of artists and intellectuals of which Strindberg was a member in the late 1870's, has always been recognized as having numerous autobiographical traits. *The Confession of a Fool* and *Inferno* are first-person novels in which it is difficult to distinguish between author and narrator, and *The Red Room*, which is narrated in the third person, has a young writer as its protagonist. This among other things makes it easy to equate the narrator's point of view with that of Strindberg himself. The point of view in *The Natives of Hemsö* is that of an omniscient, detached narrator who is very similar to Strindberg, the summer guest on Kymmendö, while the fishing inspector Axel Borg, the center of consciousness in *By the Open Sea*, is a man who in most regards corresponds to the Nietzschean ideals that Strindberg advocated at the time.

It is indeed no wonder that the author was so frequently identified with his protagonists. Seemingly oblivious to the cost to his personal happiness and appallingly disrespectful of the right to privacy of those who were close to him, Strindberg consistently turned his life into art.

THE RED ROOM

Strindberg published *The Red Room* in 1879, when he had already had some minor successes as a serious writer but also had expended much effort on a variety of minor assignments for various newspapers and magazines. He was thoroughly acquainted with life among Stockholm's younger artists and intellectuals, however, and was thus well equipped for the task of writing the book.

Although the short span of narrated time in *The Red Room* (it covers only about a year and a half), together with its episodic structure, makes it difficult to fit the novel completely into the genre of the bildungsroman, the book may well be regarded from that perspective. The main character, Arvid Falk, is a young civil servant turned writer and journalist, and the book tells about his experiences while attempting to come to terms with society. Falk is a naïve idealist whose soul is larger than the destinies that Swedish life in the 1870's have to offer him, and his process of education therefore becomes one of a gradual loss of illusions. As a reporter, he gains insight into the hollowness and deceit of government, the Church, the newspaper industry, book publishing, the insurance industry, banking, charitable organizations, higher education, and the arts. Through this bildungsroman, Strindberg attempts to educate the reader in the true state of contemporary society by portraying his protagonist's education in disillusionment.

The book may also, however, be regarded as a novel experiment akin to the naturalistic novel. Strindberg does not conduct an experiment that, like the typical Scandinavian novel of a few years later, is designed to illustrate the thesis that biological inheritance and social environment determine human development and behavior; rather, *The Red Room* constitutes an experiment with ideas and standpoints. Strindberg tests the validity of the attitudes toward life that inhere in the philosophies of idealism, realism, and nihilism, and it is this process of testing that is of most interest to today's readers.

The standpoint of idealism is represented chiefly by Falk, the protagonist. In the beginning of the novel, he strikes one as a very young, indeed immature, man whose idealism manifests itself as a naïve sympathy with the oppressed and a vague desire for social justice, unaccompanied by serious commitment to specific causes. This naïve idealism is untenable, and Falk is faced with two choices: He may abandon idealism completely and turn to pessimism and nihilism, or he may subject his idealism to reflection and develop it in the direction of a considered realism, which would entail serious commitment on his part.

The pessimistic, nihilistic stance is represented by two characters, the actor Falander and the sculptor Olle Montanus. Falander is a decadent figure, a seducer of the young whose ideas are transmitted to Falk through Montanus. Montanus commits suicide, which might be a sign of Strindberg's dismissal of his philosophical outlook, but the matter is more complicated than that. Falander is a nihilist in that he attacks societal values, but he is also, as Johannesson has pointed out, a Christ figure: His destiny is to identify himself with others and to suffer with and for them through his compassion. Strindberg's later works show that he was far from finished with this character type.

In *The Red Room*, however, the philosophical possibilities represented by Falander are at least temporarily repressed. Falk's idealism becomes increasingly fanatic, and his demand becomes one of all or nothing. Eventually recognizing this as an impossible situation, he allows himself to be convinced by a more realistic friend to forget all thoughts of improving the world. He reenters polite society as a minor government official and teacher at a school for girls, living only for his coin collection, a few quietistic friends, and later, his fiancé. His end is thus that of the hero of the traditional bildungsroman; namely, apparent integration into society, represented by the acquisition of a respectable position and matrimony. One wonders, however, if this is Strindberg's final word concerning his hero. Falk has passed from a naïve and later desperate idealism to its opposite, an equally desperate quietism. The next stage could be a realistic synthesis of the two, a stance that indeed seems to be implied by Strindberg. The novel is open-ended on this point, for Strindberg's purpose is not as much to suggest answers as to pose questions. The book does so in a most effective manner.

The Natives of Hemsö

The Natives of Hemsö is a novel that fits rather poorly into Strindberg's largely autobiographical authorship, and it may well be regarded, as the author himself regarded it, as an "intermezzo scherzando." Its well-told story, its colorful and uncomplicated characters, and its vivid pictures of life in the Stockholm archipelago have given it the status of a Swedish classic.

The plot is simple. An enterprising farmhand named Carlsson arrives at the island Hemsö in order to help the middle-aged widow Flod put her farm in order. Marriage to the widow would make Carlsson the master of the farm, so he becomes his employer's suitor, and the two are married. Carlsson's main problem is now the widow's son Gusten, who is obviously not interested in being deprived of his inheritance. Gusten becomes a formidable antagonist, especially when Carlsson begins to mismanage the farm and spends most of his time trying to persuade his wife to make a will that would, in effect, disinherit her son. In the end, Carlsson loses in the conflict because of his weakness for one of the servant girls. His wife discovers his infidelity, catches pneumonia, and dies. Carlsson drowns accidentally, and Gusten is left as the farm's unchallenged ruler.

The novel is almost totally free of political and social ideas. It exhibits a kind of limited naturalism, however, for Strindberg depicts his characters as formed by their natural and social environment. At the same time, the book is imbued with a comic spirit, which manifests itself both in the events portrayed and in the depiction of Carlsson's character. Carlsson is uncomplicated and without inner conflicts, and his death is only another instance of the old giving way to youth in life's endless chain. He is simply a man who tried and failed, and his failure has no philosophical implications. As the book's point of view is consistently that of the community, which stands in opposition to the outsider, the ending leaves the reader with a feeling of contentment: The conflict has been resolved in accordance with the order of nature.

The Confession of a Fool

In *The Confession of a Fool*, Strindberg returns to his general artistic project with full force. His search for truth focuses on the human psyche and the effects of interpersonal relationships on it. When read strictly as a work of fiction, the book becomes a powerful and engaging psychological novel. Many critics, however, have found it difficult to regard the book from this perspective. Both the contemporary reading public and later scholars have been painfully aware that the novel tells in detail about Strindberg's relationship with his first wife, Siri von Essen. It can be argued that the book is a piece of autobiography, but if it is to be regarded as such, it quickly becomes clear that many of the events related have been significantly distorted. Strindberg used the experience he had gained in his relationship with Siri, but because he knew that he was writing fiction, not autobiography, he felt no obligation to adhere strictly to what had actually taken place in every instance.

A key to the understanding of both *The Confession of a Fool* and the novel *By the Open Sea* is to be found in an essay written by Strindberg in 1887 on Henrik Ibsen's drama *Rosmersholm* (pb. 1886; English translation, 1889). Titled "Själamord" ("Psychic Murder"), the essay explores the ways in which modern human beings destroy one another by a variety of means infinitely more sophisticated than old-fashioned physical violence. Today's psychic murderer uses public opinion, hypnotism, and suggestion to destroy his victim; more specifically, he makes the victim ridiculous, robs him of his ability to make a living, and, if possible, drives him insane. *The Confession of a Fool* tells the story of such a crime.

The first-person narrator of the book is a Swedish writer named Axel, who, with his wife, Maria, lives in exile somewhere in central Europe. He suspects that Maria, who he believes has done her best to isolate him from the world in order to destroy his reputation as a writer, is now trying to kill him by causing him to go insane. In order to defend himself both against the rumors that he fears his wife has spread about him and against other and more direct threats to his mind, he begins an investigation into their relationship. The book is the record of this investigation, and it is designed to serve as his final word to the world in case his wife should succeed in her design.

The novel's point of view is consistent throughout; Strindberg never departs from the perspective of his narrator. From this viewpoint, Maria becomes a villain of the highest order who no doubt has been doing everything in her power to rob her husband of his sanity. The discerning reader also understands, however, that there is a considerable difference between the story as told by the narrator and the author's version of it. Because the point of view is consistently that of the first-person narrator, the views of the author can be reconstructed only through a careful reading. Such an analysis will make it clear that Maria is indeed innocent and that her husband, who can be classified only as a madman, is in the process of committing psychic suicide. The value of the novel lies in the tension between these two perspectives and the careful psychological portrayal that is necessary for their creation.

Some critics have argued that Strindberg indeed shared the perspective of his narrator and that he involuntarily revealed the fact that he, like his narrator, was insane during the period when the novel was written. This view is the result of an inability to distinguish between reliable and unreliable narrators. The narrator in *The Confession of a Fool* is insane, but he either does not know it or is unwilling to admit it. The novel's author is, of course, not in the same situation, and he has to find a means of transmitting his view to the reader.

This difficult task Strindberg has handled in a sophisticated manner by creating a complex ironic structure. The novel is thus a thoroughly modern one, both in terms of the author's use of psychology and in its narrative technique.

BY THE OPEN SEA

Strindberg continues his search for truth concerning the human psyche in *By the Open Sea*, one of his most underrated novels. Set in the Stockholm archipelago, the book is nevertheless free of the comedy and lightheartedness of its predecessor in the same setting, *The Natives of Hemsö*. The author now has taken up a most solemn subject—namely, the process by which an individual may descend from superhuman strength and intelligence to complete disintegration of the personality. Although the novel's center of consciousness, the fishing inspector Axel Borg, is also the person through whose eyes most of the action is seen, the telling is done by a third-person narrator virtually indistinguishable from Strindberg himself. This makes the transmission of norms from the author to the reader more easily accomplished than in *The Confession of a Fool*, where Strindberg chose to employ a first-person narrator.

One day in spring, Borg arrives at a tiny, isolated island in the archipelago where he is to teach modern fishing techniques to the inhabitants. Borg is an outsider both geographically and socially; in addition, he views himself as a superman in the spirit of Nietzsche. As a character, he could be attractive only to those who fancy themselves to be of the same kind, and the stage is set for a constant battle between him and the natives. While they are creatures of instincts and feelings, Borg worships logic and reason. The battle thus also becomes one between two different attitudes toward life.

In the first part of the novel, Strindberg describes the intellectual virtues of his protagonist. The fishing inspector is an eminent scientist whose training and native intellect combine to make him an ideal type. Compared to him, the islanders are nothing; they do, however, have the advantage of belonging to a community, a group, while Borg is isolated. Borg's state of isolation constitutes both a strength and a weakness. It is necessary in order to keep him from too much contact with inferior minds, but his lack of access to a community of his equals tends to make him lose the ability to cope with the world of human beings.

A decisive change in Borg's mental state is brought about by his relationship with a young female summer guest. Her name is Maria, and she has a function that is similar to that of the female antagonist by the same name in *The Confession of a Fool*. The cerebral Borg, unable to repress his instincts, seeks Maria's company and, as he believes, allows his intellect to be degraded through their association. Knowing that the relationship is harmful to him, he attempts to liberate himself but discovers that he can accomplish this only by seducing the girl. He does so with the effect that the intended liberation is achieved, but the seduction is also a fatal surrender to his own bodily nature.

Maria leaves, but a new challenger has already arrived. He is a preacher, an old acquaintance of Borg, and his function is to bring the fishing inspector's fears and suppressed feelings of guilt to the surface. Borg's scientifically grounded rejection of religion immediately places him at odds with the man of God, and a battle of the brains follows. The preacher proves to be the stronger; Borg capitulates by asking him to say prayers for him and tell his folktales. At the end of the novel, Borg has receded into insanity. In a moment of clarity, he goes down to the sea, finds a boat, and sails to his death.

By the Open Sea can be read as a novel about the conflict between the conscious and the unconscious and the need to arrive at a state of balance between the two. Borg's personality unravels because the unconscious has been excluded from it. Strindberg, like Carl Jung after him, uses the male-female opposition as a metaphor to describe this conflict. When the book's perhaps trivial story is regarded from this perspective, this often underrated work reveals itself to be a powerful psychological novel.

INFERNO

Like *The Confession of a Fool*, the equally autobiographical novel *Inferno* is narrated in the first person. Because the book ostensibly tells about Strindberg's life in Paris during the years 1894 to 1897, it has been customary not to distinguish between Strindberg and the narrator and Strindberg the author. The lack of distinction between the two is strongly reinforced by the author/narrator, who at the end of the novel offers his diary as proof that the novel is factual. When this claim is taken at face value, however, it becomes clear that Strindberg's perception of reality during the period covered by the novel is such that the author would have to be regarded as mentally ill. The lack of distance between the novel's "experiencing self" and the self that later narrates the events, furthermore, indicates that Strindberg suffered from the same defects at the time of the book's composition.

The reader may accept Strindberg's claims at face value or may subject the book to a less orthodox reading. If, for example, the events of the novel are compared with those that are narrated in Strindberg's diary, it soon becomes clear that the diary strongly discredits the novel's claim to factuality. By inviting comparison with the diary, Strindberg offers the reader a clue that will lead to the reconstruction of a story that is radically different from what appears on the book's surface. The novel thus becomes a fundamentally ironic one, and its aesthetic value lies largely in the elegant way in which the irony is constructed. Strindberg's purpose is, in fact, to fool those of his readers who allow themselves to be taken in by the description of his supposed madness, while at the same time he wishes to commune secretly with those who are sufficiently perceptive to realize what he is up to. The structure of the narrative situation thus closely parallels the general structure of irony, with Strindberg being the author and most readers being victims of the irony, and with those few who really understand constituting its audience.

Such a narrative strategy entails a high degree of risk to the author, who by most readers will be considered a madman. Strindberg compensates for this risk by using his persona to express some important verities regarding his perception of his own destiny, much as the medieval fool often was able to express profound truths. Thus, the victims of the irony will simultaneously allow him to experience a sense of intellectual superiority and provide him with an audience that, despite its inferiority, is capable of being instructed. Those who reconstruct the irony and become part of his more sophisticated audience, on the other hand, allow him to feel a sense of community in his exalted intellectual station. At the same time, they have seen through the structure of norms offered to the victims and consequently also possess those truths that Strindberg offers to his least enlightened readers. *Inferno* thus places Strindberg in a position where he cannot lose in his relationship with the reader.

The truths that are expressed by Strindberg's first-person madman concern both how it feels to be losing one's sanity and an antidote against the disintegration of the personality that Strindberg, strictly on an experimental basis, began to administer to himself during the 1890's. This antidote, which was intended both to prevent any loss of mind and to enhance the writer's creative powers, consisted in a religious interpretation of life. Religion was becoming popular among both Scandinavian neo-Romantics and reformed Continental decadents, so Strindberg was in good company. His experimental religiosity was centered on a belief in supernatural powers that were guiding his life and in relationship to which he was a former rebel who was now being chastened and turned into a suffering sacrificial victim not dissimilar to the actor Falander in *The Red Room*. By viewing himself as a proxy for humanity, Strindberg was able to reinterpret his life in Paris as a myth of the human predicament. *Inferno* thus becomes both the story of humanity's passing through Hell and the exceptional individual's rise above his torments by virtue of his intellect.

Strindberg's career stands at the juncture between the nineteenth and the twentieth centuries. Rooted in a Romantic view of the world, Strindberg passed through the Scandinavian literary realism of the 1870's and the naturalism of the 1880's and ended in the neo-Romanticism of the 1890's. His oeuvre is dedicated to the search for truth, particularly with reference to the nature of his own identity. Although his dramas have influenced twentieth century theater to a greater extent than his novels have affected their genre, he is nevertheless an important figure when viewed in the context of the modern psychological novel. Above all, however, Strindberg was a man whose life, in its joy and pain, may well serve as a paradigm for modern people.

Jan Sjåvik

OTHER MAJOR WORKS

SHORT FICTION: *Svenska öden och äventyr*, 1882-1892; *Giftas I*, 1884; *Utopier i verkligheten*, 1885; *Giftas II*, 1886 (*Married*, 1913; also known as *Getting Married*, 1973; includes *Giftas I* and *Giftas II*); *Skärkarlsliv*, 1888; *Legender*, 1898 (*Legends*, 1912); *Fagervik och Skamsund*, 1902 (*Fair Haven and Foul Strand*, 1913); *Sagor*, 1903 (*Tales*, 1930); *Historiska miniatyrer*, 1905 (*Historical Miniatures*, 1913).

PLAYS: *Fritänkaren*, pb. 1870; *I Rom*, pr., pb. 1870; *Hermione*, pb. 1871; *Den fredlöse*, pr. 1871 (*The Outlaw*, 1912); *Mäster Olof*, pb. 1878 (*Master Olof*, 1915); *Gillets hemlighet*, pr., pb. 1880; *Anno fyrtioåtta*, pb. 1881 (wr. 1876); *Herr Bengts hustru*, pr., pb. 1882; *Lycko-Pers resa*, pr., pb. 1883 (*Lucky Peter's Travels*, 1912); *Fadren*, pr., pb. 1887 (*The Father*, 1899); *Marodörer*, pr. 1887; *Fordringsägare*, pb. 1888 (in Danish), pr. 1889 (in Swedish; *Creditors*, 1910); *Fröken Julie*, pb. 1888 (*Miss Julie*, 1912); *Kamraterna*, pb. 1888 (with Axel Lundegård; *Comrades*, 1912); *Hemsöborna*, pr. 1889 (adaptation of his novel); *Paria*, pr. 1889 (*Pariah*, 1913); *Den starkare*, pr. 1889 (*The Stronger*, 1912); *Samum*, pr., pb. 1890 (*Simoom*, 1906); *Himmelrikets nycklar, eller Sankte Per vandrar på jorden*, pb. 1892 (*The Keys of Heaven*, 1965); *Bandet*, pb. 1893 (in German), pb. 1897 (in Swedish; *The Bond*, 1960); *Debet och kredit*, pb. 1893 (*Debit and Credit*, 1906); *Första varningen*, pr., pb. 1893 (*The First Warning*, 1915); *Inför döden*, pr., pb. 1893 (*In the Face of Death*, 1916); *Leka med elden*, pb. 1893 (in German), pr. 1897 (in Swedish; *Playing with Fire*, 1930); *Moderskärlek*, pb. 1893 (*Mother Love*, 1910); *Till Damaskus, forsta delen*, pb. 1898 (*To Damascus I*, 1913); *Till Damaskus, andra delen*, pb. 1898 (*To Damascus II*, 1913); *Advent, ett mysterium*, pb. 1899 (*Advent*, 1912); *Brott och Brott*, pb. 1899 (*Crime and Crime*, 1913; also known as *There Are Crimes and Crimes*); *Erik XIV*, pr., pb. 1899 (English translation, 1931); *Folkungasagan*, pb. 1899 (*The Saga of the Folkungs*, 1931); *Gustav Vasa*, pr., pb. 1899 (English translation, 1916); *Gustav Adolf*, pb. 1900 (English translation, 1957); *Carl XII*, pb. 1901 (*Charles XII*, 1955); *Dödsdansen, första delen*, pb. 1901 (*The Dance of Death I*, 1912); *Dödsdansen, andra delen*, pb. 1901 (*The Dance of Death II*, 1912); *Engelbrekt*, pr., pb. 1901 (English translation, 1949); *Kaspers fet-tisdag*, pr. 1901; *Kristina*, pb. 1901 (*Queen Christina*, 1955); *Midsommar*, pr., pb. 1901 (*Midsummertide*, 1912); *Påsk*, pr., pb. 1901 (*Easter*, 1912); *Ett drömspel*, pb. 1902 (*A Dream Play*, 1912); *Kronbruden*, pb. 1902 (*The Bridal Crown*, 1916); *Svanevit*, pb. 1902 (*Swanwhite*, 1914); *Gustav III*, pb. 1903 (English translation, 1955); *Näktergalen i Wittenberg*, pb. 1904 (*The Nightingale of Whittenberg*, 1970); *Till Damaskus, tredje delen*, pb. 1904 (*To Damascus III*, 1913); *Brända tomten*, pr., pb. 1907 (*After the Fire*, 1913); *Oväder*, pr., pb. 1907 (*Storm*, 1913); *Pelikanen*, pr., pb. 1907 (*The Pelican*, 1962); *Spöksonaten*, pb. 1907 (*The Ghost Sonata*, 1916); *Abu Casems tofflor*, pr., pb. 1908; *Bjälbo-Jarlen*, pr., pb. 1909 (*Earl Birger of Bjälbo*, 1956); *Riksföreståndaren*, pr. 1909 (*The Regent*, 1956); *Siste riddaren*, pr., pb. 1909 (*The Last of the Knights*, 1956); *Stora landsvägen*, pb. 1909 (*The Great Highway*, 1954); *Svarta handsken*, pb. 1909 (*The Black Glove*, 1916); *Genom öknar till arvland, eller Moses*, pb. 1918 (wr. 1903; *Through Deserts to Ancestral Lands*, 1970); *Halländarn*, pb. 1918 (wr. 1902); *Hellas: Eller, Sokrates*, pb. 1918 (*Hellas*, 1970); *Lammet och vilddjuret: Eller, Kristus*, pb. 1918 (wr. 1903; *The Lamb and the Beast*, 1970); *Toten-Insel: Eller, Hades*, pb. 1918 (*Isle of the Dead*, 1962); *Six Plays*, 1955; *Eight Expressionist Plays*, 1965.

POETRY: *Dikter och verkligheter*, 1881; *Dikter på vers och prosa*, 1883; *Sömngångarnätter på vakna dagar*, 1884.

NONFICTION: *Gamla Stockholm*, 1880; *Det nya riket*, 1882; *Svenska folket i helg och söcken, krig och fred, hemma och ute eller Ett tusen år av svenska bildningens och sedernas historia*, 1882; *Tjänstekvinnans son: En s äls utvecklingshistoria*, 1886 (4 volumes; *The Son of a Servant: The Story of the Evolution of a Human Being*, 1966, volume 1 only); *Vivisektioner*, 1887; *Blomstermalningar och djurstycken*, 1888; *Bland franska bönder*, 1889; *Antibarbarus*, 1896; *Jardin des plantes*, 1896; *Svensk natur*, 1897; *Världshistoriens mystik*, 1903; *Modersmålets anor*, 1910; *Religiös renässans*, 1910; *Världsspråkens rötter*, 1910; *Folkstaten*, 1910-1911; *Tal till svenska nationen*, 1910-1911; *Öppna brev till Intima Teatern*, 1911-1912 (*Open Letters to the Intimate Theater*, 1959); *Zones of the Spirit: A Book of Thoughts*, 1913.

BIBLIOGRAPHY

Carlson, Harry Gilbert. *Out of "Inferno": Strindberg's Reawakening as an Artist*. Seattle: University of Washington Press, 1996. Discusses Strindberg's reemergence as a major literary figure after the 1897 publication of *Inferno*, the novel that recounts some of his harrowing experiences during his six-year exile. Includes bibliography and index.

House, Poul, Sven Hakon Rossel, and Göran Stockenström, eds. *August Strindberg and the Other: New Critical Approaches*. Atlanta: Rodopi, 2002. Collection of essays (originally papers delivered in 2000 at a conference titled "Strindberg at the Millennium—Strindberg and the Other") focuses on interpreting the motif of "the other" and "otherness" in Strindberg's work. Includes analyses of his novel *A Madman's Defense* and his autobiographical prose.

Lagercrantz, Olof. *August Strindberg*. Translated by Anselm Hollo. New York: Farrar, Straus and Giroux, 1984. Thorough and accessible biography recounts the events of Strindberg's life and the circumstances in which he created his plays and novels. Includes illustrations, bibliography, and index.

Martinus, Eivor. *Strindberg and Love*. Oxford, England: Amber Lane Press, 2001. Examines Strindberg's letters and diaries, among other sources, to describe his relationships with women and how these relationships are reflected in his literary works. Includes bibliography and index.

Meidal, Bjorn. "Ola Hansson and August Strindberg." In *Poe Abroad: Influence, Reputation, Affinities*, edited by Lois Davis Vines. Iowa City: University of Iowa Press, 1999. Discussion of Strindberg and Swedish poet Ola Hansson is part of a collection of essays devoted to the examination of Edgar Allan Poe's impact and reputation outside the United States.

Robinson, Michael. *Studies in Strindberg*. Norwich: Norvik Press, 1998. Critical analysis sets Strindberg's achievements as a playwright against his accomplishments as an autobiographer, painter, letter writer, and theater director. Includes a discussion of the difficulties Strindberg encountered when he sought to place his life experiences into his literature.

_______, ed. *The Cambridge Companion to August Strindberg*. New York: Cambridge

University Press, 2009. Collection of essays analyzes Strindberg's work and places it within the context of his life and times. Includes Ulf Olsson's essay "Learning to Speak: Strindberg and the Novel."

_______. *Strindberg and Genre*. Norwich, England: Norvik Press, 1991. Good selection of essays on Strindberg's writing in various genres. A majority of the essays analyze his plays, but some examine the novel *Inferno* and other nondramatic works. Includes bibliographical references and an index.

Robinson, Michael, and Sven Hakon Rossel, eds. *Expressionism and Modernism: New Approaches to August Strindberg*. Vienna: Edition Praesens, 1999. Collection of essays (most originally papers delivered at the Thirteenth International Strindberg Conference in October, 1997) provides wide-ranging examination of the literary works of Strindberg. Includes bibliography and index.

Schoolfield, George C. "Sweden: August Strindberg." In *A Baedeker of Decadence: Charting a Literary Fashion, 1884-1927*. New Haven, Conn.: Yale University Press, 2003. Chapter on Strindberg discusses his novels *The Red Room*, *The Madman's Defense*, and *By the Open Sea* as part of a larger study of Decadent literature.

Steene, Birgitta, ed. *Strindberg and History*. Stockholm: Almqvist & Wiksell International, 1992. Collection of essays is devoted to the examination of the theme of history in Strindberg's works. Includes bibliography and index.

ANTHONY TROLLOPE

Born: London, England; April 24, 1815
Died: London, England; December 6, 1882

PRINCIPAL LONG FICTION

The Macdermots of Ballycloran, 1847
The Kellys and the O'Kellys, 1848
The Warden, 1855
Barchester Towers, 1857
Doctor Thorne, 1858
The Three Clerks, 1858
The Bertrams, 1859
Castle Richmond, 1860
Framley Parsonage, 1860-1861 (serial), 1861 (book)
Orley Farm, 1861-1862 (serial), 1862 (book)
The Small House at Allington, 1862-1864 (serial), 1864 (book)
Rachel Ray, 1863
Can You Forgive Her?, 1864-1865 (serial), 1864, 1865 (book)
Miss Mackenzie, 1865
The Belton Estate, 1865-1866 (serial), 1866 (book)
The Claverings, 1866-1867 (serial), 1867 (book)
The Last Chronicle of Barset, 1867
Phineas Finn, the Irish Member, 1867-1869 (serial), 1869 (book)
He Knew He Was Right, 1868-1869 (serial), 1869 (book)
The Vicar of Bulhampton, 1869-1870 (serial), 1870 (book)
The Eustace Diamonds, 1871-1873 (serial), 1872 (book)
Phineas Redux, 1873-1874 (serial), 1875 (book)
The Way We Live Now, 1874-1875 (serial), 1875 (book)
The Prime Minister, 1875-1876 (serial), 1876 (book)
The American Senator, 1876-1877 (serial), 1877 (book)
Is He Popenjoy?, 1877-1878 (serial), 1878 (book)
John Caldigate, 1878-1879 (serial), 1879 (book)
The Duke's Children, 1879-1880 (serial), 1880 (book)
Dr. Wortle's School, 1880
Ayala's Angel, 1881
The Fixed Period, 1881-1882 (serial), 1882 (book)
The Landleaguers, 1882-1883 (serial), 1883 (book)
Mr. Scarborough's Family, 1882-1883 (serial), 1883 (book)

Other literary forms

The novels of Anthony Trollope (TRAHL-uhp) were frequently first published in serialized form in various periodicals such as the *Cornhill Magazine* and *The Fortnightly Review.* They appeared subsequently in a two- or three-volume format. Trollope wrote several books of cultural reportage that were more than mere travelogues: *The West Indies* (1859), *North America* (1862), *Australia and New Zealand* (1873), and *South Africa* (1878), along with the more impressionistic *Travelling Sketches* (1865-1866). Three volumes of short stories appeared: *Lotta Schmidt, and Other Stories* (1867), *An Editor's Tales* (1870), and *Why Frau Frohmann Raised Her Prices, and Other Stories* (1882). He wrote sketches of clerical men in *Clergymen of the Church of England* (1865-1866) and detailed biographies of William Makepeace Thackeray, a longtime friend (*Thackeray*, 1879), and Lord Palmerston, the prominent politician (*Lord Palmerston*, 1882). His *Autobiography* appeared posthumously in 1883. He tried his hand at classical translation in an edition of *The Commentaries of Caesar* (1870). Many of Trollope's letters were collected in a 1951 volume edited by Bradford A. Booth, but a number of complete and fragmentary letters remain unpublished at Princeton University.

Achievements

Anthony Trollope was acknowledged during his lifetime as a prominent though not necessarily a weighty or enduring writer. He wished to entertain and he did so, at least until the late 1860's, when *He Knew He Was Right* turned out to be a failure. His posthumous reputation was harmed by his *Autobiography*, which claimed that he wrote automatically, that his characters were imitations of commonly observed types, that he transcribed reality without much aesthetic control, and that he forced his production by his methodical habits of composition whatever the circumstances. These admissions brought upon him the wrath of the next generation of writers in the 1880's and 1890's who were imbued with more aesthetic doctrines of carefully contrived and consistent viewpoints, detailed representation of interior states, a conscious interplay of ideas, and a complex style to suit a more complex method of storytelling.

Later, Trollope suffered from those who deemed him a pedestrian realist padding his work with creaking plots, flat characters, prosaic situations, and dull prose. He was, and still is for much of the public, the novelist of a single work, *Barchester Towers*, but other writers and critics have not forgiven him for writing more than thirty novels and setting himself a goal to exceed in quantity if not in quality. Despite what seems to be a simple theory of fiction—the writer tries as closely as possible to make the reader's experience approximate his own, to make his characters and events appear to parallel actual life—Trollope was more sophisticated than many have allowed.

According to scholar Walter Kendrick, before *He Knew He Was Right*, Trollope's works do not distinguish inner thought from outer events, consciousness is presented chronologically, and characters, at least by implication, appear without authorial interven-

Anthony Trollope
(Library of Congress)

tion. After *He Knew He Was Right*, character becomes "a zone of space on a canvas" with changes of age, feeling, and appearance even while outside the narrative. Various linear plots create a spatial unity for the reader, and they become a mosaic on which the character exists. Fiction writing becomes a subject in the novel, and the characters are a warning against efforts to define their existence with the narrative. This view sees the characters as a complex interplay between narrative and reader. Nathaniel Hawthorne had a very different view of Trollope, equating him to a giant hewing a great lump out of the earth as the earth's inhabitants go about the business of putting it under a glass case. This comment leads, unfortunately, in the direction of Henry James's evaluation, made after Trollope's death, that Trollope had "a great deliberate apprehension of the real" but that his "great fecundity is gross and importunate."

Trollope is a mixture of several kinds of writer, sometimes realistic in the sociological way of Honoré de Balzac, analyzing class and caste, sometimes a comedian of manners and mores like Henry Fielding, at times a sentimental melodramatist like Charles Dickens, fairly often an ironist deliberately breaking fictional illusions like Thackeray, often introspective if not as equally learned as George Eliot, and periodically a brilliant chronicler of dementia like Joseph Conrad. This mixture is what creates havoc with critical response. Trollope is a master of convincing and accurate dialogue, good at retrospective interior analysis, and gifted with varieties of ironic voices. The building of his reputation, aided by Michael Sadleir's biography in the 1920's, was materially assisted by *The*

Trollopian (now *Nineteenth-Century Literature*), a journal devoted to studies of his novels, further work by scholars, such as Ruth apRoberts, Robert M. Polhemus, and James R. Kincaid, and new critical techniques, which have given Trollope his present reputation as a leading English novelist.

BIOGRAPHY

Anthony Trollope, born on April 24, 1815, in London, seems to have owed his boisterous energy, booming voice, quarrelsome touchiness, and reticent sensitivity to a childhood of offhanded upbringing. C. P. Snow refers to him as "weighed down by 20 years of neglect and humiliation." His father was a tactless and impractical barrister who had pretensions about being a landowner in Harrow. There, he established his family in an elegant though quickly declining farm, Julians, later the model for the experimental Orley Farm in the novel of that name. Trollope's mother, Frances, was the driving force of the family; she was closer to Trollope's oldest brother, Tom, than to Anthony: Anthony received neither much encouragement nor much regular affection from her. After starting his education at Sunbury School, with a brief stint at Harrow, Anthony was sent to Winchester, his father's old school, for three years. In 1827, the family was forced to move into a smaller house in Harrow for financial reasons.

Meanwhile, his mother made the acquaintance of a zealous utopian reformer, Fanny Wright, and went with her and three of her children—Henry, Cecilia, and Emily—to the United States. Their experiences there border on black comedy. Among other misfortunes, Frances, without past experience or common sense, started a fancy emporium or bazaar in Cincinnati; the building evolved into a grand structure modeled on an Egyptian temple. The enterprise only succeeded in making the family penniless. Through the efforts of a painter friend, her husband, and son Tom, they managed to piecemeal their way home to England.

Anthony was removed from Winchester in 1830, which deprived him of the chance to enter Oxford University, from which he might have entered into the clergy, the usual course at that time. He returned as a day student to Harrow School, where the intense and entrenched snobbery made the shabby boy the butt of ridicule and persecution, and perhaps began his lifelong pattern of irritability. Also at that time, Trollope's father sank into petty miserliness and self-pitying moroseness, becoming more obsessively preoccupied with his scholarly work, an ecclesiastical encyclopedia.

The success of Frances's *Domestic Manners of the Americans* (1832), a book adversely critical of American society, temporarily kept the family from bankruptcy, but her husband's financial mismanagement created more debts. To prevent his arrest for bankruptcy in 1834, the family, without Anthony, went to Bruges, Belgium. Any possible happiness they might have found was destroyed by tuberculosis, which killed Anthony's father, brother Henry, and sister Emily between 1834 and 1836. Frances Trollope was obviously too occupied with nursing to pay much attention to Anthony, but she did get him a tutoring position in Belgium for a short time. He returned to England, where he survived in squalid lodgings in Marylebone, London, at a clerk's job in the main post office for seven years. At age twenty-six, he got the chance that changed his life, obtaining the post of deputy surveyor, the overseer of mail service, in western Ireland.

At Banaghar, he found a comfortable social milieu for the first time, though his manner with carriers and postmasters was brusque and his temper was at times violent. Trollope became a man jovial with companions, truculent with superiors, bullying with inferiors, and tender with close friends and family. In 1842, he married Rose Heseltine, an Anglo-Irish woman. Her bank-manager father, like one of Trollope's own shady characters, was an embezzler. A trusted partner, Rose handled Trollope's financial affairs, edited his manuscripts, and accompanied him on his journeys around the world. The portraits of solid, sensible, and compassionate wives and mothers found throughout his work, such as Lady Staveley in *Orley Farm*, suggest the type of woman Trollope had found in Rose.

Irish scenery and politics, and the models of his mother and his brother, Tom, led Trollope to his own fiction writing. Thus, not coincidentally, his first two novels have an Irish theme. In these years, Trollope also began rearing a family, two sons. Henceforth, Trollope's career ran on a dual path, pursuing his duties for the postal service and his writing.

Posted to southwest England in 1851 to correct faults in rural delivery, Trollope and his family led a roving existence for three years until he became his own boss as full surveyor in Belfast, at age thirty-nine. The experience of sleepy country towns and a current topic—the Anglican Church's misuse of endowed charity funds to create sizable incomes for administrators—resulted in the writing of *The Warden*, finished in Belfast and published in 1855; it was his first major success. When Trollope moved his family to Dublin, he established a daily routine of writing. The successor to *The Warden*, *Barchester Towers*, his best-known novel, is a social comedy in the eighteenth century mock-heroic vein of Henry Fielding or Oliver Goldsmith.

During a visit to see his mother and brother in Italy, Trollope met a young American woman, Kate Field, and began a long and close friendship, mostly carried out by correspondence. C. P. Snow thinks that Trollope was impressed by the independent and self-assertive woman, who was rather unlike English women. Intrigued by Kate's advocacy of female freedom, in *Orley Farm*, Trollope presents a woman who affronts social and moral conventions by an act of forgery to save the inheritance of her infant son. The motivation is a bit slick, but the fact that the resolute heroine succeeds against a determined male antagonist suggests that Kate's independence was sympathetically perceived.

Trollope went to North America during the early years of the American Civil War (1861-1862), a trip that resulted in a travel book. Like his mother's work, the book took a negative stance toward American institutions. He then published, among others, *Rachel Ray*, *The Last Chronicle of Barset*, and *The Claverings*, which gained Trollope his biggest sales price ever. His works were also being serialized in various periodicals, such as *The*

Fortnightly Review. It became obvious, however, that Trollope's continued output led him to repeat themes and recycle characters.

Immersed as he was in writing and somewhat resentful of his position at the post office, Trollope resigned in October, 1867, after receiving the offer of the editorship of a new journal, *St. Paul's Magazine*. He continued to do some work on behalf of the post office, however; he went to Washington, D.C., to negotiate a postal treaty in 1868. Trollope ran *St. Paul's Magazine* for three years before it went under financially. He was not temperamentally suited to deal with authors.

In his own writing, Trollope tended, as Walter Kendrick has noted, to turn toward more sensational materials that other authors had discarded, but he was also experimenting in the psychological novel. In *He Knew He Was Right*, Trollope treats the subject of insanity and he presents a fascinating study of psychosis. Ruth apRoberts has praised the novel for its economy and the supporting relationships among its closely knit characters. Trollope's work began to command less popular attention, however, and he increasingly turned to the political world. He created Phineas Finn, an Anglo-Irish politician, who appears in the novel of that name in 1869 and reappears in *Phineas Redux*, part of the loose series sometimes referred to as the Palliser novels. Trollope, however, did not give up what is really his chief subject: conflict between the sexes.

In 1871, having sold Waltham House and given up his editorship, Trollope and his wife embarked on an eighteen-month visit to New Zealand and a stay with their son, Fred, a relatively unprosperous sheep-farmer in Australia. Trollope continued to write during their stay in the primitive sheep-station. A travel commentary and materials for *John Caldigate* were the result of the voyage, as well as further work on the novel *The Eustace Diamonds*. The Trollopes then settled in London, where he wrote on the current topic of "the condition of England" in *The Way We Live Now* and *The Prime Minister*. Trollope presented his skeptical views about the ability of a democratic society to govern itself effectively.

The final stage of Trollope's life was a restless one in his sixties. He took another trip to Australia for eight months in 1875, returning through the United States and meeting with Kate Field. Then, he immediately went to South Africa to inspect the Boer territory with the encroaching British settlement based on gold and diamond exploitation. The Trollopes again returned to the land by moving into a refined farmhouse at Hartung, near Hastings, where Trollope worked on his autobiography. Along with other fiction, he wrote a mystery novel, *Mr. Scarborough's Family*, which was serialized before his death but published posthumously in 1883. Farm living aggravated Trollope's asthma and thus drained his energy, causing him to return to London. He was enjoying club life, dinners, and letters to his son, Henry, who was also a writer, when Trollope suffered a sudden stroke in the fall of 1882 that left him paralyzed. A month later, on December 6, 1882, he died, at the age of sixty-seven.

Analysis

Twentieth century criticism of Anthony Trollope acknowledged his affinity with comic satirists of the eighteenth century, and this affinity is reflected in his best-known work, *Barchester Towers*. There are two distinct worlds in the novel: that of London vanity, represented by Mr. Slope, the London preacher who comes to Barchester as the protégé of Mrs. Proudie; and that of the smaller, conservative rural world, represented by Archdeacon Grantly of Barchester Cathedral, who opposes Mr. Slope with "high and dry" Anglicanism. At the end, Slope is rejected but so is the siren of the comic interlude, Signora Madeleine Vesey Neroni, daughter of the gentlemanly but parasitic, self-indulgent Dr. Vesey Stanhope, canon of the cathedral.

Barchester Towers

The novel is concerned with the pursuit of Eleanor Bold, a young prosperous widow and daughter of Mr. Harding, by Obadiah Slope, a brash and unctuous social climber. The newly vacant position of warden provokes a struggle between the Grantly forces and the Proudie forces (including Mr. Slope), with Mrs. Proudie at the head. In this strand of the plot, the mock-heroic or mock-epic combat parodies the Miltonic epic tradition, with Grantly and his supporters as the rebel angels struggling against the tyrant Mrs. Proudie, with Slope as a kind of fallen angel. Slope is first supported by Mrs. Proudie in his efforts to prevent the return of the vacant post to Harding, but Slope, in his effort to attain favor with Eleanor Bold, eventually gets the position for Harding.

Slope is emasculated by Signora Neroni, who transfixes him with her bright eyes and silvery laughter during rural games and festivities at Ullathorne, the ancient seat of the Thornes and center of a static pastoral world. Seduced by her witchery, he is humiliated by this demoniac Eve and defeated by the godlike rebuff of Eleanor, who slaps his face as he presses his suit upon her. Further, he incurs the wrath of his patroness, Mrs. Proudie, with his attentiveness to Signora Neroni, who, although crippled, rules from a couch where she resides in state like Cleopatra. In this world of sham battles, Grantly celebrates his triumph, including a dean's position for Mr. Harding in a solemn conclave of the clergy.

The disputants in these mock exercises practice their feints around innocent third parties: Bishop Proudie between Slope and Mrs. Proudie; Quiverful, the other candidate for the wardenship, a pathetically comic father of numerous children, between his determined wife and Slope; and Harding between Slope and Grantly. In this formally ordered structure, it is appropriate that Eleanor and Frances Arabin, the naïve Oxford academician, be matched by Miss Thorne, reaffirming the power of the old order, yet still contending with Proudies. The marriage of Eleanor and Arabin asserts the two worlds, old and new, country and city, innocent and corrupt.

The novel has a rich galaxy of minor characters. For example, there is Bertie Stanhope, the dilettante sculptor, who is pressed into proposing to Eleanor, but he undermines his own courtship by the candid admission of his motives; Mr. Harding, the unwilling tool of both Slope and Grantly, who takes such delight in the cathedral music that he mechanically saws an imaginary cello during moments of partisan plots and counterplots; and Mrs. Quiverful, who functions like a wailing chorus in a Greek tragedy, piteously reminding the world and Mrs. Proudie of the cruel difficulties of pinched means and a large family. Although Trollope did write important novels on more serious themes, *Barchester Towers* remains his best known, with its effective comic scenes, the balletlike entrances and exits, the lively irony, and the mock-heroic bathos. The orchestration of speaking styles ranging from the pomposity of the Archdeacon to the vacuity of Bertie Stanhope is another example of the buoyancy and playful wit that Trollope achieved only intermittently thereafter.

ORLEY FARM

Orley Farm was written during Trollope's middle period. Its central situation revolves around the plight of Lady Mason, the second wife of a rich man, who, twenty years earlier, forged a codicil to her dying husband's will so that it leaves Orley Farm, her sole economic support, to her and her young child, Lucius. The possession of the farm has become a matter of regret, as the suspicions of the legitimate heir, Joseph Mason, otherwise the inheritor of considerable wealth, eventuate in a trial to break the will. The effort fails only because Lady Mason commits perjury. Using the omniscient viewpoint, Trollope shows both her guilt and her anguish in trying to provide security for her infant son. Lucius, as the novel opens, is a proud, priggish young man given to notions of scientifically reforming agricultural practice; he is well educated, theoretical, and self-righteous.

The novel's unusual perspective poses two main themes: first, how justice can be accomplished, and second, whether justice can actually be achieved. In setting human rights against legal rights, Trollope portrays Lady Mason's crime in the light of vested interests and the selfish motives of various people. Like C. P. Snow in a novel such as *The Masters* (1951), Trollope displays in *Orley Farm* an abstract ideal distorted and transformed by human emotions, calculations, and egotism. Joseph Mason is more concerned with defeating Lady Mason than with enjoying the actual property; Sir Peregrine Orme, a highly respected landowner, proposes marriage to Lady Mason in order to extend the protection of his name, but even he is forced to realize the stain on his honor if the truth should come out, and after Lady Mason refuses his offer, he, having been told the damning truth, keeps his promise to support her in her new trial. Another perspective is provided through Mr. Dockwrath, the country lawyer who discovers the evidence that necessitates the new trial and hopes it will prove lucrative and will enhance his legal reputation. Lady Mason's solicitor, Mr. Furnival, carefully avoids definite knowledge of her guilt, though he suspects it, while also wishing she were proven guilty so that he might forgive her with pleasure. A less selfish attitude is seen in Edith Orme, Sir Peregrine's widowed daughter-in-law, who recognizes with compassion the necessity for Lady Mason's crime and the suffering it has entailed for her.

Trollope reveals some of his other typical thematic concerns in the subplots of *Orley Farm*. He explores various attitudes toward marriage and money in the romances of Peregrine, Jr., Lucius Mason, and Felix Graham, a poor barrister, with a variety of modern young women. The women's responses to the gentlemen's advances run from prudent calculation of worldly advantages to prudent reticence in acknowledging love until family wisdom approves it. Also, Trollope's impulses toward indulgence of children are exemplified in Lord and Lady Staveley, who, having made their way without worldly advantages, are willing to offer the same chance to their children by permitting the engagement of a daughter to Felix Graham, whose success has been impeded by his honesty. Trollope's conservatism is revealed through the reluctance of these young people to avow their love until they have consent from the Staveleys.

With regard to the central theme of moral and legal justice, purely through the oratorical skills of the trial lawyer, Lady Mason is found innocent of perjury, a finding wholly incorrect. The trial frees the guilty, turns the truthful into villains, makes the innocent bear the burden of deceit, challenges the loyalty of lawyers, and implicates the idealists' posturings. The system has turned Lady Mason's desperate chicanery into heroism. It is somewhat anticlimactic that Trollope has the pure Edith Orme take Lady Mason to her heart and, from a sense of Christian charity, refuse to render judgment against her.

Meanwhile, Lady Mason's greatest trial has been alienation from Lucius, who, unaware of her guilt, has attempted vigorous countermeasures to defend her honor rather than respecting her dignified silence. His discovery of the truth cuts deeply into his priggish pride, destroys his dreams of becoming a gentleman-farmer, and makes him restore the farm to Joseph Mason before departing abroad with his mother. Again, Trollope makes an ambivalent statement through this conclusion. Although forgiveness implies repentance and restitution, Lady Mason has not been, at least in public, repentant, and the restitution is as much a matter of pride as of justice. The effect is a tacit denial of Lady Mason's innocence and thus the aborting of the whole effort to save her reputation.

CAN YOU FORGIVE HER?

If the power of money, or the distortions of human choice and desire that money brings, is Trollope's major concern, the warfare of the sexes and the frustrations that warfare brings are secondary themes in his novels. *Can You Forgive Her?*, the first of the Palliser series—which includes *Phineas Finn*, *Phineas Redux*, and *The Prime Minister*, each grounded in politics—raises the issue of what sort of love a woman wishes in marriage or indeed whether marriage is a suitable institution. The novel presents the case of Alice Vavasour, a "new woman" who does not know what she wants in life but resents the demands of social propriety. She especially resents the expectation that she accept the marriage proposal of John Grey, whom she really does love, merely because everyone knows him to be a suitable partner. Her cousin, the heiress Lady Glencora McCluskie, has married Plantagenet Palliser, the dull younger son of a ducal family, to support his Liberal political career with her money; but she has fallen in love with the handsome Burgo Fitzgerald, an unconventional, ruinous, yet passionate charmer. Alice reinstitutes her former affection for her cousin George Vavasour, another charmingly irresponsible man who needs her money to campaign to keep his seat in Parliament. For Alice, the masculine excitement of politics makes George attractive, although she honestly admits his desire for her money.

The novel has low-comedy relief in Alice's aunt, Arabella Greenow, and her two suitors, a grocer with money and a retired military officer without it. Arabella means to have her own way, giving her lovers only as much liberty as she desires, choosing the officer because of "a sniff of the rocks and the valleys" about him. The comedy underscores the desire of Alice and Glencora, who, if they had a choice, would put themselves at the mercy of weak men.

In a melodramatic turn of the main plot, George knocks down his sister, Kate, for refusing to assist him in overturning their grandfather's will, which had left all the family property to her. This turn of the plot demonstrates, through George's furious masculine rage, the falsity of the normal economic subjugation of women, which has been reversed in Kate's case. Arabella Greenow, for her part, is also financially independent and can bargain her way into a satisfactorily romantic liaison balancing "rocks and valleys" against "bread and cheese."

Glencora, aware of being sold into matrimony, almost runs off with Burgo but is dissuaded at the last minute by the vigilance of Alice, who makes clear to Plantagenet the temptation he has given to his wife by his conduct. In an improbable reversal that displays Trollope's own romanticism, Plantagenet sacrifices his political hopes for a cabinet appointment in order to take her away from the scenes of her misery after she has confessed her infatuation. Indeed, he is even willing to provide Burgo, who becomes a frequenter of gambling tables, with an allowance at her behest when they encounter him abroad.

Plantagenet can make a sacrifice for Glencora because he has money and social position; George Vavasour, by contrast, is defeated in politics and exiled for lack of money. John Grey, meanwhile, has interposed himself in Alice's arrangement with George so that her fortune is not at stake. This conduct, chivalrous in one sense, paternalistic in another, results in George's challenging him to a duel. The Victorian world is not that of Regency rakes, however, and George's blustering challenge is physically rebuffed, and he is sent away degraded. Alice finally accepts John Grey in a contrite mood. Although Grey has kindly intentions, Alice's undefined longings for autonomy anticipate those Henrik Ibsen made memorable through Nora Helmer in *Et dukkehjem* (1879; *A Doll's House*, 1880), where Nora sacrifices love in the effort to mold her own destiny.

If the future of his heroines seems to lie within conventional marital arrangements or respectable spinsterhood secured by inherited money, Trollope's questioning title for the novel seems to turn the issue of feminine aspiration somewhat ambivalently to the reader. He has shown women challenging the decorum of prudent emotions and affections based on money, but only the ungenteel Mrs. Greenow succeeds in mastering her destiny through financial manipulation.

THE EUSTACE DIAMONDS

In *The Eustace Diamonds*, Trollope shows the psychologically damaging effects of survival in an upper-class and aristocratic hierarchy, a society that channels affections and loyalties in terms of property and money, where people struggle for ascendancy, domination, and power while subscribing to Romantic illusions of unfettered expression and creative self-development. The narrator ironically undercuts the Romantic pretensions as the novel delineates the unrealistic strategies of men and women coping with the moral corruption of social ambition. They seek security, status, prestige, and elegance while evincing pretentiousness, snobbery, envy, and parasitism. Trollope takes an anarchic pleasure in those egotistical characters who subvert institutions by undermining the rules of conduct, stretching them to the point of fatuity.

In the novel, Lizzie Eustace appropriates the diamonds without specific authority from her late husband, Sir Florian, and uses them as weapons against the respectable family lawyer, Mr. Camperdown, and the man she intends as her second husband, the morally honorable Lord Fawn. The diamonds become a symbol of Lizzie's inner rage against the world, a rage arising from self-doubt prompted by the excessive demands of her own idealized views of herself. While denying that ownership of the necklace gives her any pleasure, Lizzie simultaneously insists that she will throw the diamonds away while guarding them zealously. When the box in which she ostentatiously houses them is stolen, Lizzie claims that the necklace has been stolen as well. The lie is psychologically predictable. The diamonds exemplify her attitudes toward herself, toward Lord Fawn whom she despises for his complete disdain of the diamonds, and toward Frank Greystock, her champion before the world, whom she has lured away from his serious attentions to Lucy Morris. The supposed theft is Lizzie's symbolic punishment for a guilt that will be lessened if the diamonds are believed stolen, but it is also an aggrandizement of her own self-esteem since secretly she knows they are still in her possession. The diamonds, however, are stolen in a second robbery, which ends Lizzie's control of the situation.

Lizzie's desire for social domination gains dimension through the narrator's ironic moral judgment and through the close-ups of the omniscient viewpoint that reveal her own rationalizations and fears. Seeking support, Lizzie confesses to Lord George, hoping that he will be cynically brutal, but instead she receives his weak acknowledgment of her supposed cunning. When the police discover the truth, Lizzie prefers the illusion of submitting to the police administrator to the reality of confronting her own self-destructive behavior. Lizzie then tries desperately to reestablish control by triumphing over someone: She reproaches Mrs. Carbuncle, her friend; breaks her engagement with Lord Fawn, ignoring his earlier efforts to end the relationship and pretending to be heartlessly jilted; offers herself to Lord George, who also refuses her; and finally bids for the attentions of

Frank Greystock through his need for money, yet Frank is simply provoked into promising he will abandon her utterly if she persists.

Yielding to a fantasy logic, Lizzie entertains a marriage proposal from Mr. Emilius, an impudent and sanctimonious popular preacher whom she had once refused. She deliberately accepts him knowing that he is a fraud and admitting that his bogus qualities attract her. Lizzie's limited knowledge of how the world operates is supported by Emilius's brazen effrontery, which will offer her a new chance for social domination.

The secondary characters are drawn with an equal sense of psychological aberration. For example, there is the cynical honesty of Lord George, which conceals a fearful vacillation that abhors responsibility yet is resolute in pushing his companion, Sir Griffin Tewett, into marriage with Lucinda Roanoke. Alternately submissive and aggressive, he turns vindictive in denouncing Lizzie for the damage she has caused his reputation by creating suspicions of his complicity in her concealment of the necklace. He is also forgiving, on the other hand, of Mrs. Barnacle, his former mistress, for her good intentions in encouraging her niece, Lucinda, to marry for money. Lord George appears cognizant of obligations assumed by others though irresolute in taking them upon himself. Further, he shows the unreality of Lizzie's dreams, but his own conduct is the model of a romantic neurosis. Other examples of psychologically crippled characters are Lucinda, who suffers from strong sexual repression and emotional sterility, and Sir Griffin, cool, vindictive, and arrogant, who is repelled by anyone who would love him.

These characters are set up in contrast to the more conventional ones, such as Mrs. Hittaway, who reflect the pathological tendencies that a materialistic society encourages. The baffled efforts of Lizzie, Lord George, Sir Griffin, and Lucinda to deal with destructive self-deception reflect the results of social forces inhibiting real creative growth in understanding. V. S. Pritchett criticized Trollope for being "a detailed, rather cynical observer of a satisfied world" and has asserted that "we recognize that he [Trollope] has drawn life as people say it is when they are not speaking about themselves." C. P. Snow commented that an exploratory psychological writer such as Trollope "has to live on close terms with the blacker—including the worse—side of his own nature." *The Eustace Diamonds* is the record of Trollope's endurance of a mental nature that was divided.

Pritchett accused Trollope of not capturing or presenting the depth of moral experience. This may reflect a demand for a more complex style, a more intensive depiction of the intricacies of moral struggle, and a more insistent emphasis on values. Snow, however, perceived the simple, direct style as cutting out everything except the truth. Trollope was not temperamental or self-advertising, but as a novelist he covers the wide range of social, institutional, and religious issues and controversies constituting the fabric of Victorian society. He dramatizes the moral and intellectual dilemmas often arising from them and has considerable insight as well as the ability to present the sheer flux of mental life, which anticipates later developments in the work of James Joyce, Virginia Woolf, and Dorothy Richardson.

Roger E. Wiehe

Other major works

short fiction: *Tales of All Countries*, 1861, 1863; *Lotta Schmidt, and Other Stories*, 1867; *An Editor's Tales*, 1870; *Why Frau Frohmann Raised Her Prices, and Other Stories*, 1882.

nonfiction: *The West Indies*, 1859; *North America*, 1862; *Clergymen of the Church of England*, 1865-1866; *Travelling Sketches*, 1865-1866; *Australia and New Zealand*, 1873; *South Africa*, 1878; *Thackeray*, 1879; *Lord Palmerston*, 1882; *Autobiography*, 1883; *The Letters of Anthony Trollope*, 1951 (Bradford A. Booth, editor).

translation: *The Commentaries of Caesar*, 1870.

Bibliography

Bridgham, Elizabeth A. *Spaces of the Sacred and Profane: Dickens, Trollope, and the Victorian Cathedral Town*. New York: Routledge, 2008. Describes how Trollope and Charles Dickens use the setting of Victorian cathedral towns to critique religious attitudes, business practices, aesthetic ideas, and other aspects of nineteenth century English life.

Bury, Laurent. *Seductive Strategies in the Novels of Anthony Trollope, 1815-1882*. Lewiston, N.Y.: Edwin Mellen Press, 2004. Presents a study of seduction in Trollope's novels. Argues that seduction was a survival skill for both men and women in the Victorian era and demonstrates how Trollope depicted the era's sexual politics.

Felber, Lynette. *Gender and Genre in Novels Without End: The British Roman-Fleuve*. Gainesville: University Press of Florida, 1995. Examination of multivolume works of British fiction focuses on Trollope's Palliser novels, Dorothy Richardson's *Pilgrimage*, and Anthony Powell's *A Dance to the Music of Time*. Includes notes and index.

Glendinning, Victoria. *Anthony Trollope*. New York: Alfred A. Knopf, 1993. Perceptive, witty biography focuses on Trollope's relationships with his parents and siblings, his wife, and his lovers. Uses incidents from Trollope's novels and other works to tell the writer's story.

Hall, N. John. *Trollope: A Biography*. Oxford, England: Clarendon Press, 1991. Discussion of Trollope's life draws heavily on the great Victorian's own words. Pays particular attention to Trollope's travel writing and the final decade of his life.

_______, ed. *The Trollope Critics*. New York: Macmillan, 1981. Critical anthology provides a good introduction to Trollope. Contains essays by twenty Trollope critics who cover a wide range of topics. Includes bibliography.

Markwick, Margaret. *New Men in Trollope's Novels: Rewriting the Victorian Male*. Burlington, Vt.: Ashgate, 2007. Examines Trollope's novels to trace the development of his ideas about masculinity. Argues that Trollope's male characters are not the conventional Victorian patriarchs and demonstrates how his works promoted a "startlingly modern model of manhood." Markwick also has published an examination of Trollope's female characters, *Trollope and Women* (London: Hambledon Press, 1997).

Mullen, Richard, and James Munson. *The Penguin Companion to Trollope*. New York: Penguin Books, 1996. Comprehensive guide describes all of Trollope's novels, short stories, travel books, and other works; discusses plot, characters, background, tone, allusions, and contemporary references and places the works in their historical context.

Pollard, Arthur. *Anthony Trollope*. Boston: Routledge & Kegan Paul, 1978. Seeks to put all of Trollope's novels and a variety of miscellaneous works within the context of his life and time. Emphasizes Trollope's evocation of his age and his guiding moral purpose. Includes index.

Wright, Andrew. *Anthony Trollope: Dream and Art*. New York: Macmillan, 1983. Brief study of fifteen of Trollope's novels sees them as contemporary fictions, transfiguring life in a certain way. Includes bibliography and index.

ROBERT PENN WARREN

Born: Guthrie, Kentucky; April 24, 1905
Died: West Wardsboro, near Stratton, Vermont; September 15, 1989

PRINCIPAL LONG FICTION

Night Rider, 1939
At Heaven's Gate, 1943
All the King's Men, 1946
World Enough and Time: A Romantic Novel, 1950
Band of Angels, 1955
The Cave, 1959
Wilderness: A Tale of the Civil War, 1961
Flood: A Romance of Our Time, 1964
Meet Me in the Green Glen, 1971
A Place to Come To, 1977

OTHER LITERARY FORMS

Robert Penn Warren wrote successfully in so many genres that Charles Bohner called him "the pentathlon champion of American literature." In addition to his novels, he published short stories, numerous volumes of poetry, and a considerable amount of nonfiction. Warren's fiction and his poetry often consider the same philosophical themes: the meaning of history, the loss of innocence and the recognition of evil in the fallen world, and the difficulty of finding a moral balance in a world in which traditional Christian values seem to be faltering. For example, in his book-length poem *Brother to Dragons: A Tale in Verse and Voices* (1953), Warren begins with a historical event—a brutal murder of a slave by Thomas Jefferson's nephew, Lilburne Lewis—and creates a philosophical examination of people's fallen nature. Warren does something very similar in his novel *World Enough and Time.* The story is based on a murder that occurred in 1825, but the novel, like the poem, becomes an examination of people's fall from innocence and the difficulty of establishing moral ideals in a fallen world.

Warren's concerns over history and morality are also evident in his earliest, nonfiction works. In his first book, a biography, *John Brown: The Making of a Martyr* (1929), Warren contends that Brown did not tread the path of morality quite so righteously as Ralph Waldo Emerson had thought he had; in his fallen condition, Brown mistook his own egotism for pure idealism. Warren's neo-orthodox insistence on people's fallen nature and his skepticism about the possibilities of pure idealism, both of which are reflected in his novels, led him to accept the traditionalist attitudes of the southern intellectuals who made up the Fugitive Group, and he contributed to the agrarian manifesto *I'll Take My Stand* (1930). Warren did, however, espouse a more liberal attitude toward racial matters in his later nonfiction works *Segregation: The Inner Conflict in the South* (1956) and *Who Speaks for the Negro?* (1965).

Warren's social criticism ultimately proved less influential than his literary criticism. His *Selected Essays* (1958) contains perceptive studies of Samuel Taylor Coleridge's *The Rime of the Ancient Mariner* (1798), Joseph Conrad's *Nostromo* (1904), William Faulkner, Ernest Hemingway, and Katherine Anne Porter. These essays are important not only for what they say about these authors but also for what they reveal about Warren's own work. Even more important than these essays, however, was Warren's collaboration with Cleanth Brooks. Their textbooks, *Understanding Fiction* (1943) and *Understanding Poetry* (1938), helped to change substantially the way literature was taught in the United States.

Warren continued to publish literary criticism at intervals throughout his life; indeed, *New and Selected Essays* appeared in the year of his death, 1989. With a poetry-writing career that spanned fifty years, however, he was at least equally well known as a craftsman in that genre. His poems have been widely anthologized, and he is recognized as one of the foremost American poets of the twentieth century.

Achievements

For most readers, Robert Penn Warren's name is probably most associated with his novel *All the King's Men*, for which he won both the Pulitzer Prize for fiction and the National Book Award. He also won the Robert Meltzer Award from the Screen Writers Guild for the play based on that novel. Warren's short story "Blackberry Winter" also has been highly acclaimed and widely anthologized. Other readers think of Warren primarily as a poet, and with good reason; he won the Pulitzer Prize for poetry twice, first for *Promises: Poems, 1954-1956* (1957), which also won the Edna St. Vincent Millay Prize and the National Book Award for poetry, and a second time for *Now and Then: Poems, 1976-1978* (1978). *Selected Poems: New and Old, 1923-1966* (1966) won the Bollingen Prize from Yale University, and *Audubon: A Vision* (1969) won the Van Wyck Brooks Award and the National Medal for Literature. Warren was elected to the American Philosophical Society in 1952 and to the American Academy of Arts and Sciences in 1959. He was named first poet laureate of the United States in 1986.

Biography

Robert Penn Warren's background and experience had a tremendous impact on the thematic concerns of his fiction. He demonstrated the need, common to so many southern writers, to cope with the burden of the past. He also wrote out of a scholar's familiarity with and devotion to certain prominent literary artists, past and present, particularly the Elizabethan and Jacobean dramatists Conrad, Faulkner, and T. S. Eliot. Warren's academic studies may have had a great deal to do with the structure of his works and their typically tragic mode. His recurring subject, however, was the peculiar experience of the South; a love-hate relationship with a dying heritage runs throughout his work.

Born to Robert Franklin and Anna Ruth Penn Warren on April 24, 1905, in the tiny Kentucky town of Guthrie, Warren grew up in an almost classic southern situation. His father, a banker and businessman struggling to support a large family, did not initially fire the young Warren's imagination as his grandfather did. The emotional bond between Warren and his maternal grandfather, Gabriel Thomas Penn, ripened during long summers spent on his grandfather's tobacco farm. Here, Warren experienced the pastoral charms of agrarian life, soaked up the nostalgic glow of the American Civil War from his grandfather, and absorbed the rhetoric and humor that permeates the southern storytelling.

Gabriel had been a cavalryman during the Civil War, and he spent many an afternoon with his grandson reliving the legendary time. It is not surprising that the boy looked upon the Civil War as America's great epic, as imbued with nobility and tragedy as Homer's *Iliad* (c. 750 B.C.E.; English translation, 1611) He was not blind, however, to the irony and ambiguity of his grandfather as representative of the values of the aristocratic horse soldier. Warren commemorated his realization that the romantic image of the Confederate cavalryman had its darker side in the poem "Court Martial" in *Promises: Poems, 1954-1956*, which is about his grandfather's hanging of bushwhackers without benefit of legal trial. Because this poem was written much later, however, it is possible that the ambiguous view of the grandfather was partially constructed from a more mature understanding. The event, however, was a true one that evidently made a deep impression on the young Warren. In any case, Warren was absorbing background for a number of later novels, such as *Wilderness: A Tale of the Civil War* and *Band of Angels*. In neither of these does he write as an apologist for the Old South, but he does expose the moral shortcomings of Northerners, much as he does in his early biography of John Brown.

Warren also was absorbing the local tales of tobacco war, when the growers of dark-fired tobacco banded together to boycott the tobacco company that regulated prices. Warren's first novel, *Night Rider*, was written from childhood memories of such local stories. Warren's brother, Thomas, who became a grain dealer, knew all the farmers of the region and was adept at repeating such tales.

The young Warren loved nature; collected butterflies, snakes, rocks, and leaves; and aspired to paint animals (an interest reflected in his poem about John Audubon). Later, he hunted with his brother and learned taxidermy. These experiences were more important, perhaps, to the content of his poetry than to his fiction. In spite of his persistent affinity for nature, he usually recognized in his fiction its essential amorality: "The blank cup of nature," he calls it in *World Enough and Time*.

In spite of the contribution to his early imaginative development by his grandfather and his agrarian milieu, the influence of Warren's father was subtle and pervasive, perhaps more significant in the long run to the human relationships explored in his novels. Ambiguous father-son relationships appear over and over in such novels as *All the King's Men*, *The Cave*, *At Heaven's Gate*, and *A Place to Come To*. None is modeled on Warren's actual relationship to his own father, but they reflect a combination of admiration, guilt, and mystery that suggests some deep personal involvement in the issues they raise.

Warren often admitted to an odd sense of guilt about "stealing his father's life." Robert Franklin Warren had wanted to be a lawyer and a poet but had become a businessman instead, because of financial responsibilities not only to his own family but also to a family of half brothers and sisters left without a provider when his father died. One of Warren's favorite reminiscences was about finding a book with some poems written by his father in it and carrying it with delight to him. His father summarily confiscated the book, and his son never saw it again. Warren thought perhaps his father had been embarrassed or pained at this reminder of a goal long since set aside. According to Warren, his father never regretted the obligations that dictated the terms of his life. Indeed, he took joy in them. Warren speaks with an admiration bordering on awe of the seemingly effortless rectitude of his father and of the ideal relationship between his father and mother.

As the result of an accident when he was fifteen years old, Warren lost his sight in one eye and was thus prevented from pursuing a career as a naval officer, as he had planned. Warren went, instead, to Vanderbilt University and came under the influence of John Crowe Ransom and the Fugitives, a group of academics and townspeople who met regularly to discuss philosophy and poetry. Ransom soon recognized Warren's unusual ability and encouraged him to write poetry.

Warren graduated summa cum laude from Vanderbilt in 1926 and pursued a master of arts degree at the University of California, Berkeley. While there, he became an ardent student of Elizabethan and Jacobean drama, which perhaps struck a responsive chord in an imagination already steeped in the violence and melodrama of southern history. He started to work on a doctorate at Yale University but left as a Rhodes scholar for Oxford, England, where he received a bachelor of letters degree in 1930.

During this period, Warren wrote his first book, *John Brown*. To some extent, this book grew out of an impulse shared with a number of his Vanderbilt friends and other writers of the Southern Renaissance. They were concerned about the exclusively Northern bias of most historians dealing with events leading up to and during the Civil War and its aftermath. Certainly, Warren presents a jaundiced view of the radical abolitionist. Brown seems to have provided a nucleus for Warren's meditations about the effects of power and the misuses of altruism that were to be explored in a number of later novels, especially *Night Rider* and *All the King's Men*. He also wrote his first fiction while at Oxford, a short story called "Prime Leaf," about the impact of the Kentucky tobacco war on an old man, his son, and his grandson. The old man has a role similar to that of the elder Todd in *Night Rider*, the wise man who bows out of the organization when it resorts to vigilante tactics.

Warren taught at a number of universities, including Louisiana State, where he lived in the legendary ambience of the southern demagogue Huey Long, whose presence lies behind the fictional Willie Stark of *All the King's Men*. Warren later said that he knew nothing about the real Long, but the mythical Long was on everyone's lips. Even casual conversations often dwelled on questions of power and ethics, of means and ends, and of "historical costs." In an essay titled "*All the King's Men*: The Matrix of Experience," in John Lewis Longley's *Robert Penn Warren: A Collection of Critical Essays* (1965), Warren writes,

> Melodrama was the breath of life. There had been melodrama in the life I had known in Tennessee, but with a difference; in Tennessee the melodrama seemed to be different from the stuff of life, something superimposed upon life, but in Louisiana people lived melodrama, seemed to live, in fact, for it, for this strange combination of philosophy, humor and violence. Life was a tale that you happened to be living—and that "Huey" happened to be living before your eyes.

These remarks demonstrate that Warren was not primarily a historical novelist; rather, he was a classicist, fascinated with the universal patterns in particular experience. He thus discouraged close comparisons between Willie Stark and Long, pointing out that he wrote the first version of the story as a verse drama in Italy, as he watched Benito Mussolini consolidate his power.

In Warren's writing career, the years from 1943 to 1950—though a dry period for poetry—were productive ones for fiction and literary criticism. In addition to *All the King's Men*, he produced *At Heaven's Gate*, about the unscrupulous liaison between government and industry, and *World Enough and Time*, about a nineteenth century murder case. When Warren was poetry consultant for the Library of Congress in 1944-1945, Katherine Anne Porter, who was fiction consultant that year, threw on his desk the confession of Jeroboam Beauchamp, hanged for murder in Kentucky in 1826. Porter announced cryptically that she was giving him a novel. This was, indeed, the germ for his most complex novel, *World Enough and Time*. Warren's dry period in poetry eventually ended after he divorced his first wife, Emma Brescia, married the writer Eleanor Clark, and fathered two children. He began writing excellent poetry and produced several more novels. A long association with Yale University began in 1950.

In 1986 Warren was named the first poet laureate of the United States, a post he held for two years. He died of cancer in 1989 at his summer home near Stratton, Vermont.

ANALYSIS

Often, what Robert Penn Warren said about other writers provides important insight into his own works. This is especially true of Warren's perceptive essay "The Great Mirage: Conrad and *Nostromo*" (in *Selected Essays*), in which he discusses the enigmatic speech of Stein in Conrad's *Lord Jim* (1900):

> A man that is born falls into a dream like a man who falls into the sea. If he tries to climb out into the air as inexperienced people endeavor to do, he drowns—*nicht wahr*? . . . No! I tell you! The way is to the destructive element submit yourself, and with the exertions of your hands and feet in the water make the deep, deep sea keep you up.

Warren interprets the dream here as "man's necessity to justify himself and his actions into moral significance of some order, to find sanctions." The destructiveness of the dream arises from humans' nature as egotistical animals with savage impulses, not completely adapted to the dream sea of ideas. The one who learns to swim instead of drowning in the unnatural sea of ideas is he who realizes that the values he creates are illusion, but that "the illusion is necessary, is infinitely precious, is the mark of his human achievement, and is, in the end, his only truth." Warren calls *Nostromo* "a study in the definition and necessity of illusion." This phrase could also describe most of Warren's works of fiction.

Warren's classification of thematic elements in Conrad's stories could also be applied to his own. Warren writes that Conrad is concerned with the person who lacks imagination but clings to fidelity and duty (like the old captain in *Youth*, 1902), the sinner against human solidarity and the human mission (like Kurtz in *Heart of Darkness*, 1902, and Decoud in *Nostromo*), and the redeemed individual (Jim in *Lord Jim* and Dr. Monygham in *Nostromo*). Warren says that Conrad is most interested in the latter—"the crisis of this story comes when the hero recognizes the terms on which he may be saved, the moment, to take Morton Zabel's phrase, of the 'terror of the awakening.'"

One might note that in Warren's novel *At Heaven's Gate*, Jerry's dirt-farmer father fits the pattern of natural rectitude, while Slim Sarrett, the nihilistic, cynical artist, is certainly the sinner against human solidarity. No one seems to be redeemed in *At Heaven's Gate*, though Jerry might have a chance in a hypothetical future, since he has acquired considerable self-knowledge. Mr. Munn in *Night Rider* has also stripped away his own illusions, but he dies, like William Shakespeare's Macbeth, without redemption. In other novels of this period, however, Jack Burden in *All the King's Men*, and perhaps even the murderer in *World Enough and Time*, achieve some kind of absolution. Warren and Conrad share this deep obsession with the need for redemption, and though the sentiment is religious and may be expressed in Christian imagery, it is consistently humanistic in emphasis. The world they both recognize is a naturalistic one, but people must live in two worlds, the world of facts and the world of ideas, which they create themselves. Warren's notion of submission to the realm of ideas is analogous, perhaps, to Hemingway's code of the hunter, the fisherman, the bullfighter, or the soldier, which provides existential meaning in a meaningless world.

Warren's early novels, particularly *Night Rider*, *All the King's Men*, and *World Enough and Time*, which critics generally agree are his best, trace a pattern of increasing complexity in the theme of people's vacillation between the fantasy of dreams and the reality of facts. After *World Enough and Time*, which is almost too densely packed and convoluted in theme, Warren relaxed his insistence that everything must be said on the subject of illusion and reality in one novel. Later works, such as *Meet Me in the Green Glen* and *Wilderness*, though not conspicuously different in theme, concentrate on a particular manifestation of the problem—on the nature of love in *Meet Me in the Green Glen*, and on the nature of altruism in *Wilderness*.

Actually, Warren's examination of the apposition between the world of ideas and the world of facts begins in his first book, *John Brown*. Warren portrays the militant abolitionist as not so much obsessed with freeing slaves as with starring in his own myth. Brown is encouraged in this role by the unqualified praise of Ralph Waldo Emerson, whom Warren believed to be a writer of empty words, with little perception of the real world; Warren quotes Emerson as saying of Brown, "He is a man to make friends wherever on earth courage and integrity are esteemed—the rarest of heroes, a pure idealist, with no by-ends of his own." Warren did not for a moment believe that Brown was a "pure idealist"; moreover, Warren had a continuing distrust of "pure idealists," whoever they might be. In his fiction, Warren was inclined to show abstract idealists as lacking in self-knowledge, capable of self-righteous violence because they refuse to acknowledge their own irrational impulses. The best example of this personality-type in Warren's fiction is Adam Stanton, in *All the King's Men*, who assassinates Willie because Willie, the man of fact, seduced Adam's sister.

John Brown, however, as one who uses exalted ideas to inflate his own self-image, is more akin to Warren's Professor Ball, Dr. MacDonald, and Mr. Munn of *Night Rider*; Bogan Murdock, the industrialist, and Slim Sarett, of *At Heaven's Gate*; and Wilkie Barron, the manipulative false friend of Jeremiah Beaumont, in *World Enough and Time*. Willie, though categorized by Jack as the "man of fact," in contrast to Adam, the "man of idea," has his own idealistic dream of the people's hospital, free to anyone who needs it. Whether that dream was truly altruistic, however, or tinged by the secret need for a personal monument to his existence, is ambiguous.

NIGHT RIDER

Warren thus suggests that the self is itself part of the dream sea of ideas. Warren's protagonists are often initially passive persons whose emptiness is filled by other more dynamic personalities. Having acquired a somewhat fictitious self under such influence, they proceed to act in the real world as though that dream were true—often with tragic results. Thus, Mr. Munn seems an innocuous, ordinary young lawyer when he first appears in *Night Rider*, but he is drawn irresistibly to his more dynamic friend, Mr. Christian, who has a legitimate concern for the plight of the tobacco growers at the mercy of the price-controlling tobacco company. Munn learns to savor his new role as labor leader. He is ripe, then, for indoctrination by more conniving, professional agitators, Professor Ball and Dr. MacDonald, who preach a secret society that will scrape the fields of uncooperative growers and punish backsliders who dare to violate the embargo.

What begins as a lawful strike by the downtrodden majority becomes lawless action by a vigilante group that destroys crops, burns warehouses, and commits murder. In the case of Munn, the crisis of this psychic change in direction comes when he realizes that his assigned task to assassinate the tobacco farmer Bunk Trevelyon, whom he once defended in court on a murder charge, is not only his "duty" to the group; it also satisfies something very personal in himself that he has not yet recognized. Trevelyon had committed the murder of which he was once accused, and the African American who was hanged for that murder was innocent. Trevelyon thus becomes the symbol for Munn's half-conscious cooperation in framing the African American, or, to use another favorite term of Warren, Munn's original sin. In this ritual of retribution, the shared myth of community justice fuses with Munn's private myth of killing the shadow self, an act of both self condemnation and deliberate concealment of a secret crime.

After this private confrontation and ritual killing of his shadow self, Munn makes no more moral objections to anything Ball and MacDonald want to do. The three lead a concerted assault on the company warehouses, which results in a number of casualties. One person who dies is young Benton Todd, who had been an ardent admirer of Munn. Moreover, Todd hoped to marry Mr. Christian's daughter, Lucille, who has been having a secret affair with Munn. If Trevelyon symbolizes the murderous shadow self that Munn has hated to acknowledge, Benton Todd suggests the lost idealism, the better dream that Munn has betrayed.

Munn's subsequent flight to the West to escape prosecution for a murder he did not commit might have resulted in redemption, but it does not. The pattern of redemption is presented to him obliquely by the story of Proudfit, the impoverished farmer who is sheltering Munn. Proudfit tells of his own checkered career in the West, as a buffalo hunter and hide-tanner, with companions as rough and wild as himself. Eventually, however, he lives in peace among American Indians. When he becomes ill, the Native Americans care for him, using all their resources of natural healing and religious ritual. In his fever, he eventually has a vision of Kentucky, where he was reared, and a young woman waiting beside a stream. His strength then begins to return, so he leaves the Native American friends and goes back to find the very woman he saw in his vision, now his wife, and the very hill he saw, which is now his farm.

Proudfit's story is both an engrossing dialect narrative and a unique version of the underlying myth of death and resurrection. Proudfit's humble redemption contrasts with the myth of sin and damnation implied in Munn's career. Both Proudfit and Munn have a period of withdrawal (Proudfit, among the American Indians; Munn, on Proudfit's remote farm), time to rethink their past lives and future goals. This experience is analogous, perhaps, to the withdrawal and contemplation that the mythic hero undergoes before he returns to his homeland as a new man. Munn, however, is not transformed. He does become mildly obsessed with the innocent African American who died in Trevelyon's stead, but he cannot even remember the man's name. Perhaps his inability to name the scapegoat is intended to suggest Munn's distance from the redemption offered by Christ's sacrifice. This does not mean that Warren was advocating Christianity; he was admitting, at least, a moral vacuum where traditional values have been eliminated in a society concerned primarily with power and wealth.

All the King's Men

The polarity of idea and fact receives more explicit development in *All the King's Men*. Again, an essentially passive person, Jack Burden, feeds emotionally on a more dynamic personality, Willie Stark. Jack calls himself—somewhat cynically—an idealist, but his idealism consists mostly of a fastidious preference for not getting his hands dirty with some of Willie's more questionable political maneuvers. Willie is good-naturedly tolerant of Jack's moral preferences, since he has Tiny Duffy to do his dirty work.

Jack considers himself a good judge of character and motives, but when a cherished image about the purity and goodness of his old girlfriend, Anne Stanton, is proven to be false, he is devastated and lost in self-doubt. Anne, who is quite a passive, unfulfilled person herself, has become Willie's mistress. Jack's first impulse is to flee, to escape, to drown, to fall into what he calls the Great Sleep. From this symbolic death, Burden is born again into a bleak but emotionally insulating belief in the Great Twitch—an understanding of the world as completely amoral and mechanistic, wherein no one has any responsibility for what happens. Here, indeed, Jack has stepped out of the fantasy of dreams into the reality of facts.

Jack can now consent to let Willie use the information he has uncovered concerning Judge Irwin's long-forgotten political crime. Jack soon discovers how brutal the world of fact can be, when Judge Irwin's suicide reveals that the judge was actually Jack's own father. Hardly recovered from this blow, Jack recognizes a measure of responsibility for the deaths of Willie and his best friend, Adam, who is shot by Willie's bodyguard after the assassination. Through his passivity and noninvolvement, Jack had virtually handed over Anne to his more dynamic boss, and thus set the stage for assassination.

The novel is a fascinating study of symbiotic relationships, of which the most striking is that between Willie, the practical politician, and Adam, the puritanical idealist and perfectionist. Warren also suggests a politically symbiotic relationship between the demagogue and the people he represents. In social terms, the world of *All the King's Men* is more complex than that of *Night Rider*. Munn's career is essentially that of the tragic hero, the good but not exclusively good man who is corrupted by power. Willie, however, is sustained not only by his own drive for power but also by the concerted will of his constituency, who feel themselves to be socially and politically helpless. He is probably more significant as an antidote to their depression than as an answer to their physical needs. Even though Willie wants to change the world of facts for their benefit—build roads, bridges, a free hospital—it is for his psychological impact, exemplifying the triumph of the common person over the privileged elite, that he is beloved. Thus, even the man of facts floats in the symbolic sea of ideas.

World Enough and Time

If the relationship between dream and reality is complicated in *All the King's Men*, in *World Enough and Time* it becomes intricately complex. Seldom have human aspirations been so relentlessly exposed, one after another, as frail illusions. Though it might be termed a historical novel because it is based loosely on an actual event, or a philosophical novel because it comments repeatedly on the abstract meaning of human behavior and aspiration, *World Enough and Time* is better termed a psychological novel, or more precisely, perhaps, an examination of the psychological motivations for philosophizing. It is certainly not, like Andrew Marvell's poem "To His Coy Mistress," to which the title ironically alludes, a neat argument for seizing pleasures while one may. It is not a neat argument for any philosophical position, but it illuminates the sequential confusion of a reasonably thoughtful, well-meaning person trying to identify himself and justify his actions.

Jeremiah Beaumont, the orphaned son of an unsuccessful Kentucky farmer in the early nineteenth century, becomes the loved protégé of Colonel Cassius Fort, a well-known lawyer and statesman of the region. Jerry's exalted view of Colonel Fort receives a cruel blow from his dashing friend Wilkie Barron, a popular man-about-town and dabbler in politics. Wilkie tells Jerry of a beautiful woman he once loved in vain, who was seduced by an older man who had come to console her when her father died. When the young woman, Rachel Jordan, had a stillborn child, the older man abandoned her. The knave who wronged her was the unimpeachable Colonel Fort.

The persuasive Wilkie succeeds in promoting in a somewhat passive Jerry a romantic vision of wronged womanhood. From this point on, Jerry creates his own drama of love and revenge, though Wilkie continues to manipulate him in ways he never understands until near the end of his life. Jerry repudiates Colonel Fort, his surrogate father, and woos and eventually wins the lovely Rachel, who is in a neurotic state of depression, not because of the supposed perfidy of Colonel Fort but because of her baby's death. Jerry, blind to the real source of her despondency, hounds her into commanding him to defend her honor. Fort refuses a duel with Jerry, however, and the honorable vengeance seems destined to fizzle. Rachel is again pregnant, and Jerry is fitting into the comfortable role of country squire. An unknown messenger brings to Rachel a slanderous handbill in which Colonel Fort, presumably denying to his political opponents his affair with Rachel, claims that Rachel had slept with a slave. Fort had gallantly claimed paternity of the child as a chivalric gesture. This shocking document, which is actually a forgery written by Wilkie, precipitates Rachel's labor, and Jerry's child is also born dead. Jerry, in remorse, kills Fort—not openly in a duel, as he had planned, but secretly, letting it appear to be a political assassination.

Jerry's trial is a bewildering process where deceit and truth become inextricably mixed. Wilkie appears, however, and reveals Jerry's vow to kill Fort, the reaction Wilkie had himself orchestrated even before Jerry had met the wronged lady. All is lost, and Jerry is sentenced to hang. Rachel comes and stays with him in his basement jail cell, where they indulge in a passionate interlude—a veritable frenzy of love in the face of imminent death.

The unpredictable Wilkie appears at the last minute, after the lovers have unsuccessfully tried to commit suicide by drinking laudanum. Wilkie rescues them and sends them west to live in the desolate island refuge of a notorious bandit. This is a return to nature, but a nature devoid of its original innocence, incapable of healing the scars of "civilization." Jerry sinks into a bestial pattern and Rachel into insanity, eventually killing herself. Jerry, who finds out that the slanderous handbill came from Wilkie, is himself murdered as he seeks to find his way back to the hangman, resigned now to the most austere prize of all—neither love nor honor, but simply knowledge.

The flight to the West seems an almost gratuitous extension of suffering, especially since the real Jereboam Beauchamp, who murdered Colonel Solomon Sharp in 1825, did hang for his crime. The real trial and death of Beauchamp and his wife, Ann Cook, were only slightly less miserable, however, than Warren's fictional account.

Warren's extension to allow further demoralization of the lovers does help to explore all possible approaches to the problem of reconciling the ideal and the real. At first, Jerry believes that the idea must redeem the world: The mental context defines the object. Unfortunately, this route leads to an idealism divorced from action and allows a further evil to develop in the world—the death of his child. Then he believes that the world will redeem the idea—that is, the act of killing Fort will vindicate the idea of honor. In his flight to the West, he commits a third error, the opposite to his first: to deny the idea completely and embrace the physical world—"to seek communion only in the blank cup of nature."

Perhaps this tortured journey through innocence and experience should arrive at some reconciliation of opposites, but, if so, that too seems more dream than reality. "There must be a way whereby the word becomes flesh," muses Jerry in his last days. Even so, "I no longer seek to justify. I seek only to suffer." If this is not a particularly lucid analysis of philosophical possibilities, it may nevertheless be true psychologically to the mental and moral confusion in which people live. Perhaps it is intended to represent the "terror of the awakening" that Warren finds in Conrad's *Lord Jim* when the "hero recognizes the terms on which he may be saved."

In his later novels, Warren continued to deal with the tension between the ideal and the real. The central mystery is usually the self, which the protagonist does not know except through a painful dialectic between exalted idea and gross fact. The protagonist also suffers from an inability to identify his real father or the real home where he belongs. Jack Burden and Jeremiah Beaumont both have several surrogate fathers, but they are responsible for the deaths of those to whom they owe the greatest filial loyalty. In *At Heaven's Gate*, Jerry Calhoun rejects his real father, the man of natural rectitude and love, and gives his devotion to Bogan Murdock, who, in Conrad's phrase, is hollow at the core.

A Place to Come To

Even in Warren's last novel, *A Place to Come To*, the protagonist's first act is to despise his father and flee from his homeland; his last is to return to his hometown and make peace with the gentle stepfather he had never wanted to meet and the deaf father who had humiliated him as a child. As Warren wrote in "The Ballad of Billie Potts," the son must always return to the father, who often represents the flawed and fallen world that is our heritage.

WILDERNESS

The struggle between the ideal and the real in Warren's later novels is most explicit in *Wilderness*, about an idealistic young Jew from Bavaria who comes to the United States to fight for the freedom of the slaves. When his father, a political prisoner in Berlin, dies, Adam Rosenzweig realizes that he has "lived only in the dream of his father's life, the father's manhood, the father's heroism." The trip to America is a way to star in his own heroic story. Adam's career in America is a progress in disillusionment; the telltale symbol of the compromising world of physical fact is his clubfoot, which he has desperately sought to hide in a specially constructed boot. If *World Enough and Time* is Warren's most complex treatment of idealism, *Wilderness* is his most direct treatment of this recurring subject, uncluttered by secondary themes or plots. Some critics prefer it for that reason, though it lacks the depth and humanity of Warren's earlier epic treatment of romantic idealism.

MEET ME IN THE GREEN GLEN

Meet Me in the Green Glen is a pastoral novel about the nature of love. The love of a homeless young Italian immigrant for a dowdy country wife begins with carnal passion devoid of any attempt to idealize sexual attraction. The ironically named Angelo has distinct similarities to Conrad's "natural man," Nostromo, who lives in the physical world with little thought of any other. In fact, Angelo protects himself from any really serious bond with Cassie, the frustrated wife of a paralyzed man, casting her in the more tawdry dream of "scarlet woman" with gifts of a tight red dress and cosmetics. Only at the last, when she pleads for his life in court by confessing to the murder of her husband, of which Angelo is accused, does he recognize a love that transcends the merely physical. Just as Adam in *Wilderness* becomes more human when he admits the strength of flawed reality, so Angelo becomes more human when he recognizes the strength of dreams. In spite of Cassie's confession, Angelo is condemned to die, because, in his ignorance of the racial situation, he violates the mores of the community. Cassie, unable to save her lover, drifts off in the dream sea of ideas, forgetting the sordid elements of their affair and only retaining the dream that transcends the body's need.

In these and other episodes in his fiction, Warren showed his fascination with what he called, in his Conrad essay, "the Great Mirage." It is a dark vision that sees all human values as illusions, yet insists—with the passion that fueled six decades of creative work—that such illusions are necessary, and that humanity must continue to invent itself.

Katherine Snipes

OTHER MAJOR WORKS

SHORT FICTION: *Blackberry Winter*, 1946; *The Circus in the Attic, and Other Stories*, 1947.

PLAYS: *Proud Flesh*, pr. 1947; *All the King's Men*, pr. 1958 (adaptation of his novel).

POETRY: *Thirty-six Poems*, 1935; *Eleven Poems on the Same Theme*, 1942; *Selected Poems, 1923-1943*, 1944; *Brother to Dragons: A Tale in Verse and Voices*, 1953; *Promises: Poems, 1954-1956*, 1957; *You, Emperors, and Others: Poems, 1957-1960*, 1960; *Selected Poems: New and Old, 1923-1966*, 1966; *Incarnations: Poems, 1966-1968*, 1968; *Audubon: A Vision*, 1969; *Or Else—Poem/Poems, 1968-1974*, 1974; *Selected Poems 1923-1975*, 1976; *Now and Then: Poems, 1976-1978*, 1978; *Brother to Dragons: A New Version*, 1979; *Ballad of a Sweet Dream of Peace*, 1980 (with Bill Komodore); *Being Here: Poetry, 1977-1980*, 1980; *Rumor Verified: Poems, 1979-1980*, 1981; *Chief Joseph of the Nez Percé*, 1983; *New and Selected Poems, 1923-1985*, 1985; *The Collected Poems of Robert Penn Warren*, 1998 (John Burt, editor).

NONFICTION: *John Brown: The Making of a Martyr*, 1929; *Modern Rhetoric*, 1949 (with Cleanth Brooks); *Segregation: The Inner Conflict in the South*, 1956; *Selected Essays*, 1958; *The Legacy of the Civil War: Meditations on the Centennial*, 1961; *Who Speaks for the Negro?*, 1965; *Democracy and Poetry*, 1975; *Portrait of a Father*, 1988; *New and Selected Essays*, 1989; *Cleanth Brooks and Robert Penn Warren: A Literary Correspondence*, 1998 (James A. Grimshaw, Jr., editor); *Selected Letters of Robert Penn Warren*, 2000-2001 (2 volumes; William Bedford Clark, editor).

EDITED TEXTS: *An Approach to Literature*, 1936 (with Brooks and John Thibault Purser); *Understanding Poetry: An Anthology for College Students*, 1938 (with Brooks); *Understanding Fiction*, 1943 (with Brooks); *Faulkner: A Collection of Critical Essays*, 1966; *Randall Jarrell, 1914-1965*, 1967 (with Robert Lowell and Peter Taylor); *American Literature: The Makers and the Making*, 1973 (with R. W. B. Lewis).

BIBLIOGRAPHY

Blotner, Joseph. *Robert Penn Warren: A Biography.* New York: Random House, 1997. Blotner began this work while Warren was still alive and had the good fortune to have the cooperation not only of his subject but also of the larger Warren family. This book is straightforward and chronological, and it makes a good beginning for a study of Warren.

Bohner, Charles. *Robert Penn Warren.* 1962. Rev. ed. Boston: Twayne, 1981. This lucid survey encompasses details of Warren's literary career and an analysis of his major themes. It also provides a study of the development of Warren's art as evidenced in his novels and short fiction, his poetry (through *Being Here: Poetry 1977-1980*), and his major essays. Includes a detailed chronology and a valuable select bibliography.

Burt, John. *Robert Penn Warren and American Idealism.* New Haven, Conn.: Yale University Press, 1988. Burt describes his book as traversing "regions" of Warren's work:

the elegies, the narrative poems, and three major novels—*Night Rider, All the King's Men*, and *World Enough and Time*. What unifies these works, Burt maintains, is Warren's ambivalence about experience, an ambivalence endemic to American idealism.

Clark, William Bedford, ed. *Critical Essays on Robert Penn Warren*. Boston: G. K. Hall, 1981. A comprehensive collection of criticism by leading literary scholars of Warren's major work as novelist, poet, biographer, and essayist. Among the contributors are Harold Bloom, Malcolm Cowley, Carlos Baker, John Crowe Ransom, and Randall Jarrell. The collection includes a valuable 1969 interview with Warren by Richard Sale.

Ferriss, Lucy. *Sleeping with the Boss: Female Subjectivity and Narrative Pattern in Robert Penn Warren*. Baton Rouge: Louisiana State University Press, 1997. A feminist analysis, focusing on Warren's novels. Ferriss argues that although Warren wrote in a traditional masculine style, his narratives contained a "female voice" with the potential to change a plot's direction.

Gray, Richard, ed. *Robert Penn Warren: A Collection of Critical Essays*. Englewood Cliffs, N.J.: Prentice-Hall, 1980. Many of the essays in this collection date from the 1960's, and about two-thirds of them deal with Warren's novels. Represented in the volume are a number of recognized Warren specialists, among them James Justus, Leonard Casper, and Victor Strandberg. A competent and comprehensive essay prefaces the volume, which contains a short bibliography helpful to general students.

Grimshaw, James A. *Understanding Robert Penn Warren*. Columbia: University of South Carolina Press, 2001. An introduction to and commentary on Warren's novels and other works. Chapter 2 focuses on the early fiction, from 1939 to 1955, while chapter 3 examines the later fiction, from 1955 to 1977. Includes notes, a bibliography, and an index.

Guttenberg, Barnett. *Web of Being: The Novels of Robert Penn Warren*. Nashville: Vanderbilt University Press, 1975. Examines Warren's nine novels from *Night Rider* through *Meet Me in the Green Glen*, with emphasis on their existential element. Advances the premise that through all the novels the individual struggles to attain the true being of selfhood through self-awareness.

Hendricks, Randy. *Lonelier than God: Robert Penn Warren and the Southern Exile*. Athens: University of Georgia Press, 2000. Hendricks examines the theme of exile in Warren's work, maintaining this subject is crucial to understanding Warren's theories of language, ideas about race, and his regionalism.

Justus, James H. *The Achievement of Robert Penn Warren*. Baton Rouge: Louisiana State University Press, 1981. A cogent study. Justus argues that Warren's work largely derives from the cultural circumstances of time and place in his career. The book is divided into four sections examining Warren's themes, poetry, nonfiction prose, and novels.

Madden, David, ed. *The Legacy of Robert Penn Warren*. Baton Rouge: Louisiana State

University Press, 2000. A collection of critical and biographical essays on Warren's life and work, including discussions of *All the King's Men*, his poetry, and Warren as a mentor and a moral philosopher. Includes bibliographical references and an index.

Watkins, Floyd C., John T. Hiers, and Mary Louise Weaks, eds. *Talking with Robert Penn Warren*. Athens: University of Georgia Press, 1990. A collection of twenty-four interviews, extending from 1953 to 1985, in which Warren talks about his work with characteristic honesty, openness, folksiness, and wit from the joint perspective of writer, interpreter, and critic. The group of interviewers includes Ralph Ellison, Marshall Walker, Bill Moyers, Edwin Harold Newman, Floyd C. Watkins, and Eleanor Clark.

ANGUS WILSON

Born: Bexhill, East Sussex, England; August 11, 1913
Died: Bury St. Edmunds, Suffolk, England; May 31, 1991
Also known as: Angus Frank Johnstone Wilson

PRINCIPAL LONG FICTION

Hemlock and After, 1952
Anglo-Saxon Attitudes, 1956
The Middle Age of Mrs. Eliot, 1958
The Old Men at the Zoo, 1961
Late Call, 1964
No Laughing Matter, 1967
As If by Magic, 1973
Setting the World on Fire, 1980

OTHER LITERARY FORMS

Angus Wilson started his literary career in 1946, at the age of thirty-three, by writing short stories. The earliest stories were published in *Horizon*. *The Wrong Set, and Other Stories* (1949), *Such Darling Dodos, and Other Stories* (1950), and *A Bit off the Map, and Other Stories* (1957) deal with the same problems and use the same imagery as his novels. Wilson also wrote drama, and in the 1970's, he became a leading reviewer of fiction. His literary journalism and criticism for *The Spectator*, *The Observer*, and *The London Magazine* center mainly on the problem of the English novel. The range of writers he discussed in articles, introductions, or lectures is wide and includes, among others, the Victorians, the Bloomsbury Group, Aldous Huxley, D. H. Lawrence, John Cowper Powys, Leo Tolstoy, Fyodor Dostoevski, Irving Shaw, Robert Penn Warren, and William Golding.

Wilson also published three full-length literary monographs: *Émile Zola: An Introductory Study of His Novels* (1952), *The World of Charles Dickens* (1970), and *The Strange Ride of Rudyard Kipling: His Life and Works* (1977). Wilson's many lectures and articles display his concern with a wide range of problems relevant to the second half of the twentieth century. Most important for the study and understanding of his art is the volume *The Wild Garden: Or, Speaking of Writing* (1963), which contains lectures given in California in 1960. Some of his criticism was collected in *Diversity and Depth in Fiction: Selected Critical Writings of Angus Wilson* (1983). Written over several decades are the essays collected in *Reflections in a Writer's Eye: Travel Pieces* (1986).

ACHIEVEMENTS

Most critics agree that by the 1980's, Angus Wilson had secured a place among the most distinguished contemporary British novelists. He even became recognized outside the English-speaking world, particularly in France. In the 1960's and 1970's, the number of interviews with the artist increased, signifying his growing recognition among critics. Whether the critics use Stephen Spender's terminology of "modern" and "contemporary" or speak of experimental, psychological, aesthetic, or modern versus the traditional, sociological English novel, they all try to assess Wilson in relation to these categories. Some contend that Wilson's main concern rests with the sociological aspects of human life, but almost all critics concede that his interest goes beyond social issues. Without abandoning his commitment to depicting reality, Wilson was always committed to probing deeper into the dark depths of the human self. This concern with the inner self separates him sharply from the "angry" writers who also wrote in the 1950's: Kingsley Amis, John Wain, and Alan Sillitoe. Wilson, however, was dedicated to experimenting both in content and method. In his novels and critical writings, he emerged as a champion for a new type of novel, standing between the traditional and the experimental.

BIOGRAPHY

Angus Frank Johnstone Wilson was born in Bexhill, Sussex, England, on August 11, 1913, the sixth son of a middle-class family. His father was of Scottish extraction; his mother came from South Africa, and he spent some time there as a child. In constant financial troubles, his parents tried to maintain pretense and appearance, which left a deep impression on Wilson: At a very early age, he became aware of the chasm separating the real world and the world of fantasy into which many people escape to avoid the unpleasant facts of their lives. Frequently lonely (he was thirteen years younger than his next older brother), he realized that his clowning ability made him popular with the schoolchildren. He attended prep school in Seaford; from there he went to Westminster School and then to Merton College, Oxford. At the University of Oxford, his history training was on the Marxist line; that fact and his left-wing political activities in the 1930's account for his Labour sympathies.

In 1937, Wilson started work at the British Museum and, with an interruption during World War II, he stayed there until 1955. During the war, he was associated with an interservice organization attached to the foreign office, and for a while he lived in the country in a home with a Methodist widow and her daughter. During this time, he had a serious nervous breakdown; his psychotherapist suggested creative writing as therapy. In 1946, Wilson rejoined the staff at the British Museum and, at the same time, started writing seriously. His first published writing, the short story "Raspberry Jam" (1946), reflects his personal crisis and foreshadows the dark atmosphere of most of his work to come. The whole experience at the British Museum, situated in London's sophisticated Bloomsbury district and especially his job as deputy superintendent at the Reading Room, provided him with an understanding and knowledge of the cultural establishment and of the management of cultural institutions, which he used later in *The Old Men at the Zoo*. Also, observing scholars, book addicts, and eccentric visitors to the Reading Room gave him material for creating some of his fictional characters, such as Gerald Middleton in *Anglo-Saxon Attitudes*.

In 1952, Wilson published his first novel, *Hemlock and After*, and a critical monograph, *Émile Zola*. He gave talks on the novel for the British Broadcasting Corporation that were later published in *The Listener*. In 1955, a contract with Secker and Warburg as well as his ongoing reviewing activity for *The Spectator* and *Encounter* made it possible for him to resign his post at the British Museum. He then retired to the Sussex countryside, thus reviving his childhood garden-dream. As a result of his freedom from job-related responsibilities, he published four novels in a rapid sequence: *Anglo-Saxon Attitudes*, *The Middle Age of Mrs. Eliot*, *The Old Men at the Zoo*, and *Late Call*. Furthermore, his participation in the cultural and literary life of England as a journalist, critic, and lecturer became more extensive. In 1963, he started his association with the University of East Anglia as a part-time lecturer, becoming professor in 1966. Also in 1966, he became chair of the literary panel of the Arts Council of Great Britain. In 1967, he lectured at Berkeley, California, and in the same year published *No Laughing Matter*.

In 1968, Wilson was made Commander of the British Empire and honorary fellow of Cowell College of the University of California, Santa Cruz. He honored the Dickens Centennial in 1970 with *The World of Charles Dickens*. Between 1971 and 1974, he served as chair of the National Book League while receiving two more distinctions in 1972, becoming a companion of literature and a chevalier de l'Ordre des Arts et des Lettres, the latter a sign of his growing reputation in France. A sixth novel, *As If by Magic*, appeared in 1973; in it he made use of his teaching experience and involvement with young intellectuals. He continued to live in the country, his many activities including travel. His Asian journey resulted in his book *The Strange Ride of Rudyard Kipling*. He was a visiting professor at Johns Hopkins University in 1974, and, in 1977, a distinguished visiting professor at the University of Delaware; he also lectured at many other American universities. In 1980, he published another novel, *Setting the World on Fire*. His manuscripts, deposited at the library of the University of Iowa, provide ample material for researchers. After suffering a stroke, Wilson died on June 1, 1991, in a nursing home in the southeast of England.

ANALYSIS

"Self-realization was to become the theme of all my novels," declared Angus Wilson in *The Wild Garden*. Self-realization does not take place in a vacuum; the process is closely linked with a person's efforts to face and to cope with the world. Wilson's childhood experience, among déclassé middle-class people living in a fantasy world, initiated the novelist's interest in the conflict between two worlds and in the possibility or impossibility of resolving the conflict. The rapidly changing scene in England as the Edwardian Age gave way to the postwar 1920's, with the cultural dominance of Bloomsbury, and then to the radical leftist 1930's, impressed on him the urgency of such a search. His encounter with Marxism at Oxford intensified his tendency to see the world as one of opposing forces. The dichotomy of town and country, of the classes, and of old and new forms the background of Wilson's fiction as the remnants of Edwardian England disappeared and the dissolution of the British Empire left the island nation searching for its place in the modern world.

In *The Wild Garden*, Wilson describes his creative-writing process in terms of a dialectic; he reveals that he "never felt called upon to declare allegiance to either fantasy or realism," but then he adds that "without their fusion I could not produce a novel." Wilson is desperately looking for syntheses to all kinds of conflicts and insists that self-realization is an absolute necessity to achieve them. His own breakdown as well as Sigmund Freud's impact on his generation pushed Wilson in the direction of psychoanalysis and the search for identity. In an age of tension, violence, and suffering, he insists on the necessity of self-realization in order to overcome despair.

Wilson's heroes all have crippled, wasted lives and broken families, and the novelist explores their "cherished evasions." Bernard Sand in *Hemlock and After* has to be shocked into self-knowledge by facing sadism in his own nature; Gerald Middleton, in *Anglo-Saxon Attitudes*, gets a new chance for a satisfactory, if not happy, life in old age when he is ready to resume responsibility as a scholar and to reveal a shameful hoax. Both of these heroes are presented in their private and public lives because, in Wilson's view, both of these aspects of life are equally important to modern people. This view of human life in the dialectic of the private and the public is even more important for Meg Eliot, the heroine of *The Middle Age of Mrs. Eliot*; after many frustrations she emerges at the end of the novel as a career woman. Similarly, Sylvia Calvert in *Late Call* discovers a meaningful (retirement) life of her own, independent of her family.

Wilson was a very "British" writer with a subtle sense for the typical English understatement, while his Hegelian drive for reconciliation of conflicts agrees with the spirit of the traditional English compromise. He was constantly searching for ways to save the remnants of the liberal, humanistic values that have remained dear to him in a world that did not seem to have any use for them. His heroes and heroines, saved from final disintegration, are restored to some kind of meaningful life through self-knowledge and are brought closer to other people in defiance of loneliness and despair.

Hemlock and After

In his first novel, *Hemlock and After*, Wilson extends the exploration of the theme of self-knowledge to both the private and public life of his hero. The novel is about Bernard Sand's troubled conscience, a most private matter; but Bernard is an important public figure, described as "the country's own ambassador to the world outside," and a successful, self-confident novelist who organizes a subsidized writers' colony, Valden Hall, in order to support young talent. Overtly successful, his family life is in shambles. His wife, Ella, lives in "neurotic misery"; his son is a staunch conservative in strong disagreement with Bernard's liberal views; his unmarried daughter, a journalist, feels lonely and unhappy. As an indication of the overhanging disaster, Bernard's first novel is titled *Nightmare's Image*.

In the title of Wilson's novel, "Hemlock" suggests poisonous wrong, evil, and even violence. Poisoning and violence occur in a "massacre of innocence," as related to Eric, Bernard's young gay partner, and to the little girl Elzie, whom the disreputable Mrs. Curry wants to make available to Hugh Rose. Wilson deliberately links the fate of the two young people by calling them both "rabbits." Rose and Mrs. Curry strike their deal at the "Lamb" Inn.

The word "After" in the title refers to the aftermath of knowledge: self-knowledge. A crucial scene occurs at the end of book 1 when a still complacent and self-confident Bernard watches the arrest of young gays at Leicester Square and is shocked suddenly by the discovery that he experienced sadistic enjoyment in watching the terror in the eyes of those youths. This discovery has a devastating effect on Bernard's life and destroys not only him but also Valden Hall. The long-awaited opening of the young artists' colony becomes a total disaster, as its erupting violence grows into a symbol of the modern predicament. Wilson describes the scene as one of chaos, disorder, disappointment, strain, and hostility.

After this startling event, Bernard's life goes downhill very rapidly; self-knowledge paralyzes his will, and he is entirely unable to act. The discovery of sadistic tendencies makes him suspect his own motives. He realizes with frightening clarity the abyss of the human soul and is driven to utter despair about the motivation behind any action. He has a horrifying vision of the subtle difference between intention and action, and as a consequence, Bernard loses his determination to deal with Mrs. Curry. At the same time, Ella almost miraculously recovers from her nervous breakdown and, after Bernard dies, acts on his behalf in arranging efficient management at Valden Hall and a prison sentence for Rose and Mrs. Curry. Rose commits suicide in prison, while Mrs. Curry earns an early release with her good behavior. It is briefly indicated that she might continue her former activity; thus the epilogue ends the novel on an ambiguous note of qualified optimism.

Anglo-Saxon Attitudes

The title *Anglo-Saxon Attitudes*, derived from Lewis Carroll's *Alice's Adventures in Wonderland* (1865), suggests a typically English atmosphere; it is Wilson's most Victorian novel, a broad social comedy. At the same time, it displays experimental technique in the use of the flashback, which provides all the background to Gerald Middleton's crisis in his private and public life. The hero, a sixty-year-old failure, is a historian. In the beginning of the novel, sitting by himself at a Christmas party given by his estranged wife, Inge, Gerald overhears broken sentences of conversation that remind him of the most significant episodes of his life. Wilson makes it very clear that self-knowledge is important for Gerald; it is both a psychological need to him and a matter of "intellectual honesty," a duty to the professional community of historians.

Gerald's crisis of conscience concerns a cruel hoax that occurred back in 1912 when he participated with a team in an excavation. Young Gilbert Stokeway, a disciple of T. E. Hulme and Wyndham Lewis and the son of the leader of the team, put a fake idol in the tomb under research at Melpham. His hoax was successful, and the fake came to be hailed as a pagan idol. At that time, Gerald was a Prufrock-like antihero: disabled physically by a sprained ankle and disabled emotionally by his love for Gilbert's wife, Dollie. His affair with her played an important role in his silence about the fake idol. Gerald's feelings of guilt center on "the two forbidden subjects of his thoughts," his marriage and the hoax. His life, "rooted in evasion," appears to him empty, meaningless, and futile. His professional career fell victim to his decision not to reveal the hoax. Because of his affair with Dollie, he evaded dealing with Inge's inadequacies as a mother.

In fact, none of the minor characters has a happy, self-fulfilling life. While Gerald still believes in the liberal tradition, neither of his sons adheres to his beliefs. His elder son, Robert, a businessman, stands rather to the right and the younger son, John, is a radical, and they have violent clashes whenever they meet. Both sons are unhappy in their personal relationships as well. Robert is married to the conventional Marie-Hélène but loves the more modern Elvira Portway. John has a short-lived sexual relationship with an unruly young Irishman, Larry, who is killed in a wild drive in which John loses a leg. Gerald's daughter, Kay, has a serious crisis in her marriage to the smart right-wing young sociologist, Donald. Wilson employs specific imagery to drive home to the reader the overwhelming atmosphere of frustration of all these people. Expressions such as "flat and dead" and "deadly heaviness" abound, referring to the behavior of people at parties when communication is impossible. Gerald's house is "noiseless as a tomb," and during the Christmas party at the home of the "Norse Goddess" Inge, all those present "shivered" in spite of the central heating.

Realizing the failure of his family, Gerald has to admit that he is to take the blame; when he selected Inge to be his wife, he decided for second-best. Yet, at the end, Gerald manages to pull himself out of his dead life. By revealing the hoax, he succeeds in restoring his professional status, and after a long silence, he becomes active again in research. The novel, however, like *Hemlock and After*, ends on a note of qualified optimism as Gerald remains estranged from his family. The picture of Gerald's life, combined with the divergent subplots, reveals a world in which relationships do not last, where options are limited.

THE MIDDLE AGE OF MRS. ELIOT

Critics believe that they can recognize Wilson in most of his central characters; the novelist, however, admits the connection only in the case of Meg Eliot, the heroine of his third novel, *The Middle Age of Mrs. Eliot*. "Meg," he says, "is in large part modelled on myself," while David Parker's nursery recalled to Wilson childhood memories of a garden of a friendly family.

Meg Eliot, a well-to-do barrister's childless, worldly, spoiled wife, experiences sudden tragedy when her husband dies from a gunshot wound as he tries to protect a local minister. The novel depicts Meg's nervous breakdown and painful recovery: her journey to self-knowledge. She is first revealed to be holding desperately to her old friends; yet, their lives are no more secure than hers. Lady Pirie in her "decaying genteel jail" is preoccupied with her son only; bohemian Polly Robinson lives a kind of "animated death"; and Jill Stokes is obsessed with the memory of her dead husband. These "lame ducks" cannot help Meg, nor can drugs. Meg's brother, David Parker, who runs the nursery with his gay partner, is sheltered in the pleasant quiet atmosphere, which suggests a return to lost innocence. Yet, Wilson is ambiguous about the validity of the garden image, since David's nursery is commercial, an irony in itself. Meg cannot share her brother's lifestyle, his abnegation of action and the human world. Wilson does not censure David for his contemplative lifestyle, but it is evident that he prefers Meg's choice "to be with people!"

Meg is determined to find meaning in life, in a life with people. She is strikingly reminiscent of George Eliot's heroines; similar to them, she used to live in self-delusion and is shocked into consciousness by the "remorse of not having made life count enough" for her husband. Moreover, again like the Victorian woman, she returns to a fuller life. Two factors are important in her recovery. First, she refuses any kind of opium, an Eliot ideal; second, she is determined to build herself a meaningful, useful life. While she admits that she "used to be Maggie Tulliver," she also resembles Gwendolen Harleth from Eliot's *Daniel Deronda* (1876). She shares with her an unhappy childhood and the horrors of remorse, but she shares also in Gwendolen's way of redemption. Like the Victorian heroine, Meg too had to learn in a painful way that the outside world could intrude into her life at any time and destroy it if she is taken unaware. As she takes a paying secretarial job, Meg is full of confidence in her farewell letter to David: "At any rate in a few years at least, the modern world won't be able to take me by surprise so easily again."

THE OLD MEN AT THE ZOO

From the omniscient narrator of his early works, Wilson shifts to a more modern device in *The Old Men at the Zoo* by creating a first-person narrator in Simon Carter. In the beginning of the novel, Simon is a gifted, dedicated yet disabled naturalist, very much like Gerald Middleton at the time of the excavation. He is prevented from continuing research in Africa because of amoebal dysentery. He joins the London Zoo as an administrator at a crucial time when the zoo itself becomes a battleground of conflicting ideas, reflecting a conflict of values in British politics. Wilson creates an armed conflict between England and Allied Europe, followed by a fascist invasion of England when all standards of civilized behavior collapse and give way to brutality. When the war breaks out, the fascists want to put on a spectacle with prisoners of war fighting the zoo animals. Simon is horrified, but as he later tries to drive the animals to safety, he finds himself killing his favorite badgers to feed a boy and his mother.

Almost an antihero, trying to avoid any kind of involvement with people, an administrator following orders, Simon emerges at the end of the novel ready to face the world, to be involved with people, even running for director. Because of his loyalty to the zoo under three different administrations, representing three different political ideologies, some are inclined to view him as a Vicar of Bray. In the twentieth century, however, many people had to face Simon's fundamental dilemma: whether to follow orders or to take up independent responsibility. Simon's American-born wife, Martha, disapproves of his behavior; she would like him to give up his job. Simon refuses, saying, "What do you think I am, a weathercock?" There is cruel irony in this remark; however, Wilson's irony is not pointed at Simon but rather at the general human predicament of a rapidly changing world in which choices are limited and people are continuously bombarded with dilemmas.

Simon's only independent action is his attempt to save the animals, which ends in disaster. In him, Wilson presents modern society struggling with despair in a desperate race to catch up with challenges. Simon's painful adjustment commands respect; he almost achieves heroic status when, after all the horrors and violence, he describes this modern world as "a demie-paradise." In this sense, *The Old Men at the Zoo* is Wilson's least pessimistic novel.

NO LAUGHING MATTER

No Laughing Matter is one of Wilson's most complex novels and requires close reading. The narrative is interwoven with dramas, enacted by the characters and reflecting various dramatic styles, including the absurd. Pastiches and parody of writers are important features of the novel, and literary references abound. A chronicle of the Matthews family like that of the family of John Galsworthy's 1922 *A Forsyte Saga*, *No Laughing Matter* is also a historical document covering the twentieth century to 1967. The father, Billy Pop, a Micawber of the twentieth century, is a failure in his writing profession and ineffectual in his family life, letting his selfish wife dominate the children. All six of them have a crippled childhood and are deprived of privacy. By the end of the novel, they all achieve some kind of success in their professional lives; some even attain fame, such as Rupert, the actor, and Quentin, the political journalist, later a celebrated television commentator. Success does not make him lovable, and his cynicism, enjoyed by a million common viewers, questions the role of the media.

The final scene, in 1967, brings the whole clan together. While Margaret and her gay brother, Marcus, an art dealer, are discussing and quarreling about Margaret's art, Hassan, who will inherit Marcus's cooperatively run scent factory, makes a final statement: the last words of the novel. He considers Marcus's ideas of a cooperative absurd. Hassan admires "ambition, high profit and determined management." His coldly calculating thoughts cast a dark shadow on the future; they underline once again Wilson's skepticism about the survival of liberal humanistic ideals in the modern world.

A strong moral sense links Wilson to Eliot, and his sense of the caricature and the grotesque shows affinities with his favorite author, Charles Dickens. At the same time, his fiction is full of experiments into new literary methods. With almost each novel, Wilson made an important step forward in his search for new techniques. Tragedy and laughter coexist in his novels; there is tragedy in the private lives of the characters, but Wilson has a grotesque view of people's behavior, and his ability to create atmosphere through concentrating on speech habits promotes laughter.

In his commitment to duty, in his moral seriousness, Wilson is definitely akin to Eliot, but he differs from the Victorian in that he cannot believe in "meliorism." Eliot firmly maintained that self-awareness would lead to self-improvement and, in consequence, to the individual's improved performance in the human community. Wilson is much more skeptical. Like E. M. Forster, he, too, is painfully aware of the decline of liberal hopes. In *The Middle Age of Mrs. Eliot*, he came to the sad conclusion that "self-knowledge had no magic power to alter," and in his sixth novel, he killed magic with finality.

As If by Magic

In *As If by Magic*, magic, the ultimate evasion, is destroyed forever for the two central characters. Moreover, this time they are not middle-aged or elderly intellectuals paralyzed by frustration; they are young people. Wilson's teaching experience in Britain and America caused him to concentrate on the young, the future generation.

Hamo Langmuir is a dedicated young scientist on a worldwide fact-finding tour to study the benevolent effects of his "magic" rice, destined to solve the problem of starvation in underdeveloped countries. His goddaughter, Alexandra Grant, in the company of her fellow hippies, is also on a world tour in search of an occult answer to all human problems. A bewildered Hamo must find out that his magic rice solution has introduced a farming method for which natives are not yet prepared and, consequently, it is causing more damage than good. Hamo falls victim to the anger of a crowd at a moment when he is ready to get involved in the human aspects of research. He, like Alexandra, who gets to Goa at the same time, had to learn through experience that the intrusion of Western ways into radically different cultures can cause disruption and many unnecessary tragedies. At the end of the novel, a sober Alexandra, cured of her hippie ways, resumes the responsibility of building a normal life for her son, a legacy of the hippie venture. A millionaire through an inheritance, she is ready to support and subsidize food research, but she knows by now that the possibilities are limited and that no easy answers are available; magic of any kind is only for the neurotics who are unable to face reality or for the power-hungry who use it to dominate others.

Setting the World on Fire

Wilson's concern with human nature and with what it means for the future of the world dominates *Setting the World on Fire*. This novel is a family chronicle like *No Laughing Matter* but more condensed, more limited in time (1948-1969) and in the number of characters. Indeed, the writer concentrates on two brothers, Piers and Tom, the last generation of an old aristocratic family. Literary references are replaced by other arts: theater, music, architecture, and painting. Piers hopes to dedicate his life to the theater, and as a promising student, he earns the admiration of family, friends, and teachers with his stage-managing and directing abilities. The final part of the novel is about the preparations for the first performance of a new play, with the younger brother, Tom, supporting Piers as best he can in the hectic work. Everything is set for success when, unexpectedly, Scotland Yard intervenes and orders the premises emptied because of a bomb threat. The author of the play, an old employee of the family, masterminded the plot, simultaneously aimed at the family and at the government.

Tom saves Piers's life by knocking him down, but he himself gets killed. On his way home from the hospital where Tom died, Piers is on the verge of a breakdown and about to give up hope as well as artistic ambitions, because what good are the wonders of art in "a chaotic universe"? He calms down, however, and decides to stage the play anyway; he must not "lose the power to ascend the towers of imagination," he says. The tragedy brought Piers to a fuller realization of his duty as an artist, which means doing the only thing left to him: to create in, and for, a world threatened by chaos, violence, and destruction.

Wilson, a mixture of a twentieth century Dickens, Eliot, and Forster, with an increasingly dark vision of the modern predicament, rededicated himself, the artist, to his moral obligation. He continued writing in a desperate attempt to impose some kind of order on chaos and, by making people aware, to try to save humankind from itself.

Anna B. Katona

OTHER MAJOR WORKS

SHORT FICTION: *The Wrong Set, and Other Stories*, 1949; *Such Darling Dodos, and Other Stories*, 1950; *A Bit off the Map, and Other Stories*, 1957; *Death Dance: Twenty-five Stories*, 1969.

PLAY: *The Mulberry Bush*, pr., pb. 1956.

NONFICTION: *Émile Zola: An Introductory Study of His Novels*, 1952; *For Whom the Cloche Tolls: A Scrapbook of the Twenties*, 1953 (with Philippe Jullian); *The Wild Garden: Or, Speaking of Writing*, 1963; *Tempo: The Impact of Television on the Arts*, 1964; *The World of Charles Dickens*, 1970; *The Strange Ride of Rudyard Kipling: His Life and Works*, 1977; *Diversity and Depth in Fiction: Selected Critical Writings of Angus Wilson*, 1983 (Kerry McSweeney, editor); *Reflections in a Writer's Eye: Travel Pieces*, 1986.

BIBLIOGRAPHY

Brooke, Allen. "The Mimetic Brilliance of Angus Wilson." *New Criterion* 15 (October, 1996): 28-37. In this biographical essay, Brooke describes Wilson's childhood and youth, his early literary career, his gay relationship with Tony Garrett, his disillusionment with communism, and his declining final years.

Cavaliero, Glen. "Matter for Laughter: Angus Wilson." In *The Alchemy of Laughter: Comedy in English Fiction*. New York: St. Martin's Press, 2000. The comic style of Wilson's novels is examined in this analysis of English fiction, in which Cavaliero discusses how parody, irony, satire, and other types of humor are evident in these works.

Conradi, Peter. *Angus Wilson*. Plymouth, England: Northcote House, 1997. A solid introduction to Wilson's work, including a biographical outline, chapters on his major novels, a section on his stories, notes, and a useful annotated bibliography.

Drabble, Margaret. *Angus Wilson: A Biography*. New York: St. Martin's Press, 1995. A detailed biography of Wilson in which his friend Margaret Drabble reveals the autobiographical sources of much of his fiction in his early years. Drabble describes Wilson's long-term gay relationship with Anthony Garrett and analyzes his obsession with the nature of evil in relationship to his mother's Christian faith.

Furbank, P. N. "No Laughing Matter: A Word on Angus Wilson." In *On Modern British Fiction*, edited by Zachary Leader. New York: Oxford University Press, 2002. Furbank discusses Wilson's fiction, including his novels *Anglo-Saxon Attitudes*, *Hemlock and After*, *No Laughing Matter*, and *The Old Men at the Zoo*.

Gardner, Averil. *Angus Wilson*. Boston: Twayne, 1985. In this general introduction to Wilson's life and art, Gardner provides biographical information and discusses Wilson's novels and short stories. Includes a bibliography and an index.

Halio, Jay L., ed. *Critical Essays on Angus Wilson*. Boston: G. K. Hall, 1985. A collection of reviews, interviews, and criticism covering Wilson's literary career. Includes influential reviews by Edmund Wilson, V. S. Pritchett, Kingsley Amis, and Anthony Burgess, as well as important essays by Malcolm Bradbury, A. S. Byatt, and Margaret Drabble. Halio's overview essay is a concise survey of Wilson's work and a critique of the criticism it has received.

Head, Dominic. *The Cambridge Introduction to Modern British Fiction, 1950-2000*. New York: Cambridge University Press, 2002. This overview of late twentieth century British fiction contains numerous references to Wilson's novels, which are listed in the index. This book helps place Wilson within the broader context of modern British literature.

Mackay, Marina. "Mr. Wilson and Mrs. Woolf: A Camp Reconstruction of Bloomsbury." *Journal of Modern Literature* 23 (Summer, 1999): 95-110. An overview of Wilson's career and works, surveyed with the career and works of Virginia Woolf.

Sinfield, Alan. "Culture, Consensus, and Difference: Angus Wilson to Alan Hollinghurst." In *British Culture of the Postwar: An Introduction to Literature and Society, 1945-1999*, edited by Alistair Davies and Alan Sinfield. New York: Routledge, 2000. Wilson's work is studied in this collection of essays examining how British literature, film, and music reflect the social, economic, and technological changes that occurred in the years after World War II.

Bibliography

Every effort has been made to include studies published in 2000 and later. Most items in this bibliography contain a listing of secondary sources, making it easier to identify other critical commentary on novelists, movements, and themes.

Theoretical, thematic, and historical studies

Altman, Janet Gurkin. *Epistolarity: Approaches to a Form.* Columbus: Ohio State University Press, 1982. Examines the epistolary novel, explaining how novelists use the letter form to develop characterization, further their plots, and develop meaning.

Beaumont, Matthew, ed. *Adventures in Realism.* Malden, Mass.: Blackwell, 2007. Fifteen essays explore facets of realism, which was critical to the development of the novel. Provides a theoretical framework for understanding how novelists attempt to represent the real and the common in fiction.

Brink, André. *The Novel: Language and Narrative from Cervantes to Calvino.* New York: New York University Press, 1998. Uses contemporary theories of semiotics and narratology to establish a continuum between early novelists and those of the postmodern era in their conscious use of language to achieve certain effects. Ranges across national boundaries to illustrate the theory of the development of the novel since the seventeenth century.

Brownstein, Rachel. *Becoming a Heroine: Reading About Women in Novels.* New York: Viking Press, 1982. Feminist survey of novels from the eighteenth century through the latter half of the twentieth century. Examines how "becoming a heroine" defines for women a sense of value in their lives. Considers novels by both men and women, and discusses the importance of the traditional marriage plot.

Bruzelius, Margaret. *Romancing the Novel: Adventure from Scott to Sebald.* Lewisburg, Pa.: Bucknell University Press, 2007. Examines the development of the adventure novel, linking it with the medieval romance tradition and exploring readers' continuing fascination with the genre.

Cavallaro, Dani. *The Gothic Vision: Three Centuries of Horror, Terror, and Fear.* New York: Continuum, 2005. Study of the gothic novel from its earliest manifestations in the eighteenth century to the early twenty-first century. Through the lenses of contemporary cultural theories, examines readers' fascination with novels that invoke horror, terror, and fright.

Doody, Margaret Anne. *The True Story of the Novel.* New Brunswick, N.J.: Rutgers University Press, 1996. Traces the roots of the novel, traditionally thought to have been developed in the seventeenth century, to classical Greek and Latin texts that exhibit characteristics of modern fiction.

Hale, Dorothy J., ed. *The Novel: An Anthology of Criticism and Theory, 1900-2000.* Malden, Mass.: Blackwell, 2006. Collection of essays by theorists and novelists. Includes commentary on the novel form from the perspective of formalism, structuralism, poststructuralism, Marxism, and reader response theory. Essays also address the novel through the lenses of sociology, gender studies, and feminist theory.

_______. *Social Formalism: The Novel in Theory from Henry James to the Present*. Stanford, Calif.: Stanford University Press, 1998. Emphasizes the novel's special ability to define a social world for readers. Relies heavily on the works of contemporary literary and cultural theorists. Provides a summary of twentieth century efforts to identify a theory of fiction that encompasses novels of many kinds.

Hart, Stephen M., and Wen-chin Ouyang, eds. *A Companion to Magical Realism*. London: Tamesis, 2005. Essays outlining the development of Magical Realism, tracing its roots from Europe through Latin America to other regions of the world. Explores the political dimensions of the genre.

Hoffman, Michael J., and Patrick D. Murphy, eds. *Essentials of the Theory of Fiction*. 2d ed. Durham, N.C.: Duke University Press, 1996. Collection of essays by influential critics from the late nineteenth century through the twentieth century. Focuses on the essential elements of fiction and the novel's relationship to the world it depicts.

Lodge, David. *The Art of Fiction: Illustrated from Classic and Modern Texts*. New York: Viking Press, 1993. Short commentaries on the technical aspects of fiction. Examples from important and minor novelists illustrate literary principles and techniques such as point of view, suspense, character introduction, irony, motivation, and ending.

Lynch, Deirdre, and William B. Walker, eds. *Cultural Institutions of the Novel*. Durham, N.C.: Duke University Press, 1996. Fifteen essays examine aspects of long fiction produced around the world. Encourages a redefinition of the genre and argues for inclusion of texts not historically considered novels.

Moretti, Franco, ed. *The Novel*. 2 vols. Princeton, N.J.: Princeton University Press, 2006. Compendium exploring the novel from multiple perspectives, including as an anthropological, historical, and sociological document; a function of the national tradition from which it emerges; and a work of art subject to examination using various critical approaches.

Priestman, Martin, ed. *The Cambridge Companion to Crime Fiction*. New York: Cambridge University Press, 2003. Essays examine the nature and development of the genre, explore works by writers (including women and ethnic minorities) from several countries, and establish links between crime fiction and other literary genres. Includes a chronology.

Scaggs, John. *Crime Fiction*. New York: Routledge, 2005. Provides a history of crime fiction, explores key subgenres, and identifies recurring themes that suggest the wider social and historical context in which these works are written. Suggests critical approaches that open crime fiction to serious study.

Shiach, Morag, ed. *The Cambridge Companion to the Modernist Novel*. New York: Cambridge University Press, 2007. Essays explaining the concept of modernism and its influence on the novel. Detailed examination of works by writers from various countries, all influenced by the modernist movement. Includes a detailed chronology.

Vice, Sue. *Holocaust Fiction*. New York: Routledge, 2000. Examines controversies generated by novels about the Holocaust. Focuses on eight important works, but also offers observations on the polemics surrounding publication of books on this topic.

Zunshine, Lisa. *Why We Read Fiction: Theory of Mind and the Novel*. Columbus: Ohio State University Press, 2006. Applies theories of cognitive psychology to novel reading, explaining how experience and human nature lead readers to constrain their interpretations of a given text. Provides numerous examples from well-known novels to illustrate how and why readers find pleasure in fiction.

Laurence W. Mazzeno

Glossary of Literary Terms

absurdism: A philosophical attitude, pervading much of modern drama and fiction, that underlines the isolation and alienation that humans experience, having been thrown into what absurdists see as a godless universe devoid of religious, spiritual, or metaphysical meaning. Conspicuous in its lack of logic, consistency, coherence, intelligibility, and realism, the literature of the absurd depicts the anguish, forlornness, and despair inherent in the human condition. Counter to the rationalist assumptions of traditional humanism, absurdism denies the existence of universal truth or value.

allegory: A literary mode in which a second level of meaning, wherein characters, events, and settings represent abstractions, is encoded within the surface narrative. The allegorical mode may dominate an entire work, in which case the encoded message is the work's primary reason for being, or it may be an element in a work otherwise interesting and meaningful for its surface story alone. Elements of allegory may be found in Jonathan Swift's *Gulliver's Travels* (1726) and Thomas Mann's *Der Zauberberg* (1924; *The Magic Mountain*, 1927).

anatomy: Literally the term means the "cutting up" or "dissection" of a subject into its constituent parts for closer examination. Northrop Frye, in his *Anatomy of Criticism* (1957), uses the term to refer to a narrative that deals with mental attitudes rather than people. As opposed to the novel, the anatomy features stylized figures who are mouthpieces for the ideas they represent.

antagonist: The character in fiction who stands as a rival or opponent to the *protagonist.*

antihero: Defined by Seán O'Faoláin as a fictional figure who, deprived of social sanctions and definitions, is always trying to define himself and to establish his own codes. Ahab may be seen as the antihero of Herman Melville's *Moby Dick* (1851).

archetype: The term "archetype" entered literary criticism from the psychology of Carl Jung, who defined archetypes as "primordial images" from the "collective unconscious" of humankind. Jung believed that works of art derive much of their power from the unconscious appeal of these images to ancestral memories. In his extremely influential *Anatomy of Criticism* (1957), Northrop Frye gave another sense of the term wide currency, defining the archetype as "a symbol, usually an image, which recurs often enough in literature to be recognizable as an element of one's literary experience as a whole."

atmosphere: The general mood or tone of a work; atmosphere is often associated with setting but can also be established by action or dialogue. A classic example of atmosphere is the primitive, fatalistic tone created in the opening description of Egdon Heath in Thomas Hardy's *The Return of the Native* (1878).

bildungsroman: Sometimes called the "novel of education," the bildungsroman focuses on the growth of a young *protagonist* who is learning about the world and finding his or her place in life; typical examples are James Joyce's *A Portrait of the Artist as a*

Young Man (1914-1915, serial; 1916, book) and Thomas Wolfe's *Look Homeward, Angel* (1929).

biographical criticism: Criticism that attempts to determine how the events and experiences of an author's life influence his or her work.

bourgeois novel: A novel in which the values, preoccupations, and accoutrements of middle-class or bourgeois life are given particular prominence. The heyday of the bourgeois novel was the nineteenth century, when novelists as varied as Jane Austen, Honoré de Balzac, and Anthony Trollope both criticized and unreflectingly transmitted the assumptions of the rising middle class.

canon: An authorized or accepted list of books. In modern parlance, the literary canon comprehends the privileged texts, classics, or great books that are thought to belong permanently on university reading lists. Recent theory—especially feminist, Marxist, and poststructuralist—critically examines the process of canon formation and questions the hegemony of white male writers. Such theory sees canon formation as the ideological act of a dominant institution and seeks to undermine the notion of canonicity itself, thereby preventing the exclusion of works by women, minorities, and oppressed peoples.

character: Characters in fiction can be presented as if they were real people or as stylized functions of the plot. Usually characters are a combination of both factors.

classicism: A literary stance or value system consciously based on the example of classical Greek and Roman literature. While the term is applied to an enormous diversity of artists in many different periods and in many different national literatures, "classicism" generally denotes a cluster of values including formal discipline, restrained expression, reverence for tradition, and an objective rather than a subjective orientation. As a literary tendency, classicism is often opposed to *Romanticism*, although many writers combine classical and romantic elements.

climax/crisis: The term "climax" refers to the moment of the reader's highest emotional response, whereas "crisis" refers to a structural element of plot, a turning point at which a resolution must take place.

complication: The point in a novel when the *conflict* is developed or when the already existing conflict is further intensified.

conflict: The struggle that develops as a result of the opposition between the *protagonist* and another person, the natural world, society, or some force within the self.

contextualist criticism: A further extension of *formalist criticism*, which assumes that the language of art is constitutive. Rather than referring to preexistent values, the artwork creates values only inchoately realized before. The most important advocates of this position are Eliseo Vivas (*The Artistic Transaction*, 1963) and Murray Krieger (*The Play and Place of Criticism*, 1967).

conventions: All those devices of stylization, compression, and selection that constitute the necessary differences between art and life. According to the Russian Formalists, these conventions constitute the "literariness" of literature and are the only proper concern of the literary critic.

deconstruction: An extremely influential contemporary school of criticism based on the works of the French philosopher Jacques Derrida. Deconstruction treats literary works as unconscious reflections of the reigning myths of Western culture. The primary myth is that there is a meaningful world that language signifies or represents. The deconstructionist critic is most often concerned with showing how a literary text tacitly subverts the very assumptions or myths on which it ostensibly rests.

defamiliarization: Coined by Viktor Shklovsky in 1917, this term denotes a basic principle of Russian Formalism. Poetic language (by which the Formalists meant artful language, in prose as well as in poetry) defamiliarizes or "makes strange" familiar experiences. The technique of art, says Shklovsky, is to "make objects unfamiliar, to make forms difficult, to increase the difficulty and length of perception. . . . Art is a way of experiencing the artfulness of an object; the object is not important."

detective story: The so-called classic detective story (or mystery) is a highly formalized and logically structured mode of fiction in which the focus is on a crime solved by a detective through interpretation of evidence and ratiocination; the most famous detective in this mode is Arthur Conan Doyle's Sherlock Holmes. Many modern practitioners of the genre, however, such as Dashiell Hammett, Raymond Chandler, and Ross Macdonald, have de-emphasized the puzzlelike qualities of the detective story, stressing instead characterization, theme, and other elements of mainstream fiction.

determinism: The belief that an individual's actions are essentially determined by biological and environmental factors, with free will playing a negligible role. (See *naturalism.*)

dialogue: The similitude of conversation in fiction, dialogue serves to characterize, to further the *plot*, to establish *conflict*, and to express thematic ideas.

displacement: Popularized in criticism by Northrop Frye, this term refers to the author's attempt to make his or her story psychologically motivated and realistic, even as the latent structure of the mythical motivation moves relentlessly forward.

dominant: A term coined by Roman Jakobson to refer to that which "rules, determines, and transforms the remaining components in the work of a single artist, in a poetic canon, or in the work of an epoch." The shifting of the dominant in a *genre* accounts for the creation of new generic forms and new poetic epochs. For example, the rise of *realism* in the mid-nineteenth century indicates realistic conventions becoming dominant and *romance* or fantasy conventions becoming secondary.

doppelgänger: A double or counterpart of a person, sometimes endowed with ghostly qualities. A fictional character's doppelgänger often reflects a suppressed side of his or her personality. One of the classic examples of the doppelgänger motif is found in

Fyodor Dostoevski's novella *Dvoynik* (1846; *The Double*, 1917); Isaac Bashevis Singer and Jorge Luis Borges, among others, offer striking modern treatments of the doppelgänger.

epic: Although this term usually refers to a long narrative poem that presents the exploits of a central figure of high position, the term is also used to designate a long novel that has the style or structure usually associated with an epic. In this sense, for example, Herman Melville's *Moby Dick* (1851) and James Joyce's *Ulysses* (1922) may be called epics.

episodic narrative: A work that is held together primarily by a loose connection of self-sufficient episodes. *Picaresque novels* often have episodic structure.

epistolary novel: A novel made up of letters by one or more fictional characters. Samuel Richardson's *Pamela: Or, Virtue Rewarded* (1740-1741) is a well-known eighteenth century example. In the nineteenth century, Bram Stoker's *Dracula* (1897) is largely epistolary. The technique allows for several different points of view to be presented.

euphuism: A style of writing characterized by ornate language that is highly contrived, alliterative, and repetitious. Euphuism was developed by John Lyly in his *Euphues, the Anatomy of Wit* (1578) and was emulated frequently by writers of the Elizabethan Age.

existentialism: A philosophical, religious, and literary term, emerging from World War II, for a group of attitudes surrounding the pivotal notion that existence precedes essence. According to Jean-Paul Sartre, "Man is nothing else but what he makes himself." Forlornness arises from the death of God and the concomitant death of universal values, of any source of ultimate or a priori standards. Despair arises from the fact that an individual can reckon only with what depends on his or her will, and the sphere of that will is severely limited; the number of things on which he or she can have an impact is pathetically small. Existentialist literature is antideterministic in the extreme and rejects the idea that heredity and environment shape and determine human motivation and behavior.

exposition: The part or parts of a fiction that provide necessary background information. Exposition not only provides the time and place of the action but also introduces readers to the fictive world of the story, acquainting them with the ground rules of the work.

fantastic: In his study *The Fantastic* (1970), Tzvetan Todorov defines the fantastic as a *genre* that lies between the "uncanny" and the "marvelous." All three genres embody the familiar world but present an event that cannot be explained by the laws of the familiar world. Todorov says that the fantastic occupies a twilight zone between the uncanny (when the reader knows that the peculiar event is merely the result of an illusion) and the marvelous (when the reader understands that the event is supposed to take place in a realm controlled by laws unknown to humankind). The fantastic is thus essentially unsettling, provocative, even subversive.

feminist criticism: A criticism advocating equal rights for women in political, economic, social, psychological, personal, and aesthetic senses. On the thematic level, the feminist reader should identify with female characters and their concerns. The object is to provide a critique of phallocentric assumptions and an analysis of patriarchal ideologies inscribed in a literature that is male-centered and male-dominated. On the ideological level, feminist critics see gender, as well as the stereotypes that go along with it, as a cultural construct. They strive to define a particularly feminine content and to extend the *canon* so that it might include works by lesbians, feminists, and women writers in general.

flashback: A scene in a fiction that depicts an earlier event; it may be presented as a reminiscence by a character in the story or may simply be inserted into the narrative.

foreshadowing: A device to create suspense or dramatic irony in fiction by indicating through suggestion what will take place in the future.

formalist criticism: Two particularly influential formalist schools of criticism arose in the twentieth century: the Russian Formalists and the American New Critics. The Russian Formalists were concerned with the conventional devices used in literature to defamiliarize that which habit has made familiar. The New Critics believed that literary criticism is a description and evaluation of its object and that the primary concern of the critic is with the work's unity. Both schools of criticism, at their most extreme, treated literary works as artifacts or constructs divorced from their biographical and social contexts.

genre: In its most general sense, this term refers to a group of literary works defined by a common form, style, or purpose. In practice, the term is used in a wide variety of overlapping and, to a degree, contradictory senses. Tragedy and comedy are thus described as distinct genres; the novel (a form that includes both tragic and comic works) is a genre; and various subspecies of the novel, such as the *gothic* and the *picaresque*, are themselves frequently treated as distinct genres. Finally, the term "genre fiction" refers to forms of popular fiction in which the writer is bound by more or less rigid conventions. Indeed, all these diverse usages have in common an emphasis on the manner in which individual literary works are shaped by particular expectations and conventions; this is the subject of genre criticism.

genre fiction: Categories of popular fiction in which the writers are bound by more or less rigid conventions, such as in the *detective story*, the *romance*, and the *Western*. Although the term can be used in a neutral sense, it is often used dismissively.

gothic novel: A form of fiction developed in the eighteenth century that focuses on horror and the supernatural. In his preface to *The Castle of Otranto* (1765), the first gothic novel in English, Horace Walpole claimed that he was trying to combine two kinds of fiction, with events and story typical of the medieval romance and character delineation typical of the realistic novel. Other examples of the form are Matthew Gregory

Lewis's *The Monk: A Romance* (1796; also known as *Ambrosio: Or, The Monk*) and Mary Wollstonecraft Shelley's *Frankenstein: Or, The Modern Prometheus* (1818).

grotesque: According to Wolfgang Kayser (*The Grotesque in Art and Literature*, 1963), the grotesque is an embodiment in literature of the estranged world. Characterized by a breakup of the everyday world by mysterious forces, the form differs from fantasy in that the reader is not sure whether to react with humor or with horror and in that the exaggeration manifested exists in the familiar world rather than in a purely imaginative world.

Hebraic/Homeric styles: Terms coined by Erich Auerbach in *Mimesis: The Representation of Reality in Western Literature* (1953) to designate two basic fictional styles. The Hebraic style focuses only on the decisive points of narrative and leaves all else obscure, mysterious, and "fraught with background"; the Homeric style places the narrative in a definite time and place and externalizes everything in a perpetual foreground.

historical criticism: In contrast to *formalist criticism*, which treats literary works to a great extent as self-contained artifacts, historical criticism emphasizes the historical context of literature; the two approaches, however, need not be mutually exclusive. Ernst Robert Curtius's *European Literature and the Latin Middle Ages* (1940) is a prominent example of historical criticism.

historical novel: A novel that depicts past historical events, usually public in nature, and features real as well as fictional people. Sir Walter Scott's Waverley novels established the basic type, but the relationship between fiction and history in the form varies greatly depending on the practitioner.

implied author: According to Wayne Booth (*The Rhetoric of Fiction*, 1961), the novel often creates a kind of second self who tells the story—a self who is wiser, more sensitive, and more perceptive than any real person could be.

interior monologue: Defined by Édouard Dujardin as the speech of a character designed to introduce the reader directly to the character's internal life, the form differs from other kinds of monologue in that it attempts to reproduce thought before any logical organization is imposed on it. See, for example, Molly Bloom's long interior monologue at the conclusion of James Joyce's *Ulysses* (1922).

irrealism: A term often used to refer to modern or postmodern fiction that is presented self-consciously as a fiction or a fabulation rather than a mimesis of external reality. The best-known practitioners of irrealism are John Barth, Robert Coover, and Donald Barthelme.

local colorists: A loose movement of late nineteenth century American writers whose fiction emphasizes the distinctive folkways, landscapes, and dialects of various regions. Important local colorists include Bret Harte, Mark Twain, George Washington Cable, Kate Chopin, and Sarah Orne Jewett. (See *regional novel*.)

Marxist criticism: Based on the nineteenth century writings of Karl Marx and Friedrich Engels, Marxist criticism views literature as a product of ideological forces determined by the dominant class. However, many Marxists believe that literature operates according to its own autonomous standards of production and reception: It is both a product of ideology and able to determine ideology. As such, literature may overcome the dominant paradigms of its age and play a revolutionary role in society.

metafiction: This term refers to fiction that manifests a reflexive tendency, such as Vladimir Nabokov's *Pale Fire* (1962) and John Fowles's *The French Lieutenant's Woman* (1969). The emphasis is on the loosening of the work's illusion of reality to expose the reality of its illusion. Other terms used to refer to this type of fiction include "irrealism," "postmodernist fiction," "antifiction," and "surfiction."

modernism: An international movement in the arts that began in the early years of the twentieth century. Although the term is used to describe artists of widely varying persuasions, modernism in general was characterized by its international idiom, by its interest in cultures distant in space or time, by its emphasis on formal experimentation, and by its sense of dislocation and radical change.

motif: A conventional incident or situation in a fiction that may serve as the basis for the structure of the narrative itself. The Russian Formalist critic Boris Tomashevsky uses the term to refer to the smallest particle of thematic material in a work.

motivation: Although this term is usually used in reference to the convention of justifying the action of a character from his or her psychological makeup, the Russian Formalists use the term to refer to the network of devices that justify the introduction of individual *motifs* or groups of motifs in a work. For example, "compositional motivation" refers to the principle that every single property in a work contributes to its overall effect; "realistic motivation" refers to the realistic devices used to make a work plausible and lifelike.

multiculturalism: The tendency to recognize the perspectives of those traditionally excluded from the canon of Western art and literature. In order to promote multiculturalism, publishers and educators have revised textbooks and school curricula to incorporate material by and about women, members of minority groups, persons from non-Western cultures, and homosexuals.

myth: Anonymous traditional stories dealing with basic human concepts and antinomies. According to Claude Lévi-Strauss, myth is that part of language where the "formula *tradutore, tradittore* reaches its lowest truth value. . . . Its substance does not lie in its style, its original music, or its syntax, but in the story which it tells."

myth criticism: Northrop Frye says that in myth "we see the structural principles of literature isolated." Myth criticism is concerned with these basic principles of literature; it is not to be confused with mythological criticism, which is primarily concerned with finding mythological parallels in the surface action of the *narrative*.

narrative: Robert Scholes and Robert Kellogg, in *The Nature of Narrative* (1966), say that by "narrative" they mean literary works that include both a story and a storyteller. The term "narrative" usually implies a contrast to "enacted" fiction such as drama.

narratology: The study of the form and functioning of *narratives*; it attempts to examine what all narratives have in common and what makes individual narratives different from one another.

narrator: The *character* who recounts the *narrative*, or story. Wayne Booth describes various dramatized narrators in *The Rhetoric of Fiction* (1961): unacknowledged centers of consciousness, observers, narrator-agents, and self-conscious narrators. Booth suggests that the important elements to consider in narration are the relationships among the narrator, the author, the characters, and the reader.

naturalism: As developed by Émile Zola in the late nineteenth century, naturalism is the application of the principles of scientific *determinism* to fiction. Although it usually refers more to the choice of subject matter than to technical conventions, those conventions associated with the movement center on the author's attempt to be precise and scientifically objective in description and detail, regardless of whether the events described are sordid or shocking.

New Criticism: See *formalist criticism*.

novel: Perhaps the most difficult of all fictional forms to define because of its multiplicity of modes. Edouard, in André Gide's *Les Faux-monnayeurs* (1925; *The Counterfeiters*, 1927), says the novel is the freest and most lawless of all *genres*; he wonders if fear of that liberty is the reason the novel has so timidly clung to reality. Most critics seem to agree that the novel's primary area of concern is the social world. Ian Watt (*The Rise of the Novel*, 2001) says that the novel can be distinguished from other fictional forms by the attention it pays to individual characterization and detailed presentation of the environment. Moreover, says Watt, the novel, more than any other fictional form, is interested in the "development of its characters in the course of time."

novel of manners: The classic examples of this form might be the novels of Jane Austen, wherein the customs and conventions of a social group of a particular time and place are realistically, and often satirically, portrayed.

novella, novelle, nouvelle, novelette, novela: Although these terms often refer to the short European tale, especially the Renaissance form employed by Giovanni Boccaccio, the terms often refer to that form of fiction that is said to be longer than a short story and shorter than a novel. "Novelette" is the term usually preferred by the British, whereas "novella" is the term usually used to refer to American works in this *genre*. Henry James claimed that the main merit of the form is the "effort to do the complicated thing with a strong brevity and lucidity."

phenomenological criticism: Although best known as a European school of criticism practiced by Georges Poulet and others, this so-called criticism of consciousness is also propounded in the United States by such critics as J. Hillis Miller. The focus is less on individual works and *genres* than it is on literature as an act; the work is not seen as an object but rather as part of a strand of latent impulses in the work of a single author or an epoch.

picaresque novel: A form of fiction that centers on a central rogue figure, or picaro, who usually tells his or her own story. The plot structure is normally *episodic*, and the episodes usually focus on how the picaro lives by his or her wits. Classic examples of the mode are Henry Fielding's *The History of Tom Jones, a Foundling* (1749; commonly known as *Tom Jones*) and Mark Twain's *Adventures of Huckleberry Finn* (1884).

plot/story: "Story" refers to the full *narrative* of *character* and action, whereas "plot" generally refers to action with little reference to character. A more precise and helpful distinction is made by the Russian Formalists, who suggest that "plot" refers to the events of a narrative as they have been artfully arranged in the literary work, subject to chronological displacement, ellipses, and other devices, while "story" refers to the sum of the same events arranged in simple, causal-chronological order. Thus story is the raw material for plot. By comparing the two in a given work, the reader is encouraged to see the narrative as an artifact.

point of view: The means by which the story is presented to the reader, or, as Percy Lubbock says in *The Craft of Fiction* (1921), "the relation in which the narrator stands to the story"—a relation that Lubbock claims governs the craft of fiction. Some of the questions the critical reader should ask concerning point of view are the following: Who talks to the reader? From what position does the narrator tell the story? At what distance does he or she place the reader from the story? What kind of person is he or she? How fully is he or she characterized? How reliable is he or she? For further discussion, see Wayne Booth, *The Rhetoric of Fiction* (1961).

postcolonialism: Postcolonial literature emerged in the mid-twentieth century when colonies in Asia, Africa, and the Caribbean began gaining their independence from the European nations that had long controlled them. Postcolonial authors, such as Salman Rushdie and V. S. Naipaul, tend to focus on both the freedom and the conflict inherent in living in a postcolonial state.

postmodernism: A ubiquitous but elusive term in contemporary criticism, "postmodernism" is loosely applied to the various artistic movements that followed the era of so-called high modernism, represented by such giants as James Joyce and Pablo Picasso. In critical discussions of contemporary fiction, the term "postmodernism" is frequently applied to the works of writers such as Thomas Pynchon, John Barth, and Donald Barthelme, who exhibit a self-conscious awareness of their modernist predecessors as well as a reflexive treatment of fictional form.

protagonist: The central *character* in a fiction, the character whose fortunes most concern the reader.

psychological criticism: While much modern literary criticism reflects to some degree the impacts of Sigmund Freud, Carl Jung, Jacques Lacan, and other psychological theorists, the term "psychological criticism" suggests a strong emphasis on a causal relation between the writer's psychological state, variously interpreted, and his or her works. A notable example of psychological criticism is Norman Fruman's *Coleridge, the Damaged Archangel* (1971).

psychological novel: A form of fiction in which *character*, especially the inner lives of characters, is the primary focus. This form, which has been of primary importance at least since Henry James, characterizes much of the work of James Joyce, Virginia Woolf, and William Faulkner. For a detailed discussion, see *The Modern Psychological Novel* (1955) by Leon Edel.

realism: A literary technique in which the primary convention is to render an illusion of fidelity to external reality. Realism is often identified as the primary method of the novel form: It focuses on surface details, maintains a fidelity to the everyday experiences of middle-class society, and strives for a one-to-one relationship between the fiction and the action imitated. The realist movement in the late nineteenth century coincides with the full development of the novel form.

reception aesthetics: The best-known American practitioner of reception aesthetics is Stanley Fish. For the reception critic, meaning is an event or process; rather than being embedded in the work, it is created through particular acts of reading. The best-known European practitioner of this criticism, Wolfgang Iser, argues that indeterminacy is the basic characteristic of literary texts; the reader must "normalize" the text either by projecting his or her standards into it or by revising his or her standards to "fit" the text.

regional novel: Any novel in which the character of a given geographical region plays a decisive role. Although regional differences persist across the United States, a considerable leveling in speech and customs has taken place, so that the sharp regional distinctions evident in nineteenth century American fiction have all but disappeared. Only in the South has a strong regional tradition persisted to the present. (See *local colorists*.)

rhetorical criticism: The rhetorical critic is concerned with the literary work as a means of communicating ideas and the means by which the work affects or controls the reader. Such criticism seems best suited to didactic works such as satire.

roman à clef: A fiction wherein actual people, often celebrities of some sort, are thinly disguised.

romance: The romance usually differs from the novel form in that the focus is on symbolic events and representational characters rather than on "as-if-real" characters and events. Richard Chase says that in the romance, character is depicted as highly stylized, a function of the plot rather than as someone complexly related to society. The romancer is more likely to be concerned with dreamworlds than with the familiar world, believing that reality cannot be grasped by the traditional novel.

Romanticism: A widespread cultural movement in the late eighteenth and early nineteenth centuries, the influence of which is still felt. As a general literary tendency, Romanticism is frequently contrasted with *classicism.* Although many varieties of Romanticism are indigenous to various national literatures, the term generally suggests an assertion of the preeminence of the imagination. Other values associated with various schools of Romanticism include primitivism, an interest in folklore, a reverence for nature, and a fascination with the demoniac and the macabre.

scene: The central element of *narration*; specific actions are narrated or depicted that make the reader feel he or she is participating directly in the action.

science fiction: Fiction in which certain givens (physical laws, psychological principles, social conditions—any one or all of these) form the basis of an imaginative projection into the future or, less commonly, an extrapolation in the present or even into the past.

semiotics: The science of signs and sign systems in communication. According to Roman Jakobson, semiotics deals with the principles that underlie the structure of signs, their use in language of all kinds, and the specific nature of various sign systems.

sentimental novel: A form of fiction popular in the eighteenth century in which emotionalism and optimism are the primary characteristics. The best-known examples are Samuel Richardson's *Pamela: Or, Virtue Rewarded* (1740-1741) and Oliver Goldsmith's *The Vicar of Wakefield* (1766).

setting: The circumstances and environment, both temporal and spatial, of a *narrative.*

spatial form: An author's attempt to make the reader apprehend a work spatially in a moment of time rather than sequentially. To achieve this effect, the author breaks up the *narrative* into interspersed fragments. Beginning with James Joyce, Marcel Proust, and Djuna Barnes, the movement toward spatial form is concomitant with the *modernist* effort to supplant historical time in fiction with mythic time. For the seminal discussion of this technique, see Joseph Frank, *The Widening Gyre* (1963).

stream of consciousness: The depiction of the thought processes of a *character,* insofar as this is possible, without any mediating structures. The metaphor of consciousness as a "stream" suggests a rush of thoughts and images governed by free association rather than by strictly rational development. The term "stream of consciousness" is often used loosely as a synonym for *interior monologue.* The most celebrated example of stream of consciousness in fiction is the monologue of Molly Bloom in James Joyce's *Ulysses* (1922); other notable practitioners of the stream-of-consciousness technique include Dorothy Richardson, Virginia Woolf, and William Faulkner.

structuralism: As a movement of thought, structuralism is based on the idea of intrinsic, self-sufficient structures that do not require reference to external elements. A structure is a system of transformations that involves the interplay of laws inherent in the system itself. The study of language is the primary model for contemporary structuralism. The structuralist literary critic attempts to define structural principles that operate intertextually throughout the whole of literature as well as principles that operate in *genres* and in individual works. One of the most accessible surveys of structuralism and literature available is Jonathan Culler's *Structuralist Poetics* (1975).

summary: Those parts of a fiction that do not need to be detailed. In *Tom Jones* (1749), Henry Fielding says, "If whole years should pass without producing anything worthy of . . . notice . . . we shall hasten on to matters of consequence."

thematics: According to Northrop Frye, when a work of fiction is written or interpreted thematically, it becomes an illustrative fable. Murray Krieger defines thematics as "the study of the experiential tensions which, dramatically entangled in the literary work, become an existential reflection of that work's aesthetic complexity."

tone: The dominant mood of a work of fiction. (See *atmosphere.*)

unreliable narrator: A narrator whose account of the events of the story cannot be trusted, obliging readers to reconstruct—if possible—the true state of affairs themselves. Once an innovative technique, the use of the unreliable narrator has become commonplace among contemporary writers who wish to suggest the impossibility of a truly "reliable" account of any event. Notable examples of the unreliable narrator can be found in Ford Madox Ford's *The Good Soldier* (1915) and Vladimir Nabokov's *Lolita* (1955).

Victorian novel: Although the Victorian period extended from 1837 to 1901, the term "Victorian novel" does not include the later decades of Queen Victoria's reign. The term loosely refers to the sprawling works of novelists such as Charles Dickens and William Makepeace Thackeray—works that frequently appeared first in serial form and are characterized by a broad social canvas.

vraisemblance/verisimilitude: Tzvetan Todorov defines vraisemblance as "the mask which conceals the text's own laws, but which we are supposed to take for a relation to reality." Verisimilitude refers to a work's attempts to make the reader believe that it conforms to reality rather than to its own laws.

Western novel: Like all varieties of *genre fiction*, the Western novel—generally known simply as the Western—is defined by a relatively predictable combination of *conventions*, *motifs*, and recurring themes. These predictable elements, familiar from many Western films and television series, differentiate the Western from *historical novels* and idiosyncratic works such as Thomas Berger's *Little Big Man* (1964) that are also set in the Old West. Conversely, some novels set in the contemporary West are regarded as Westerns because they deal with modern cowboys and with the land itself in the manner characteristic of the *genre.*

Charles E. May

Guide to Online Resources

Web Sites

The following sites were visited by the editors of Salem Press in 2009. Because URLs frequently change, the accuracy of these addresses cannot be guaranteed; however, long-standing sites, such as those of colleges and universities, national organizations, and government agencies, generally maintain links when sites are moved or updated.

American Literature on the Web

http://www.nagasaki-gaigo.ac.jp/ishikawa/amlit

Among this site's features are several pages providing links to Web sites about specific genres and literary movements, southern and southwestern American literature, minority literature, literary theory, and women writers, as well as an extensive index of links to electronic text collections and archives. Users also can access information for five specific time periods: 1620-1820, 1820-1865, 1865-1914, 1914-1945, and since 1945. A range of information is available for each period, including alphabetical lists of authors that link to more specific information about each writer, time lines of historical and literary events, and links to related additional Web sites.

Books and Writers

http://www.kirjasto.sci.fi/indeksi.htm

This broad, comprehensive, and easy-to-use resource provides access to information about hundreds of authors throughout the world, extending from 70 B.C.E to the twenty-first century. Links take users from an alphabetical list of authors to pages featuring biographical material, lists of works, and recommendations for further reading about individual authors; each writer's page also includes links to related pages on the site. Although brief, the biographical essays provide solid overviews of the authors' careers, their contributions to literature, and their literary influences.

The Canadian Literature Archive

http://www.umanitoba.ca/canlit

Created and maintained by the English Department at the University of Manitoba, this site is a comprehensive collection of materials for and about Canadian writers. It includes an alphabetical listing of authors with links to additional Web-based information. Users also can retrieve electronic texts, announcements of literary events, and videocasts of author interviews and readings.

A Celebration of Women Writers

http://digital.library.upenn.edu/women

This site presents an extensive compendium of information about the contributions of women writers throughout history. The "Local Editions by Authors" and "Local Editions by Category" pages include access to electronic texts of the works of numerous writers, including Louisa May Alcott, Djuna Barnes, Grazia Deledda, Edith Wharton, and Virginia Woolf. Users can also access biographical and bibliographical information by browsing lists arranged by writers' names, countries of origin, ethnicities, and the centuries in which they lived.

Contemporary Writers

http://www.contemporarywriters.com/authors

Created by the British Council, this site offers "up-to-date profiles of some of the U.K. and Commonwealth's most important living writers (plus writers from the Republic of Ireland that we've worked with)." The available information includes biographies, bibliographies, critical reviews, news about literary prizes, and photographs. Users can search the site by author, genre, nationality, gender, publisher, book title, date of publication, and prize name and date.

Internet Public Library: Native American Authors

http://www.ipl.org/div/natam

Internet Public Library, a Web-based collection of materials, includes this index to resources about writers of Native American heritage. An alphabetical list of authors enables users to link to biographies, lists of works, electronic texts, tribal Web sites, and other online resources. The majority of the writers covered are contemporary Indian authors, but some historical authors also are featured. Users also can retrieve information by browsing lists of titles and tribes. In addition, the site contains a bibliography of print and online materials about Native American literature.

LiteraryHistory.com

http://www.literaryhistory.com

This site is an excellent source of academic, scholarly, and critical literature about eighteenth, nineteenth, and twentieth century American and English writers. It provides numerous pages about specific eras and genres, including individual pages for eighteenth, nineteenth, and twentieth century literature and for African American and postcolonial literature. These pages contain alphabetical lists of authors that link to articles, reviews, overviews, excerpts of works, teaching guides, podcast interviews, and other materials. The eighteenth century literature page also provides access to information about the eighteenth century novel.

Literary Resources on the Net

http://andromeda.rutgers.edu/~jlynch/Lit

Jack Lynch of Rutgers University maintains this extensive collection of links to Internet sites that are useful to academics, including numerous Web sites about American and English literature. This collection is a good place to begin online research about the novel, as it links to hundreds of other sites with broad ranges of literary topics. The site is organized chronically, with separate pages for information about the Middle Ages, the Renaissance, the eighteenth century, the Romantic and Victorian eras, and twentieth century British and Irish literature. It also has separate pages providing links to Web sites about American literature and to women's literature and feminism.

LitWeb

http://litweb.net

LitWeb provides biographies of more than five hundred world authors throughout history that can be accessed through an alphabetical listing. The pages about each writer contain a list of his or her works, suggestions for further reading, and illustrations. The site also offers information about past and present winners of major literary prizes.

The Modern Word: Authors of the Libyrinth

http://www.themodernword.com/authors.html

The Modern Word site, although somewhat haphazard in its organization, provides a great deal of critical information about writers. The "Authors of the Libyrinth" page is very useful, linking author names to essays about them and other resources. The section of the page headed "The Scriptorium" presents "an index of pages featuring writers who have pushed the edges of their medium, combining literary talent with a sense of experimentation to produce some remarkable works of modern literature." The site also includes sections devoted to Samuel Beckett, Umberto Eco, Gabriel García Márquez, James Joyce, Franz Kafka, and Thomas Pynchon.

Novels

http://www.nvcc.edu/home/ataormina/novels/default.htm

This overview of American and English novels was prepared by Agatha Taormina, a professor at Northern Virginia Community College. It contains three sections: "History" provides a definition of the novel genre, a discussion of its origins in eighteenth century England, and separate pages with information about genres and authors of nineteenth century, twentieth century, and postmodern novels. "Approaches" suggests how to read a novel critically for greater appreciation, and "Resources" provides a list of books about the novel.

Outline of American Literature

http://www.america.gov/publications/books/outline-of-american-literature.html

This page of the America.gov site provides access to an electronic version of the ten-chapter volume *Outline of American Literature*, a historical overview of prose and poetry from colonial times to the present published by the U.S. Department of State. The work's author is Kathryn VanSpanckeren, professor of English at the University of Tampa. The site offers links to abbreviated versions of each chapter as well as access to the entire publication in PDF format.

Voice of the Shuttle

http://vos.ucsb.edu

One of the most complete and authoritative places for online information about literature, Voice of the Shuttle is maintained by professors and students in the English Department at the University of California, Santa Barbara. The site provides thousands of links to electronic books, academic journals, association Web sites, sites created by university professors, and many, many other resources about the humanities. Its "Literature in English" page provides links to separate pages about the literature of the Anglo-Saxon era, the Middle Ages, the Renaissance and seventeenth century, the Restoration and eighteenth century, the Romantic age, the Victorian age, and modern and contemporary periods in Britain and the United States, as well as a page focused on minority literature. Another page on the site, "Literatures Other than English," offers a gateway to information about the literature of numerous countries and world regions.

ELECTRONIC DATABASES

Electronic databases usually do not have their own URLs. Instead, public, college, and university libraries subscribe to these databases, provide links to them on their Web sites, and make them available to library card holders or other specified patrons. Readers can visit library Web sites or ask reference librarians to check on availability.

Canadian Literary Centre

Produced by EBSCO, the Canadian Literary Centre database contains full-text content from ECW Press, a Toronto-based publisher, including the titles in the publisher's Canadian fiction studies, Canadian biography, and Canadian writers and their works series, *ECW's Biographical Guide to Canadian Novelists*, and *George Woodcock's Introduction to Canadian Fiction*. Author biographies, essays and literary criticism, and book reviews are among the database's offerings.

Literary Reference Center

EBSCO's Literary Reference Center (LRC) is a comprehensive full-text database designed primarily to help high school and undergraduate students in English and the humanities with homework and research assignments about literature. The database contains massive amounts of information from reference works, books, literary journals, and other materials, including more than 31,000 plot summaries, synopses, and overviews of literary works; almost 100,000 essays and articles of literary criticism; about 140,000 author biographies; more than 605,000 book reviews; and more than 5,200 author interviews. It also contains the entire contents of Salem Press's MagillOnLiterature Plus. Users can retrieve information by browsing a list of authors' names or titles of literary works; they can also use an advanced search engine to access information by numerous categories, including author name, gender, cultural identity, national identity, and the years in which he or she lived, or by literary title, character, locale, genre, and publication date. The Literary Reference Center also features a literary-historical time line, an encyclopedia of literature, and a glossary of literary terms.

MagillOnLiterature Plus

MagillOnLiterature Plus is a comprehensive, integrated literature database produced by Salem Press and available on the EBSCO*host* platform. The database contains the full text of essays in Salem's many literature-related reference works, including *Masterplots*, *Cyclopedia of World Authors*, *Cyclopedia of Literary Characters*, *Cyclopedia of Literary Places*, *Critical Survey of Long Fiction*, *Critical Survey of Short Fiction*, *World Philosophers and Their Works*, *Magill's Literary Annual*, and *Magill's Book Reviews.* Among its contents are articles on more than 35,000 literary works and more than 8,500 writers, poets, dramatists, essays, and philosophers, more than 1,000 images, and a glossary of more than 1,300 literary terms. The biographical essays include lists of authors' works and secondary bibliographies, and almost four hundred overview essays offer information about literary genres, time periods, and national literatures.

NoveList

NoveList is a readers' advisory service produced by EBSCO. The database provides access to 155,000 titles of both adult and juvenile fiction as well information about literary awards, book discussion guides, feature articles about a range of literary genres, and "recommended reads." Users can search by author name, book title, or series title or can describe the plot to retrieve the name of a book, information about the author, and book reviews; another search engine enables users to find titles similar to books they have enjoyed reading.

Rebecca Kuzins

GEOGRAPHICAL INDEX

SUBJECT INDEX